The Sovereigns and The Admiral

A biography of Isabel, Ferdinand and Columbus

by

Jon Bauman

To Philip + Jerry Henderson
Two good friends
[illegible]
Sept 19, 1992

The Sovereigns and The Admiral

A biography of Isabel, Ferdinand and Columbus

by

Jon Bauman

Epigram Press
P.O. Box 1647
515 S. First Street
Lufkin, Texas 75901

ISBN 1-878096-23-0

First Printing, 1991

Epigram Press
P.O. Box 1647 • 515 South First Street
Lufkin, Texas 75901

Dedication

My thanks to:

Diane McNulty and Sally Estes for their enthusiasm and support.

Jane Roberts Wood and Fran Vick for holding the hand of an old lawyer determined to write a book.

Susan and Lea Bauman for their editing and criticism.

Number one, Lou.

Table of Contents

Family Tree of the Sovereigns

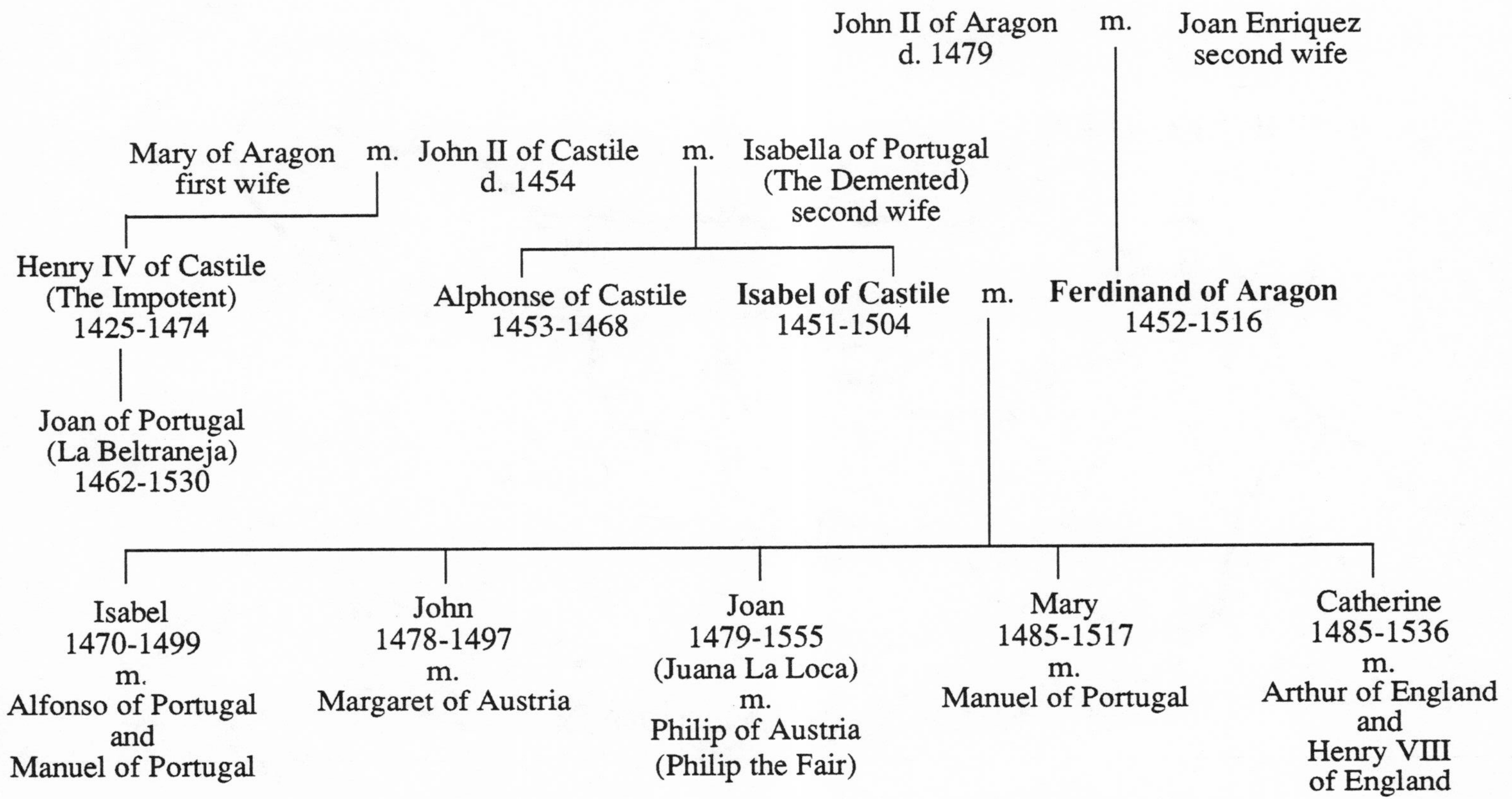

KINGDOM OF GRANADA, 1484

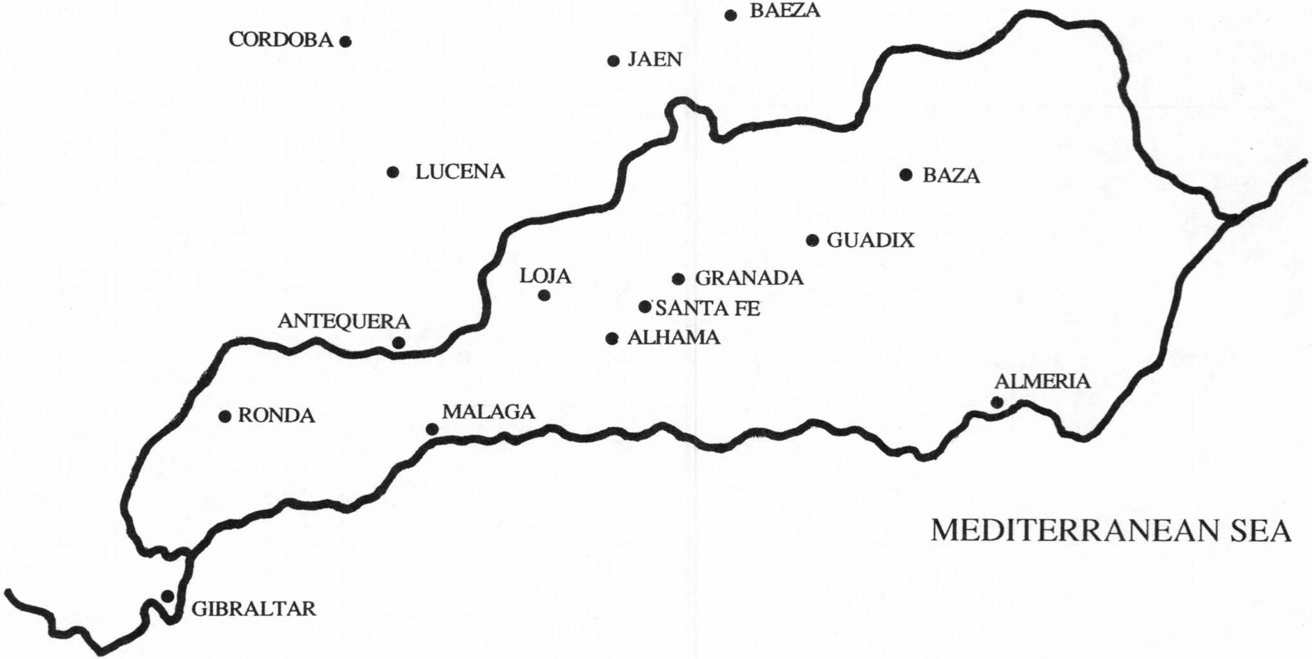

SPAIN AND PORTUGAL

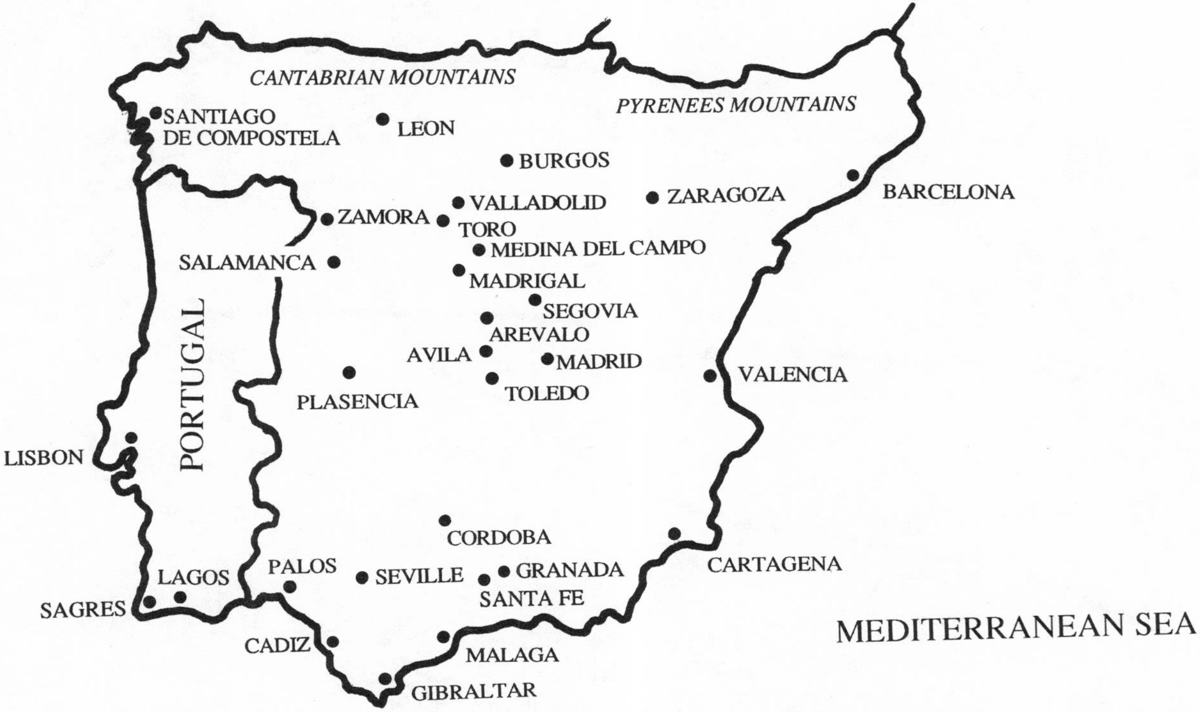

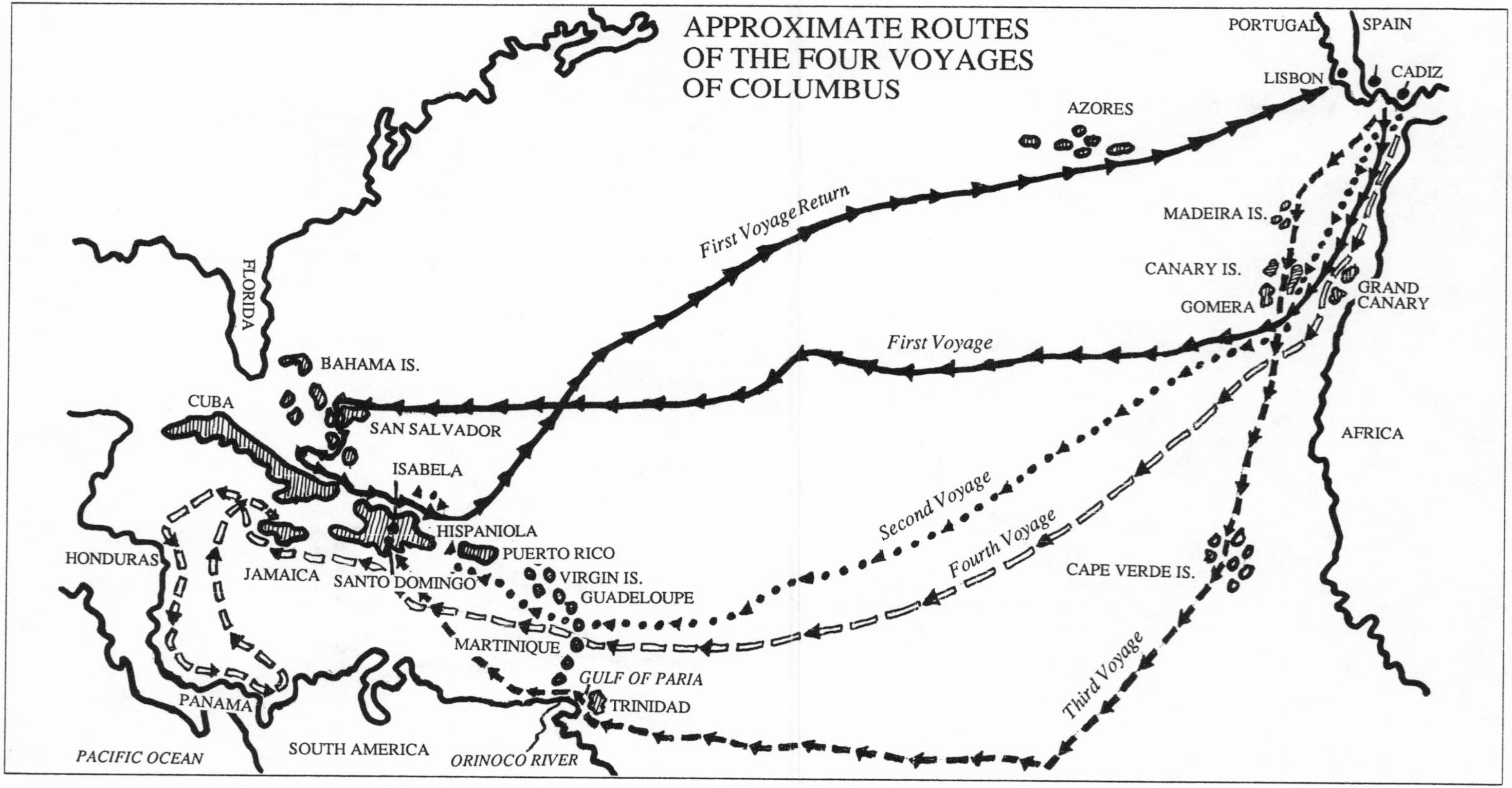
APPROXIMATE ROUTES
OF THE FOUR VOYAGES
OF COLUMBUS
PORTUGAL
SPAIN
LISBON
CADIZ
AZORES
MADEIRA IS.
CANARY IS.
GOMERA
GRAND CANARY
AFRICA
CAPE VERDE IS.
First Voyage Return
First Voyage
Second Voyage
Fourth Voyage
Third Voyage
FLORIDA
BAHAMA IS.
CUBA
SAN SALVADOR
ISABELA
HISPANIOLA
PUERTO RICO
VIRGIN IS.
GUADELOUPE
HONDURAS
JAMAICA
SANTO DOMINGO
MARTINIQUE
GULF OF PARIA
TRINIDAD
PANAMA
PACIFIC OCEAN
SOUTH AMERICA
ORINOCO RIVER

PREFACE

Three truly dramatic characters, Isabel, Ferdinand and Columbus, helped to pry open Europe's doors and direct its attention beyond the narrow world of the Mediterranean Sea. The achievements of the Sovereigns and the Admiral were among the first steps that created what is now called the global village.

Isabel and Ferdinand, with their reforms, and Columbus, by serving up the riches of the New World, allowed Spain to commence a global expansion which made it the most potent force in Europe for almost two hundred years. Their legacy directly impacts the lives of North and South Americans, yet we know little or nothing about them.

It is difficult to understand why the three principle characters in this book are such shadowy figures to the twenty-two million Hispanics who live in North America and to the non-Hispanics who want to understand their Hispanic neighbors. They were fascinating, if sometimes unlikable, and their accomplishments and mistakes are indelibly stamped on our culture. Columbus accidentally discovered ("encountered" some say) a New World, and changed the way Europeans thought about themselves.

True, many of those who followed the Admiral of the Ocean Sea transported medieval Europe's diseases and materialism to the civilizations of the New World. But, even though the Spanish brought many of Europe's evils across the Atlantic, they also introduced the wheel, horses and metal tools.

What the Spanish found in the New World was a sometimes gentle, sometimes savage new frontier. An American historian,

Walter Prescott Webb, elaborated on the theory that the wildness of the North American frontier shaped the character of its people. It can be argued that the Spanish had already developed a "frontier mentality" during their eight century struggle with the Arabs for control of Iberia. In the no man's land that separated Christians and Moors from 711 to 1492, the Spanish knights created a unique character, the military entrepreneur, who cloaked himself in the robes of medieval chivalry which sanctioned his warrior behavior. The Spanish exported this personality type, in the person of the conquistadors, to their colonies in the New World.

Isabel and Ferdinand made this colonization, the most extensive in history, possible by remodeling Spain's institutional framework. During their thirty-five-year marriage partnership, the Sovereigns harnessed the powerful aristocrats who had sunk the nation into chaos. They gained control of the independent cities which functioned as mini-kingdoms outside the royal grasp. The King and Queen reformed the corrupt judicial system, the inefficient government and the incoherent laws. Under their sponsorship, the first grammar of a modern European language was published, making Castilian Spanish an instrument of empire. They fought a civil war, the War of Succession, and a holy war, the War of Granada, to achieve their ultimate goal — the unification of Spain.

But, like most people obsessed with an overriding objective, they made mistakes in their fervor to bind their nation together. Isabel and Ferdinand launched a campaign to impose strict religious homogeneity on their subjects. Most of the impetus for enforcing fundamentalist Christianity came from Isabel, who believed that religious tolerance was a vice, an evil to be punished with unswerving severity.

Wrapping her zealous religious beliefs around her political philosophy, Isabel instituted the measures necessary to eradicate non-believers who she felt threatened to destroy or undermine her cherished conformity. She gave minorities, Jews and Moors, two choices, convert to the Holy Faith or be expelled from Spain. Those who chose exile deprived Spain of a large segment of its most brilliant intellectuals, merchants and bankers. Without a corps of men to handle money and create industries, Spain squandered the wealth flooding in from the New World.

Many of those who remained and converted to Christianity did so in name only, creating a fifth column of what Old Christians viewed as subversives. To ferret out these infidels, Isabel and Ferdinand unleashed the Inquisition. Its success in rooting out Jews and Moors, and later Protestants, was almost complete.

The Inquisition quashed all heretical thinking, and, in the process, shielded Spain and its colonies in the New World from the two most significant waves of Western thought between 1400 and 1900, the Renaissance, which gave thinkers and doers an outlet for their individual creativity, and the Enlightment, which paved the way for liberal democratic ideas of government and economic theories which resulted in the Industrial Revolution. After the gold and silver mines played out, Spain and Latin America remained agricultural and poor.

Because the Inquisition allowed only limited access to these two great intellectual movements, Latin America struggled under medievalism's legacy. Despots and dictators toppled one another with brutal regularity. For centuries the Catholic Church dominated intellectual and political life in much the same way that Islam permeates Iran. Medieval chivalric precepts survived in the form of *machismo, personalismo* and romantic, idealized love of women, primarily as sex objects.

Another hang over of chivalry, *pundonor* (a point of honor), still exists. As Professor Luis Martin of Southern Methodist University says, it is the "unique Hispanic conception of the self, a vivid, almost blinding awareness of one's unmatched inner reality and worth."

When translated into politics, *pundonor's* sense of individual dignity sometimes drowns Hispanics in anarchy, which, in turn, sends them scrambling for its opposite, authoritarianism. It is no accident that the Anarchist Party in the 1930s was the largest political party in Spain, and that Francisco Franco's dictatorship served as a counter weight. "Spaniards are always tempted by extremes. They hate the center," one commentator says.

When translated into daily living, *pundonor's* imperative of pride can sometimes result in self-destruction. Professor Martin tells the true story of a Spanish beggar slumped in his dirty, ragged clothes in front of the Cathedral of Seville. "For the love of God, please let me have some money to eat," the tramp cried. "I'm dying of hunger." A passer-by agreed to give the emaciated man a few *pesestas,* but stipulated that the beggar must spend the money on a sandwich for lunch and soup for dinner. "Take your money back, Senor," the beggar said. "I, and I alone, will determine how to handle my own hunger."

When I began research for this book, I had no idea that so many of the ways of thinking and doing in 1492 Spain still exist in the Hispanic world. The parallels in attitudes, prejudices, institutions and values of five hundred years ago persist, sometimes modified, but at their core the same. The United States still carries the baggage and benefits of English and French traditions, but most of these stem from the liberal Enlightenment of the 1700s and 1800s, not from the remnants of medievalism in the late 1400s.

To understand modern-day Hispanics it is, I believe, necessary to begin with the footprints made in 1492, and to begin with the three remarkable personalities whose careers intertwined and overlapped to play an important role in the next five hundred years of history for millions of their successors.

Machiavelli lauded Ferdinand as the perfect medieval prince; underhanded, deceitful and cruel if necessary. His wife was a strong woman obsessed with unifying her nation and obsessed by the Holy Catholic Church.

Columbus could be equally obsessive, but his goal was different. With his monumental ego, he convinced himself that God ordained him to be the man to find the route west across the Ocean Sea to the riches of the Indies, China and Japan. Having been brought up in the primitive capitalism of Genoa, Columbus had all the instincts of a bourgeois businessman. He yearned for wealth and glory, and would lie, beg or flatter to achieve his aims. He was a man you may not have liked, but who you would have to admire.

Columbus' objective was personal, glory for himself. Isabel's was national, glory for her country. Despite this difference, the Queen and her Admiral shared many traits. They were both unquestioning in their devotion to Christ and the Virgin Mary. They both had forceful, determined personalities. Because Columbus and Isabel were so similar in many ways, a strange, almost mystical, attraction developed between them. Not love, as a few scholars claim, but a deep emotional bond between two people who recognized the traits in the other which would produce success.

Against a medieval background, the Sovereigns and the Admiral proved that individuals do make a difference, that force of personality can prevail and that history is not merely a series of random events that would inevitably happen.

1

ISABEL, FERDINAND, THE EARLY YEARS

Ferdinand and Isabel's dynasty, the Trastamara, began with a bloody stabbing. In 1369, Peter the Cruel sat on the throne of Castile. Consumed in a paranoic mist of distrust and suspicion, Peter the Cruel murdered nobles, churchmen, relatives and, many believed, his own wife. In that year, Peter's illegitimate half-brother, Henry of Trastamara, barged his way into Peter's tent, and, after a furious hand-to-hand fight, sank a dagger into Peter's chest. With the tyrant deposed by fratricide, the Castilian aristocrats, who suffered under the "terror and punishments" of the aptly named Peter, threw their support to Henry. As Henry II, he ruled for ten years, and, upon his death, was followed by two rather inconsequential successors, John I and Henry the Sickly. When Henry the Sickly died at age twenty-seven, his minor son, John II, became King in 1406 at age two.

During the first years of John II's forty-eight-year reign, regents ran Castile's affairs on behalf of the boy-King. When John II reached age fourteen, the regency ended, and, although John II was now empowered to govern his realm, the young man had little interest in his nation's business. The King continued his boyhood passion for intellectual pursuits, reading the Roman classics in the original Latin and writing poetry in Castilian. He also "loved painting and played, sang and danced well." With the King's approval, many courtiers indulged in arts and letters. John

II's private secretary dedicated a compilation of ancient Spanish songs *(cancioneros)* "For the pleasure and amusement of His Highness, the King, when he finds himself too sorely oppressed with the cares of state."[1] Perhaps because of his carefree youth, perhaps because he was lazy and perhaps because he was incompetent as a leader, John II disdained, even hated, his royal duties.

As a dedicated aesthete, and a hopeless politician, John II forfeited the active governance of Castile to favored nobles. One, Alvaro de Luna, emerged to fill the void. Luna, the bastard son of a noble family, had entered the royal service as a pageboy. He was the same age as King John, and Luna's proficiency in music and poetry drew them close. Luna was friendly, and almost everyone liked and admired the young man. A biographer claims that Luna could ride, fence, dance and sing better than any cavalier at court. But Luna's facade of insinuating amiability and good manners masked a consummate liar, a man grasping for power and money and a schemer of the first order.

Armed with these skills, Luna planned his ambitious plots, and executed them with cold, efficient precision. He wheedled his way into King John's confidence, and persuaded the Sovereign to appoint him Grand Master of the Order of Santiago and Constable of Castile. With these exalted titles, coupled with John II's default and Luna's own adroit political manipulation, he became the de facto King of Castile. Without Luna's blessing, appointments to Church, military and government posts were almost impossible, and most of those jobs went to his relatives and supporters. With a network of beholden henchmen spread throughout Castile, Luna's power grew to the point that he arrogantly dictated *pragmaticas* (royal decrees) to his secretary and gave them to King John for signature. Often, the King, more interested in a new poem, didn't bother to read Luna's laws. As Luna's sway over the King grew, so too did his abuse of power, turning many aristocrats against him.

Luna alienated the rich bourgeois in the cities by appointing representatives to the Parliament *(Cortes)*, in clear violation of laws allowing the townsmen to freely elect their representatives. And, with another back of the hand to ancient traditions, Luna imposed taxes on the cities without Parliamentary approval. Like most men with unchecked authority, Luna stumbled over his own greed, becoming the "most notorious legal thief in history...[with an] appetite for land and money [that] was so voracious that after a few years he amassed one and a half million coins of Spanish gold...."[2] As Luna's power grew, his insolence kept pace, and his opponents eventually coalesced into an anti-Luna party. Backed by rich merchants and clergymen, groups of nobles organized cabals to depose Luna.

Odium exploded into civil war between the pro- and anti-Luna factions. Even King John's son and eventual heir, Prince Henry, joined an unsuccessful confederacy against his father and Luna. Although the royal forces, directed by Luna, won, during his thirty years of ascendancy the jealousy and hatred of nobles, clergy and merchants periodically forced the King to banish his favorite from court until the storms subsided. Every time Luna's opponents convinced King John to exile him, he managed to ingratiate himself back into King John's confidence and returned more arrogant and triumphant than ever. Superstitious commentators of the time attributed the King's blind infatuation with Luna to sorcery or witchcraft. But, more likely, Luna's dominance resulted from his strong and willful mind eclipsing John II's weak, pleasure soaked mind.

Even though his mastery over King John was almost total, the haughty Luna finally blundered. Shortly after the death of John II's first wife in 1445, the King set his mind on a marriage to the daughter of the French monarch. But Luna, without consulting King John, opened negotiations with Portugal to marry him to the Princess Isabella.[3] With little argument, the King agreed and married the high strung Isabella of Portugal.

This time the fox outfoxed himself. Miscalculating, Luna thought Queen Isabella would remain in his debt for putting her on the Castilian throne. Instead, the young Queen developed a true affection for the aging King, and her resentment of Luna's ascendency over her music-loving husband quickly grew into hatred. Luna's avarice also drew her ire. "He is stealing the nation," Queen Isabella told the King.[4] Finding a sizeable cadre of nobles to support her, Queen Isabella launched a merciless campaign to get rid of Luna. At first the King resisted. After years of dominance, John II automatically, almost instinctively, backed his favorite. But Queen Isabella's arguments gradually persuaded the King.

Luna, scenting the Queen's loathing and the King's shift against him, made a strategic retreat from court. With Luna away from court, Queen Isabella badgered John II into summoning Luna back to court under a royal letter of safe conduct. Thinking he was once again in the King's favor, Luna returned. The King's men promptly arrested Luna for the ambiguous crime of "treachery." The charges and evidence against Luna were so trivial that, one historian says, "If the King had dispensed such justice to all of his nobles who deserved it...there wouldn't have been anybody left to reign over."[5] Nevertheless, the King's tribunal found Luna guilty and sentenced him to death. But King John was so enslaved by Luna that he twice issued orders to pardon his old friend. Relentlessly, Queen Isabella kept the pressure on her husband. The King even cried, arguing that Luna was no more selfish than the rest of the nobles, and that, even if Luna had stolen millions, he was generous in dispensing his loot. Again, the determined Queen quashed all backsliding.

On the day of the execution, in 1453, Luna was paraded through the streets on a mule preceded by the King's herald shouting to the crowd Luna's crime and its punishment. Along the way, Luna saw one of Prince Henry's servants and shouted to the servant " [Tell the Prince] to reward the affection of his (Henry's) servants with something better than that which King John has given to me." Luna was serene, fully composed. Even though he was illegitimate, he would go out following the aristocratic code of honor, *Vivir bien. Morir bien.* (Live well. Die well.)

As he climbed the scaffold steps, dressed in a blue cloak lined with fox fur, he paused and surveyed the crowd and the executioner. "No manner of death brings shame if it is supported by courage," Luna said. On the platform, Luna knelt and placed his head on the block. With a savage blow, the executioner plunged his sword into Luna's throat, and then severed the head from the body. The head and corpse were left on display for several days until his mutilated remains were buried in a cemetery for criminals. Luna's family later moved the body to a tomb in a chapel in Toledo where they erected a life-sized mechanical statue of him. From under the chapel floor, a servant tugged on a set of chains that caused Luna's statute to stand, sit and kneel. No doubt, some of his enemies attending mass at the chapel must have appreciated the irony of the great manipulator being himself manipulated after death. Luna's legacy to Castile was a feeble crown scorned by much of the nation and a host of incompetents holding important positions in the government, army and Church.

Queen Isabella and King John had two children during their short marriage, a son, Alphonse, and a daughter, Isabel. The official announcement of Princess Isabel's birth read: "I, the King ...make known to you that by the grace of Our Lord, this Thursday just past (April 22, 1451), the Queen, Dona Isabella, my dear and well-beloved wife, was delivered of a daughter; [and I am telling you this so] that you may give thanks to God."[6] Shortly after her birth, Princess Isabel Trastamara was baptized under the gilded cupola in the Church of San Nicolas in Madrigal de las Altas Torres (Madrigal of the High Towers). Madrigal was a sun-baked medieval town surrounded by a defensive wall punctuated by several towers. Its narrow streets rambled past houses and churches that sent the sound of their morning and evening bells tolling over the tawny, bleak plains surrounding the city. Inside the city's walls, Princess Isabel spent her first three years in a windowless, ugly palace owned by her father.

In 1454, King John died, leaving his son by his previous marriage, Henry, as his heir. On his deathbed, John II lamented that "[I was] not born the son of a mechanic, instead of King of Castile." Considering his anemic reign, some of his subjects might have wished the same. As the sovereign, King John was a fumbling failure, causing one historian to sneer that "King John did one thing and one thing only for posterity, and that was to leave behind him a daughter (Isabel) who in no way resembled her father."[7]

Shortly after King John died, dowager Queen Isabella took her auburn-haired daughter and infant son to Arevalo, about twenty miles east of Madrigal. Arevalo was a town of low, monotonous buildings, many churches and a brooding royal castle where the widowed Queen and her children spent the next eight years. Here, mourning her husband's death, Queen Isabella sank into a state of morbid religious obsession. She would sit comatose for hours, staring at the stone walls of her apartments. And, as her madness deepened, she alternated between warm displays of tenderness and love for her children and screaming fits directed at their childish antics. In Spanish history, she is known as "Isabella the Demented."

In this forbidding atmosphere, churchmen carefully instructed Princess Isabel in the lessons of medieval piety and religious devotion. Hooded priests helped her understand the mysteries of the Bible and taught her that only through the Christian religion can man find his true value. For amusement, she drew pictures of Biblical subjects in her prayer book. She loved books, which she collected all her life.[8] With a nod to the new Renaissance traditions, she studied Latin, and read Cicero, Livy and Seneca.[9] Seneca, a Spaniard by birth, was the favorite Roman author of the Castilians. From her ancient countryman, Princess Isabel learned a homey, practical morality. In Livy's histories she read the edifying stories of the lives of famous Romans. From Cicero she learned the necessity of enduring sacrifices to gain one's ends, and she became acquaintedwith the disturbing concepts of republicanism.

From her Castilian teachers, Princess Isabel developed her basic political philosophy—that the divinely ordained crown was at the apex of a hierarchy administered by bureaucrats faithful only to the sovereign. After she came to power, her view would clash with that of many aristocrats, who felt that they and the crown were partners in government. Although Isabel blanched at the idea of sharing power with her nobles, her political philosophy was tempered by her belief that, even though the crown had the God-given right to exercise royal power, the monarch also had a duty to every member of society.

Mixing politics and religion, Princess Isabel subscribed to the idea that her Christian God intervened directly in the affairs of His chosen monarches, and that all nonbelievers were the enemies of God and crown. As a result, Isabel thought the Moors were "murderers who kill without piety...who impiously murdered Christians whenever they could."

In the princely style demanded by Castilian etiquette, Princess Isabel rode horseback and went hunting and hawking with a train of attendants. Like most young noblewomen, she learned to stitch fine needlework and embroidery, and many churches and cities proudly displayed the altar cloths and emblazoned banners she made. When she wasn't bending over her embroidery frame, Princess Isabel read the evangelic mythology of the Reconquest (*Reconquista*), the eight century struggle to rid the Iberian Peninsula of the Moors.

To her, the Reconquest meshed the driving themes of medieval Castile, war and religion, into one glorious cause that pitted the Cross against the Islamic Crescent. The young girl knew the stories of Pelayo, the Christian general who led his men to the first victory over the Infidels in the mountains of northern Spain. In 722, at the Battle of Covadonga, the Moslems advanced through a narrow mountain pass. From the high ground, the Christians opened the battle by heaving boulders and rocks down on the invaders. They then charged downhill, killing many Moors by the sword. Other Infidels were thrown into the fast running mountain stream in the valley below.[10]

Even more inspiring to Princess Isabel were the tales of St. James, the Moor Slayer (Santiago Matamoros), the Patron Saint of Spain whose name became a battle cry for the Castilians in their Holy War against the Moslem forces. In legend, mounted on his great white horse, wielding his terrible broadsword, the warrior-Saint was believed to wreak havoc in the enemy ranks. In Santiago Matamoros, nationalism and religion welded together to form a mighty weapon to crush the alien culture. While Santiago guaranteed a place in Heaven to those who died in the Holy Cause, the crown rewarded Christ's warriors with land and wealth.

By the late 1400s, Rodrigo Diaz was the most dashing Christian hero of legend. To Isabel, his romantic deeds embodied all that was good in a chivalrous Christian. Castilians idolized Diaz as a knight errant, a Spanish Robin Hood and an ever-loyal Christian who slaughtered the Sons of Islam with abandon. In truth, Diaz was a mercenary who fought for Christians or Moors, depending on what was in his best interest at the moment. He had been born about 1042, and was a true product of his age—a military entrepreneur. At that time, there were no real estate or industrial empires to conquer. Had Donald Trump or Henry Ford been born in 1042, these ambitious men would have been soldiers. Just like Diaz, they would have strapped on breastplates, honed their swords and set out on massive war horses to do battle for money and glory. Diaz, the son of minor Castilian nobility, entered the service of King Ferdinand I and, at an early age, distinguished himself as a valiant warrior.

When Ferdinand I died, his two sons battled for the right to succeed their father. Diaz fought, at different times, for both sons, but wound up on the side of the eventual winner, King Alphonse VI of Castile. For the next seven years, Diaz generaled the King's battles, but his aggressive, acquisitive ways alienated Alphonse VI. And, in 1079, the King banished Diaz from Castile. Exiled and broke, Diaz tried to find work with other Christian potentates in the Peninsula, but was snubbed. Finally, he took the only course left, and hired on as a soldier of fortune with the Moslem ruler of Zaragoza.

Now in Moslem service, he earned his historic name, El Cid (from the Arabic word *Sidi* [Lord]). For several years, El Cid fought for the Moors with distinction, defeating Christian princes with regularity, and, in the process, earning himself the additional sobriquet of *Campeador* (Champion). Although the Muslim ruler allowed El Cid Campeador and his mercenaries to keep large shares of the booty, it wasn't enough for the avaricious general. Already his name drew up images of panache and audacity, and stories circulated in the Iberian Peninsula of the hairy, muscular El Cid charging into battle with sword flailing, his cloak flying from broad, armored shoulders. Success in fighting and plundering for the Moorish cause attracted many restive knights to his banner, and, increasingly, El Cid fought for his own enrichment and aggrandizement. "His power grew enormous, and there was not a district he did not ravage," an Arab historian wrote. "Nevertheless, this man, the scourge of his day, because of his love of splendor, boldness of character and dauntless courage, was one of the marvels of God."[11]

Eventually, El Cid turned his greed toward the rich Mediterranean port city of Valencia. Three rival factions schemed to gain control of the city, and, somehow, El Cid convinced each that he was their friend. "But everybody's friend was nobody's ally." He attracted recruits to his cause with the alluring message that "Those who want to stop their toil and get rich, come to me to conquer and populate the land."[12] With new men under his flag, he used lies and diversionary pitched battles as tactics as he fought to conquer Valencia. When El Cid drew up his army in front of Valencia, the stubborn Moslem defenders of the city held fast. To induce a hasty surrender, El Cid instructed his men to roast a few of the captured Moors on the Christian campfires and to hunt others with packs of vicious hounds. Finally, the Arab defenders agreed to a treaty which permitted El Cid to enter Valencia peacefully. After only a few months, he broke the treaty, burned the Muslim leader alive and proclaimed himself King of Valencia.

Despite several attempts to unseat him by a new, fanatic band of North African Arabs sweeping into Spain, El Cid ruled Valencia until his death in 1099. His wife held on, but the hordes of fierce desert Berbers chanting Allah's name forced her to yield after three years. In defeat, she strapped El Cid's body, which had been embalmed in spices, to his favorite war horse, tied his sword in his hand and took El Cid's remains for burial at his birthplace near Burgos.

When Princess Isabel read the epic "Poem of El Cid" 350 years after his death, his brutality and service to the Infidels was no longer part of the myth. That he razed mosques and churches with equal abandon and fought for whoever paid the most had faded into history. By the 1300s and 1400s, El Cid's legend had grown to the point that a Castilian king tried to have him canonized as a saint. In the Christian mind, and myth, El Cid Campeador was a swashbuckling, undefeatable vanquisher of the hated Moors.

Because of the disgust for the impotent reign of John II and his minion Luna, Castilians welcomed the accession of his son, Henry IV, to the throne in 1454. A new reign, a new young King to replace his fifty-year-old father. People liked the affable young man and noted that Henry IV was kind, even familiar, with his inferiors. By nature, he didn't like confrontation or conflict, and preferred negotiation and compromise whenever possible. Although, as a prince, King Henry took part in a plot against his father, people shrugged this off to inexperience and youthful spirit. Contrary to the parsimonious John II, the new King was open-handed and generous, being nicknamed "Henry the Liberal" early on in his reign. When his treasurer goaded him for spending too freely, Henry replied, "We must give to our enemies to make them friends, and to our friends to keep them so." He enjoyed the pomp of kingship, and the people delighted in reviewing his splendidly outfitted personal bodyguard of thirty-six hundred lances, officered by the sons of favored nobles. Henry IV gained more support when he proclaimed a Holy Crusade against the Moors, and the people cheered his newly adopted coat of arms which included the pomegranate, the ancient symbol of the Muslim Kingdom of Granada.

But the honeymoon period didn't last long. Henry IV's half-hearted forays against the Moors produced no victory of significance. His unsuccessful armies of up to forty thousand men lived off the land, plundering orchards and fields of the Castilian peasants, causing some to complain that "the war was carried on against us, not against the Infidels." After a few years of abortive battles, the troops began to doubt their King, and, after one unwarranted retreat, attempted to arrest Henry to prevent him from disbanding the army.

To finance the Crusade, he levied heavy taxes and collected Papal indulgences. Priests sold the indulgences, which pardoned a man's sins and reduced the time spent in purgatory before entering Heaven, for two hundred maravedis apiece. Although the money from the sale of indulgences was to be shared with the Church, most of it was diverted to Henry IV's pockets. And, to fund his extravagant spending on clothes and jewelry, the King dipped into money intended for the Holy Brotherhood (*Santa Hermandad*), Castile's rural police force.

In addition to squandering money on personal pleasures, Henry IV's monetary policy further debased the Castilian maravedi. When Henry became King, only five royal mints existed, all controlled by the crown. In a few years, the five had grown to one hundred fifty mints, almost all controlled by Henry's favorites. The glut of coinage depreciated the maravedi six hundred percent, creating economic chaos.[13]

Because of his lackadaisical interest in government and his indulgence in the sweet life, political power soon passed to a few favorites who wormed their way into Henry IV's confidence. These friends abused their privileges and openly accepted bribes, sometimes from foreign kings. The most notorious favorite was Juan Pacheco, Marquis of Villena, a wily intriguer who was "deaf to the voice of patriotism or personal loyalty to the King." One historian says, "[Villena] knew how to conceal all other vices except for his greed, which he could neither conceal nor moderate."[14]

While Henry IV's coddled favorites ran the government for

their own benefit, the King permitted and encouraged the debauchery of the Castilian court. Even as a young man, Henry "[relished] the brutish pleasures of a voluptuary." Morals degenerated, sexual depravity was blatant. "In him (Henry IV), desire had the mastery over reason," Pulgar, a court historian, wrote.[15] Where his father spent his idle time listening to poems or ballads, Henry spent his time with whores and courtesans.

After twelve years of a childless marriage, in 1452 Henry pressured the Archbishop of Toledo into voiding his union with Blanche of Aragon because of "the impotence of both parties, owing to some malign influence." In 1455, the year after he became King, Henry married the beautiful Portuguese Princess Joan, who, in the bloom of youth, "was possessed of personal graces and a lively wit which...made her the delight of the court of Portugal."

On her entry into Castile, Joan and her entourage of maids of honor were greeted by military pageants and magnificent parties. Stories circulated that, at one welcoming party, she danced with the French ambassador who was so smitten with her that he vowed never to dance with another woman.[16] Even though his new young wife was beautiful, the philandering Henry's instincts prevailed. He scandalized the court by seducing one of Queen Joan's maids of honor, and openly kept her in regal splendor as his mistress. Forgetting royal dignity, Queen Joan engaged in a shouting, slapping cat fight with the King Henry's paramour. Finally, the King sent his mistress to the country. But it wasn't long before the hot-blooded Henry further shocked the court by appointing another discarded mistress as abbess of a convent in Toledo, saying that the convent needed reform.

Even though Queen Joan lived in an era when the code of chivalry demanded that wives remain chaste, she couldn't resist temptation. Her wandering husband's disappearances from the marriage bed disappointed the beautiful, high spirited young Queen. "[Queen Joan] was a woman to whom love speeches were pleasant," one historian said. "[And] she delighted more in the beauty of her face than in the glory of her reputation."[17] Not long after her arrival in Castile, court gossips linked Queen Joan with one of Castile's handsomest nobles, Beltran de la Cueva. Beltran, a favorite of Henry IV, held the title of Lord High Steward and the King later elevated him to the Dukedom of Albuquerque.

The future Duke personified the dash and audacity of romantic chivalry. To pay homage to his unnamed "fair lady," Beltran challenged all comers to a passage of arms *("paso")*; jousts on horseback with lances. Several knights accepted the challenge, and many lances were broken that day. To commemorate the noble occasion, King Henry established the monastery of San Jeronimo del Paso (St. Jerome of the Passage of Arms) on the site of the jousting field. The courtiers whispered that the unnamed "fair lady" was Queen Joan.

In 1462, after seven years of marriage, Queen Joan became pregnant, catching King Henry's detractors off guard. His old nickname, "Henry the Liberal," had long since been discarded. His enemies now used the behind-the-back gibe "Henry the Impotent," referring as much to the King's inability to run the government as to his failure to produce an heir during nineteen years of marriage to two different women.

Fearing plots against him by the Castilian aristocrats sickened by the debauchery of the court and the chaos in the government, Henry the Impotent seized custody of his half-sister and half-brother, Princess Isabel and Prince Alphonse. The King moved them into a royal palace under the guard of men loyal to him. The professed reason Henry gave for taking the Princess and Prince away from their mother was so that "they could be better brought up and learn more virtuous customs than away from His Majesty's presence." With this direct exposure to the corrupt and licentious court, the eleven-year-old Princess Isabel heard the rumors about her new cousin.

When Queen Joan gave birth to a daughter, the rumors claimed that the baby girl was Beltran's child, not the King's. As political propaganda, Henry IV's enemies branded the infant *La Beltraneja* (Beltran's bastard daughter). The King and Queen named her Joan, after her mother. Princess Isabel attended Princess Joan's baptism, and was named a god-mother to her cousin. And, despite La Beltraneja's questionable parentage, Henry IV recognized her as his legitimate heir, and required the nobles to swear an oath to support his only child. Now, with two possible heirs to the throne, the stage was set for a breakup of the Castilian nobles into opposing parties—the supporters of Henry the Impotent and La Beltraneja and those of Prince Alphonse and Princess Isabel.

With an incompetent cuckold on the throne, and his daughter a suspected bastard, the court fell into contempt. Because of Henry IV's feeble rule, and the greed of his favorites, Castile had collapsed into a state of hopeless anarchy and weakness. There was no law and order, the government was inefficient and the national prosperity and power were at a low point. While nobles ran amuck, churchmen guzzled and fornicated and judges turned a blind eye to justice or held out their hands for bribes. Princess Isabel looked on—revolted by the degradation and immorality swirling around the crown.

A small group of powerful aristocrats, convinced of La Beltraneja's illegitimacy and disgusted by the economic and moral anarchy in Castile, formed a coalition supporting Princess Isabel's brother Alphonse as the rightful heir to the throne. The rebellious nobles issued a manifesto listing their grievances against Henry IV. The King, they said, was lax in religious matters, debased the coinage, appointed corrupt judges and allowed his personal bodyguard to commit unchecked violence. And, since Henry IV's only goal seemed to be the avoidance of risk, his enemies interpreted this as weakness. Alphonse's supporters swore never to reenter the King's service until he righted the wrongs and recognized Prince Alphonse as heir apparent. At first, Henry rejected the brazen attempt to force him to admit the illegitimacy of La Beltraneja. But the rebellious nobles knew their man, and gambled that the King's well-known fear of civil war would force him to back down.

Since the rebels were a minority, Henry's supporters urged him to crush the recalcitrants by force. When the Bishop of Cuenca urged him to fight, the King snapped, "You priests, who don't have to fight, are very liberal with the blood of others." The Bishop, unafraid of the King, snapped back, "Since you are not true to your own honor at a time like this, I will live to see you become the most degraded monarch in [Castilian history], and you will live to be sorry for your cowardice." Despite the pleas of his supporters, Henry wavered and sought compromise.

In 1464, King Henry delivered custody of Prince Alphonse to the rebels and agreed to recognize his half-brother as heir, on condition that Alphonse marry La Beltaneja when they reached majority. Henry also appointed a five-man commission to reform the abuses of power. The commission's report slashed the King's power "to such an extent that they (the commission) left him almost nothing of his powers except the title of King, without power to command or any preeminence."[18] The normally passive King Henry became roused at last. He disavowed his agreement to recognize Alphonse as his heir, rejected the commission's report and sent a threatening letter to the belligerents. The anti-Henry party defiantly told the King's messenger: "Go tell your King that we have had enough of him and his affairs. Henceforward, he will see who is the true Sovereign of Castile."

The plotters proclaimed Alphonse king, and Castile began choosing up sides. Toledo, Seville and Cordoba in the south defected to Alphonse. But most of the Castilian cities and nobles in northern Castile remained loyal to King Henry, recalling his generous disposition and blaming most of the corruption on his evil advisors. Henry's counsellors told him that his supporters were "eager to come to blows with those tyrants who have dishonored their natural Lord," and pressed him into issuing a call to arms. Thousands rallied to Henry's cause, and ferocious fighting broke out all over the Kingdom. But, despite his superiority in arms and men, the vacillating King again chose conciliation and appeasement.

King Henry met with the Marquis of Villena, who had deserted his patron and was now a leader of the confederates. Henry first requested that both sides disband their armies. Villena agreed. Then Villena reminded the King of the treasury's depleted state. He offered an enormous sum of money to replenish the royal coffers, in return for Henry's recognition of Prince Alphonse as heir to the throne. Henry agreed. And, in doing so, admitted La Beltraneja's illegitimacy. Next, Villena had the effrontery to propose that Princess Isabel marry Villena's brother. Henry agreed, even though the Villena family were upstarts in the Castilian nobility, much inferior to the Trastamaras. To seal the bargain, the rebels and the King signed a truce in 1465 that lasted almost two years.

Anxious to implement the agreement, Villena's forty-three-year-old brother, the Grand Master of the powerful Calatrava military order, immediately began wedding plans. The Grand Master was twenty-nine years older than Princess Isabel, and, even more loathsome to the devout Isabel, the Grand Master lived a notoriously debauched life. He had a reputation as a voluptuary, even being accused of making indecent proposals to Princess Isabel's demented mother.

After hearing the news of her betrothal, the fourteen-year-old Isabel couldn't eat or sleep for days and spent long hours praying to God for relief. When Princess Isabel told her best friend, Beatriz de Bobadilla, of the proposed marriage, Beatriz said, "God will not permit it, and neither will I." Beatriz then drew a dagger from her skirts, and vowed to assassinate the Grand Master. Princess Isabel, her prayers seemingly answered, experienced her first piece of political luck. While the Grand Master was traveling in splendid state to meet his intended for the wedding, he died, some thought by poison.

During the two-year truce, the rebels consolidated their support, and renewed their demands against King Henry. After months of squabbling over, and backtracking on, the truce, it fell apart. The confederates proclaimed Alphonse King, and civil war broke out. The two armies met on the plains of Olmedo in August of 1467. Before the battle began, a rebel knight sent a message through the lines to Henry's favorite, Beltran de la Cueva, warning Beltran to stay off the field because forty of the noble rebels had sworn to kill him. Ever chivalrous, Beltran sent back a note describing in detail what he would wear during the battle.

At Olmedo, on a hot summer day, the knights, clad in full armor, sweltered inside their iron suits. The rebels rode by the side of their fourteen-year-old King Alphonse. King Henry didn't participate in the fighting, but looked on from afar. As the lines of sword-swinging men ebbed and flowed, at the first sign of a reversal in his troops' fortunes, King Henry fled, sure that the battle was lost. Late that evening, a messenger found Henry hiding in a nearby village. When the messenger told Henry that his army was still intact, the King rejoined his army. Because the Battle of Olmedo was indecisive, civil war spread across the nation. The opposing forces skirmished for almost a year until Alphonse died suddenly in 1468. Some claimed that he had been fed a poisoned trout. With her brother's death, all eyes turned to Princess Isabel. The political chess board was altered. Now, she was the centerpiece of the confederates' plots.

At the beginning of the civil war, King Henry had held Princess Isabel in his custody. After the Battle of Olmedo, the rebels conquered Segovia, where Princess Isabel was being kept under guard, and she slipped away to rejoin the faction loyal to Alphonse. When Alphonse died, the Princess moved to a convent at Avila, surrounded by white robed nuns in the peaceful seclusion of the cloister. The rebels, thinking they could easily influence the Princess, sent a delegation to Avila. With their lives and property at stake, they leaned hard on the teen-aged girl, pressuring Isabel to accept the title of Queen of Castile and continue the fight. They needed a figurehead, a rallying point. But, even at her age, Princess Isabel was already a shrewd judge of situations and men. She knew the aristocrats were perfectly capable of shifting their loyalties on a whim and of backing off their promises overnight.

At seventeen, when some modern American girls' only worry is whether they will be elected cheerleader, Princess Isabel faced hard decisions. Would she agree to be the puppet of the rebels or reconcile with Henry IV? If she reconciled with the King, would he recognize her or La Beltraneja as his heir? Should she declare herself Queen of Castile? For Princess Isabel, the last question was easy. For her to sanction a rebellion against the crown, even if she won, would stigmatize her as a usurper—illegitimate, illegal. And it would open the door for future rebels to use the precedent against her. No, she would not be a party to a naked attempt to remove a sovereign by force of arms. The rebels pressed her. She resisted. "While Henry lives, none other has the right to the crown," she told them. "The country has been divided long enough under the rule of two competing monarches, and Alphonse's death may, perhaps, be interpreted as a sign from Heaven that [God] disapproves of the [rebel] cause."[19]

Without Isabel's support, lacking a focal point, the rebels' only course was clear—negotiate. Knowing Henry's conciliatory nature, the rebel commanders were sure they could make a good deal, and they did. In the Treaty of Toros de Guisando, King Henry, in return for a guarantee of his throne for life, granted a general amnesty to the confederates. He also agreed to divorce Queen Joan and send her and La Beltraneja back to Portugal. Then, Henry recognized Princess Isabel as heir to the crown of Castile. For the second time, La Beltraneja's purported father declared her illegitimate. Although the Treaty put Isabel first in line, the clauses related to her marriage was of almost equal importance to the young woman. Having narrowly escaped a marriage to the aged Grand Master of Calatrava, Princess Isabel insisted that she could not be forced to marry anyone against her will. On the other hand, Isabel agreed that she would not marry without King Henry's permission.

To formalize the Treaty, Henry and Isabel met on September 9, 1468, at Toros de Guisando, the little town for which the Treaty was named. Surrounded by their coteries of nobles and prelates, brilliantly dressed in brocades, rich silks and their finest jewels, the King and Princess embraced affectionately. Henry solemnly proclaimed Isabel his rightful heir, and commanded the assembled aristocrats and churchmen to kiss her hand and swear allegiance to his half-sister. Shortly thereafter, the Castilian Parliament ratified the succession "because they [the deputies to Parliament] had been informed by witnesses worthy of credence of the adultery of the Queen [Joan] and the impotence of the King." For the time being, Isabel was the sole, legitimate heir to the throne, with the title of Princess of Asturias.

As next in line, her marriage plans became the single most important political issue in the Kingdom. Both her supporters and her enemies had a vital interest in knowing who would join Isabel on the Castilian throne when Henry IV died. With free and clear title to the crown, Isabel was a prized plum. For years, Henry IV and his advisors had been negotiating possible marriages. When Isabel had been only nine, King Henry had agreed to her betrothal to Charles of Aragon, Ferdinand's forty-year-old half-brother. But Charles died before the wedding took place. The Castilians held serious discussions with the English to marry Isabel off to the hunchback who would later become Richard III of England. Isabel declined. Henry IV put forward the Duke of Guienne, the French King's brother, thinking that a French marriage might remove Isabel from the Castilian chess board and pave the way for La Beltraneja's return. Isabel declined, after receiving a report that the French Duke was "feeble, effeminate...with limbs so emaciated as to be almost deformed...and eyes so weak and watery as to incapacitate him for the ordinary exercises of chivalry."

King Alfonso of Portugal, who had proposed a marriage to Isabel four years before, renewed his suit. Isabel declined. Her supporters floated the name of Ferdinand of Aragon, and it appeared that Ferdinand was amenable to the match. Intrigued, Isabel sent her private chaplain to investigate. "Ferdinand...[is] possessed of a comely, symmetrical figure, a graceful demeanor, and a spirit that [is] up to anything," the clergyman reported. "He is well suited to anything he may want to do."[20] The more she heard of this daring seventeen-year-old who was already fighting at the side of his father, King John of Aragon, the more interested she became.

In addition to Ferdinand of Aragon's stout character and favorable physical aspects, Isabel and Ferdinand were of common stock, their grandfathers having been brothers. They spoke the same language and they had similar traditions. Their backgrounds meshed, and, if she was lucky, there might be love.

Still, however, the faction controlling Henry IV heavily touted King Alfonso of Portugal. Isabel analyzed the political implications. If she married the Portuguese King, she would be a foreigner in Castilian eyes, reducing her chances of gaining the Castilian crown. Since Alfonso of Portugal already had an heir, Isabel's children could not hope to succeed to the throne of Portugal. And, although Portugal was a sea power, it faced the unknown wasteland of the Atlantic Ocean. On the other hand, the great maritime power of Aragon, with important ports at Valencia and Barcelona, would help cut off the Moors in Granada by sea, and would open Castile to the prosperous trade in the Mediterranean. Also, a marriage to Ferdinand would unite Castile and Aragon under one rule, creating a country that could compete to join the first rank of European nations. Henry IV tried persuasion. Isabel wouldn't budge. He threatened to throw her in prison if she didn't marry King Alfonso of Portugal. Isabel's blue-green eyes didn't blink.

By late 1468, it was no secret that Isabel had her mind, and heart, fixed on Ferdinand. Young men in Castile paraded with banners emblazoned with the coats of arms of Aragon and Castile, and made up satirical poems contrasting the aging Portuguese monarch with the youthful graces of Ferdinand. But there was one major obstacle. In the Treaty of Toros de Guisando, Isabel agreed that Henry IV had the right to approve her mate. It would be risky to break her agreement with the King, even though he had not fulfilled many of his pledges. Isabel cautiously lined up supporters for the Aragonese match, chief among them being the Archbishop of Toledo and the Admiral of Castile, Ferdinand's maternal grandfather. With these, and other, powerful men backing her, in early 1469, Isabel sent her ambassador to Aragon with a favorable, but secret, reply to her suitor.

King John of Aragon was delighted. He and Henry IV had long been rivals for control of Navarre, and King John hadn't forgotten his humiliation when Henry IV divorced King John's daughter Blanche and sent her back to Aragon. A marriage of Ferdinand and Isabel was an opportunity to foil Henry IV's plan to fuse Portugal and Spain, and to carry out John of Aragon's grand design of uniting his country with Castile. To enhance his son's status, and to increase Aragon's bargaining position in the negotiation of the marriage contract, King John bestowed one of his titles, King of Sicily, on Ferdinand.

After his first wife's death in 1447, John of Aragon married into the Enriquez family, headed by the powerful Admiral of Castile. His new Castilian wife, Joan Enriquez, was "of consummate address, intrepid spirit and unprincipled ambition," the historian William Prescott says. Five years after the marriage, in 1452, Queen Joan of Aragon presented her husband with a son, Ferdinand.

Even before Ferdinand's birth, Queen Joan had feuded with her step-son Charles, the heir to the Aragonese crown.[21] After the birth of Ferdinand, the struggle between the first and second families intensified. But, when Charles died in 1462, King John proclaimed the ten-year-old Ferdinand heir to the Aragonese crown.

While Princess Isabel and Henry IV were in Ocana attending a meeting of Parliament in late 1469, a rebellion broke out in Andalusia in the south. Before leaving Ocana with his army, Henry IV extracted a promise from Isabel that she would take no "new" steps regarding marriage until he returned. She gave her promise, reasoning that, since she had already, but secretely, committed to marry Ferdinand in early 1469, there was no "new" arrangement.

While the King and his army marched south, Isabel sent word to Henry IV that she was taking her brother Alphonse's body to Avila to be buried in state. After a brief pause in Avila, she moved farther north to her birthplace at Madrigal to be with her mentally ill mother. Suspicious of his half-sister's movements, King Henry appointed the Bishop of Burgos to spy on Isabel, and bribed many of her household servants to report her activities to Henry's men. The reports were not favorable.

Convinced that Isabel was plotting against him and that she might be moving forward with a marriage to Ferdinand, King Henry sent an armed force to Madrigal to arrest Isabel. At the same time, the King sent a letter to the city fathers of Madrigal telling them that he would treat any favor shown to Isabel as an act of treason. The situation became so tense that Isabel's best friend, Beatriz de Bobadilla, urged her to break off the Aragonese marriage. But, Isabel said, her course was set.

Using the threat against her person as a pretext to repudiate her agreement to obtain Henry IV's approval of her marriage, Isabel issued a call to arms to her supporters. The Admiral of Castile and the Archbishop of Toledo hastily assembled a small army which got to Madrigal before the King's men arrived. Surrounded by loyal troops, Isabel threw out Henry's spies. She and her entourage then moved farther north to Valladolid, the headquarters city of the Admiral of Castile. Isabel's rejection of the Treaty of Toros de Guisando and calling men to arms were major gambles. Had she read the cards right? Had the shrewd judge of political circumstances, of friends and enemies, trumped at the right time? Isabel's bet now depended on Ferdinand playing his part in the drama.

Isabel sent two envoys to Ferdinand to urge him to come to Valladolid immediately. The timing couldn't have been worse. John of Aragon and Ferdinand were putting down a civil war that had broken out in Barcelona, and the Aragonese treasury was almost drained. The urgency was clear, but King John's choices were to divert money and men from the fight with Barcelona to accompany Ferdinand, or to send his only son, unprotected, to Castile. King John knew that if Henry IV stopped fighting in Andalusia and returned with his army to capture Isabel the marriage would never take place. King John told his son that he couldn't make the decision for him.

Excited by the danger and romance of such a chivalrous adventure, Ferdinand quickly devised a plan. He sent a messenger to Isabel to tell her he was coming. As a diversion, King John publicly announced that he was sending ambassadors to Henry IV to discuss the situation, and, amid much pomp and display, the decoy embassy left for Castile over the main roads. Ferdinand disguised himself as a servant, and he and six of his officers, posing as merchants, set off for Valladolid. To carry out the deception, at stops along the way Ferdinand took care of the mules and served his companions their meals.

Although Henry IV's supporters controlled the fortresses along the Castilian-Aragonese border, the seven-man party crossed the frontier with no difficulty. In Castile, squadrons of Henry IV's cavalry combed the countryside to arrest Ferdinand before he joined Isabel. The party eluded Henry's troops and made its way to a small Castilian town garrisoned by Isabel's partisans. Arriving late on a chilly October night, Ferdinand banged on the town gate. The guards on the battlement, not knowing who was creating the ruckus, showered stones down on the party, narrowly missing Ferdinand's head. Finally, Ferdinand identified himself and the guards lowered the gate. Accompanied by Isabel's supporters, Ferdinand arrived at Valladolid on the night of October 15, 1469. Even though it was late, he went immediately to Isabel's apartments. It was the first meeting of the two young people who would shape Spain's destiny.

After her meeting with Ferdinand, Isabel wrote to Henry IV, telling the King that Ferdinand was in Valladolid and that she intended to marry him. To justify breaking her agreement to obtain Henry's approval of her marriage partner, Isabel told the King that he breached the Treaty of Toros de Guisando first by sending armed forces to arrest her. Isabel then pointed out the political advantages of uniting Aragon with the Castilian throne, and noted that many Castilian nobles heartily approved the marriage. In a final effort at conciliation, she concluded by asking Henry IV's approval, and assured him that she and Ferdinand would remain loyal to the King. Henry's curt reply was that "[I will] take counsel with my Ministers," a response just short of an open declaration of war.

Before the marriage ceremony could take place there was one more formality. Ferdinand and Isabel were second cousins and, under Church law, could not marry without a bull of dispensation from the Pope. Knowing that the deeply religious Isabel would never marry in violation of the laws of the Church, Ferdinand produced a spurious Papal bull with a forged signature. King John had anticipated the problem, and, in collusion with the Archbishop of Toledo, prepared the document and concealed its falsity from Isabel. With the religious issue seemingly cleared, Ferdinand and Isabel married on October 19, 1469. The ceremony took place in Valladolid at the palace of a noble supporter, with the Archbishop of Toledo performing the nuptial rites. It was a simple ceremony, partly because it was organized in only a few days, and partly because the bride and groom didn't have enough money to pay for an elaborate wedding.

Isabel and Ferdinand signed their marriage contract, and it

was read aloud to the gathered witnesses. The contract granted Isabel a dowry, and Ferdinand agreed to treat Isabel's mother with reverence. Although it was a marriage contract, it was, at the same time, a political document. To quiet the fears of Henry IV and his clique, Ferdinand and Isabel agreed that Henry IV was the rightful King, and that Henry's followers would not be stripped of their property or titles. To assure that Ferdinand would not upset Castilian traditions, he swore to respect the laws and customs of Castile. He also promised to live in Castile and not to leave the country without Isabel's permission.

Then came the provisions that struck the delicate political balance between the couple. The contract prohibited Ferdinand from making war or alliances without Isabel's approval. In order to make government and military appointments, and to issue new laws, both of their signatures would be required. Isabel reserved to herself the exclusive right to make appointments to posts in her treasured Catholic Church.

The marriage contract set the basic structure under which Ferdinand and Isabel would jointly rule for thirty-one years. The watchword that would govern their relationship was *Tanto monta, monta tanto, Isabel como Fernando.* (The one as much as the other, Isabel and Ferdinand are equal.) It was to be a marriage partnership of equals—astonishing in an age when women's rights were almost nonexistent.

In medieval thought, women existed primarily for men's pleasure and for bearing children to keep the family line alive. Isabel would perform these roles, but, in concert with her husband, she would mold Spain into a country that would stand at the apex of European nations for the next two hundred years. "The will and actions of Ferdinand and Isabel complemented each other, so that life in Spain seemed to be governed by a single mind," a historian writes of their reign. "It is not only difficult...but [almost] impossible to distinguish the personal role of either monarch in governmental decisions."[22]

Working in tandem, their partnership created the foundation which permitted Spain to conquer global empires and to become the first nation in Europe. To do this, the Sovereigns would tame the rapacious aristocrats who splitered Castile into chaos. They would join Castile and Aragon, bring Muslim Granada under Chistian control and assert their royal authority over Spain's institutions. But, before achieving these goals, the teen-aged couple would face years of struggle.

2

THE ROAD TO SUCCESSION

Even though the Treaty of Toros de Guisando and Parliament confirmed the newlyweds' title to the Castilian throne, Ferdinand and Isabel spent their first years together enmeshed in a tangle of plots and counterplots spun by deceitful nobles and churchmen. To buy loyalty, Henry IV had a store of lands, titles and money to shower on the aristocrats and clergymen. While King Henry passed out largess freely, Ferdinand and Isabel had little more than risky expectations of future rewards to offer their supporters.

Ferdinand's father, John of Aragon, had promised a rich dowry in the marriage contract, but his years of fighting civil wars and the French left him struggling to find enough money to keep his kingdom together. The young couple was so poor they had trouble paying ordinary living expenses and moved their small court to an out-of-the-way village north of Valladolid.

Almost penniless, Ferdinand and Isabel lived mostly off the charity of their noble and clerical patrons, primarily the Archbishop of Toledo. From his vast Church income, the Archbishop doled out sufficient funds for Ferdinand and Isabel to pay their household needs. But there was a price. The Archbishop demanded absolute loyalty and deference from Ferdinand and Isabel. If the couple became too cozy with another advisor or refused to take his advice, the jealous Archbishop reminded them of his constant, and continuing, support.

Isabel bridled at the domineering prelate's attempts to control her. But not even Isabel's ire stopped the heavy-handed Archbishop. Finally, Ferdinand told him, "[I will] not be put in harness like so many of the other sovereigns of Castile [have been]." When the wily old King of Aragon got wind of the rift between the impoverished nineteen-year-olds and their principal financial backer, King John wrote a letter counselling them to choke down their pride, to placate the Archbishop. Ferdinand and Isabel, understanding that there were too many risks and uncertainties to openly break with one of the most powerful men in Castile, took King John's advice, for the time being.

Although their attempts at independence nettled the Archbishop of Toledo, early on he remained loyal to Ferdinand and Isabel. Henry IV did manage to seduce the couple's erstwhile friend, the Marquis of Villena, back to the royal side by dangling the Grand Mastership of Santiago before the Marquis. Now in charge of the predominant military order in Castile, the new Grand Master and his potent family were, once again, staunch supporters of the King and La Beltraneja. And it didn't take the Grand Master long to oil his way into the position of Henry IV's chief advisor.

Back in the King's good graces, the cunning Grand Master convinced Henry to issue a manifesto in October of 1470 declaring Isabel's rights to the throne void because she violated the Treaty of Toros de Guisando when she married Ferdinand without the King's approval. The manifesto also branded the marriage illegal due to the forged Papal bull used to sanction the union.

As part of the Grand Master's grand design, Henry IV declared La Beltraneja his legitimate heir and simultaneously announced the nine-year-old Princess' betrothal to the rheumy-eyed, emaciated Duke of Guienne, the King of France's brother whom Isabel rejected as a mate two years before. The Grand Master convinced Henry to agree to the French marriage with arguments that France would end its conspiracies to wrest control of two Basque provinces in northern Castile, and that the full power of France would back La Beltraneja's claim to the throne. Henry IV's supporters swore an oath of allegiance to La Beltraneja, but Castilian law and custom required Parliament's approval. Henry summoned the deputies. They refused to come. He summoned them again. They stayed home.

In that same month of October, 1470, Isabel gave birth to her first child, a daughter, who the couple named Isabel after her mother, as was common at the time. Isabel was enraged by the claim that her marriage, and therefore her new baby, were illegitimate. Barely out of the birthing bed, Isabel countered Henry's manifesto. As proof of her loyalty, she said, she had declined the crown when her supporters offered it to her after her brother Alphonse's death. She entered into the marriage with Ferdinand, Isabel claimed, on the advice of the wiser and larger segment of the leading nobles. Her right to the crown, she said, were valid, and it couldn't be nullified by a stroke of the King's pen, particularly when that pen was being manipulated by the Grand Master. As required by law, she had Parliament's blessing. Answering Henry's charge that she breached the Treaty of Toros de Guisando, Isabel counterclaimed that Henry breached it first by sending armed forces to arrest her at Madrigal in 1469.

Although legal rights were important, they meant little without power and political muscle. Enticed by Henry's favors and liberal grants of privileges, the Mendoza, Pacheco, Zuniga, Velasco and Pimentel families lined up with the King and La Beltraneja. Ferdinand and Isabel, like many politicians with few favors to pass out, launched a negative propaganda campaign.

Playing on the emotional and religious appeal of her legitimacy, and with the odor surrounding La Beltraneja's parentage still hanging in the air, Isabel took direct aim at La Beltraneja's alleged bastardy. Isabel was without question a legitimate Trastamara. She knew who her father was. With these appeals to legality and offers of riches and privileges when the couple succeeded to the throne, powerful noble families in the south kept most of Andalusia in Isabel and Ferdinand's camp. The new Pope, Sixtus IV, favored Ferdinand and Isabel, and the Enriquez and Guzman families sided with the Archbishop of Toledo behind them. The Basque provinces in the north, fearing an alliance between King Henry and France that would lead to their domination by the French, supported Ferdinand and Isabel. But perhaps the couple's greatest appeal came from Ferdinand and Isabel's strong characters which, their supporters hoped, would result in a wise, orderly administration when they became King and Queen.

The loyalties of nobles, clergy and cities wavered with the shifting fortunes of the contending parties. Henry IV caused a major swing of the political pendulum when he transferred custody and protection of La Beltraneja from the Mendoza family to the family of the Grand Master of Santiago. Shortly after the transfer, Cardinal Mendoza entered into correspondence with Isabel. Cardinal Mendoza did not openly sever his ties with Henry IV, but he began the dangerous game of currying favor with Isabel. Behind the scenes, Ferdinand performed favors for the Duke of the Infantado, the head of the Mendoza family.

While the thin constancy of some prelates and nobles waxed

and waned, others attempted mediation. Isabel's closest friend, Beatriz de Bobadilla, had married the officer in charge of King Henry's Royal Treasury at Segovia. With Henry's approval, the officer, Andres de Cabrera, persuaded his wife to write Isabel proposing a reconciliation with the King. Isabel wrote back that she would entertain a meeting with Henry, but that she was suspicious of a trick.

To show that the peace effort was sincere, Beatriz disguised herself as a peasant and rode to Isabel's court to make a personal appeal. Trusting her good friend's assurances that Henry wanted an end to the hostilities, and knowing that Henry's fear of civil war could very well lead to a truce, Isabel went to Segovia, accompanied by the Archbishop of Toledo and his troops. They arrived before dawn on a cold December morning in 1473 to meet with Henry IV. The King was already out hunting, but returned to Segovia that evening to find Isabel and her entourage. The good-natured King embraced his half-sister warmly, and assured her of his pleasure at seeing her.

The next day's talks began on a favorable note, and Henry, to show his good will, condescended to appear in public leading Isabel's saddle horse by its bridle. Ferdinand, who was in Aragon fighting the French with his father, returned to join Henry and Isabel in Segovia. After one of the many elaborate parties and dinners held to celebrate the hoped-for peace treaty, Henry IV became ill. The Grand Master of Santiago moved quickly. He reminded the King that the dinner was arranged by Isabel's friends, Beatriz de Bobadilla and her husband, and insinuated that Ferdinand and Isabel were trying to poison Henry. The attempt at reconciliation, the Grand Master said, was nothing more than a ruse to assassinate the King. Following the Grand Master's lead, King Henry issued orders to arrest the couple. Before the King's men came, Isabel's spy network discovered the scheme, and she and Ferdinand managed to escape.

When the attempt at compromise collapsed, political maneuvering surged again. To put one legal issue to rest, Ferdinand and Isabel obtained a Papal Bull of dispensation from their ally, Pope Sixtus IV, approving their marriage. And La Beltraneja's cause lost ground when her fiancee, the Duke of Guienne, died, cutting off her support from France. With the French door open, Ferdinand and Isabel sent an embassy to King Louis XI in early 1474 to propose an engagement of their three-year-old daughter, Isabel, to the Dauphin of France. The French King entertained the couple's ambassadors lavishly, while at the same time preparing for an invasion of the territories of Roussillon and Cerdagne, in northern Aragon. The marriage negotiations ended when Louis XI invaded, and John of Aragon, Ferdinand's father, sent for his son to come immediately with troops and supplies.

Shortly after Ferdinand joined King John at his headquarters in Barcelona, his father sent him to the Aragonese city of Zaragoza to raise more men and materiel. A nobleman, Jimenez Gordo, ran Zaragoza as its virtual dictator. When Ferdinand asked Jimenez Gordo to send aid to King John, the arrogant aristocrat delayed. Ferdinand summoned Jimenez Gordo to the royal palace. When Jimenez Gordo arrived, Ferdinand greeted him with great deference and invited him to the royal apartments for a friendly discussion. Ferdinand opened the door to the royal apartments and ushered the nobleman inside. There, standing beside a gallows made of fresh wood, were the public hangman and a priest. An official read a list of Jimenez Gordo's alleged crimes and summarily pronounced him guilty. Jimenez Gordo pleaded for forgiveness, but Ferdinand replied that only God could forgive him, and that the priest was ready to take his last confession. That afternoon Jimenez Gordo's corpse was displayed in the public marketplace.[1]

Between 1472 and 1474, Castile suffered severe famine, and the prices of basic necessities skyrocketed to the point that only the affluent could afford them. Many of the poor survived only by crime. Violence and theft multiplied dramatically in both the cities and the countryside. Without armed bodyguards, no one was safe. Rapacious nobles exacerbated the chaos. For more than fifty years, the weak Castilian kings were unable or unwilling to keep the aristocrats from engaging in vicious internecine warfare for control of lands, serfs and towns. In Andalusia, two hot-blooded young men heading the houses of Guzman and Ponce de Leon revived an ancient clan feud which their fathers had let lie. The battles were so destructive that in one block by block battle in Seville fifteen hundred houses of the Ponce de Leon faction were burned to the ground. As the nobles' personal armies swept back and forth over the countryside, the land lay dormant, desolate and unproductive. Scavenging soldiers decimated vineyards, wheatfields and orchards.

Sapped by debauchery and diverted by the struggle over succession, Henry IV and his corrupt, incompetent officials failed to quell the anarchy. By 1474, with the nobles savaging one another and the peasants starving, Castile was ready to crater. In November of that year, the Grand Master of Santiago died, and King Henry followed his cohort to the grave a month later, a few weeks short of his fiftieth birthday. Equivocating to the last, when his counsellors questioned him on his deathbed about the succession, the King refused to answer. Even though the succession was the primary political issue during the last days of Henry's reign, the "driveling imbecile with his usual improvidence" died without a will designating a successor.

Isabel wasted no time. Ferdinand was in Aragon, but two days after Henry's death she proclaimed herself and Ferdinand King and Queen of Castile on December 13, 1474. Fortunately, Isabel was in Segovia where her friend Andres de Cabrera guarded what little remained of the royal treasure. Cabrera turned the money over to Isabel, and she rewarded him with a golden goblet from her table service and later raised him to the rank of Marquis of Moya.

The Segovians hastily arranged a coronation, and the nobles, clergy and city fathers donned their ceremonial robes to pay homage to the twenty-three-year-old Isabel. Dressed in her finest clothes, Isabel mounted a Spanish pony whose bridle was held by two Segovian officials. An officer of the court, carrying a naked sword symbolizing sovereignty, took up his position to lead the procession from the castle of Segovia through the narrow streets to the *Plaza Mayor* (Main Square). With great dignity, Isabel mounted the platform, hung with rich embroidered cloth, and, for the first time, took her seat on the the throne of Castile. A court herald shouted "Castile for the King, Don Ferdinand, and his wife, Dona Isabel, Queen proprietor of these Kingdoms."

In the ancient ritual of feudalism, the aristocrats, prelates and government officials knelt, kissed her hand and swore fealty and obedience. To these medieval men, the idea of loyalty to a nation-state was a vague, obscure concept. To them, only the direct, personal bond of a man to his lord guaranteed the loyalty needed to gel society. Once the *personalismo* (personal relationship) between subject and sovereign was sealed with an oath, disobedience thereafter constituted a breaking of the faith, an act of treason, a felony. After receiving the oath of allegiance from her vassals, Isabel, in recognition of her duties back to them, reciprocated with an oath to defend their rights and liberties. With the rituals completed, the crowd cheered, pages unfurled the royal banners, church bells rang and salvos of canon fire saluted the new Queen.

The procession then made the short walk from the *Plaza Mayor* to the Cathedral of Segovia for a mass to add the Church's blessing to the royal couple's succession. The devout Queen prostrated herself before the altar and gave thanks to God for His protection. Then, she prayed for Him to watch over she and her husband and to give them the wisdom to govern with fairness and justice.

When Ferdinand heard the news of Henry IV's death, he left his father in Aragon and returned to Segovia, arriving on January 2, 1475. Cardinal Mendoza and the Archbishop of Toledo served as a reception party for the new King, riding out to escort him into the city. The crowds were so large that it was past sunset before Ferdinand reached the castle. "He was a young man of twenty-three," the city historian of Segovia wrote. "His face [was] grave but handsome and of a fair complexion, his hair chestnut in shade but somewhat spare on the temples...his eyes bright with a certain joyful dignity...[And] he carried himself boldly both on horse and foot."[2] It was too early for his subjects to gauge Ferdinand's character, but there was no hint of Henry IV's vacillating aura, and it was clear that Ferdinand would not fail due to indecision or lack of courage.

After Ferdinand's arrival in Segovia, the royal couple had their first, and only, serious dispute. Supported by his grandfather, the Admiral of Castile, Ferdinand declared that, as the nearest male representative of the Trastamara dynasty, he was entitled to the exclusive sovereignty. To support his claim, Ferdinand cited the ancient Salic law which said that only men could hold power. With history books in hand, Isabel's legal advisors answered that the Salic law didn't apply in Castile, even though it did in Aragon, and that women could, and had, ruled in Castile. The pitch of the argument grew nasty, and the couple called on Cardinal Mendoza and the Archbishop of Toledo to arbitrate. Ruling in Isabel's favor, the two churchmen based their decision on Castilian tradition, the agreements reached by the couple in their 1469 marriage contract and the practical fact that Isabel's supporters outnumbered Ferdinand's.

When Ferdinand learned that his power in Castile would be derived through his wife, he was furious, to the point that he appeared ready to reject the arbitrators' decision. Isabel, after five years of marriage, understood her husband's stubborn nature, and, more importantly, she knew how to handle him. When they met, she opened with *palabras dulces* (sweet words). "Sir, this matter need never have been discussed, because of the union between us. By the grace of God, there can be no real dis-agreement." Isabel told her husband that she was his wife and that she would act with obedience as such. She reminded him that the distribution of power was more nominal than real, and that their interests were indivisible. All royal laws and decrees would be signed by them jointly, their coat of arms would bear the emblems of Castile and Aragon and the Kingdom's coins would have both of their images. *Tanto monta, monta tanto, Fernando como Isabel.*

The fact that she was the Queen made her no less a woman, she said, and she was ready to share with him all her goods and dignities. No matter what the law said about the distribution of power, they would be equals. Then Isabel turned the conversation to the cold realities of their mutual self interest. Because the Castilian nobles looked to her as the Sovereign, it would be politically dangerous to formally legalize their equality. Because they had a daughter, Princess Isabel, adoption of the Salic law by Castile threatened their only child's future. When Princess Isabel married, her consort could claim the authority of the crown, and, if their son-in-law were a foreigner, he might bring troops to Castile to take the nation by force. If they split over this issue, Isabel said, La Beltraneja's coalition was still strong, and any division between them would surely cause them both to lose. The combination of hard political facts and *palabras dulces* worked. "The King,"a chronicler wrote, "having heard the Queen's reasons was highly pleased, because he knew them to be true; and both he and she gave orders that there should be no more talk of this matter."[3]

After the euphoria of the coronation, the Marquis of Villena, who was as devious as his late father, the Grand Master of Santiago, approached Ferdinand and Isabel. Even though he was a principal leader of La Beltraneja's faction, he offered to drop his support of La Beltraneja, but only with certain conditions. In the settlement negotiations, Villena demanded that the King and Queen appoint him to follow his dead father to the more powerful position of Grand Master of Santiago.

Villena also wanted a royal confirmation of his lands and castles and the payment of two million maravedis a year. Other supporters of La Beltraneja, including the Duke of Arevalo, the Marquis of Cadiz and the Grand Master of Calatrava, made similar demands. At first, Ferdinand and Isabel were inclined to grant most of what the noblemen asked, but the confederates went too far. They issued an ultimatum that La Beltraneja receive the title of Princess of Castile and be next in line to the throne. Agreement to this stipulation by Ferdinand and Isabel would disinherit their own daughter. Never. The negotiations aborted.

Villena began scheming to strengthen the coalition behind La Beltraneja's claim to the throne. His first target was the Archbishop of Toledo. It would be difficult, Villena knew, to convince the Archbishop to defect from Ferdinand and Isabel's cause. After all, the Archbishop was the man who galloped to Isabel's rescue in Madrigal, who forged the Papal Bull of dispensation permitting the marriage, who married the couple in 1469 and who arbitrated

Ferdinand and Isabel's dispute over power. Shrugging aside the old ties between the Archbishop and the royal couple, the calculating Villena had a clear picture of his quarry. He knew that the Archbishop was an amateur alchemist who spent huge sums trying to turn ordinary metals into gold. Villena promised the prelate land and gold. Villena knew that the jealous Archbishop was sulking because Cardinal Mendoza's influence over Ferdinand and Isabel was on the rise, and the Archbishop's delicate vanity was severely bruised. Carefully analyzing his prey, Villena understood that the slightest glimmer of insult or neglect raised the Archbishop's hackles. At court, the new King and Queen had increasingly refused to kowtow to his advice and demands. As Ferdinand and Isabel tired of their old ally's carping, Cardinal Mendoza eclipsed his rival for influence. The Archbishop's loyalty wavered, and finally snapped. He left the court and returned to his palace at Alcala to connive secretly with Villena.

The royal couple knew that losing so powerful an ally was dangerous. They were the King and Queen, but they still faced powerful opposition. Ferdinand persuaded his father, King John of Aragon, to write a letter to the Archbishop of Toledo, pleading with the clergyman to remain loyal to the Sovereigns. Although Isabel resented the Archbishop's apparent defection, she decided to visit him at his palace in Alcala to try one last time to bring him back to court. The Queen's advisors told her that the Archbishop's resentment was too strong. He would never change his mind. Isabel's counselors told her that humbling herself to go to the Archbishop would demean her royal status.

Isabel, trusting in *personalismo*, and buoyed by the force of her logic which had recently convinced Ferdinand to cede his claim to total authority, had full confidence in her powers of persuasion. She well knew the depth of the sullen Archbishop's conceit, but she felt that her appeal to their long history together would win him back. "I would blame myself if I did not at least try to convince him in person that he is about to follow a false road," she said. Isabel sent the Constable of Castile to Alcala to soften up the Archbishop, but appeals to his conscience and wounded pride failed. Bursting into a storm of passion, the Archbishop shouted at the Constable: "If Isabel enters Alcala by one gate, I will leave by another." Even though the Archbishop did not openly break with Isabel, she now understood the depth of the his bitterness, and the proposed meeting did not take place.

While the conspirators wooed Castilian leaders, they simultaneously lined up foreign support for La Beltraneja. In secret correspondence with King Louis XI of France, they offered as bait

Castile's Basque provinces of Guipuzcoa and Biscay, knowing that the French monarch had coveted those provinces, bordering on France, for years. Next, Villena and the Archbishop of Toledo hatched a scheme to net King Alfonso of Portugal. They lured King Alfonso with an offer of the hand of La Beltraneja. The aging Portuguese King already held a grudge against Isabel for twice refusing to marry him. Uniting Portugal and Castile under his rule had long excited his imagination.

Villena and his henchmen told King Alfonso that many important Castilian nobles would readily follow him, and that more were waiting in the wings to depose Ferdinand and Isabel if it appeared that La Beltraneja had enough support. Further, fourteen important cities opposed the Sovereigns, and other towns were in disarray, bleeding from internal feuds between aristocratic families. In those cities, one of the warring factions would surely side with King Alfonso if he gave them a few promises of riches and support against their enemies. The confederates said Ferdinand and Isabel were almost penniless, and King Alfonso, with his wealth and that of his Castilian allies, could easily outspend the Sovereigns.

Appealing to Alfonso's vanity, Villena's followers reminded the Portuguese King of his three successful military campaigns against the Moors in Africa which had earned him the nickname of *El Africano*. His prowess in the field, they said, would prevail over the two inexperienced usurpers. And saving the honor and dignity of his niece, La Beltraneja, appealed to Alfonso's chivalric, romantic nature.

Alfonso's practical-minded counsellors cautioned him that Castile was much larger than Portugal, that Villena and the Archbishop of Toledo had repeatedly proven they were untrustworthy and that not only was he a foreigner but a bitter rivalry had existed between Portugal and Castile for almost one hundred years. Despite these warnings, Alfonso's dreams of glory overwhelmed his judgment. He agreed to join the rebels.

In early May of 1475, King Alfonso invaded Castile with a relatively small force of cavalry and foot soldiers, crossing the border and taking the town of Plasencia in the western province of Extremadura. While waiting at Plasencia to be joined by the forces of the Marquis of Villena and the Duke of Arevalo, Alfonso sent purses of money to Castilian nobles he thought would join him. One noble, the Duke of Alba, took the Portuguese money and used it to raise troops for Ferdinand and Isabel. The rebels brought La Beltraneja to Plasencia to announce the proposed marriage to King Alfonso, pending receipt of a Papal Bull of dispensation for the wedding of uncle and niece. The confederates proclaimed "Castile for Don Alfonso of Portugal and Dona Joan (La Beltraneja), the rightful owner of these kingdoms." After a delay in Plasencia, the Portuguese-rebel army moved north to the town where Isabel spent much of her childhood, Arevalo. Alfonso stayed at Arevalo for two months waiting for reinforcements from his Castilian allies. With rising self-confidence, the plotters told themselves that Ferdinand and Isabel would never dare to confront them, and that in all probability the couple was already scurrying away to Aragon for safety. "Before gaining the victory, they divided the spoil," Pulgar said sarcastically.

Ferdinand and Isabel were unprepared for the invasion, and, at the outset, could only bring five hundred cavalry into the field. The young couple were far from contemplating flight. Even though she was pregnant, Isabel assumed the role of quartermaster general of her army. She worked feverishly through many nights dictating letters pleading for troops. On horseback, she rushed from town to town shoring up allegiances and obtaining men and supplies. She rode to Toledo to raise troops. She mobilized elements of the rural police force, the Holy Brotherhood, into a fighting force. She sped west to rescue Leon from a governor suspected of treachery. When Isabel got word of Louis XI's plan to invade the Basque provinces, she collected troops and sent them north to defend against the French King. She was indefatigable, riding from one stronghold to another, encouraging the garrisons by her presence. Isabel's furious efforts gave many of her subjects the chance to see their new Queen for the first time. What they saw, and were inspired by, was a vigorous young woman of dauntless spirit and daring.

While Isabel crisscrossed Castile, Ferdinand brought all his energy, negotiating skills and resourcefulness to bear as he bargained with nobles and cities for support. Although the Sovereigns were still short of funds, support for the them grew daily. Because of Isabel's intense activity, the days and nights in the saddle, she miscarried in the summer of 1475, making the little Princess Isabel, their soul heir to the throne, doubly precious.

Ferdinand assumed command of the army and mustered their forces at Valladolid. Intense hatred of the Portuguese, who defeated the Castilians in a vividly remembered battle in 1385, and love of their new King and Queen, caused many towns to send soldiers at their own expense. From northern Castile, nobles in full suits of armor, light cavalry, archers of the Holy Brotherhood and footmen joined with the troops Isabel raised on swings through Segovia, Avila and Toledo. But the army was undisciplined, little more than a civilian militia. Ferdinand's military experts, many imported from Aragon where they had gained years of experience fighting for King John, had little time to whip the soldiers into combat shape.

After a two-month delay at Arevalo, King Alfonso put his army on the march from Arevalo north and westward to the town of Toro, a formidable stronghold perched on a red cliff overlooking the Duero River. By prearrangement with the renegade governor of Toro, the town surrendered to the invaders. Zamora, just west of Toro on the Duero, then agreed to betray the Sovereigns, and Alfonso sent troops to occupy the town and its fortress. With these two bases in western Castile secured, Alfonso established his line of communication with Portugal, about twenty-five miles west of Zamora.

Even though his hastily assembled army was ill trained, Ferdinand marched on Toro and drew up his men in battle order in front of the city's walls on a hot summer day in 1475. Alfonso refused to come out of the fortified town, and Ferdinand had little artillery, battering rams or catapults to lay siege. Frustrated, Ferdinand sent a messenger through the lines challenging King Alfonso to personal combat, *mano a mano* (one on one). "Since our armies cannot reach a conclusion," Ferdinand said, "let you and me duel in the old manner. And the lady of the winner will become Queen of Castile."

The forty-three-year-old Alfonso accepted the challenge from his twenty-three-year-old counterpart. It would have been a sublime moment of the highest chivalric romance: two kings pitted against one another for the honor of their lady fair, with the fate of nations at stake. But the agents of the two kings wrangled over the rules of combat and safeguards against cheating, and reached no agreement.

Ferdinand called a council of war at a small church outside of Toro. In the dark sanctuary of the little country church, Ferdinand's officers angrily debated whether to retreat or attack. Over strident objections from many of his officers, Ferdinand decided to retreat. As a military decision, it may have been correct, but politically it was a dangerous decision which "...unsettled every man's political principles, [because] the allegiance of even the most loyal hung so loosely about them, that it was difficult to estimate how far it might be shaken by such a blow occurring at this crisis."[5] Taking the retreat as a lack of Ferdinand's resolve, a few fence sitters crossed over to the side of the rebels and their Portuguese allies. The most important defector was the Archbishop of Toledo, who came out openly for Alfonso and La Beltraneja, saying "[I] rescued Isabel from her spinning wheel, and [I] will send her back to it."

Although Ferdinand's withdrawal from the field cost the Sovereigns some support, most Castilians held fast for Ferdinand and Isabel, repelled by the thought of a Portuguese King and a bastard Queen ruling over them. As Ferdinand's army retreated from Toro, squadrons of Castilian light cavalry raided across the border into central and southern Portugal. Many of King Alfonso's Portuguese officers grumbled that while they were cooped up in Toro and Zamora the Castilians were ravaging their homeland. Worried, Alfonso sent a messenger to Ferdinand and Isabel with an offer to give up his and La Beltraneja's claims to the Castilian crown if Ferdinand and Isabel would pay him a large sum of money and cede to Portugal the northwestern province of Galicia and the cities of Toro and Zamora. Reportedly, Ferdinand was almost ready to accept the offer, but Isabel refused to give up a single hectare of Castilian territory.

The Sovereigns began reorganizing their army, but they had exhausted almost all of their money in the first foray against Toro. While Ferdinand and Isabel scratched to raise funds to pay their troops, King Alfonso sent his emissaries throughout Castile with bags of money.

To counter the bribes, King John of Aragon advised Ferdinand and Isabel to make liberal grants of titles and lands which, the crafty old man said, they could take back or expropriate after defeating the enemy. The royal couple rejected this ploy, and called for Parliament to meet in August of 1475 to levy new taxes. The delegates met at Medina del Campo, but claimed that Henry IV had so impoverished the nation that the people had nothing left to give. Another suggestion, which the Sovereigns turned down, was that the army could fend for itself by looting and scavenging off the countryside. Finally, under pressure, the Castilian Church agreed to loan Ferdinand and Isabel half of its substantial store of silver plate.

With fresh funds, during the fall and early winter of 1475, Ferdinand and Isabel organized and trained a new army, equipping it with artillery and siege weapons. The royal couple ordered Castilian forges to produce double-edged swords, battle axes, pikes and spears. The forges also turned out cumbersome harquebuses and smoothbore matchlock rifles that were so heavy they required a prop to hold up their long iron barrels. Arming and equipping the troops was expensive. It cost eight thousand maravedis to outfit a single man-at-arms of the heavy cavalry with a full suit of armor and padding for his war horse. To equip a light cavalryman with a visored helmet and spear, it cost seven thousand maravedis.[6] Iron caps, shields, daggers and swords for the infantry were less costly.

With his soldiers better armed and disciplined, Ferdinand led his forces on a winter march. Bypassing Toro, where King Alfonso had his headquarters, Ferdinand sent his army eighteen miles farther west to Zamora to cut Alfonso's supply line to Portugal. Zamora, known as *la bien cercada* (the well-walled city), sits on a bluff on the north side of the Duero River. Ferdinand's men surrounded the heavily garrisoned town and prepared for a siege.

During the night of February 17, 1476, Alfonso marched his men across the Roman-built bridge at Toro to the south side of the Duero River and arrived before dawn at Zamora. As the sun rose, the Castilians looked across the Duero to see Portuguese battle flags waving and the enemy's battle armor and artillery glittering in the cold morning sun. King Alfonso intended to relieve the siege at Zamora, but he was trapped on the south bank of the Duero, which ran swift with the runoff of winter rains. Castilian canons, ready to spew a murderous fire of stone balls and metal shards, were aimed at the only crossing, a single bridge.

With the bridge blocked, King Alfonso settled his troops into camp on the south side of the river. While the main bodies of the armies stared at each other across the swollen Duero, the Castilian light cavalry harassed Alfonso's army from the rear, curtailing its supply line. On the north side of the Duero, fresh recruits raised by Isabel joined Ferdinand's army. After two weeks of stalemate, Alfonso decided to pull back to Toro.

As the sun rose on March 1, 1476, King Alfonso's forces decamped and started the march east to Toro. Before leaving, Alfonso's engineers destroyed the south side of the bridge at Zamora to cover his army's retreat. After a three-hour delay while the bridge was being repaired, the Castilians crossed the Duero in hot pursuit. At quick march, the Castilian advance guard caught up with Alfonso a few miles west of Toro on an open plain where the Portuguese King formed his troops in a line of battle. As winter storm clouds built over the battlefield, Ferdinand called a war council.

There were strong arguments against an attack. The Portuguese could be easily reinforced by the garrison at Toro. Ferdinand's men had trudged more than fourteen miles and hadn't eaten all day. The speed of the march had forced the Castilians to leave most of their artillery behind, and the heavy infantry got bogged down on the road. Still stinging from his retreat the summer before, Ferdinand ordered an immediate assault.

King Alfonso anchored his right wing on the Duero River, and took personal command of the center. Ferdinand put the Duke of Alba in charge of his left, and the King squared off against his rival in the center. Up and down the Castilian lines, their ancient war cry *Santiago y Castilla* (St. James and Castile) split the air. The Castilian right advanced into a fusillade of harquebus fire from the Portuguese, forcing the Castilians to fall back. Ferdinand sent part of his reserves to stiffen his right and his officers rallied their men to attack again. As Ferdinand's right wing rushed forward, he sent the center and left on the offensive. Both Ferdinand and Alfonso rode into the melee to encourage their men. Cardinal Mendoza, in Ferdinand's service, and the Archbishop of Toledo, riding with Alfonso, traded their priestly robes for suits of armor and joined in the battle, clergyman against clergyman.

The shock troops, the lancers, clashed. Pikemen hooked the steel spurs of their weapons under the joints in the armor of the opposing cavalrymen and, with mighty jerks, brought the knights crashing to the ground. Steel clanged against steel. Horses, covered with white sweat, snorted strings of mucus from their noses. With the horses' eyes rolling wide with fear, their flailing hooves crushed the chests of fallen men. Iron tipped arrows peppered the enemy. The experienced crossbowmen of the Holy Brotherhood fired their weapons with deadly accuracy. It became a vicious three-hour hand-to-hand fight with swords, maces and battle axes hacking and cutting human flesh, brute strength assailing brute strength, so close each could smell the other's breath.

After a bitter struggle, the Duke of Alba turned Alfonso's flank. As the Duke's troops rolled up the rebel's right wing, Alfonso's men fled in total disarray. Panicked, some of Alfonso's men tried to cross to the north bank of the Duero and drowned, their bodies floating down river as a warning to their brothers-at-arms occupying Zamora. Other rebel soldiers made it to the narrow Roman bridge to cross to the safety of Toro, and became trapped. The Castilians surrounded Alfonso's army, stacked up at the bridge, and slaughtered many rebel soldiers. Night and a driving rainstorm allowed some of Alfonso's troops to escape, but the victory was decisive. Reports that King Alfonso had been killed proved false, and he and a small force fought their way back to Portugal.

There would be three more years of skirmishing before the opposing sides agreed to a final truce, but the Battle of Toro determined the future of the Iberian Peninsula. If Ferdinand had lost, there would have been no royal couple to set the course of Spanish history.

Isabel received the news in Tordesillas. To honor their glorious conquest, the pious Queen walked barefoot to the church of St. Paul to give thanks to God for the victory and for the favor He had shown she and her husband. When they reunited, the Sovereigns moved the court to Toledo to celebrate their triumph. At nine in the morning, the procession of clergy, nobles and officials walked to Toledo's cathedral to present the trophies of war. Isabel wore a skirt of white brocade, stitched in gold thread with the castles and lions of Castile and Leon. Around her throat, she wore a necklace of rubies, the largest of which was said to have belonged to King Solomon. Setting off her auburn hair was a golden crown blazing with gemstones. The magnificent ermine cloak she draped from her shoulders required two pageboys to carry the train to keep it out of the garbage-strewn, muddy streets.

Trumpets blared and royal banners unfurled as the Sovereigns entered the cathedral and took their places before the great altar. They heard mass in the shadowy temple, surrounded by massive pillars resembling a mysterious grove of stone trees. To memorialize their victory at Toro, the King and Queen placed tattered Portuguese battle flags on the tomb of an ancestor who the Portuguese had defeated decades before. To further commemorate their victory, Ferdinand and Isabel laid the corner stone of the church of San Juan de los Reyes (St. John of the Kings). Although it took many years to build, the church was always Isabel's favorite, and she enriched it with chalices, crosses and altar cloths made with her own hand. In the church's marble and granite, the stonemasons chiseled the arms of Castile quartered with those of Aragon and the initials "F" for Ferdinand and "Y" for Isabel (*Ysabel* in medieval Castilian).

Although it took three years for Castile and Portugal to sign a peace treaty, inside Castile the bulk of Villena's rebel coalition collapsed almost overnight. To blot out their sins, the Duke of Arevalo, the Grand Master of Calatrava, the Marquis of Villena and the Archbishop of Toledo scurried into the Sovereigns' presence to beg forgiveness. With most, Ferdinand and Isabel were lenient, but they stripped Villena and the Archbishop of much of their wealth and privileges. The rebel fortresses at Zamora, Burgos, Madrid and Baeza surrendered, and, by early 1477, there was only scattered resistance.

A few fortified castles in western Castile still flew the Portuguese flag, and some nobles, harnessed by the royal yoke for the first time, chafed in secret conspiracies that occasionally flamed into open rebellion. In one revolt, supporters of the Bishop of Segovia took to the streets and attacked the forces of Segovia's royal governor, Andres de Cabrera. To put down the violence, Isabel, accompanied by Cardinal Mendoza and a mounted bodyguard, made the seventy-five-mile trip on horseback from Tordesillas to Segovia, where her only heir, Princess Isabel, was guarded by Cabrera. To protect the little girl, Cabrera surrounded her with armed men in the city's fortress, the Alcazar.

As Isabel's party ascended the steep road to Segovia, she could see the Alcazar, sitting on the edge of a sheer cliff, jutting up from the granite like the prow of a ship. Before her entourage reached the city's gate, the leaders of the insurgents came out and begged Isabel to turn back because, they said, her entry into Segovia would incite the mob. Unyielding, Isabel responded, "Tell the knights and citizens of Segovia that I am the Queen of Castile, that this city is mine by inheritance and that I accept no orders from my rebellious subjects."

Isabel, with Cardinal Mendoza at her side, entered Segovia and rode through a hostile crowd to the Alcazar. Her soldiers closed the Alcazar's heavy doors behind her, as the mob in front of the fort screamed for Cabrera's death. Despite Cardinal Mendoza's advice, Isabel ordered the doors opened, and the Bishop of Segovia's supporters swarmed inside the large courtyard. Isabel appeared—alone—at the top of a staircase over-looking the courtyard. She paused a moment, and, in a clear voice, said, "Tell me your grievances my good people, and I will do what I can to redress them. What is for your good is also for mine and for the welfare of your city." Magnetized by the cool courage of their Queen, the crowd quieted, and their leaders meekly told her of their dissatisfaction with Cabrera and his minions.

"I will entrust it [the governorship of the Alcazar] to one of my servants, who will be loyal to me and to your honor," she replied, "[and I will] render justice to any wrongdoers."

Mollified, the crowd shouted *Viva la Reina!* (Long Live the Queen), and returned to their houses. Her fearless grit having put an end to the violence, Isabel quickly arranged trials for Cabrera and his followers. She punished or dismissed the men who had been particularly brutal or greedy, but she cleared Cabrera of the charges and restored him to the governorship.

While Isabel stamped out domestic strife, Ferdinand organized an army and marched on the Basque provinces to drive out the French forces of Louis XI. As Ferdinand approached, the French, already harried by the citizens' guerilla warfare, withdrew without a fight. France and Castile finally signed a peace treaty in 1478. In it, Louis XI broke his alliance with Portugal and agreed to give no further support to La Beltraneja. To further seal off La

Beltraneja's claims, Castile and Aragon pressured the pliant Pope Sixtus IV into issuing a new Bull revoking the Church's dispensation for the marriage of King Alfonso and La Beltraneja.

In Portugal, King Alfonso refused to make peace, and continued his threats against Castile. In the spring and summer of 1478, a few noble families in Castile continued to foment clan warfare or collude with the Portuguese. Isabel, pregnant again, mobilized troops and moved her headquarters to Seville to mop up the remaining resistance along the Portuguese border. While she was in Seville, two important events occurred. On June 30, 1478, the royal couple's prayers were answered when a son, John, named after his paternal and maternal grandfathers, was born. Shortly after the birth of his grandson, the pugnacious King John of Aragon died. With his death, Castile and Aragon, which had been separate kingdoms for more than four hundred years, were united under the rule of Ferdinand and Isabel.

In Seville Isabel put her personal stamp on the administration of the law, holding court every Friday to settle civil disputes and to punish criminals. Sitting on a raised dais covered with cloth of gold, she dispensed harsh justice to those who engaged in the bloody clan warfare that ravaged the city. Because so many of Seville's citizens took part in the rampant violence, a large part of the city's population could be labeled as criminals. "They [the acts of violence] were so numerous that, in my opinion, there were few persons in Seville free of fault; some for having committed some offense, others for having kept it silent," wrote Pulgar, the Sovereigns' official court historian. Rather than face the Queen's punishment, thousands of Sevillians packed their belongings and fled the city. To stop the exodus, Isabel granted a general amnesty for all past offenses—except heresy.

Even though King Alfonso was still rattling swords in Lisbon, after six months of being badgered by his advisors, Alfonso finally agreed that he could not win a new war, and, in September of 1479, the King of Portugal signed the treaty. In the document, Ferdinand and Isabel renounced any claims they might have to the Portuguese throne, and Alfonso gave up his and La Beltraneja's pretensions to the Castilian crown. To unify Portugal and Castile, Alfonso's grandson would marry Princess Isabel of Castile when she reached majority. To settle the first of many future territorial disputes, the two kingdoms ratified Castile's ownership of the Canary Islands, and Portugal's rights to the Azores, Madeira and Cape Verde Islands, Guinea and all regions beyond the Canary Islands.[8]

The treaty gave La Beltraneja six months to decide whether to leave Portugal forever, to retire to a Portuguese convent for life or to marry the one-year-old Prince John of Castile when he reached marriageable age. During her seventeen years, the people controlling La Beltraneja's destiny had proposed nine matches. She was bleary from the stream of suitors seeking, and then rejecting, her hand for their own selfish interests. And she was sick of being a puppet in the hands of ruthless kings and deceitful courtiers. La Beltraneja became a nun. Gowned in religious habit, she lived another fifty-one years in the comfort of the cloister.

It was over. The struggle for the throne, which had begun when Isabel was a baby, was at an end. In the pious Isabel's mind, her beloved Christian God paved the way for her and her husband to bring about the moral and material redemption of their nation. God pulled the threads together. God suppressed the internal strife. God quashed the French and Portuguese threats. God joined Castile and Aragon. Now, with the Heavenly hand on their shoulders, she and Ferdinand could weave their way through the maze of remaining obstacles to make Castile into Spain. To symbolize her earthly desires, Isabel chose as her personal emblem a tightly tied bundle of arrows, signifying unified power. Ferdinand chose the yoke, which he intended to impose on the Moors.

3

TIGHTENING THE GRIP

A medieval Castilian city could be disgusting. The slaughterhouse was usually located just outside the city's walls. When the wind blew from the wrong direction, the odor of decaying offal drifted over the town. Pigs dined in garbage-filled ditches in the middle of the unpaved streets. In addition to using the streets as garbage heaps, the townsmen mucked them with human waste thrown out of second story windows. Pedestrians hugged close to the walls of buildings to escape the liquid refuse dumped from chamber pots.

Some cities passed laws requiring people to shout *"Agua va!"* ("Here comes the water!") before throwing their waste into the streets. Wealthy men wore high boots to keep the filth off their cloths, and servants carried their wives in litters to avoid the slops. The stench was overpowering, particularly on humid summer days when clouds of flies swarmed to their feast.

The unsanitary conditions spawned disease, and the faces of most men and women carried the permanent scars of smallpox. Epidemics decimated the population every few years, including the most feared plague, the Black Death. "It was called the 'Black Death' because of the large, black blotches that appeared on the body," an historian writes.[1] "There were also swellings of the glands in the armpits, the groin and the neck, where painful lumps as large as eggs often appeared. The body was covered with smaller boils and carbuncles, and the sick person often vomited blood. The vast majority died within two or three days." Although the filth and odors of the Middle Ages might appall twentieth century men, medieval Castilians might be equally revolted by today's rotten egg smell of catalytic converters, brown clouds of smog and refineries belching sulfuric smoke.

Despite the lack of hygiene, Castile's cities had a charm that still attracts modern men to visit its ancient towns. " The buildings...were as bright and clean as a medieval illumination...because they were usually white-washed with lime, so that the colors of the image makers, in glass or polychromed wood, would dance in reflection on the walls. The town was an ever-present work of art, and the very clothes of its citizens on festival days were like a flower garden in bloom," Louis Mumford says in his somewhat poetic description of a Middle Age city.[2]

Although the towns had charm, the city fathers also designed them to meet practical needs. Defensive walls with strategically placed towers belted the cities to keep out marauding bandits, aggressive noblemen and, in Andalusia, raiding Moors. In Seville the Romans built the original walls, the Moors improved them and the Castilians added the latest in military engineering after they retook Seville in 1248.

While the massive walls were imposing, a town's Alcazar and Cathedral dominated the cityscape. In cities reconquered from the Arabs, the Castilians often converted mosques into churches, a tradition followed by the Spaniards when they built churches over Indian temples in the New World. Seville's Cathedral, which took almost one hundred years to build, incorporates the Giralda, an Islamic minaret. Inside the churches, skilled craftsmen carefully decorated places that did not show to the public because, they thought, even if the people could not see these hidden places, God could.

The *Plaza Mayor* (Main Square) was the center of town. From the *Plaza Mayor*, a maze of narrow, winding streets opened into smaller squares or branched off into blind alleys. During the summer in Seville, the townsmen continued the Islamic custom of hanging curtains across the streets to shade them from the Andalusian sun. In the most ancient towns, Roman-built aqueducts provided water to fountains and wells. Tailors, silversmiths and other craftsmen plied their trades in specific streets they reserved for themselves. The craftsmen incorporated themselves into monopolistic guilds that enforced guild rules and prohibited nonmembers from encroaching on their trade. The cities were also divided into parishes, and a group of parishes formed a quarter. In the 1200 and 1300s, the free cities, which received their charters directly from the crown, prohibited aristocrats from owning real estate inside their walls. Over the years, the powerful nobles infiltrated the cities and built huge mansions and palaces with enclosed courtyards where fountains gurgled and oranges ripened.

Seville, with a population of about fifty thousand, was medieval Castile's queen city. Before the Guadalquivir River mudded up years later, oceangoing ships navigated upstream to Seville's docks. Goods from the Middle East, Italy, France and England jammed its warehouses and shops, warranting the old Arab proverb that, "If one were to ask for bird's milk in Seville, he would be able to get it." The Castilian General Chronicle, written in the late 1200s, says:

> "Seville was a great, noble and very rich city, replete with every comfort and all luxurious things....There were beautiful streets and wide plazas where all kinds of stores and shops abounded, each trade or business occupying its own section, and all neatly distributed and well ordered....No place so wealthy or so beautifully adorned had ever been seen before....The walls of the city were the greatest that had ever been seen. They are high and strong and wide, with great towers guarding them at regular intervals, all constructed with tremendous effort."[3]

The lives of ordinary people in the cities was hard, but, on fair and festival days, Christian townsmen mingled with bearded Jews, turbaned Moors, dark-skinned gypsies and foreign merchants from Genoa, Venice, France and Flanders. At the fairs the city's constables looked on suspiciously, arresting gypsy pickpockets and breaking up brawls between Christians and Moors. Beggars, many maimed by birth defects or amputations at the hands of the Holy Brotherhood's harsh justice, pleaded for alms. Tonsured Franciscan friars in brown wool cloaks and noblemen in their silk and gold finery "pushed and sweated, pointed and shouted" along with the guildsmen, laborers and farmers.

Religious fraternities, following priests in scarlet and white robes, paraded richly garbed statues of Holy Mary and local saints through the narrow streets to the doors of churches. Smitten lovers waited on church steps to catch a glimpse of their ladies fair. Married women, most of whom were perpetually pregnant, shopped for spices and cosmetics, while their husbands, satisfied that their wives were providing heirs and were safe from infidelity, bargained for weapons and mules. Toothless widows in their black weeds, broken from years of almost nonstop pregnancies and miscarriages, jostled to get closer to the entertainers at the fairs.

Minstrels and troubadours, playing lutes, goatskin bagpipes, flutes, Moorish guitars, drums and tambourines, sang the ancient ballads romanticizing the deeds of Pelayo and El Cid.[4] Taverns and public bath houses provided whores and games of dice and cards to fairgoers seeking more immediate pleasure. Jugglers, bear tamers and bullfighters entertained the crowds, and noblemen drew cheers for acts of bravery at jousts and tournaments. Mystics told "rhymed stories of local saints and mundane miracles [in exchange for] a good glass of wine." Although the Church condemned performers as *infames* or *instrumenti damnations*, the entertainers recited risque lines from the *Book of Good Love:*

> "Aristotle says, and it is true,
> The world labors for two things.
> First, to have food and shelter.
> The other, to copulate with a pleasing female."

At night, torches lighted the miracle or mystery plays in the *Plaza Mayor*. The actors played the parts of blessed saints fighting to save their souls from fanged devils with horns, while the director stood to the side with his baton to direct the action and to prompt the performers if they forgot their lines.

When the towns-people weren't shopping at the fair, they listened as storytellers repeated the wonderful tales about the mythical Christian preacher king, Prester John, who ruled an Asian kingdom as rich and powerful as it was just and peaceful. The storytellers amazed the gawking crowd with their accounts of the English traveler, John Mandeville, who reported on the monsters of the mysterious orient. There were Sciapodes who could walk on their one foot "so quickly that they are a wonder." The single foot was so large that a Sciapode could lie down, stick his foot in the air and shade himself from the sun. Monoculars were giants with one eye in the middle of their forehead who ate nothing but raw meat and fish. There were people "with bodies so horrible, and of natures so wicked, that they have no heads and have their eyes in the middle of their chests. Their mouths are like twisted horseshoes."[5] The storytellers also told tales of Antilia and St. Brendan's Isle, strange lands to the west, across the vast wasteland of the Atlantic Ocean.

To protect the merchants traveling to fairs and festivals, the policemen of the Holy Brotherhood, dressed in their forest green capes, patrolled the highways leading into the city. The merchants shouted and popped their whips over the backs of mules carrying sacks of wool cloth and brassware. They prodded the oxen, straining in their leather harnesses to pull carts loaded with goods from all over the known world. Slaves rowed galleys from the Middle East across the Mediterranean, the "sea between lands," to bring golden threaded silks and herbs to Castilian ports. Genoese caravels slipped past Arab pirates operating out of Tripoli and Tunesia to shuttle perfumes and gold jewelry from the Black Sea.Chunky merchant ships brought Russian furs from the Baltic Sea.

When the world's goods arrived in the *Plaza Mayor,* some Christian traders organized their books of account with a special column under the name of the Lord to keep track of the amount of tithe owed to God and the Holy Catholic Church. In the *Plaza Mayor* and its surrounding streets, merchants set up stalls and tables to display their wares.

Included in the array of goods were cosmetics in terracotta jars. One beauty treatment called for applying minced toad to the face. Midwives sold love potions to stimulate both men and women to greater potency. Stag's tears were supposed to be an aphrodisiac, but nobody explained how one gathered the precious fluid. The merchants peddled herbal medicines to heal sores, and, for the rich, ground up pearls and gemstones to ward off diseases. Traders did a brisk business selling charms and miraculous salves which protected against claw-footed demons, witches who ruined crops or prevented pregnancies and evil women who turned themselves into owls and sucked the blood of humans.

Vendors offered salt to preserve food and pepper to mask the flavor of slightly rancid meat. Merchants sold olive oil, wine, plows, rakes, weapons, armor, slaves and, in cities with a strong Moorish influence, eunuches. Aproned women carrying baskets and pitchers of water on their heads scurried among the crowds. Booksellers tempted the literate with illuminated manuscripts; romantic tales of chivalry, Old and New Testaments and the Koran. Farmers hawked the virtues of their vegetables and kicked away the dogs roaming the streets. Crafty traders dealt in falcons, horses and mules, bargaining prices to the last maravedi. Buyers grumbled about the high cost of spices and other goods from Asia, blaming the infidel Turks who captured Constantinople in 1453, making access to the Orient's products more difficult, and expensive.

The Castilian traders, Christians, Jews and Moors, haggled with foreign merchants from Italy, England, Flanders and France, creating a multilingual symphony of commerce. Gold and silver coins from all over the world required verification and weighing to calculate the precious metal content. Florentine florins, Venetian ducats, Portuguese cruzados, Genoese genovinos and English half nobles crossed the tables. When arguments broke out over a coin's value, the city's controller of weights and measures arbitrated the dispute.

As was true all over Europe, in Castile the nobles and the Church owned and controlled the towns and villages located in their domains. Cities created by royal charters *(fueros)*, however, were free of aristocratic and ecclesiastical control. The designation of "city" usually meant that it was a regional capital owning a large slice of surrounding land over which the city had jurisdiction. The city's domain included its towns, villages, communal pastures, fields, vineyards and forests which supplied wood for cooking and heating. The townsmen carved out portions of the common land for use for public threshing and winnowing of grain, trash dumps and slaughterhouses. With their lands and their towns and villages, these regional capitals formed self-sustaining city-states. Villages *(aldeas)* were small, usually with less than thirty households. Towns *(villas)* were larger in population, but their territory was normally confined to the land within their walls.

Although medieval Castilian cities were similar to other European cities, they developed in a unique way. During the Reconquest, as the Christian kings captured Moorish cities, they pushed the Sons of Islam further south. Because some cities suffered heavy damage in the sieges, and much of the area conquered was a wild frontier, the Christian sovereigns were forced to grant special favors to induce Christians from the north to immigrate the captured territory. The kings wanted the newcomers to implant the wisdom of their New Testament God in the cities, and to create strongholds capable of resisting counterattacks by the Arabs.

To entice Christians to leave the safety of their homes and families in the north, the Christian kings granted royal charters to the cities which contained "numerous...tempting concessions and favors." The royal charters varied from city to city, but most authorized the cities to govern themselves, build fortresses, maintain local militias, tax themselves and send delegates to Parliament. As a result, delegates from the Castilian Third Estate sat in Parliament one hundred years before English townsmen had the same rights and two hundred years before the French. The city of Leon received the first royal charter in 1020, to be followed during the next centuries by such cities as Toledo, Cordoba, Burgos and Seville. Over time, fifteen cities and three towns came to enjoy the independence and privileges authorized by the royal charters.

To further induce the immigrants, the kings gave individuals fields and houses expropriated from the Moors and set contributions to the royal treasury at low levels.[6] The commerce carried on in the towns and cities supplied taxes to pay municipal officials, build bridges and support the militia. Self-sufficient, the cities developed proud local traditions, and adopted strict citizenship laws based on place of birth and ownership of property.

The unusual freedom enjoyed by Castilian cities created an inward-looking mentality, and, for many people, their universe was no larger than their city or town. Even though the kings tried to retain a measure of control in the cities, the combination of insularity, personal liberty and administrative autonomy produced a feeling of fierce independence from the power of both the crown and the nobles. In the early Middle Ages, nobles were almost *persona non grata* in the cities. The townsmen excluded aristocrats from the ownership of property in the cities, and the kings willingly accepted the cities' anti-aristocratic bias as a counterbalance to the power of the noblemen. Mostly, the civic militias fought with the kings against the more rapacious aristocrats, but, on occasion, the cities formed alliances to fight against the crown.

Although the kings periodically meddled in the cities' affairs, the governmental structure of the free Castilian cities and towns provided their inhabitants with a measure of democracy not seen in most of the rest of medieval Europe. Heads of families formed a general assembly *(consejo abierto)* which elected the members of the city council. The city council administered the city's business and appointed the commander of the militia, the controller of public weights and measures, the keeper of public records, the tax farmers, the constables, the judges and other officers. Even though royal charters granted broad freedoms to the cities, the sovereign's presence was always there. In Toledo, the king named the president of the city council, but the citizens elected the other members. In Seville, the crown designated certain administrative officials and the commander of the militia, but the city council picked all other officials.

This independence of the Castilian cities blossomed during the 1200s and 1300s, but, as the incompetent Trastamara kings of the early 1400s came to the throne, the nobles grew more powerful and audacious. The civic militias and the nobles fought mini-wars for control of the cities' treasured common lands outside their walls. Gradually, the old restrictions against aristocrats owning property in the cities broke down. The nobles began infiltrating the cities, building palaces which served the dual purposes of shelter for their families and strong points to foment violence and plots to increase their power. As aristocratic influence in the cities increased, the Trastamara kings, to counter this growing power, schemed to enhance their royal prerogatives in the cities. In many cities, the aristocrats came to dominate the city councils, and, in others, rival factions fought bitter battles for control of the parishes and quarters. The great lords hired soldiers and criminals to fight in their private armies, turning the streets into battlefields. In Toledo, high and low nobility, merchants, New Christians, Jews and demagogue-led masses struggled for advantage. In Cordoba, the Count of Cabra made war on the noble Aguilar family. In Seville, the bitter feud between the Ponce de Leon and Guzman families caused an anonymous poet to write:

> "Unhappy Seville, bathed in the blood of its children...
> Where are the men who maintained you in peace and justice?
> Where are they, those stern city councilmen?
> Where are those brave officials who never bent their knee before an aristocrat?
> Where are your judges, those zealous hearts who kept you safe from all evil and harm?
> The Ponce de Leons and the Guzmans resided within your walls before, but never did they place a yoke on your neck."[7]

The battlefield wasn't limited to the violence in the streets. The aristocratic factions maneuvered to control the city councils, rigging elections and buying votes. While chaos reigned in most cities, the wealthy merchants of Burgos, the center of Castile's wool trade, bought peace by trading their ancient democratic traditions for a tight, self-perpetuating oligarchy of a few men who controlled the city council with iron fists.

By the time of Isabel and Ferdinand, the "age of happy independence" had ended. The cities had a choice—submit to the rule of violent, vicious noblemen or that of the royal couple. The cities could either continue with the anarchy of the aristocrats or give up much of their cherished—but decayed—automomy to their new Sovereigns, who promised order and stability.

To carry out the royal policy, Isabel, who took primary responsibility for domestic affairs, employed a panoply of economic and political weapons. In some cases, she used a divide and conquer strategy of meting out rewards or punishments to one or the other noble faction. If this didn't work, Isabel intervened personally to arbitrate the peace. To favored cities, the Queen granted tax reductions or exemptions and duty-free rights at fairs. To the uncooperative, she coerced them by increasing the crown's share of taxes, confiscating goods and property or imposing stiff fines for civic misdeeds. With her uncanny skill as a propagandist and psychologist, Isabel had no hesitation in playing on her subjects' emotions, prejudices and pride to gain their support. The Queen reminded them often of the glorious victory at the Battle of Toro, and promised to crush the Moors in a Holy Crusade. To awe her subjects, she staged elaborate royal ceremonies and processions, impressing on her people the dignity and majesty of their new Sovereigns.

Perhaps the strongest weapons in Isabel's arsenal were her person, her vigor, her energy. By her presence, her *personalismo,* the majesty of the Queen's power dazzled her subjects. Wherever she was, the sovereignty was. To put her personal stamp on Castile's affairs, she traveled the breadth of her nation to attend sessions of Parliament and National Assemblies of the Holy Brotherhood. If revolts broke out in Andalusia in the south, or if noblemen's greed flared in Galicia in the north, she and her household guard were on the road to put down the violence.

Isabel gave birth to her five children in five different places, and she made many trips on horseback during pregnancy. When she was expecting her last child, Isabel's labor pains began while she was sitting at a table conducting a council of war. From that pregnancy she bore twins, one of which was stillborn.

During her thirty-year reign she visited every corner of Castile and Aragon, in some years traveling more than twelve hundred miles by horse or mule. One scholar, Henry Kamen, prepared a map of Castile and Aragon with dots at the places visited by Ferdinand and Isabel. The map looks like someone spilled a jar of pepper on it. In the late 1400s, Castile had no fixed capital city. The capital was wherever the Sovereigns resided at the moment.

When Isabel visited a village, town or city, what her subjects saw was a woman who could be extravagant in her dress but whose personal habits were mostly frugal, who ate lightly and seldom drank wine. Her vassals also saw a petite, auburn-haired woman with blue-green eyes and fair skin inherited from her English grandmother. Her devoted contemporaries lavishly describe her as beautiful, but the few surviving portraits of the Queen belie that description. Her round, soft face was not beautiful, but maternal. More likely, her attraction was in her personality, in the same way a Margaret Thatcher or Barbara Bush become beautiful when their personalities emerge.

Isabel's natural intelligence drew her to intellectual activities.

She studied and read Latin throughout her life, and encouraged the ladies and maidens of her court to read and study. She was receptive to new ideas, but before acting on them, she considered them carefully and deliberately. She was not "temperamentally inclined to hasty or rash action or to blindly accept the advice of her advisors." Only with the greatest reluctance did she delegate authority to subordinates. These traits, and her inclination to involve herself in decisions related to the most minor matters, sometimes delayed the wheels of government for months or years. Although Isabel was slow to make decisions, if she sensed the slightest possibility of infringement on her royal prerogatives, she acted quickly and decisively.

Isabel's contemporaries commented over and over about her "unruffable, unflappable" demeanor that let her deal with even the most tense situation in a judicious, calm manner. The Queen's presence of mind in dangerous situations, her "grace under pressure" and her bravery are constantly noted by scholars. Even though Isabel was inclined to be serious and earnest most of the time, she could be gay. Graciousness *(con blandura)* was her watchword.[8] The Queen was gracious to the military escorts who guarded her on a journey, gracious in distributing alms and gracious as she chatted with her courtiers and her subjects.

In her personal dealings with courtiers and her people she was generally honest, but, as with most politicians, honesty necessarily gave way to political reality when the situation warranted. Isabel had a sixth sense about human nature, an essential characteristic for a good politician. She was a shrewd, intuitive judge of men's characters, often surprising her counselors with her ability to accurately sum up a man she had just met. She used this gift to the fullest, surrounding herself with good and loyal advisors. Because she was a quick reader of men and their natures, when she coupled this with her graciousness and subtle tact, she was an excellent persuader. She could sense what a man wanted to hear, address his concerns and convince him to do what she wanted. At her best, she could make him think her idea was his own.

Isabel used her femininity with an "inspired virtuosity" that caused writers of her time to praise her pious gentility, which, in turn, appealed to Castilian notions of chivalry and gallantry. "This incomparable women who far transcends all human excellence, the mirror of every virtue, the shield of the innocent and an avenging sword to the wicked," Peter Martyr wrote.[9] But the chroniclers report no instances of the Queen abusing her femininity to gain her ends. Because of the moral degeneracy and sexual abuses she observed as a girl at Henry IV's court, Isabel developed a strong sense of decorum that caused her to look askance at the moral flaws of adultery and vulgar language, and to prohibit the time-honored services of prostitutes in army camps.

Isabel was capable of strong, tenacious affection. She loved Ferdinand "stubbornly and passionately" all her life. Except for matters related to her treasured Church and morality, she placed great trust in her husband's judgment. When she miscarried or one of her children died, Isabel would be grief stricken for weeks. But when her duties as Queen required her attention, this strong, active woman brushed aside the most acute personal grief and consideration for her own health.

As were many women of her time, Isabel was deeply religious, steadfast in her devotion to the teachings of the Catholic Church.[10] In her pious mind, religion and politics were inextricably linked, and her political goal of unity translated into absolute "religious conformity and the enforcement of the most rigid religious orthodoxy." To Isabel, religion demanded that society be homogeneouse, meaning that only Old Christians and true converts to the Faith received her favor. The Muslim and Jewish cultures must be stamped out, by expulsion, torture or death. At the beginning of her reign, Castile was steeped in factionalism, isolationism and separatism, and Isabel saw spiritual conformity as a powerful tool to unify her country. "For those [persons] who were even vaguely tainted with heresy, Isabel had [no] sympathy," one writer says.[11]

"As a girl, [Isabel knew] the hardships of war, the treachery of conspiracy, the malice of disloyal courtiers, the compliments of flatterers; she...even experienced poverty," historian Paolo Taviani writes.[12] Against this background, she became tough-minded and intense when her interests were at stake. Even obsessive. Any threat to her dignity or power brought an instant, harsh response. Any threat to her cherished religion or her zeal for reform met stubborn resistance.

With her tremendous store of energy, Isabel actively pursued her two primary political goals; unifying Castile and reforming its institutions. She was uncompromising in her struggle for centralized authority. Controlling, binding the arrows together in tight unity, was her nature—her instinct. In the early days of her reign, before she solidified her power, she was forced to treat the issues of unification and reform with great delicacy. The crown had no standing army, no organized bureaucracy, no reliable source of income. Isabel intended to reshape, to mold and to consolidate all of Castile's institutions. Even though she began her reign in weakness, when she died the phrase "by my royal absolute power" appeared seven times in her will.

Although some writers criticize Isabel as "absolutist," her concept of sovereignty was medieval. It was more a notion of lordship or stewardship than one of an absolute monarch. The Queen believed that her authority undoubtedly came from God, but also from her people. Because her subjects gave the Queen their trust, Isabel felt she had a clear duty to protect and defend them, to act in what she perceived to be her peoples' best interests. Even when she reached the peak of her power, Isabel tried, whenever possible, to rule with the consent of her vassals.

To govern by consensus required a direct network of personal relationships between the Sovereigns and their people. Isabel made considerable efforts to convey to her subjects the sense of obligation she felt toward them, and her people reciprocated with an the intense personal loyalty to their Sovereigns. "They [Ferdinand and Isabel] were kings of this realm alone, of our speech, born and bred among us...." the Admiral of Castile wrote nostalgically in 1522 after the Sovereigns were dead. "They knew everybody, always gave honors to those who merited them, travelled through their realms, were known by great and small alike, could be reached by all...."[13] Over time, the royal couple's understanding of their subjects' aspirations permitted them to shape Castile's institutions to their own design. While the King and Queen made both the high and low born feel that they were participating in the restructuring of the nation, it was a two-way street. The hopes, desires and prejudices of Isabel and Ferdinand's vassals shaped and molded their Sovereigns.

Ferdinand and Isabel wanted to strengthen the local communities, to make them into viable, homogeneous towns and cities, but always under royal supervision. The Sovereigns realized that, without strong local communities below, there was little or nothing to rule over from on high.

As is true today, drawing the fine line between central and local control automatically created tension. In 1476, the King and Queen called Parliament into session at Madrigal. They introduced a measure which would permit the crown to appoint a *corregidor* (royal governor) to represent the national interest in each town and city. The idea was not new. Previous kings implemented the same system with varying degrees of success. Politically, Ferdinand and Isabel's position on the throne was too tenuous in 1476, and the city fathers beat back the Sovereigns' attempted intrusion on local control.

Four years later, in 1480, when the King and Queen had stifled most domestic opposition, they pushed a *corregidor* bill through the Parliament of Toledo. The new law gave the crown the right to appoint royal governors to preside over city council meetings, to administer local justice and to provide the essential link between the communities and the crown. To minimize the possibility that the *corregidores* would become too cozy with the citizens, the new law limited their terms to two years, and they could be recalled at any time. In practice, it was not unusual for Isabel and Ferdinand to reappoint a *corregidor* to subsequent terms.

To distance the *corregidores* from the city fathers, the royal governors took an oath that they would not ally themselves with any faction or accept bribes or other favors. To further avoid entangling alliances, the new law forbid the *corregidores* from selecting officials from among citizens of the city they were governing. To make sure that the *corregidores* didn't sink into corruption, Ferdinand and Isabel appointed royal inspectors *(veedores)* and commissioners *(pesquisidores)* to look over the shoulders of the *corregidores.*

The royal commissioners and inspectors visited each town and city at least once a year to take secret testimony regarding the royal governors' conduct and to verify any complaints or accusations against the *corregidores*. At the end of a royal governor's term, he was required to remain in the city for thirty days to answer any charges brought against him. If there were accusations of abuse of power or corruption, the *corregidor* stood trial before the Royal Council of Justice.

Despite their attempts to maintain clean government, Isabel and Ferdinand made one mistake with their new system. To keep the *corregidores* off the royal payroll, the cities paid their salaries, building in a division of loyalties. Even though the royal couple attempted to sanitize the *corregidores,* there were many cases of the royal governors accepting bribes or permitting their wives and children to accept them.[14]

The Sovereigns made other changes. To avoid the bloody internecine battles caused by elections in some cities, Isabel and Ferdinand suppressed free elections wherever they could. In 1477, Isabel went to Caceres, in western Castile, to put down rioting that grew out of local elections. She suspended the town's laws and ordered that all town officials should be chosen for life by lot, not by election. To secure civic stability in Barcelona in the late 1480s, Ferdinand threw out the city council and appointed his own men to govern the city.

For cities and towns where she was politically unable to abolish elections, Isabel drew up a list of qualifications for holding office. When they could, the Sovereigns replaced corrupt city officials with well-educated, intelligent men *(letrados)* from humble backgrounds, infuriating the nobles who put their friends in positions of authority and the local officials the royal couple tossed out of their lucrative jobs.

To stop city officials from charging exorbitant fees for civic services, Isabel drew up a schedule of fees and set severe penalties for officials who charged anything in excess of the scheduled amounts. At the Sovereigns' direction, the Parliament of 1480 ordered each town and city to build a town hall, to keep written copies of all laws and to revoke all hereditary rights to hold office. In some cities and towns, Isabel usurped their rights to appoint many municipal officials. One story, which may not be true, holds that one of Isabel's servants saw a note written in her own hand which said: "The office of public crier in the town of X...is reserved for Mr. X...because he has a better voice."[14] It is doubtful that the Queen was interested in naming a town crier, but the story points up her attention to the smallest detail and her interest in extending royal control deep into the society.

Although all of Isabel and Ferdinand's attempts at reform of the free cities and towns didn't take, by the end of their reign the power of the nobles was mostly broken and the crown had sufficient control over the municipal governments to make them instruments of national policy.

4

COLUMBUS, 1451—1476

Genova la Superba. Genoa the Superb, the Proud. In the early 1450s, Genoa had good reason to be proud. Running east from Monaco about 150 miles along the coast of northern Italy, its widest point only twenty-five miles inland, this tiny maritime republic was a dominant power in international trade. Sleek caravels, galleys and fat-bellied merchant ships [1] from all over the world crowded the city-state's quays and wharves.

From this small crescent-shaped sliver of land, the Republic of Genoa's merchant seamen maneuvered their vessels through the forest of masts in its harbor, set sails and probed west to Spain, then through the Pillars of Hercules to Portugal, France, Belgium, Holland and England. Genoese captains also pointed their prows east across the Mediterranean Sea, past Constantinople, through the Straits of Bosporus and into the Black Sea; "Genoa's lake" some called it. Backing the east and west trade, the Republic's bankers eagerly extended liberal credit to finance convoys that would bring back cargoes of Malabar pepper or English wool.

With a population of only a few hundred thousand, the Genoese established trading colonies in the Aegean and Black Seas. Where they didn't have colonies, Genoa's merchant princes sent traders to bargain for gold, grain and aphrodisiacs. In the thick accents of their Genoese dialect, they haggled prices with Russians for furs, with Syrians for prunes and with Portuguese for ivory from Portugal's West African colonies. When they couldn't pierce the language barrier, the traders used a sign language to make deals in "mute markets." So numerous were Genoa's sons in some cities, like Lisbon and Seville, they crowded together in what the natives called "the Genoese quarter."

From their outposts, Genoese agents sent merchant convoys threading their way through fleets of Tunisian pirates and Aragonese corsairs, their holds filled with aromatic spices; ginger, cinnamon, nutmeg, cloves and vanilla. They bought dyes, such as indigo for blue, saffron for yellow, gallnut for black, brazilwood for red. Before goods filtered into Genoa's trading network, colorful Bedouin cloth, Persian gold filigree and Mongolian leather sometimes changed hands twelve times.

The Genoese moved some products directly from the Middle East or Northern Europe to other points in their business empire. On these trades, Genoese shipowners made handsome profits for transporting the goods, and the Republic's merchants earned fortunes, buying cheap in Constantinople and selling high in Cordoba. Genoa's businessmen shipped many of the bulk products back home where the Republic's armorers hammered iron into shields, shoemakers cobbled hides into boots and weavers loomed wool into cloth. If the craftsmen couldn't sell all their production at home, they exported it to the rest of Italy and Europe, selling it at a nice markup.

To finance Genoa's industrial base and worldwide trade, sophisticated bankers used profits earned by the merchants and artisans to extend credit and issue guarantees of payment. Gold served as the primary medium of exchange, but many goods changed hands under the barter system. Although the Catholic Church frowned at the high interest rates charged by the financiers, there was too much money to be made, and Genoa's Renaissance money lenders flourished. While many Christian nations bogged down in obeyance to the Church's restrictions on loaning money, the bankers in Genoa provided the engine for their Republic's success. It was the bold, calculating bankers and proud, flinty businessmen who dominated Genoa and set the pattern for its success.

It was into this world of rampant commerce and primitive, but free-wheeling, capitalism that Christopher Columbus was born in the fall of 1451, about six months after Isabel's birth in April, 1451, in Spain.[2] In other parts of Italy, Fra Angelica was at his height as a painter, Bellini was beginning his career and, while Christopher was still in his cradle, Leonardo da Vinci was born in 1452.[3]

Columbus' mother, Susanna Fontanarossa Colombo, the daughter of a weaver, married a weaver, Domenico Colombo, in 1445.[4] Because she was a private citizen and, even worse in the medieval scheme, a woman, almost nothing was written and little is known about Susanna. She bore at least five children, one of whom died as a young man. Those who survived were her first born, Christopher, Bartholomew a year or two later, the only sister Bianchetta and Diego,[5] about seventeen years younger than his eldest brother.

Although Susanna Colombo's life is shadowed in obscurity,[6] Christopher's father was another matter. At least seventy-seven documents [7] mention his business affairs and lawsuits. At about age eleven, Domenico's father apprenticed him to a master weaver, and at age twenty-one the ambitious young man opened his own cloth shop in Genoa. The Republic's acquisitive entrepreneurs were among the world's best, and Domenico learned the rules of commerce well. As a master weaver and a respected member of the Guild of Weavers, Domenico became a skilled businessman, buying raw wool from Genoa's importers and selling the finished cloth from his looms at home and abroad.

The comfortable income from his business wasn't enough for this energetic risk-taker who aspired to working his way out of the lower middle class. He needed more. During his life, he speculated in any number of sideline businesses, a tavern, a cheese shop and real estate. Genoa's official records[8] show him buying and leasing houses when he had money, and selling when he needed cash. In 1450 he bought a house and, on the same day, leased it back to its former owner, a "sale-leaseback" that modern financiers would be proud of.

Like many men whose restless ambition and optimism lead them to gamble their money in ventures they know nothing about, Domenico often found himself in financial trouble. His own son-in-law, his daughter Bianchetta's husband, sued him for nonpayment of her dowry. The Mayor of Genoa clapped Domenico, hounded by his creditors, in debtor's prison, but a judge later released him when he posted a bond to cover his fine. To pay his fine, he sold off a piece of land, part of his wife Susanna's dowry. Even this resulted in a squabble. Susanna's brother claimed that he had rights to the family land, but Susanna obediently ratified the sale by her husband to keep him out of jail.

In 1470, Domenico's credit was so bad that a lender required Christopher, then nineteen, to guarantee his father's loan. Evidently an optimistic investor to the last, when he died sometime around 1500 Domenico's creditors tried to foreclose on a piece of land he owned.[9] Even though Domenico lacked skill as a speculator, his son Christopher must have loved him, naming his capital city in the New World, Santo Domingo, after his father's patron saint.[10]

No stranger to the risks and vagaries of litigation and the courthouse, Domenico Colombo was equally unafraid of the dangers of Genoese politics. Although Shakespeare wrote "Romeo and Juliet" more than a century later, he could have easily used Genoese politics in the 1450s as a model for the Capilets and Montagues. Two principal families jockied for power in Genoa, the Adornos and the Fregosos. Because Genoa was so small, and because its tight-fisted merchants refused to tax themselves for the expense,[11] the Republic lacked the military power to back up its economic empire, leaving an inviting power vacuum for outsiders to exploit.

The Adorno clan sided with Ferdinand's father, King John of Aragon, while the Fregosos lined up support from France and King Rene d'Anjou. Genoa's western neighbor, Milan, and its trade rivals, Florence and Venice, added to the turmoil by meddling in Genoese affairs. Even within the Adorno and Fregoso parties, bitter factional struggles sometimes erupted in civil war.

Although Genoa called itself a republic, the name was a fraud. Power didn't come from the voting booth, but from bloody coups d'etat and force of arms. In the year Christopher was born, the Fregosos hanged a man for treason, and pinned a note to his foot saying: "This man said things that must not be said." During rioting when Columbus was eight, the youth may have heard the screaming supporters of the Fregosos calling for the death of the Adornos or seen the mangled bodies left to rot in the streets.

To survive the risks and intrigues of Genoese politics, a cautious man stayed on the sidelines out of harm's way. An audacious man willing to gamble his fortune and, perhaps, his life, became a party stalwart. Domenico Colombo, the political activist, placed his bet with the Fregosos, and won. When the Fregosos gained control of Genoa after a clan war, the Doge appointed Domenico Keeper of the Gate of Olivella at a salary of eighty-four Genoese lire a year. "The illustrious and excellent [Giano Fregoso], by the grace of God Duke of the Genoese, has elected to the keeping of the tower and gate of Olivella his beloved Domenico Colombo," the appointment read.

Despite the internal feuds, the city-state was still *Genova la Superba*. She was justly proud, even arrogant. She survived the political turbulence fomented by the Fregosos and the Adornos. The plagues of the late 1300s decimated her population, but she kept on going. Militarily weak, with powerful, avaricious neighbors, her ships kept on sailing thousands of miles east and west to bring enormous wealth to her citizens. Her burghers, merchants and bankers enjoyed a warm feeling of superiority over their medieval European cousins who lived in squalor.

The Genoese were Renaissance men, convinced by humanism's teachings that they controlled their own destiny. Self-assured, living in a boom economy of luxury and splendor, Genoa's swaggering traders appeared invincible. They might not be able to send an army or navy to enforce their will. But, when they couldn't buy their way out of trouble with bribes or pragmatic alliances, they could persuade, cajole, lie. In the quiet of their counting houses, they could negotiate secret financial arrangements to calm a caliph or a king. Secret loans, secret treaties. As good businessmen, Genoa's elite concealed their affairs from governments that might tax, or take, what they had. With their suspicious businessmen's nature, they veiled their dealings from competitors like the Venitians whose ships might beat them to a Black Sea port and buy honey, timber or nourishing dates at a lower price.

Although Genoa's materialistic businessmen prospered under the Renaissance and humanist doctrines which underpinned their crafty dealings and blessed their acumen, the influence of the Catholic Church permeated their lives. Romanesque and Gothic churches dominated Genoa's skyline. Young boys like Christopher could visit the cathedrals to see the wash basin in which Jesus supposedly washed his hands during the Last Supper and the silver box containing John the Baptist's ashes.[12] In Christopher's day, the church where the Knights of the Order of Saint John of Jerusalem organized the Fourth Crusade still stood, conjuring up images in a boy's mind of armor-clad men planning the Infidel's defeat.

When the weaver's son was eight years old, construction began on the Gothic chapel of Saint John the Baptist, and he must have watched the stonemasons climbing up the spindly scaffolding to build its spires—fingers pointing toward Jesus and the Virgin Mary in heaven. Jesus and John the Baptist were powerful figures in Genoa, but its faithful worshipped the Virgin Mary with a fervency that equaled that of Portugal and Spain. While Christopher shared his countrymen's ardent devotion to the cult of the Madonna, he also dwelled on his namesake, Saint Christopher, the Bearer of Christ, the patron saint of travelers.[13]

Most boys in Genoa knew the story of the Syrian pagan who hoisted the Christ child on his shoulders to carry him across a swift river. In mid-stream, Saint Christopher stumbled and almost fell into the torrent, but made it to the other side where Christ turned the saint's wading staff into a beautiful date palm. "Thou hast borne upon thy back the whole world and Him who created it. I am the Christ," Jesus told Saint Christopher. Columbus would take to heart the story's moral that, despite obstacles, perseverance would result in Christ's reward.

During Columbus's childhood another event stirred Christian zeal. In 1453, Mohammed II, "The Magnificent," Sultan of the Turks, stormed eastern Christendom's bastion at Constantinople. In the fighting, the Turks killed the Christian Emperor Constantine, whose body was never found among the massacred corpses, and captured the two hundred-year-old Genoese trading colony in the city.[14] Some Genoese ships escaped to the Republic's colony on the Aegean island of Chios and spread word of the disaster. In a letter to the Doge of Genoa, the governor of the Genoese colony at Constantinople wrote: "No longer will our ships be able to sail toward the Black Sea bearing our goods. The [rights of our] trading companies are worthless."[15] The loss of their colony, and the stories of the Turkish atrocities, beheading Christians and throwing holy relics into the sea, instilled hatred and a desire for revenge in the Genoese. The fall of Constantinople to the Ottoman Turks regenerated the old crusading urge to reconquer the sacred lands of Jerusalem and the Holy Sepulchre and to reunite the world under Jesus' banner.

When Christopher visited Jesus' wash basin and John the Baptist's ashes, the hooded priests no doubt told him that it was the Genoese who recovered these holy articles during the First Crusade 350 years earlier. In the First Crusade it was a victorious Genoese general who captured so much loot that every soldier received forty-eight *soldi* of silver and two pounds of pepper.[16] Christopher would understand the morals of these stories too—crushing the heathens would purify the world for Christianity and it would bring glory and riches to the man who did it.

Mohammed II's victory at Constantinople was not only a disaster for the Christian religion, it sealed Genoa's trade routes through the Straits of Bosporus to the Black Sea and its colonies in the eastern Mediterranean. Now, Allah's disciples controlled access to the Orient's silks and spices. Now, before these coveted goods passed into the hands of Genoa's merchants, Islam's traders marked up the price one more time, cutting into Genoa's profits.

Faced with the Saracen threat, the Genoese's businessmen's instincts, and their lack of military power, brought them to the negotiating table. They paid tribute and taxes to the emirs and bribed Muslim courtiers to give them favorable treatment. While they compromised and rearranged their relationships in the east, increasingly the Genoese began sending their convoys of merchant ships to the west, to Spain and Portugal and farther north to France, England, Holland and Belgium.[17]

Trade. Religion. Politics. All with a peculiar Genoese twist. These were Christopher Columbus' legacy from his native land. There was another legacy. Hemmed in by the Appennines Mountains, no wider than twenty-five miles, the Republic of Genoa faced the sea, was wedded to the sea, received its wealth from the sea. "Genoa..can give you nothing, locked as it is among the mountains, landless: nothing but harshness, fertile only in scrub grass and stunted bushes twisted by the marine wind," Taviana writes.[18] "And because the city can give you nothing, she drives you to the sea, on which she depends totally, from which she receives everything and which demands...tenacity and commitment...."

The wind brought the constant smell of the sea. The setting sun glared off the sea. And the dark blue sea brought the hope of adventure and wealth to Genoa's ambitious young men. "At a very young age, I went to sea, navigating, and I have continued until today," Columbus wrote years later in a letter to Ferdinand and Isabel.[19] As did many Genoese boys, Christopher may have gone on the short voyages up and down the Italian coast, maybe as far as Corsica or Sicily, buying raw wool and selling cloth for his father. Or he may have boarded a fishing vessel at night to net sardines by torchlight.

Exactly when Christopher first went to sea is not known. It is known that his father, Domenico, leased a house near the Gate of Saint Andrea in 1455 when Columbus was four years old. On the ground floor of his ten-foot-wide, four-story house,[20] Domenico ran his wool business. Up the staircase, Susanna padded about on the wooden plank floors, stoked the fireplace, cooked and looked after her children. From the upper windows, she would hang her washing on poles that stuck out past the eaves of the gray slate roof to catch the little sunlight that shined into the narrow streets. In the back yard, she would tend her vegetable garden and draw water from the well. When Christopher was a little boy, Susanna might have held his hand while she went on her rounds to the fishmonger, butcher, vegetable and bakery shops.

As Christopher grew older and went out into the narrow streets by himself, he would have to scrunch his back to the walls to make way for Genoa's elegant ladies in sedan chairs, merchants on horseback and pack mules carrying olive oil and fire wood. In residential areas, the red-headed boy would walk by ordinary men's houses, built of red bricks or stones.[21] The rich men built their mansions of hand quarried marble and stone, some of which had eighty-foot-high towers to provide protection during an intra-city war—and to raise them above the stench of the streets. Wandering through the four-foot-wide back streets, the tall young man would pass the shops of goldsmiths, sword makers, dyers and blacksmiths. In the banking section, he would see the palatial headquarters of the Banco di San Giorgio, with its stream of agents and messengers arriving or departing on trips to its branches in Europe and the Middle East.

When Christopher would walk down to the port he would come to a broad avenue. There, magnificent buildings housing the great trading companies faced the harbor. He could mingle with the foreign and Genoese merchants who gathered in knots under the porticos fronting the buildings to bargain prices and negotiate loans. He would have heard the in-coming sailors telling the merchants the latest news from faraway places. In 1469, when Christopher was eighteen, he may have heard the businessmen discussing the political and commercial implications of the marriage of Isabel of Castile and Ferdinand of Aragon.

Masts, spars and yardarms studded the harbor, flying flags of many nations. Ships rigged to carry triangular lateen or square sails bobbed alongside Genoa's piers. The ships' slack running lines snapped in the breeze coming down from the Apennine Mountains, and thick hemp hawser ropes strained at the incoming and outgoing tide. Oarsmen moored their galleys, and stevedores unloaded the world's goods on the docks.

In their Genoese dialect, the young boys[22] would struggle to make themselves understood by the gangs of foreign sailors crowding the wharves.[23] Across the harbor, facing the sea, Christopher could see the jetty the Genoese built to protect the port from storms and which they fortified with towers to ward off marauding pirates and corsairs. High on a hill, Genoa's lighthouse shined miles out to sea to pilot its mariners home.

On warm humid days, warehouses gave off the smell of sage and thyme. Near the docks, the shipping industry's suppliers sweated in their factories, making anchors, sails, oars, pulleys and barrels to store wine and grain, and selling straw, pitch and tar to protect the wooden ships against seepage and seaworms. In the shops of Genoa's famed mapmakers, Christopher could see the detailed drawings used by sea captains all over the Mediterranean, and hear the stories of Genoa's sons who had worked for Prince Henry in Portugal making maps of Africa's west coast.

Other stories circulated in Genoa when Christopher was a boy. Marco Polo's book, *Il Milione*, written when Polo was a prisoner in a Genoese jail,[24] piqued a young man's sense of adventure, and greed, with its tales of golden roofs and gemstones. At the court of Kublai Khan in China, Polo said he saw scented flowers, exotic fruits, spices and herbs galore during his twenty-four-year trip. Polo talked about a vast Ocean Sea stretching from China past Japan to the east.

An imaginative boy could well have asked if that same Ocean Sea went all the way around the world to Europe. At about the same time Marco Polo was in China, Genoa's sons left its harbor in 1291 to circle Africa and find a new route to the Orient. Captained by two Genoese brothers, Ugolino and Vadino Vivaldi, their two ships never returned. Supposedly, the stories said, one ship went went down off the west coast of Africa and the other made it to Ethiopia where the legendary Christian king, Prester John, captured its crew.[25] Dante romanticized the ill-fated trip, casting the Vivaldi brothers as epic voyagers who were swallowed up by the waves. In the 1300s, Italians discovered, or rediscovered, the Madeira, Canary and Azores Islands. By Christopher's time, in the mid-1400s, discovery was in the air.

What was not in the air for the weaver's son was much formal education. As a youth Christopher received only a rudimentary education, probably at the school run by the friars of Santo Stefano[26] or by the weaver's guild, of which Domenico Colombo was a member.[27] Christopher may have learned the basics of reading, writing and arithmetic, and a smattering of seamanship, mapmaking and navigation, since most Genoese schools at the time included nautical subjects in their curriculum. Although he spent little time in the classroom, Christopher undoubtedly worked for his father as a boy, carding wool or watching over a loom.[28] But the romance of the sea, the excitement of discovery and the stories, both truth and legend, circulating during his youth must have tugged on Christopher's imagination. No more sticky wool down his shirt collar. No more worrying about his debtor father. Christopher went to sea.[29]

At twenty-three, in 1474, Columbus sailed past the jetty protecting Genoa's harbor as either an ordinary seaman or a merchant.[30] With Genoa's flag, a red cross on a white background, flapping in the wind, the fleet's white sails powered it past Mt. Etna and around the tip of Italy's boot, then east to the Island of Chios, a Genoese trading colony in the Aegean Sea just off the coast of Turkey.[31]

When squalls whipped up the Mediterranean Sea, it could be dangerous. But, for the most part, there was little risk. For thousands of years, sailors had charted the shoals, coastlines, islands and trade routes of the Mediterranean. Its winds, tides and currents were a known quantity. Ships seldom lost sight of land for more than a day or two. A sailor knew that, if he just kept heading in any direction, he would eventually find the shore. On board the small vessels a curious, intelligent passenger like Christopher would discuss the mysteries of navigation and seamanship with the mates and captain.

During their years at sea, mariners learned to use their noses as part of the tools of their trade. They could smell a storm before they saw it, could identify an island by is scent. As the Genoese convoy approached Chios, Christopher may have picked up the odor of the island's aromatic mastic trees. When the convoy arrived at Chios, Columbus most likely checked in with the Maona, the Genoese shipowner's corporation which had a monopoly over the island's trade.[32]

From Chios, on a clear day, he could see the Turkish coast. There he was at the gateway of Genoa's opening to the exotic Orient. There he may have learned to purchase cargoes of commodities, to barter, to make a profit.[33] There he may have heard of the Castilian King Henry's death and learned that a young couple about his own age, Isabel and Ferdinand, claimed the throne. When he wasn't gossiping about world events, Christopher must have discussed Chios' most valuable product. Mastic, a gooey resin harvested from evergreen trees on the island, was highly prized as a medicinal remedy to purify the blood and treat rheumatism and as a component for varnishes and adhesives.

To protect their enormous profits from Chios' mastic trade, the Genoese paid tribute to the Sultan of Turkey. So valuable was mastic that, years later, Columbus incorrectly claimed he found the therapeutic resin in the New World to prove to Ferdinand and Isabel that they had not wasted their investment.

The false claim that he found mastic in the New World is only one of the instances when Columbus appeared ready to fudge the truth. In a January, 1495, letter, Columbus wrote to Ferdinand and Isabel that he served as the captain of a corsair in the service of King Rene d' Anjou. Supposedly, sometime in the early 1470s King Rene chartered Genoese ships to prey on Arab pirates along the Barbary Coast in North Africa and the merchant ships of King John of Aragon.

Corsairs were not pirates, but, like mercenary soldiers on land, hired themselves out to anyone willing to pay them, and split their loot with their sponsor.[34] Bankers often financed corsair captains, charging fifty percent and sometimes one hundred percent interest. Since King Rene was an ally of Domenico Colombo's party in Genoa, the Fregoso, it would have been natural for Christopher to attack the Aragonese, who supported the rival Adorno party. But Columbus' claim, Professor Morison argues, that he was a captain at about age twenty couldn't have been true, and that, writing twenty-five years later, Columbus promoted himself to a rank more in keeping with his then title of Admiral of the Ocean Sea.[35] Allegedly, when King Rene ordered the small fleet of corsairs to attack a larger fleet off the coast of Tunisia, the crew refused to go. So, Columbus gleefully claimed, "I was forced to resort to a subterfuge...I changed the feed" of the needle of the compass to make it point south rather than north to deceive the crewmen. All or part of that story is not true. What is true, is that Columbus was willing to point out with pride that he would lie, would perpetrate a hoax, when it served his purposes.

5

COLUMBUS, 1476-1848

Tall, red-headed, almost twenty-five-years-old. In the summer of 1476 Columbus joined a Genoese merchant fleet bound for Lisbon, England and Belgium with a cargo of Chios mastic. The winds sweeping down from the Appennines Mountains caught the five ships' sails, powering them out of sight of Genoa's lighthouse. On board, the cargo ships carried cannons and small arms for protection against the pirates and corsairs stalking the route they would follow. The calm seas in summertime made it the best sailing season. But the pirates and corsairs, knowing that most commercial fleets sailed in summer, made the Mediterranean dangerous at that time of year.

Once the Genoese fleet was in the open sea, the captains set their course west toward the Pillars of Hercules. If the convoy put in at a Spanish port for supplies and fresh water, they no doubt heard the news that, earlier that year, Isabel and Ferdinand's forces defeated King Alfonso of Portugal and La Beltraneja at the Battle of Toro. The reports would have also confirmed that the royal couple were still clearing out pockets of resistance in Spain, and that King Alfonso was heading for France to form new alliances with Louis XI. Columbus, working as a business agent for one of Genoa's great trading houses, may have wondered how these events would effect the profitability of his voyage.[1] After taking on water and supplies, the convoy sailed through the eight-mile wide Straits of Gibraltar. On his left, Columbus could see Ceuta in Africa and, on his right, the 1400-foot-high Rock of Gibraltar.

When the Genoese fleet passed through the Straits of Gibraltar, Columbus entered the Atlantic Ocean for the first time. About two hundred miles past the Straits, Columbus saw Cape St. Vincent jutting out from the extreme southwestern tip of Portugal.[2] There, on August 13, 1476, an armada of fifteen corsairs chartered by the French and Portuguese attacked the Genoese fleet. As the corsairs closed in on the merchant ships, the sailors hurled pots of burning oil at their attackers. The corsairs pressed in close, locking on to the merchant vessels with grappling hooks. Whipped by ocean winds, fire spread from the decks and masts of the corsairs to the Genoese convoy, sending up flames that could be seen on shore. Hundreds of men died during the fierce ten-hour battle.

Some, clad in armor, drowned after they jumped overboard to escape the fires. Five corsairs went down and three merchantmen, including Columbus' ship, sank.[3] Even though he was wounded during the battle, Columbus jumped off his sinking ship and grabbed an oar floating among the wreckage. Using the oar as a life preserver, he swam about six miles to the beach near the fishing village of Lagos. Exhausted, Columbus recuperated in Lagos, and may have gone to the fishermen's church to offer his prayers of thanks to the statue of the Madonna.

After regaining his strength, Columbus traveled to Lisbon, a two-day horseback ride. In 1476, Lisbon was one of the most exciting cities in Europe. Portugal's mapmakers, astronomers and mathematicians made it the European capital of nautical science. These scientists taught Portugal's sailors the latest techniques of celestial navigation so they could pick their way through the watery desert of the open sea. Using this new learning, the mariners mapped the West African coast and charted the Atlantic's winds and currents, earning them a reputation as the world's best ocean seamen. Almost every year, Portuguese pilots and captains extended the boundaries of the known world and returned to be idolized by their countrymen.

Each spring, Portugal's ships left Lisbon headed for West Africa with holds loaded with trading goods; falcon's bells, red wool caps, glass beads and horses. They returned home with Africa's bounty; slaves, chests of gold dust, spices and elephant tusks. With these rich cargoes piling up on Lisbon's docks, the city bristled with optimism, enthusiasm, the excitement of discovery. Mariners and merchants from Iceland to Ghana crowded its streets, swapping stories of the exotic things they saw and repeating tales of the mysterious lands to the west. Ships from a dozen nations tied up in the port at the mouth of the Tagus River. Italian and Jewish bankers advised their aristocratic Portuguese clients of how well their investments were doing, and negotiated loans to corsair and merchant captains.

When Columbus arrived in this vibrant country facing the Atlantic, he felt almost at home. Since the Genoese and Portuguese languages had Latin roots, it wasn't hard to learn the new tongue. There were so many Genoese in Lisbon that the Portuguese called one section of the city the "Genoese quarter." Some Portuguese suspected Genoese spies of stealing copies of the new maps of the valuable trade routes and other secrets of the ocean.[4]

Despite rumors of industrial espionage, Genoa and Portugal allied themselves politically against Aragon, and the two nations established important commercial ties. Genoese ships working the north European trade routes made Lisbon a major port of call. Genoa's powerful Banco di San Giorgio extended credit and issued letters of payment from its Lisbon branch. Genoa's powerful Di Negro and Spinola families set up mercantile houses in Lisbon to sell Genoa's products and buy Portugal's goods coming in from Africa and the Madeira Islands.

Because the Di Negros and the Spinolas supported the Fregoso party in Genoa, Domenico Colombo's political contacts with the Fregoso party would have made Christopher welcome at their Lisbon offices.

Comfortable in this foreign country, the young Genoese could not have avoided the infectious "boom mentality" of Portugal. And Columbus could not have helped being inspired by the Portuguese sea captains who became overnight heroes, rewarded by their King with recognition and riches. When Columbus arrived in Lisbon, the memory of the man who made Portuguese discovery and its bounty possible was still fresh.

Prince Henry the Navigator died sixteen years before Columbus swam ashore near Lagos. But Prince Henry's legacy left his tiny nation of one million people in the forefront of Atlantic and African exploration. A cold, fanatically pious man, Prince Henry heard and read the ancient and medieval wisdom that a fiery hell awaited anyone who tried to penetrate the "torrid zone" near the equator where human life was impossible.

Many of the great thinkers and geographers, Aristotle, Ptolemy and Albertus Magnus, taught that blazing heat made the lands to the south uninhabitable. Prince Henry knew that the never-ending sand dunes of the Sahara Desert almost sealed off land travel to the south. Muslims controlled North Africa, ready to murder

Christians who might try to make a trip across the Sahara. Many camel drivers disappeared in the treeless wastes, dying of thirst or at the hands of wild North African tribesmen.

If the Portuguese wanted to open sea routes to the Middle East, the pirates and corsairs in the Mediterranean lay in wait, and Portugal would risk possible wars with competing European trading nations. After the fall of Constantinople in 1453, the Ottoman Turks slammed the eastern door, threatening the already well-established commercial traffic controlled by Genoa and Venice. Going west presented the problem of crossing an ocean that might be endless. Some European scholars theorized that, if ships went west on the same latitude as the Sahara, there would only be a trackless wasteland of sand and rocks on the other side. Prince Henry also knew that the Genoese Vivaldi brothers lost their lives in the late 1200s when they tried to take the southern route and circle Africa.

Even though the austere Prince understood the risks, there were temptations. The camel caravans which made the round trip across the Sahara brought back gold and ivory. Legends of a magical kingdom somewhere to the south told of the Christian ruler, Prester John, who was supposedly richer and more powerful than any European king.[5] If he could link up with Prester John, the devout Prince Henry thought, Christ's banner would lead their coalition against the infidel Sons of Islam. In addition to the religious appeal, Prince Henry had another powerful medieval motivation. As a young man, astrologers read Prince Henry's horoscope and predicted he was destined to make great discoveries.

To bring wealth to his nation, Prince Henry could only go west or south through the ocean.[6] In his passion for discovery, he sent his ships probing west in a vain search for the legendary islands of St. Brendan. During one voyage, the Portuguese explorers accidently stumbled on the Azores Islands about seven hundred miles out to sea. But with the exception of a few ventures westward, Prince Henry directed the prows of his ships south.

Prince Henry, the third son of the Portuguese King, had little chance of mounting the throne. So the monkish young man turned his ambition to converting souls to Christ, defeating the heathen Muslims and finding treasure to enrich his nation. If he could unite his Christian kingdom with Prester John, not only would it bring wealth, but the Christian forces could attack the Infidels from the rear. Along the way, he could spread the True Faith to Africa's black natives and lead them to Christ's kingdom of paradise. Although his crusading spirit blended neatly with his passion for discovery, Prince Henry coupled his broader vision with a practical, pragmatic infatuation with systematic organization. Before the age of science, most medieval men's minds wandered in nebulous, disorganized confusion. With his orderly mind, Prince Henry formulated an intricate, step-by-step plan to achieve his goals.

In the early 1400s, Henry moved his household to Sagres at the southern-most tip of Portugal, some 150 miles away from the intrigues and conspiracies at the court in Lisbon.[7] In remote Sagres there would be no outside distractions to divert attention from his visionary plan to explore Africa's west coast. Prince Henry brought men of all faiths from all over to staff his research and development operation; Jews, Muslims, Portuguese, Italians, Germans, Scandinavians and Arabs from as far away as the Persian Gulf. He built a town to house the army of mapmakers, astronomers, ship captains, navigators, pilots and scientists.

Prince Henry sent his agents throughout Europe buying maps, charts and books on navigation, shipbuilding and geography to create an extensive library on nautical subjects.[8] His agents collected compasses, astrolabes and other navigational tools for his instrument makers to study and improve. When he finished, Prince Henry had created the greatest institution for the study of navigation and seamanship that the world would see for centuries to come. Strangely, this man who loved the sea, who developed discovery into an organized science, never made a single voyage into the open sea.

From his command headquarters at Sagres, Prince Henry ordered his naval engineers and architects to set up a shipyard at the port of Lagos, about fifteen miles away from Sagres. At Lagos, where Columbus swam ashore years later, the Prince's men developed a new class of ship, designed specifically for discovery. They successfully combined the cargo carrying capability of an Arab "dhow" with the maneuverability of vessels used in northern Portugal. The new ships could carry a full crew and enough supplies to make the long expeditions out and back home again. Rigged with triangular lateen sails, they could cruise with the wind at their backs or head directly into the breezes the vessels would confront in the undiscovered latitudes. Of shallow draft, these specially designed craft could explore close to shore and could be easily beached for repairs and recaulking.

While the naval architects sketched detailed plans for the new ships of discovery, Prince Henry's astronomers spent their nights in the observatory he built them. There they charted the constellations, and made precise notes on the movements of the stars that would guide the Prince's crews. Prince Henry put a Catalan Jew in charge of splicing together maps and charts.[9] After the geographers and astronomers gathered, checked and rechecked the data, they trained the pilots who would embark on the voyages to unknown lands. Before his daring young captains and navigators left on their trips, they received careful instructions on the keeping of accurate logbooks to document every detail of their expeditions. When the seamen brought their precious information back to headquarters in Sagres, the scholars and scientists collated the scraps of information and added it to the store of data already on hand.

Prince Henry's instrument makers perfected the astrolabe, and developed other tools to help the sailors calibrate their position in the ocean. His scientists developed and perfected the use of "tables of declination" to make it easier for the navigators to mark their routes through the uncharted waters of the open sea. As part of his long-range planning, Prince Henry's explorers established a line of forts and supply bases in the islands and along the coasts they discovered as they pressed farther south.

From the world's most sophisticated academy of ocean science, Prince Henry's mariners rediscovered the Madeira Islands. Portuguese colonists planted grapevines and sugar cane in Madeira's rich soil, and, eventually, began producing the sweet, full-bodied wine for which the islands are still famous. To administer the neighboring island of Porto Santo,[10] Prince Henry appointed Bartolomeo Perestrello as governor.

Between 1424 and 1434, the Prince sent his crews on fifteen missions to round Cape Bojador, the huge bulge of northwestern Africa.[11] As they skirted Africa's coast, they saw nothing but the rock and sand of the barren Sahara Desert. Because of the climatic conditions, huge cloud banks built up for forty to fifty miles offshore, shrouding the coast in mist and fog. Even though the explorers inched southward, their fear of the "torrid zone" caused them to return to Sagres with their assignment uncompleted. To excuse their failure to round Cape Bojador, mariners told Prince Henry that treacherous reefs and unmanageable currents made their mission impossible. A Portuguese chronicler tells the story:[12]

> "Although many set out...none dared go beyond the Cape Bojador]....[T]o tell the truth, this was not from cowardice...but from the novelty of the thing and the wide-spread and ancient legends about this Cape.... Although these legends were not true, the idea of discovering if they weren't [true] seemed full of menace; and it was doubtful who would be the first to be willing

> to risk his life in such an adventure....But, being satisfied of the peril, and seeing no hope of honor or profit, they left off the attempt. For, said the mariners, this much is clear, that beyond this Cape there is no race of men nor place of inhabitants...and the sea is so shallow that a whole league from land it is only a fathom deep, while the currents are so terrible that no ship, having once passed the Cape, will ever be able to return."

Prince Henry persisted. Finally, in 1434, a ship captained by Gil Eannes rounded Cape Bojador and broke the deadlock of fear. There, they found lush tropical vegetation and black men living their lives, putting the lie to the myth of the "torrid zone." In addition to this break-through, Prince Henry's men found the Cape Verde Islands, the Azores Islands and pushed as far south as present-day Senegal in West Africa.

Prince Henry died in 1460 after forty years of work on his project of discovery. Devout to the last, this man who lived his life almost as a monk, wore a hair shirt on his deathbed, and reportedly died a virgin. After his death, the isolated colony at Sagres disintegrated, but the tradition he established lived on at Lisbon. When Columbus arrived in Portugal in 1476, Prince Henry's successors had sailed as far as modern-day Ghana and established a fort at St. George of the Mine.

After the sea battle off Cape St. Vincent, Columbus spent several months in Lisbon before signing on for a voyage to England. The flotilla of merchant ships docked at London in the winter of 1476. Columbus then made his way to Bristol, England's principal port for its trade with Iceland. From Bristol, ships carried grain, salt, wine and honey to exchange for dried fish, wool and down for pillows. Even though it was winter, Columbus boarded an English ship bound for Iceland in February of 1477. It would be a twelve or fourteen-day trip, counting the stopover in Galway, Ireland.

Several years later Columbus noted in one of his books that, "Many remarkable things have we seen, particularly at Galway in Ireland, a man and a woman of most unusual appearance adrift in two boats [from a wreck]."[13] Columbus speculated that the two bodies came from China, but, more likely, they were Laplanders or other persons with Mongol features. In Ireland Columbus may have heard the legend of the Irish monk, St. Brendan, who supposedly sailed west in the 500s to discover the "Promised Land of the Saints." In the 1000s a chronicler wrote the tale of St. Brendan who, convinced that paradise lay to the west, sailed into the Atlantic to find the beautiful island of unsurpassed fertility. So strong was the legend that St. Brendan's Island showed up on maps long past Columbus time, and the story was translated into at least nine languages.[14]

After the stopover in Galway, the merchant ships shoved off, headed north on the 825-mile trip to Iceland; Columbus' first long voyage in the vastness of the open sea. "I sailed in the year of 1477," Columbus wrote in his memoirs, "in the month of February, a hundred leagues beyond Thule Island (Iceland), whose northern part is 73 degrees distant from the equator, and not 63 degrees as some will have it to be. Nor does it lie upon the line where Ptolemy's west begins, but much more to the westward; and to this island, which is as big as England, come the English with their goods to trade, especially from Bristol. At the time when I was there, the sea was not frozen, but the tides were so great that, in some places, it swelled 26 fathoms, and fell as much."[15]

For a man who grew up in the sunny Mediterranean and its relatively calm seas, the stormy North Atlantic and the black lava beaches of Iceland, framed by snowy mountains, must have been a strange and exotic sensation. Here there was no grain because there was little sun, no honey because there were few flowers and no timber, only scrubby bushes. Iceland's people were Christians, but they were a tough, almost savage, people clad in furs and rough woolens, living in houses made of peat with moss covered roofs. Struggling to communicate with the island's people in his rudimentary Latin, English or Portuguese, Columbus may have heard the nordic sagas of men who had been west to Greenland and Newfoundland.

Some five hundred years before Columbus' visit, a habitual criminal named Eric the Red escaped from his native Norway after being outlawed for murdering a servant. Once he got to Iceland, he murdered several more men and was banished for three years. In the late 900s, Eric the Red sailed west about five hundred miles, and touched the coast of Greenland. On Greenland's west coast, the Viking found fertile land, abundant game and plenty of fish. After his three years of banishment, Eric the Red returned to Iceland and recruited twenty boatloads of colonists to join him in a new expedition.

From his base in Greenland, Eric the Red's son, Leif Ericsson, made voyages to Baffin Island, Labrador, Nova Scotia and Newfoundland. Over time, the western colonies failed, and, by Columbus' day, were only the subject of legends, poems and songs.[16] Fighting the language barrier, Columbus may have had difficulty understanding the confusing Viking tales. But he did learn that there was no abyss to the west; that there was land. And he may have reasoned that, if there were western lands in the north, why couldn't there be land to the west on the same latitude as Portugal or Africa?

After experiencing the tides of Iceland and seeing signs of the Gulf Stream that warms northern Europe, by the spring of 1477 Columbus was back in Portugal. He may have supported himself by working with his younger brother Bartholomew in Lisbon as a map maker or book seller until the next summer, when he went on his first voyage to the Madeira Islands. The sugar cane Prince Henry introduced to the islands flourished in the volcanic soil, making many men rich.

In July of 1478, the Di Negro family of Genoa hired Columbus as a business agent to go to Madeira to buy a cargo of sugar for their customer, Ludovico Centurione. During the voyage, Columbus learned more about the play of the winds and currents in the open sea, the unpredictability of the weather and the intricacies of navigation. While Columbus learned valuable nautical lessons, he also learned a bitter lesson about business.

In a lawsuit brought in Genoa in 1479, Ludovico Centurione claimed that Paolo Di Negro had cheated him. In the suit, Centurione said he paid Di Negro 1290 ducats to buy sixty thousand pounds of sugar. Di Negro gave Columbus only 103 ducats in cash, promising to forward the rest of the money later. Columbus arrived in Madeira, and arranged to buy the full shipment.

When the merchant ship chartered to pick up the sugar docked at Madeira, Columbus still hadn't received the promised money from Di Negro. Since the Madeirian merchants wouldn't extend credit, Columbus was forced to return to Genoa with only about ten percent of Centurione's order.

Furious, with only ten percent of the sugar he ordered and the rest of his money in Di Negro's pocket, Centurione sued. On August 25, 1479, Columbus appeared in a Genoese court to testify. He stated that he was about twenty-seven, a Genoese citizen, a resident of Lisbon and that he was returning to Lisbon the next day. This was to be his last visit to his native city, and the last time he would see his father and sister.

A few weeks later, Columbus was back in Lisbon. On Sundays he attended mass at the chapel of the All Saints Convent, overlooking the Tagus River. Years before, the Knights of the Military Order of Santiago established the convent to house their wives and daughters while they were away fighting. By 1479, it was a sort of boarding school for the daughters of Portuguese aristocrats. Strict chaperons guarded unmarried girls, and many young men, including Columbus, attended services at the convent's chapel, one of the few places they could catch a glimpse of a prospective mate. On one Sunday, Columbus saw the woman who would be his only wife, Felipa Moniz de Perestrello, the daughter of Bartolomeo Perestrello, the man Prince Henry appointed governor of Porto Santo some thirty years before.[17]

Somehow Columbus arranged an introduction to the twenty-five-year-old Felipa, and, as he later told his son, it was a "love match." They met at mass and at vespers until, Columbus' son said, "She became so familiar and friendly with my father that she became his wife."

But why would the daughter of an aristocratic family marry a foreigner and even worse, a weaver's son? Columbus, who lied more than once during his life to get what he wanted, may have fudged the truth about his background and claimed noble lineage.[18] On her side, Felipa's father, Bartolomeo, died twenty years earlier, leaving little money to support the family. Even though Felipa's brother was the governor of Porto Santo, it was a poor island, producing only a meager income.

The self-confident Genoan with blue-gray eyes didn't demand a dowry. At twenty-five, Felipa was considered almost middle-aged, and may have had few prospects among the Portuguese noblemen. Perhaps, this intense, dynamic weaver's son who dreamed of dangerous voyages to reap the riches of the Indies attracted Felipa, and she convinced her mother to approve the match.

Whatever the reason, for Columbus the marriage was a coup, a step up from his lower middle class past. Marriage to an aristocrat, and the entree it would bring into powerful court circles, were no doubt strong motivations for the ambitious man. Status obsessed Columbus all his life, and now he would have it. The couple married in the fall of 1479.

Shortly after the marriage, the newlyweds went to Porto Santo to live with Felipa's brother. There, their only son, Diego, was born in 1480. To pass the time on the lonely island, Columbus studied his deceased father-in-law's sea charts and notes on sailing. During chats with his brother-in-law and his new wife, Columbus may have speculated on the reports of Portuguese sea captains who said that, while sailing in the open sea, they used flocks of land-based birds as navigational tools to lead them to the safety of land.

From 1480 to 1484, the details of Columbus' life are sketchy. He may have continued working for the Di Negro family as a merchant. If he wasn't employed as a businessman, his brother Bartholomew may have employed him in Lisbon as a map maker.

Or, with his new status as the husband of a noblewoman, he may have felt it was beneath his dignity to engage in trade. Whatever he did, Columbus apparently made little money, and may have scraped by on the few funds Felipa's family could spare. Although the dates are not certain, during that four-year period Columbus traveled to Lisbon, the Azores and the Canaries. He made at least one trip to the Cape Verde Islands, and sailed to St. George of the Mines, Portugal's Gold Coast in what is now Ghana. On his voyage to Africa, for the first time he saw the constellation of stars forming the Southern Cross, and the gold, ivory and slaves that were making the Portuguese rich. He also learned that, in the "torrid zone," men could live and work in the equatorial heat and humidity.

Perhaps, when he saw first hand that the ancient wisdom and myths about the "torrid zone" were not true, Columbus began to wonder whether the medieval theories and fables about the west were incorrect. He may have questioned the stories about snake-like sea monsters, demon sea pigs and whales with rhinoceros tusks they used to gore holes in wooden ships. Just possibly, Columbus may have thought, St. Augustine's theory, that men didn't live in the west because they couldn't be descendents from Adam, was wrong.

Whether the theories were right or wrong, the long voyages served as a training ground. From direct experience, Columbus learned that in the Canary Islands the winds blew predominantly from east to west, and that, farther north in the Azores, the winds blew from west to east. Each trip increased Columbus' knowledge of seamanship and navigation. How to handle a ship in a head wind. What kinds of food wouldn't spoil. How to stow supplies to balance the load. How to read the compass and plot a course through the open sea. Just as important, Columbus watched the experienced captains handle and discipline their tough, sometimes unruly, crewmen.

Although he learned the lessons of the sea scientifically, from experience, in the Azores he heard the story of the corpses of two men "differing in aspect from Christians" which washed ashore. Inhabitants of the islands Columbus visited told him they found strange things on the beaches; "bean of the sea" plants, limbs of pine trees and large canes unknown in Europe. To Columbus, who was by then searching for clues to prove that a voyage west to the Indies was feasible, each voyage produced new evidence that there was land not too far to the west. Finding the large canes substantiated the great geographer Ptolemy's story about joints of canes from India that could hold two quarts of wine. The islanders claimed the waves occasionally washed up intricately carved wood which could only have been worked by human hands. A sailor in Madeira told Columbus about a storm that blew sailor's ship miles to the west where he saw three mysterious islands.

Everywhere he went, the rumors of land to the west abounded. But, while Columbus seized on every shred of hearsay to build his case, at the same time he gathered scholarly proof that his ambition was more than a dream.

Sometime in the early 1480s, Co-lumbus obtained a copy of a letter written in 1474 by a well-known geographer to a close advisor of King Alfonso of Portugal. The Florentine geographer, Paolo Toscanelli, included a map with the letter. On the map, Toscanelli traced the route from Europe to Japan and China, and noted his calculation of the distance from the Canary Islands to the Indies.[19] The letter and the map were bombshells.

Toscanelli agreed with Marco Polo that the Orient lay much closer to Europe than anybody, including the revered Ptolemy, thought. By Toscanelli's reckoning, only five thousand miles separated China from the Canary Islands. And the mythical island of Antilia, two thousand miles out, and Japan, three thousand miles, would serve as convenient ports of call.[20] A trip across the Ocean Sea was not only possible, but, Toscanelli said, must be made in order to free Christendom from the Ottoman Turks' stranglehold on trade with the east.

Although Toscanelli worked primarily as a physician in Florence, he, as did many doctors of the day, also developed a distinguished reputation in other sciences. He collected books on cosmography and astronomy and maps from Genoa, Venice and Northern Europe. Toscanelli read the written accounts of world travelers and, when these men visited Florence, he discussed their travels and listened to their accounts of dark-skinned men in the east who traded in spices. By the time he wrote the 1474 letter, Toscanelli was an old man. Almost eighty, he had studied geography for more than fifty years.

Nobody knows how Columbus obtained Toscanelli's map and letter from the Portuguese archives. He may have gotten them from influential friends at court after swearing to keep them secret. Or, since there were many foreign spies in Lisbon trying to get copies of Portugal's invaluable maps of its island colonies and Africa, he may have gotten his hands on stolen copies. In either event, Columbus transcribed Toscanelli's letter in Latin in his own hand. "...I [Toscanelli] have very often discoursed concerning the short way [by sea from Europe] to the Indies, where the Spice is produced, which I look upon to be shorter than [you may think]...."

To Columbus, the letter and map confirmed his own thinking. "That map set Columbus' mind ablaze," his biographer Las Casas says.[21] In the letter, Toscanelli discussed the map "drawn with my own hand" which he enclosed, and added:

"I have also marked down in the said Chart several places in India, where ships might put in upon any Storm or contrary Winds, or any other accident unforeseen .... [And] you must understand that none but Traders live or reside in all those Islands, and that there are a great Number of Ships and Seafaring people with merchandise...particularly in a most noble Port called Zaiton, where there are every year an Hundred large ships of Pepper loaded and unloaded...[and] other Ships that take on Spice."[22]

His mind ablaze, Columbus wrote to Toscanelli asking for more details and a copy of the 1474 letter. Toscanelli answered:

> "To Cristobal Columbo, Paolo the Physician, greeting: I observe your great and noble ambition to pass over to where the spices grow, wherefore in reply to your letter I send you a copy of another letter which some time ago I wrote to a friend of mine, a servant of the most serene King of Portugal, before the wars of Castile...and I send you another sea-chart like the one which I sent to him...."

Still wanting more details, Columbus wrote back to Toscanelli, who responded in a second letter:

> "I Received your Letters with the things you sent me, which I take as a great Favor, and commend your noble and ardent desire of Sailing from East to West, as it is marked out in the Chart I sent you....[T]he Voyage laid down [by Columbus] is not only possible, but true, certain, honorable, very advantageous and most glorious among all Christians. [W]hen the said voyage is performed, it will be to Powerful Kingdoms, and to most noble Cities and Provinces, Rich, and abounding in all sorts of Spice in great quantities and store of Jewels. This will moreover be Grateful to those Kings and Princes [of the Orient], who are very desirous to Converse and Trade with Christians of these our Countries...[and it may be that] some of them [will] become Christians...."

Now, an eminent, world-renowned scholar was telling Columbus that the voyage he conceived could, and would, be successful. Toscanelli, personally, confirmed he was not a dreamer, not crazy. Toscanelli, a friend of the Medici family, an intimate of the greatest Renaissance scientists, put his seal of approval on Columbus' plan. Even with Toscanelli's blessing, there was more work to do.

Piece by piece Columbus gathered evidence to prove there was land to the west and that a voyage was feasible. He improved his Portuguese, Castilian and Latin.[23] He read, he watched and he listened. During his sea voyages, Columbus patiently studied the currents, winds, stars and skies. He seized on every clue to support his grand design, noting on maps the location of St. Brendan's Island and Antilia. He poured over academic and Biblical materials. He discussed and analyzed the data. To his scientific approach to the problem, he overlaid his instincts, his imagination, his energy.

With Felipa and his son Diego, Columbus returned from Madeira to Lisbon in 1483; the vision, the great enterprise, clearly crystallized in his mind. In Lisbon, Columbus no doubt heard the latest news from Spain about the war Isabel and Ferdinand launched against the Moors. Obsessed with his plan, Columbus had other things on his mind.

At the time, Columbus was approaching medieval middle age at thirty-two. His red hair had gone white, and the ocean sun had freckled his light skin. He was getting old, time was short, he must get on with his plan. Columbus probably contacted Felipa's friends in the Portuguese nobility, pulling every possible string to arrange an audience with King John of Portugal, who had succeeded his father, King Alfonso, in 1481. Finally, he finagled a meeting with King John sometime in late 1483 or early 1484.[24]

Columbus exuded total confidence. "[H]e had conceived of a project which appeared to him to be...magnificent," historian Cecil Jane writes. "He had been impelled to offer to dare that which others shrank from daring...he had been assured in his own mind that he would succeed where others had failed....To him, those lands, concerning which others could offer no more than vague conjectures, appeared as clearly as if he had personally visited them."[25]

Drawing on all his powers of persuasion, Columbus tantalized King John with stories of the gold and spices he would bring back to Portugal from India, China and Japan. Somewhere in the Indies he would find the valuable cloves Europeans thought cured the Black Death. Columbus spoke of the other great sovereigns, Alexander the Great and Nero, who sponsored exploration. Next, Columbus flattered King John, telling him that he "understood discovery better than any other man." Then he expressed the arrogance of most Europeans, assuring King John that the potentates of the Orient would readily submit to Portuguese sovereignty.

If Columbus obtained the Toscanelli letter and map legally, he may have shown them to King John to prove that it would be an easy journey across the Ocean Sea. If he obtained them by bribing a royal official, Columbus may have only cited unnamed scholars and Marco Polo, who thought the earth's large land masses were close together.

Columbus mentioned the corpses with oriental features that had washed ashore on the Azores, and the pines, large canes and hand-carved wood. And, Columbus said, the trip would serve Christianity. Missionaries would convert the heathens, and the conquest of the Orient would open the back door for the Christians to defeat the Muslim hordes in the Middle East. After asking King John to pay the full cost of the voyage, Columbus named his price for bringing all this wealth and glory to Portugal; a noble title and a healthy share of the riches.

Columbus' timing was bad. In a palace revolt, a cabal of Portuguese aristocrats tried to unseat King John. To keep his throne, the King executed the powerful Duke of Braganza, and personally assassinated the Queen's rebellious brother. In foreign affairs, Portugal's territorial squabbles with Ferdinand and Isabel still simmered. Historically, the Portuguese looked south, not west, for their route to the Orient. For sixty years, beginning with Prince Henry, Portuguese merchant fleets sailed to Africa with cheap trinkets, and returned with cargo bays full gold and ivory. Almost every year, a Portuguese captain went farther down the West African coast to find new treasure, and, in 1484, a Portuguese mariner discovered the Congo River.[26]

Why, King John could ask, should he pay for the ships and crews that Columbus demanded, when other rich merchants financed their own voyages? Why grant Columbus' ultimatum for the title of perpetual Viceroy and Governor of newly discovered lands and ten percent of the profits? The King's sea captains, who requested much less, were making Portugal one of Europe's most powerful nations by going south, to Africa. By underestimating King John's very viable southern alternative, and by overestimating his own worth, Columbus' tripped over his own Genoese businessman's greed.

Annoyed by Columbus' avarice, King John thought the Genoan pushed too hard. He came across as too haughty, vain and, worst of all, too much of a dreamer.

"The King," a Portuguese historian wrote, "seeing that this Christovao Colom was a big talker, and very boastful in setting forth his accomplishments, and [more] full of fantasy and imagination as to his Cipango island (Japan) than certain of what he was talking about, had little faith in [Columbus]. Still, because of his constant insistence, the King had him confer [with a three-man committee of experts] to whom he [King John] had entrusted such questions of cosmography and discovery."[27]

Columbus had a different view of King John's reluctance: "God closed [King John's] eyes and ears...for I failed to make him understand what I was saying."[28]

Even though Columbus' persistent, hard-sell pressure irritated King John, rather than give an outright "no," the King used an old ruse—he referred the matter to committee.[29] The royal committee questioned Columbus closely. They rehashed the issues and considered the tall Genoan's demands for men, ships, titles and profits. And, evidently, the scholarly committee shredded Columbus' scientific arguments. To the Portuguese experts, Columbus was a pretentious upstart. "Navigationally, he was a novice," historian Alan Lloyd says. "Academically, he was an ignoramus; socially, he was a climber of dubious origin. Professionalism is a harsh critic." In late 1484, the committee denied his request.

In that same year, Columbus suffered another blow. Felipa died.[30] And, because of his single-minded dedication to his great enterprise, he and his small son were living in poverty. With his plan rejected, his wife dead and his creditors hounding him, Columbus' dream of a voyage west seemed at an end. With these depressing events, most men would have crumbled, but not Columbus. His unswerving tenacity, and his unshakeable conviction that God chose him to complete his divinely endowed mission, drove him forward.

Instead of backing off, Columbus used his rejection as a learning experience, a building block. Even though the validity of his great enterprise was, to him, self-evident, he decided he must arm himself to combat the prejudices and arguments of the scholarly "harsh critics." He must do more research, have an answer for every question, be prepared to rebut every challenge. He must enhance his scientific and nautical credentials. There were some lessons Columbus didn't learn in Portugal; to reduce his demands for titles and money, to curb his missionary instinct to push too hard and to disguise his haughtiness toward those who couldn't, or wouldn't, understand the rightness of his God-inspired cause. The traits of a Genoese businessman were ingrained.

6

COLUMBUS, THE SPANISH YEARS

Depressed, almost penniless, a four-year-old son to care for, Columbus considered his future. He felt at home in his adopted country after having spent most of his young manhood in Portugal. He spoke fluent Portuguese even though he spoke it with a Genoese accent. Between 1476 and 1485, he had built a network of friends, and persuaded his younger brother Bartholomew to move to Lisbon. Although his wife Felipa was dead, Columbus still had supporters in the Portuguese aristocracy, and he could always fall back on his contacts in the "Genoese quarter."

If he wanted, he could probably revive his financial fortunes in Lisbon by taking a job as a business agent for a Genoese company or working in his brother Bartholomew's map shop. Even though the door to King John's audience chamber appeared closed to further discussion of his great enterprise, his friends who opened that door once might be able to do it again. For a cautious, conservative man, the easiest course would be to stay in Lisbon.

But, driven by his unquenchable willpower, the "Enterprise of the Indies" obsessed Columbus. Possibly he approached Genoa's flinty bankers to support his mission. If he did, they showed no interest in financing such a speculative plan. Perhaps he considered asking King John for a rehearing, but that could be years away, maybe never. As Atlantic nations, England or France might back his mission, but Columbus knew no one in the cold north.

With these alternatives ruled out, Columbus turned to neighboring Spain. He spoke some Castilian, and, since Castilian and Portuguese both stemmed from Latin, mastering the new language presented no problem. He didn't know many Spaniards, but Felipa's sister and her husband lived in southern Spain, and Seville's "Genoese quarter" might provide a base of support.

Although Isabel and Ferdinand made the War of Granada their first priority, with the lull in the fighting during 1485, Columbus may have thought he could get their attention. Even if eradicating the Moors diverted the royal couple for a while, the Infidels couldn't hold on to their tiny kingdom much longer. After the Muslim's certain defeat, Spain, much larger and with more resources than Portugal, would surely become a player in the game of discovery. Everyone knew of Ferdinand and Isabel's appetite for expansion.

With Portugal's lock on the southern route to the Orient, and the Ottoman Turks sealing off the Middle East, Spain had nowhere to go but west. To the west, the Spanish already controlled the Canary Islands, where the winds blew to the west, making it an ideal place to launch a voyage to the Indies. And, with a colony in the Atlantic to use as a stepping stone, surely his project would interest the Spanish monarches.

With his little son Diego in tow, Columbus secretly boarded a ship bound from Lisbon to the Spanish port of Palos in 1485.[1] Columbus left Lisbon in secret, his biographer Las Casas says, because he was afraid that King John "might [have sought Columbus] out in order to hold him, and there was no doubt that he would have held him...and, desiring to resume cautiously the enterprise, he (King John) wanted to regain the favor of Christopher Columbus, either to draw from him greater and more certain evidence...or to conclude negotiations with him."[2]

After sailing about one hundred miles past Cape St. Vincent, Columbus' ship entered the estuary of the Saltes River. As the vessel nosed its way upstream, it turned to the right into the Tinto River and passed a whitewashed monastery sitting on a high bluff before finally docking at Palos.

Although Palos was a few miles inland, it was a seafaring city full of adventurous sailors, including Martin Alonso Pinzon. In Palos, Columbus must have asked for directions to the monastery he saw from the river. Since monasteries frequently provided room and board to travellers at no cost, Columbus and his son walked about an hour from Palos to La Rabida.[3] The Franciscan brothers at La Rabida assigned Columbus and Diego to a white plastered monk's cell, and later that evening, perhaps at dinner, Columbus met the cleric in charge of the monastery, Father

Antonio Marchena.

By sheer luck, Columbus stumbled across one of the men who would be pivotal to his career. Not only was Marchena a well-respected churchman with contacts at the court of Isabel and Ferdinand, he also had a substantial reputation as an astronomer, cosmographer and student of nautical science. In Marchena, Columbus found a soul-mate. Scrupulously pious, both men dedicated themselves to the teachings of St. Francis of Assisi; Columbus from his days as a student of the Franciscan friars of St. Stefano in Genoa, and Marchena from his choice of holy order. In addition to the religious bond, the mysteries of the stars and the earth gripped the intellects and imaginations of both men. In conversations together, they could dissect the wisdom of Ptolemy's geography and the theories of other ancient thinkers.

At first, Columbus no doubt held back many of the details of his great enterprise. While sipping wine in La Rabida's garden courtyard and on strolls through the monastery's shadowy corridors, Columbus grew to trust Marchena. Overcoming his suspicious nature, Columbus gradually unveiled his plan to the brown-robed priest. After swearing Marchena to secrecy, Columbus told him of the Toscanelli map and of the Florentine's letters confirming the scientific underpinnings of a voyage to the west.[4] He revealed the evidence he collected during his trips as far north as Iceland and as far south as Ghana, and his theories of winds and currents.

As he rolled out his thoughts, Columbus' dynamism, his force of personality, his enthusiasm, his certainty, apparently overwhelmed the academically inclined Franciscan. This was no madman, no dreamer. Yes, Marchena must have thought, Columubus was insistent, maybe even pushy, but his ideas made sense to the scholar-priest. Marchena believed. Years later, in a letter to Isabel and Ferdinand, Columbus wrote: "Your Highnesses know that I spent seven years at your Court...[and] never in all that time was there found a pilot, or seaman, or philosopher, or men of any other science, who did not, all of them, say my enterprise was worthless, except for Fray Antonio Marchena...."[5]

Columbus also met Father Juan Perez at La Rabida. At the time Columbus arrived, Perez served as the monastery's prior. He had begun his career as a royal accountant, then joined the Franciscan order and eventually became Queen Isabel's personal confessor.[6] Columbus, perhaps aided by Marchena, convinced Father Perez of the feasibility of the great enterprise. With Father Perez as a confirmed supporter, Columbus no doubt sought his advice about the personalities of the King and Queen and the subtle nuances of getting things done at the Spanish court.

Columbus asked for, and got, Perez and Marchena's agreement to introduce him to the powerful nobles and clergymen who could help advance the cause. As the three men developed a plan of action, they may have called in Spanish seamen from the nearby ports of Palos and Huelva to discuss the practical problems of seamanship and navigation. Several veteran mariners lived in Palos, men who participated in the corsair raids the Duke of Medina Sidonia sponsored against Portugal's Africa trade, and members of the well-respected Pinzon family whose merchant ships carried Spanish cargoes over the trade routes. These experienced sailors could confirm Columbus' statements that the winds in the Canaries blew mostly to the west, and that some Portuguese explorers made their discoveries by following flights of birds to land.

Exhilarated by his recruitment of Marchena and Perez, Columbus then made the short journey from La Rabida to the port of Huelva to expand his network of contacts.[7] There, he joined his brother-in-law, Miguel Muliart, the husband of Felipa's sister.[8] Evidently, the two brothers-in-law got along, but history does not record that Muliart gave much assistance to Columbus. After visiting his relatives, Columbus traveled to Seville. In Seville's "Genoese quarter" many traders, including the Di Negro and Spinola families, bought and sold marble, sugar, silk and spices. No doubt, Columbus called on acquaintances from his native country to see if they knew someone in power.

Although Columbus sought help from his Genoese friends, Father Marchena's letter of introduction which plugged Columbus into Spain's "old boy" network was his primary reason for going to Seville. As part of their plan of action, Marchena wrote to the Duke of Medina Sidonia, one of Spain's most powerful and richest *grandees*, recommending Columbus and his project.[9]

Marchena knew that, out of his own pocket, the Duke had more than enough money to pay for a voyage west. The Duke's family, the Guzmans, owned lands and castles in Andalusia, and shipyards near Palos. For years, corsair fleets financed by the Guzmans raided Portuguese ships engaged in their monopoly trade with West Africa. Knowing of the Guzman's vast wealth and interest in shipping, Columbus, with Marchena's letter of introduction in hand, approached the Duke of Medina Sidonia to promote his plan. The Duke liked the project, but, after feuds broke out between his family and that of the Ponce de Leons, Isabel banished the Duke of Medina Sidonia from Seville.

His contact with Medina Sidonia broken, Columbus next

gained an audience with the Marquis of Medina Celi at his headquarters in Cadiz in the fall of 1485.[10] Medina Celi, who owned dozens of merchant ships, liked the plan, and agreed to furnish Columbus "with three or four well-equipped caravels, for he asked for no more."

Although Medina Celi enthusiastically supported the plan, he was leery of the Sovereigns' reaction if he sponsored the trip without their prior approval. Dutifully, Medina Celi wrote to Isabel asking permission to underwrite the voyage with four thousand ducats. "As I saw that this project was so important as to warrant the decision of our lady the queen," Medina Celi said later, "I wrote to Her Highness about it. She replied by telling me to send this man (Columbus) to her." [11] Isabel made her point; the exploration and conquest of new lands were not matters to be handled by individual dukes or marquises. Now they were matters of state.

Finally, Columbus, network worked. After almost a year of meetings and discussions with Spanish aristocrats and prelates, Columbus' audience with Isabel and Ferdinand would be a reality. He knew that, to support the grand scale of his project, he needed the backing of monarches, not petty noblemen. If he sailed under the flag of a duke or a count, they had no power to grant him the riches and titles he so ardently desired. If he found the splendid Orient, without the power of an entire nation behind him, another king could attack and oust him from his new domains. "Although I know but little," Columbus wrote in 1500, "I do not think that anyone considers me so foolish as not to realize that, even if the Indies were mine, I would not be able to sustain them without the aid of some Prince."[12]

With a royal summons, Columbus left Seville for the one hundred mile trip to Cordoba to meet the King and Queen, arriving on January 20, 1486.[13] The court, following the ancient custom of moving from place to place, had gone to Madrid. Disappointed, Columbus presented himself at the residence of a powerful court official, Alonso de Quintanilla. To gain access to this influential man, Columbus produced a letter of introduction from Father Juan Perez, who, before becoming a priest, had worked as an accountant for Quintanilla. After reading the letter from his old friend, Quintanilla gave Columbus a small sum of money to tide him over until he could meet with the Sovereigns.

During the rest of the winter of 1486, Isabel and Ferdinand moved the court from town to town, raising money for the War of Granada. They called on the faithful to support the holy crusade by buying the indulgences authorized by Pope Innocent VIII's bull to support the holy crusade. When necessary, the royal couple mortgaged crown revenues and pawned Isabel's jewelry. After a winter of twisting the arms of reluctant "lenders" and badgering their subjects for funds to pay for men and supplies, Isabel and Ferdinand returned to Cordoba in the spring of 1486.

There, with Andalusia's gardens in bloom, the Sovereigns received the Genoan in the formal audience chamber of Cordoba's fortress. It was late in the evening, but, from the audience chamber's windows looking out over the Guadalquiver River, Columbus could see the sturdy Roman bridge built 1,500 years before during the reign of the Emperor Augustus. After noting the imprint left by his fellow Italian, Columbus struggled to make his opening remarks in his newly-adopted language. In his heavily accented Castilian, he summarized the great enterprise for the King and Queen. "He (Columbus) told them (the Sovereigns) his dream, but they remained skeptical. He spoke with them and said that what he was saying was true. Then he showed them a map of the world. In this way, he aroused their desire to hear more about those lands," Columbus' friend Bernaldez wrote.[14]

At some point during the meeting, Ferdinand left. Always pragmatic, the King was more interested in the practical problems of fighting Moors and protecting Spain's flanks from France. To Ferdinand, now was not the time to waste on some nebulous dream of voyages to the Indies. Since Castile had jurisdiction over the Atlantic, and Aragon over the Mediterranean, this was Isabel's project. While Ferdinand focused on Italy, Sicily and the Mediterranean, as a Castilian Isabel turned her mental gaze west, to the "Sea of Darkness."

Isabel and Columbus were both thirty-five, fair skinned, and each had vivid blue eyes. Columbus, much taller than the diminutive Queen, presented an imposing figure as he pointed to the seas and lands on the map drawn by him and his brother Bartholomew. Even though he was selling his plan, he probably held back many of the details. No doubt, Father Marchena warned Columbus of Ferdinand's deceitful tendencies, making the King a man perfectly capable of stealing Columbus' ideas. Remembering the rumors of King John of Portugal's theft of his secrets, Columbus wouldn't have disclosed too many essential facts or shown Isabel the Toscanelli map.

But there was an even more important reason Columbus avoided bogging down the Queen in minutia. Having dealt at the highest levels in Portugal, Columbus knew that monarches have little patience for academic palaver. He must sell the Queen on his concept. He must make his vision her vision. With new worlds ripe for discovery, Columbus may have said, Spain's glory would know no limits. The gold and spices of the Indies lay waiting for the sovereign bold enough to sponsor his voyage.

As he built his case, he piqued Isabel's intellectual curiosity until the brilliant flashes of his vision became her own. Columbus spoke with authority of winds, currents and tides, impressing the Queen with his credentials as a navigator. In broad strokes, he painted his view of the world's geography. Columbus, briefed by Fathers Marchena and Perez on Isabel's fervent piety, spoke of his desire to save the millions of heathen souls thirsting for deliverance by Christ and the Holy Virgin. Perhaps, to the Queen, his name, Christopher, the Christ bearer, was more than symbolic.

Convinced that Columbus' devotion to the Catholic Church matched her own, in many other ways they shared a common mind set. Piety was essential. Although Isabel brooked no challenge to the teachings of the Holy Church, the Renaissance's spirit of inquiry and scientific investigation dusted the minds of both the Queen and the foreigner standing before her. Their minds worked easily at the conceptual level. They both solved problems pragmatically, businesslike. They both clearly defined, and steadfastly pursued, their goals; hers to unify and glorify her nation, his to make a voyage west. Despite adversity, they both conceived grand dreams and stuck to them. They both shared an instinct to run the "divine risk." Both had the ability to crystalize their intuition into an idea, their idea into a plan and their plan into an obsession.

In addition to their intellectual solidarity, Columbus' personality, his vitality, daring and iron will, attracted the Queen. His boldness, gravity and bearing, traits then and now much admired in Spain, struck a harmonious chord. Despite the magnetism of his personality, part of the darker side of Columbus' nature may have shown through. After his experience with King John, when his more annoying traits offended the Portuguese monarch, Columbus may have tried to hold down his pushiness, his haughtiness, his vanity.

But even if he was too aggressive, too boastful in the Queen's presence, it probably didn't offend her. All her life, Isabel had dealt with proud, imperious aristocrats, and she knew exactly how to handle men swelled with an overabundance of pride. With her experience, and her ability to analyze human nature, by 1486 the Queen was a shrewd judge of men.

Ever since she assumed the throne twelve years before, Isabel had been picking the right man for the right job. By this point in her life, she could cut through Columbus' more irritating traits and concentrate on his true character. To Isabel, this tenacious man's speculations stirred a vision of empire, of riches, of bringing her treasured faith to the Infidels in the Orient. Somehow, Columbus' sincerity and conviction sparked a mystical attraction between them. "In all men there was disbelief," Columbus later wrote, "but to the Queen, my lady, God gave the spirit of understanding and great courage...."

During the interview, as always, Isabel was gracious. Even though Columbus' eloquence and persuasiveness impressed her, the cost of forging cannons, building military roads and rounding up herds of oxen and mules for the War of Granada preoccupied the Queen. Since the Genoan's project would require the diversion of money from the war effort, she must discuss the proposal further with Ferdinand. After seventeen years of marriage, the Queen knew her marriage partner would never make a snap decision based on the vague promises of a foreigner. Ferdinand would insist on careful, deliberate consideration of this new idea.

Even though Isabel appreciated the broad outline of the great enterprise and its implications for Spain, the judgment of experts would be necessary. The Queen didn't say yes. She didn't say no. She said maybe, and referred it to a committee. In the summer of 1486, the Queen established a royal commission "to hear Cristobal Colon in more detail, and [to] investigate the quality of his proposal and the proofs that he gave of its possibility...to confer and discuss it, and...to make a full report to their Majesties."[15]

To chair the royal commission, Isabel appointed a man the crown held in highest esteem, Hernando de Talavera. At the time, Talavera held the dual posts of prior of a Jeronymite monastery near Valladolid and confessor to the Queen.[16] In addition to his priestly duties, Talavera served as a sort of royal troubleshooter to investigate matters of importance to the royal couple.

As one of Isabel and Ferdinand's most trusted servants, Talavera conducted delicate diplomatic negotiations with Portugal, dealt with Parliament regarding tax questions and convinced powerful nobles to accept crown control over all of the Canary Islands. Dr. Rodrigo Maldonado also served on the royal commission. Maldonado, another man in whom the Sovereigns placed confidence, may have been appointed because of the knowledge he gained when he participated in negotiating the 1479 treaty under which Portugal ceded the Canary Islands to Spain.[17] Although the names of the other committeemen are not known, it is believed that some were professors from the University of Salamanca and others were mariners and seamen.[18]

With Talavera presiding, the royal commission met first at

Cordoba in 1486, but moved to Salamanca, Spain's most venerable university town, in the winter months, where Columbus spent Christmas of 1486. In Salamanca Columbus won a new supporter to his cause, the Dominican priest Diego de Deza. As a younger man, Deza taught theology at the University of Salamanca, but, by 1487, he was the tutor of Prince John, the royal couple's only son.

Even though Columbus, networking at court was gaining him new friends, he still needed to convince the royal commission. He presented the committeemen with just enough information to tantalize them, but not so much that they could take his data and give it to somebody else. Ever secretive, he held back many of his most important "proofs."[19] After it heard Columbus' proposals over a period of several months, the committee of "wise and learned men and mariners...discussed what [Columbus] said about his going to the said islands, and...all of them agreed that what [Columbus] said could not possibly be true...[but Columbus] persisted in his intention of going there."[20] On the micro level, the committee did its job. It investigated Columbus' plan and found it lacking.

Even with this negative report, Isabel did not render a definite yes or no decision. The Queen, deliberately vague, let it be known that, for the time being, the Sovereigns couldn't afford the project because of the urgency presented by the War of Granada during that spring of 1487. From a broader policy standpoint, Isabel may have been afraid that, by sponsoring Columbus, it might enrage the Portuguese if she invaded what they considered to be their territory, the Atlantic. At that particular time, Isabel couldn't risk a two-front war, with the Portuguese in the west, and the Moors in the south.

In addition to her war worries, the Queen may have also been concerned that, if she didn't keep Columbus in Spain, he might take his project to another monarch or persuade the Genoese to finance the voyage. Since Columbus was almost destitute, Isabel ordered her accountants to dole out a small stipend. The entry in the royal account books read: "Today, May 5, 1487, given to Christopher Columbus, foreigner, 3,000 maravedis, since he is performing some services for Their Highnesses." Even though he now had enough money to pay his expenses for a few months, and had the honor of being in the royal service, the commission's report and Isabel's ambivalence bitterly disappointed Columbus.

During the next few bleak years, Columbus may have supplemented the Sovereigns' meager payments by selling books and maps in partnership with his brother Bartholomew, who joined him in Spain sometime in 1487 or 1488. It would have been a good business because Ferdinand and Isabel reduced taxes on imported books and passed other laws to stimulate the printing of books. Or he may have gotten handouts from the Marquis of Medina Celi, the monks of La Rabida or other patrons. The royal treasurer, Quintanilla, agreed to feed "the Genoese from his larder" and ordered that Columbus be given food "and all that was necessary to alleviate him from his poverty."[21]

At some point in 1487, Columbus returned to Cordoba where he met another friend who gave him more than mere financial solace. Through Genoese friends living in Cordoba, Columbus met Beatriz Enriquez de Harana, a fresh, attractive girl of twenty. Even though he was sixteen years older than Beatriz, the tall, blue-eyed Genoan who spoke of fantastic voyages and enormous wealth attracted the young woman. As he poured out his story to the young girl, the couple strolled Cordoba's narrow streets, passing the centuries-old remnants of Arab buildings.

In the old Moorish capital, they may have heard the tales of the sensuous pleasures of the Muslim harems, and the debauchery in the bathhouses during the Caliphate. Beatriz, the daughter of a farmer who owned vineyards in the hills about 15 miles outside of the city, was an orphan living in Cordoba with her uncle when she met Columbus. Either her family or her uncle must have had some money because, unlike most medieval women, she could read and write, and education would have been too expensive for a poor family. With her education, Beatriz could follow at least the general outline of Columbus' theories. Evidently, she accepted them and became a believer in the great enterprise.

During those trying years, Beatriz Harana lived openly as Columbus' mistress, not unusual at at time when Ferdinand, to Isabel's disgust, had uncounted mistresses, and Cardinal Mendoza publicly bragged of his liaisons.[22] Beatriz' relatives apparently had no difficulty with the arrangement, because her brother and cousin later served Columbus during voyages to the New World. In August or September of 1488, Beatriz gave birth to their illegitimate son, Ferdinand, who would later become his father's biographer.[23] Although Columbus never married Beatriz, in his will he instructed his legitimate son Diego to "take good care of Beatriz Enriquez (de Harana), mother of my son Don Fernando, so that she can live honorably, because she weighs heavily on my conscience, though I am at present unable to tell you why." [24]

Even though he had an intelligent lover as a confidant, for the next five years Columbus lived as an uncertain a ward of the court, kept on Isabel's tether with occasional encouragement and dribbles of money. He moved with the court from place to place, visiting the siege camps at Malaga and Baza, using every opportunity to make friends in high places. During this itinerant period, he gained supporters in Isabel's closest friend, Beatriz de Bobadilla, who served the Queen as her first lady in waiting, and Juana de Torres, the governess of Prince John.[25]

Columbus courted the favor the King's chamberlain and the royal treasurer, Luis de Santangel.[26] He cultivated Spain's "third King," Cardinal Mendoza, who explained to Columbus that every spare maravedis was being used for the War of Granada. Irritated, Columbus snapped that it made no sense to withhold financing for his project when the Orient burgeoned with gold and silver, just waiting for him and the Sovereigns to pluck it from the heathen potentates. Even though Cardinal Mendoza could offer no financial help, "The cardinal began to grant audience to Columbus and learned how wise he was, and what a good speaker and how he supported what he said. And he found him a man of intelligence and of great ability. Having realized this, he formed a good opinion of him and wished to favor him."[27]

Although he developed many powerful friends, other noblemen and clerics sneered that he was crazy or a crackpot adventurer promoting a ridiculous scam. Because he challenged parts of St. Augustine's teachings, some called him an atheist. Many hangers on at court suffered scorn and sarcasm, but Columbus came in for an inordinate share.

The contempt and, even worse, neglect took its toll on the proud Genoan. "He began to sustain a terrible, continued, painful and prolonged battle," Las Casas says, "[and] weapons would not have been so sharp and horrendous as that which he had to endure from informing so many people of no understanding...and replying patiently to many people who did not know him nor had any respect for his person, receiving insulting speeches which afflicted his soul."[28] Columbus himself said: "For eight years I was torn with disputes, and, in a word, my proposition was a mockery."[29] Although Cervantes wrote Don Quixote almost a century later, many Spaniards must have thought of this Genoan, in his scruffy clothes and obvious poverty, as a foolhardy man tilting at windmills.

Columbus self-induced at least part of his problems. Falling back on his Genoese businessman's instinct for secrecy, Columbus gave evasive answers to questions about the details of his plan. If the royal commission asked about the exact route he planned to follow, all they got was a vague reply that he would start from the Canary Islands. With little trust in anyone outside his immediate circle of intimate friends, Columbus' indefinite answers may have caused the panel of experts to think he was cloaking his ignorance. Or that this foreigner was nothing more than a smooth-tongued adventurer spewing out exaggeration and hyperbole to mask his quackery. Even more annoying, this vain man who revealed almost nothing, refused to compromise his demands for exalted titles and wealth. Why, the committeemen could ask, should they agree to make him rich and famous, when he wrapped his great enterprise in secrecy.

Columbus' lack of candor only fueled the suspicion of those aristocrats and clergymen who already resented his vaulting ambition and haughty arrogance. As he presented his messianic vision that God chose him as His special ambassador, Columbus' opponents may have written him off as a mad dreamer or, at best, a man consumed by self-deception. As in all personal relationships, the simple issue of whether a person is liked or not can become a decisive factor. This boastful, self-promoting weaver's son would have offended many of the sober, stoic Spanish nobles and clerics.

Even though his critics pummeled him, Isabel kept Columbus on a string, dangling a few maravedis now and then and receiving him in the royal presence to flatter his ego. From time to time, the Queen permitted him to present his evidence and arguments to formal and informal panels of experts.[30] Knowing that Columbus was the Queen's protege, rather than say no, the committeemen and bureaucrats shuffled Columbus back and forth, frustrating this man of action almost to the breaking point. For Columbus, waiting for a reply that never came must have been maddening. With his aggressive nature, sitting on the sideline as a passive spectator was impossible. He had to make something happen.

During this painful period, his anxiety and his self-imposed pressure to succeed may have clouded his judgment, may have caused him to make statements or do things that justified his critics calling him a "madman." If he told people that he was a servant of Heaven called to fulfill a holy mission, that implied that anybody who disagreed with him disobeyed God's wishes, making them servants of Satan. In his insecurity, Columbus made extravagant claims, bragged too much and shaded the truth. To Columbus, it was all justified. He was risking all, taking a supreme gamble to achieve glory, sacrificing his life in near poverty to achieve his goal.

He hated poverty, and later said: "Gold is a thing most excellent, for he who possesses it may have what he will in this world." He rankled at being forced to humble himself and beg for favors and money from the Castilian aristocrats. Reduced to living on handouts, he became depressed, soured, paranoid; suspicious of supposed enemies, and quick to take offense at slights, real or imagined. "[If] I should build churches," Columbus wrote, "I would be accused of building hideouts for robbers." Feeling backed into a corner, Columbus attacked as malicious enemies the nobles and clergymen who differed with him or who merely gave less than enthusiastic support. In his own mind he was extraordinary, convinced that God endowed him with special abilities that made him uniquely capable of great deeds.

While Columbus had his troubles with doubting clerics and aristocrats, Isabel and Ferdinand also struggled to bring Castile's unruly dukes, marquises and counts under their royal control.

7

THE ARISTOCRACY

For seventy years, during the anemic reigns of John II and Henry IV, the Spanish aristocrats seeped into a gaping political vacuum, seizing control of the military orders, Church, economy, Holy Brotherhood and judiciary. Power was dispersed among fifteen families and their surrogates, who served as advisors to the kings, directing the affairs of state to suit their own whims and self-interests.

When Isabel and Ferdinand ascended the throne in 1474, Spain was paralyzed by anarchy, by such severe chaos that the foundations of society were threatened. The historian Prescott paints the bleak picture of a Spain "dismembered by faction, her revenues squandered on worthless parasites, the grossest violations of justice unredressed, public faith a joke, the treasury bankrupt, the court a brothel and private morals too loose and audacious to seek even the veil of hypocrisy."[1] There was no control, no central authority. The crown was discredited, almost void of power—political, economic or moral.

Those aristocrats who benefited from Henry IV's favor remained loyal to him, but many barons directed their disdain at both his public and private life. Because he fathered no heirs to the throne, the nobles, sneering, nicknamed him "Henry the Impotent." In an age when taking mistresses was commonplace, almost expected, Henry scandalized his courtiers by appointing a discarded lover as abbess of a convent in Toledo to make room for a new paramour. While his licentiousness was legend, his young Portuguese wife carried on an open affair with the handsome cavalier, Beltran de la Cueva. Then, and now, one of the strongest, and most insulting, epithets in Spain is "cuckold."

Henry IV's conduct of public affairs was equally scorned. Sometimes he signed laws without reading them, and he even permitted certain nobles to co-sign public documents.[2] Although he sponsored a few feeble attacks on the Moors, he never brought home a victory. Excusing his lack of military prowess, he said, "[I] prized the life of one of my soldiers more than those of a thousand Muslims."

Even the Moors held Henry in contempt. After several years of ineffectual forays, Henry had the temerity to demand tribute from the Muslim King of Granada, who replied: "In the first years of his (Henry's) reign, I would have offered him anything, even my children, to preserve my dominions. But now I will give him nothing."[3] Due in part to Henry's lavish spending (he once said, "Kings, instead of hoarding money like ordinary men, are duty bound to spend it...."), the currency was completely debased. To support his prodigal lifestyle, Henry sold bonds, mortgaging the royal income. But the bondholders had little or no faith they would be paid, and the value of the bonds plunged, selling for as low as one year's income. At one point, the royal credit rating was so bad that Henry IV had to pledge public revenues to obtain a paltry one thousand maravedis loan.

Contempt led a group of the nobles into open revolt against the incompetent cuckold. During this attempt to depose Henry and replace him with his brother Alphonse, the clique of rebellious aristocrats erected a scaffold in an open field near the city of Avila. In a somewhat theatrical display of derision, the nobles set up a throne and seated on it an effigy of King Henry. The dummy was dressed in sable robes which bore the royal insignia, and its head was covered with a crown. Its straw arm held a scepter and a sword was buckled around its waist.

After reading to the crowd a manifesto listing the tyrannical actions of the King, the Archbishop of Toledo tore off the crown, the Marquis of Villena ripped away the scepter, the Count of Plcencia the sword and the Count of Benavente the regal insignia. All of these items, and Henry's effigy, were thrown off the scaffold into the dust to the cheers of the spectators. The eleven-year-old Alphonse was then seated on the vacant throne, and the *grandees* knelt to kiss his hand. Luckily for Henry, enough of his supporters stuck by him to save him, and Alphonse died shortly thereafter.

In addition to the destabilizing cabals against the King, the grasping barons fought among themselves to enhance their personal power and estates. With a weak King who couldn't enforce central authority, feuds between noble families often erupted into savage, internecine warfare. Sometimes, families joined with other families in ever-shifting confederacies that kept them looking over their shoulders at the moment's ally.

In the 1400s, Spain didn't have a strong tradition of loyalty to the crown, and it was not unheard of for a nobleman to renounce his obedience to the king by merely sending a messenger to announce: "Sir, in the name of the Count of [fill in the blank], I kiss your hand, and, henceforth, he is no longer your vassal." For many barons, ensconced in their castle strong-holds around the country, loyalty ran first to family, community and region, and last to the sovereign and the nation. Feeling themselves a special, exalted caste in the state, the nobles battled for their own self-aggrandizement, their own self-interest, not that of Castile.

In Cordoba, the Aguilars made bitter war on the Fernandez de Cordobas. In Toledo, four thousand houses were burned to the ground in one familial battle. In Seville, the struggle between the Guzmans and the Ponce de Leons saw house-to-house warfare, with residents from one block fighting their neighbors in the next block.

There was no law or order, and some of the more unscrupulous barons even sponsored gangs who split their stolen or extorted riches with their aristocratic bosses. When the policemen of the Holy Brotherhood tried to arrest the gangsters, a rogue aristocrat would shelter them in his stone fortress. One corrupt noble in southern Spain stooped to capturing Christians, both men and women, and selling them as slaves to the infidel Moors in Granada. The words "murder, robbery, arson, tumults, brawls and conspiracy" drip from the pens of contemporary historians. One writes: "Cities and towns were undermined by thieves, murderers, adulterers. Some took justice into their own hands. Others, gluttons and layabouts, shamelessly violated wives, virgins and nuns. Some seized lands and castles belonging to the crown, using their advantage to violate their neighbors. They also kidnapped many people, whose relatives were required to pay ransom."[4]

Highwaymen ruled the countryside, causing travelers and merchants to venture outside city walls only when accompanied by armed guards. The thieves, who were often farmers whose crops and houses had been destroyed, sometimes sold their plunder publicly the day after a robbery in a nearby town. Violent lords enslaved Galicia, in remote northwest Spain, stealing from the churches, terrorizing the towns and forcing villagers to pay protection money. The violence and lawlessness was so bad that many bishops fortified their churches and kept armed men inside the holy buildings to guard them from being sacked by the outlaws. When Ferdinand and Isabel sent police to quell the chaos in 1481, the Galicians told them hopelessly that royal power alone wasn't sufficient protection, that the crown's policemen would need powers directly from God.

When they became King and Queen in 1474, Ferdinand and Isabel stepped into this muck of anarchy. The government was almost nonexistent, and, what there was of it, was graft ridden or given over to ineffectual favorites of Henry IV. The court was "abandoned to corrupt or frivolous pleasure," and powerful nobles openly accepted bribes in exchange for their influence. The economy was on the verge of bankruptcy. Food was scarce. Prices soared. There was no nation—no Spain.

The royal couple's mission was clear; to restore the balance of power between crown and aristocrats, to tame their imperious nobles and reestablish order. At the beginning of their reign, the Sovereigns were cautious, careful, using a delicate blend of veiled threats and *palabras dulces* (sweet words). Ferdinand and Isabel were only twenty-three-years-old when they became King and Queen. Ferdinand was almost a foreigner, from Aragon, which had different traditions from those of Castile. Isabel had led a sheltered, virtually captive, life as a young girl. The Sovereigns needed time to study their swaggering barons before putting them in harness.

Like most institutions in Castile, the nobility was divided into a carefully defined hierarchy. At the bottom were the *hidalgos.* The title, a contraction of *hijos de algo* (sons of somebody), brought with it the right to be addressed as *Don. Don Juan, Don Cristobal.* In Spain today, calling someone *Don* is merely a courtesy, but five hundred years ago it set a man apart from the common herd; it told the world that he was "somebody." To further broadcast their superior status, *hidalgos* emblazoned their clothes, houses and tombs with their family coat of arms.

Some *hidalgos* were rich, owning land and serfs. Others, reduced to poverty, were forced to serve a rich and powerful master. During war, the poor *hidalgos* fought under their lord's orders, and, during peace, they served as retainers in the shadow of the feudal castles as masters of the horse, majordomos or bailiffs. The impoverished but proud *hidalgo*, armed at all times with his sword and dagger, insensible to suffering, refusing to break the noble code of honor and work for a living, is a stock character in Spanish literature. Writing in the 1700s, Jose Cadalso sketches a down and out provincial *hidalgo*, muffled in his worn cloak, stalking majestically through the sad square of his town, contemplating his family coat of arms above the door of his tumbledown house, but giving thanks to God for making him *Don* Diego. Honor, pride, dignity and status were not to be violated, no matter what the earthly price.

Because of the enhanced status of the aristocracy, and the myriad privileges that went along with it, the rich bourgeois devoted substantial time and considerable mental gymnastics to reconstructing, or fabricating, aristocratic ancestry. Traditionally, the only way into the aristocracy was by birth or distinguished military or government service. Skilled forgers carried on a brisk traffic in manufacturing immaculate lineages for hundreds of Spaniards. As an instrument of policy, Isabel and Ferdinand gave out, or sold, almost one thousand noble titles during their reign, infusing the aristocracy with new blood, new blood loyal to them.[5] For their impoverished royal treasury, selling titles was a quick and easy way to raise money.

One Spanish merchant who made the leap into the aristocracy was the grandfather of St. Teresa of Avila. This diligent commoner amassed a fortune in the silk and cloth trade. Even though he was accused by the Inquisition in 1485 for Judaizing practices, he married into a noble family and managed to marry all of his children into the local gentry. Later, St. Teresa's father steered the family fortunes away from disgusting middle class trade to the aristocratic businesses of administration of land rents and tax farming.

Next on the caste ladder was the *caballero*. Literally, *caballero* means horseman. The word probably took on noble distinction because horses were scarce and expensive, and anyone who could afford a horse was due the proper respect. Most *caballeros* owned property and lived at ease in their castles or town houses. They formed the bulk of the urban elite, and staffed the military orders and the government.

At the pinnacle of the Spanish aristocracy were the men whose names were preceded by Duke, Marquis or Count. As a group, these haughty, powerful men were known blatantly as *ricos hombres* (rich men) or *grandees* (great men). Under Ferdinand and Isabel, the beatified *grandees* had the extraordinary privileges of keeping their hats on and remaining seated in the presence of the King and Queen, having Isabel rise to greet them and being called "cousin" by the royal couple. Like the Sovereigns, the *grandees* quartered a crown on their escutcheons, were attended by mace bearers as bodyguards and, when in procession, had a drawn sword carried before them. They used the royal plural, advising their vassals "It is our will..." or "On pain of our displeasure...."

At this level, blood counted more than money. During Isabel and Ferdinand's reign there were two theories as to how a man could enter the ruling class. The first was that the nobility must continually be regenerated by men of intellectual ability and proven honor. Ferdinand and Isabel often followed this line to bolster their power, promoting talented scholars, lawyers, diplomats and merchants into the rarified society of the nobility. The King and Queen knew that this cadre, plucked out of their lowly station, would follow their Sovereigns' orders, and would not be prone to plot against them. Ferdinand and Isabel appointed these clever men judges, royal advisors, governors of towns, military officers and tax farmers, posts that traditionally went to the blooded nobles.

To protect their inherited status, the old-line nobles argued that too much social mobility threatened the stability of the state. "States are destroyed by men wishing to change their status," the Spanish author, Lope de Vega, wrote.[6] True nobility, the blooded aristocrats said, with its sanctified traditions of chivalry, honor and virtue, cannot be learned, it comes from years of breeding. Over time, the old-line nobles grew to despise their recently anointed brethren as grasping upstarts. One Spaniard ridiculed men "who the day before yesterday were peasants, yesterday merchants and today 'caballeros'...." Ultimately, the argument that blood counted for more than money became perverted, resulting in the doctrine of "*limpieza de sangre*" (purity of blood), which the Inquisition used to justify its attacks on Jews and Moors.

Although blood tainted by Moses or Mohammed usually slammed the door on admission to the nobility, bastardy did not. Bastardy was not a cause for shame in medieval Spain. King Ferdinand saw to it that his illegitimate son, Alonso de Aragon, was titled and properly educated. Columbus had no hesitation in recognizing his bastard son, Ferdinand, who later wrote one of the definitive biographies about his father. A number of *grandees* left bastard males as their only heirs.

Illegitimate daughters didn't fare as well. Apparently, there was concern that bastard females might meet up with an adventurer, and have children who might make messy claims to hereditary rights. These unfortunate girls were often shipped off, at age five or six, to convents to be raised as nuns. The portraits of two of King Ferdinand's bastard daughters, in religious garb, still hang in a convent in Madrigal de las Altas Torres, the same building in which Isabel was born.[7]

In the 1470s and 1480s, fifteen families sat at the apex of Spanish society. These families, along with their other noble friends, owned fifty percent of the land in Spain, most of the rest being controlled by the Church, the military orders and the crown. Galicia was dominated by the Counts of Monterrey and Lemos, Leon and Zamora by the Counts of Luna and Benavente, Salamanca by the Duke of Alba and Burgos by the the Duke of Frias. The family names included Enriquez, Toledo, Manrique, Cardenas, Ponce de Leon, Zuniga, Guzman, Mendoza and Pacheco.

The Pacheco family, whose leader was titled Marquis of Villena, held estates covering one million acres that stretched some 225 miles from Cuenca in central Spain to Almeira on the south coast. The Pacheco's income was about sixty thousand ducats a year, at a time when a laborer's annual wages were twenty ducats, and some 150,000 vassals worked on the Pacheco's land to fill the family coffers.[8]

The founder of the dynasty was Juan Pacheco, of Portuguese extraction, who started life as a page boy in the house of the Constable of Spain during the reign of King John II. He was a subtle, polished intriguer who ingratiated himself with the King. He was also a risk taker, willing to indulge in the dangerous intricacies of court politics. His fleet mind and clever maneuvering, and the influence of his uncle, the Archbishop of Toledo, eventually won him the Marquisate of Villena. Later, during Henry IV's reign, Villena's constant plotting got him into trouble more than once. He participated in the public humiliation of Henry IV outside the city of Avila, but quickly switched back to the King's side, supporting Princess Joan, La Beltraneja, against Isabel, and even threatened to put Isabel in prison.

Ever one to drop a bit of poison, Villena convinced Henry IV that Isabel's faction was out to assassinate the King. While in Henry IV's favor, he wheedled an appointment as Grand Master of Santiago, the most powerful of the military orders, and resigned his Marquisate in favor of his son. The new Marquis of Villena continued the wily scheming of his father, and was made Duke of Escalona in 1469. During the War of Succession, the Duke fought against Ferdinand and Isabel, but, when the war ended, he was able to buy his way out of trouble by ceding a substantial portion of his estates to the Sovereigns. After this nimble switch of allegiances, the Duke of Escalona became a staunch supporter of

Ferdinand and Isabel.

Although the Duke of Escalona was a powerful man, the oldest Dukedom in Spain, that of Medina Sidonia, controlled vast domains in Andalusia in the south.[9] Established in 1460, the Dukedom's estates yielded 55,000 ducats a year, much of which the family squandered over the decades in a Capulet and Montigue style death struggle with the Ponce de Leon family. During the Sovereigns' reign, there were many powerful families, but the greatest noble family in Spain was the Mendoza clan. Within a year after Ferdinand and Isabel seized power in 1474, they elevated their loyal supporter, Diego de Mendoza, from the Marquisate of Santillana to the Dukedom of the Infantado.

The Dukedom drew its name from once having been the property of the *Infantes* (Crown Princes) of Spain. From his castles in the province of New Castile in central Spain, the Duke of the Infantado ruled his domains almost as if they were an independent state. He controlled eight hundred towns and villages and nominated more than five hundred public officials to help him govern his mini-nation. In his jurisdictions, the Duke's word was law.

Some ninety thousand vassals sweated to supply the senior branch of the Mendoza family with annual revenues of one hundred thousand ducats. When the Duke visited his estates, he could chose from one of several sumptuous palaces. Even though Spain was a poor country at the time, the Duke of the Infantado was surrounded by tapestries and silver plate and was clad in elegant fabrics, gold and jewelry. In his private chapel, accomplished singers and musicians soothed him with hymns and other religious music. For entertainment, he enjoyed his falcons, packs of hounds and fine stud horses. In times of trouble, the Duke and his allies could summon huge armies.

The founder of the Mendoza dynasty was Inigo de Mendoza, who was described as the "glory and delight of the Castilian nobility." For his services to the crown, King John II named Inigo Marquis of Santillana in the mid-1400s. He was heavily involved in politics and war, but, with a virtue rare in such rapacious and turbulent times, he somehow maintained a reputation for loyalty, honor and purity of motive. Inigo loved letters, surrounding himself with scholars and writers who he rewarded handsomely. As a patron of arts and letters in the Renaissance tradition, his house was a watering spot for intellectual Europeans who visited Spain. He even turned his own hand to poetry and is credited with introducing the Italian sonnet form into Castilian. His descendents can still leaf through volumes of his writings and read what, to modern eyes, is somewhat turgid poetry.

When Inigo died in 1458, he left a legacy of six sons, all of whom participated in the consolidation of power and influence in the Mendoza family. His eldest son, Diego, inherited the Marquisate. With Diego as head of the family, his brother Pedro eventually became the Archbishop of Toledo, Primate of Spain and Grand Chancellor of Castile. Another brother became the Count of Tendilla, Viceroy of Granada and Governor of the Alhambra. At one point, there were two Marquises and five Counts with the illustrious Mendoza name.

Like his father, Diego Mendoza loved books and is lauded by contemporary historians for his magnanimity, chivalrous honor and loyalty. Even though loyal, Diego was not afraid to challenge the Sovereigns. Shortly after Ferdinand and Isabel came to power and began building the power of the Holy Brotherhood to quash violence on the highways, Diego Mendoza wrote Ferdinand and Isabel demanding that they abolish the Holy Brotherhood "as an institution burdensome to the nation." Mendoza also demanded that four *grandees* be appointed to a council to direct the affairs of state. This bold opposition to the Sovereigns' power drew a quick and blunt response.

"The Holy Brotherhood is an institution most salutary to the nation, and it is approved by it (the nation) as such. It is Our province to determine who are best entitled to preferment, and to determine which (institutions) have merit. You may follow the Court, or retire to your estates, as you think best; but, so long as Heaven permits to us to retain the rank with which We have been entrusted, We shall take care not to imitate the example of Henry IV, in becoming a tool of our nobility."[10] Despite his immense power, Mendoza bowed to this sharp and clear statement of the royal policy, and remained a loyal subject of his Sovereigns.

While his brother Diego tended to the family's business, Pedro de Mendoza labored in the Church's vineyard. Under Henry IV, Pedro was named Archbishop of Seville.[11] Following the Mendoza's tradition of loyalty to the king then in power, the family, including Cardinal Mendoza, initially favored King Henry's daughter, Princess Joan (La Beltraneja), over Isabel and Ferdinand to succeed Henry. For this, Henry rewarded the Mendozas by granting them custody of Princess Joan. Shortly before Henry's death, the King transferred custody of the Princess from the Mendoza family to the Marquis of Villena's family. This, along with considerable wooing of the Mendozas by Ferdinand (who was related to the Mendozas), caused the Cardinal to enter into private correspondence with Isabel.

Cardinal Mendoza remained loyal to Henry IV but, when the King died in 1474, Cardinal Mendoza threw his whole weight to the cause of Ferdinand and Isabel. When the War of Succession broke out, Cardinal Mendoza wasted no time in exchanging his priestly robes for a suit of armor, and took his place at Ferdinand and Isabel's side at the decisive Battle of Toro in 1476, where he was seen swinging a sword in the thick of hand-to-hand combat. Later that year, the Sovereigns awarded him a seat on the Royal Council, Castile's most powerful governing body. Cardinal Mendoza's early support of the Sovereigns won him their confidence, and they consulted him on many private matters and on almost all affairs of state.

So great was Isabel's trust in Cardinal Mendoza that, in 1475, she called on her advisor to accompany her to Segovia where she successfully put down a threatened revolt. When the Sovereigns needed someone to handle an issue with delicacy and tact, Cardinal Mendoza was their man. In 1480, because Henry IV had borrowed money from many noble families and issued mortgage bonds which established liens on a substantial slice of the royal income, Ferdinand and Isabel were desperate for money. At the Parliament of Toledo that year, the Sovereigns, somewhat naively, asked the aristocrats to forego their mortgage bond claims on the regal purse.

The nobles protested so strongly that the royal couple asked Cardinal Mendoza to investigate, and to arbitrate whether King Henry granted the noblemen liens on the royal income for services rendered or as bribes for political favors. Finding that the issuance of many of the mortgage bonds was unwarranted, the Cardinal ruled that the Duke of Medina de Rioseco must give up 240,000 maravedis, the Duke of Alba 575,000 maravedis and the Duke of Albuquerque 1,400,000 maravedis. With total impartiality, Cardinal Mendoza then ordered that the house of Mendoza disgorge thousands of maravedis.

In 1482, when the Sovereigns were quarreling with Pope Sixtus IV over control of the Spanish Church, Cardinal Mendoza brought his diplomatic skills to bear to patch up the dispute, resulting in a Papal Bull authorizing Isabel and Ferdinand to nominate persons to higher Church offices in Spain. When Pedro Mendoza's predecessor died in 1483, the royal couple named him Archbishop of Toledo, the highest post in the Spanish Catholic Church, and Grand Chancellor of Castile.

By granting these clerical and state titles, Isabel and Ferdinand invested Cardinal Mendoza with immense prestige and power. He was the first among equals; the King and Queen's chief counselor.

The people called him *El Gran Cardinal* (The Great Cardinal) or, only mildly in jest, *El Tercer Rey* (The Third King). During the last months of 1491, Cardinal Mendoza presided over a committee meeting at the siege camp at Santa Fe, in front of Granada, which debated whether to grant money to a somewhat boastful Genoan to sail west to find the Indies. Although Cardinal Mendoza's position on the issue was ambiguous, it appears that he may have supported a grant of royal funds for Columbus' first voyage. On January 2, 1492, when the Moorish Kingdom of Granada collapsed, the prelate-soldier headed the column of the Sovereigns' household troops which passed through the gate of Los Molinos into Granada and occupied the Alhambra. Solemnly, he raised the huge silver cross carried by the King and Queen during the war and raised the banners of Castile and Santiago triumphantly from the red towers of the Islamic stronghold.

Just as the clash of arms lured the Primate of Spain out of his priestly robes, so too did the ladies. Cardinal Mendoza fathered several children by two ladies of rank, spreading his seed to some of the most prestigious houses of Spain. Although clerical dalliance was common at the time, one saintly priest delivered a sermon, with the Cardinal in attendance, in which the priest chastised the lack of celibacy amongst his brethren in general and made a specific reference which was clearly directed at Mendoza. The Cardinal's supporters were furious, urging him to punish the impertinent priest. Instead, Mendoza sent him a gift of food and a purse full of gold coins. In his next sermon, the worthy priest made it clear that his remarks were misunderstood, and that he was not referring to the Primate of Spain. The matter was dropped.

After he became the Primate of Spain, Mendoza indulged his inclination for pomp. His palaces were filled with elegantly liveried pages, selected from the noblest families in Spain, and he maintained a large body of armed men which he used for protection and for show. Although he maintained elaborate households, he devoted a considerable part of his enormous income to founding the College of Santa Cruz at Valladolid and to other institutions which served the people.

At this time in Spain, it was not uncommon for the very poor to murder their unwanted babies by throwing them into wells or pits, or leaving them exposed in a field to die of starvation. The more compassionate left their offspring at the doors of churches, hoping that the priests and nuns would find the infants before the town's dogs did. To remedy this vile problem, Cardinal Mendoza ordered a home for foundlings to be built in Toledo.

Cardinal Mendoza was an expansive man of generous faults

and virtues. He spent lavishly on worldly pomp, but he also distributed part of his wealth for the public good. In the heat of battle, Cardinal Mendoza could be as violent as most of the military entrepreneurs of his day, but he was also a kind and generous friend to those he loved. Although he shared most of the religious prejudices of medieval Spaniards, he seems to have exhibited little of the spiritual bitterness that perverted the Inquisition.

In 1494, Mendoza developed an abscess of the kidneys which confined him to bed. As death grew near, Ferdinand and Isabel moved the court to Guadalajara to be near their trusted advisor during his final days. As testimony of the respect she had for the sixty-six-year-old Cardinal, Isabel visited his bedside often and did him the honor of agreeing to act as the executor of his estate.

During these visits, Isabel sought his counsel one last time on the issue of who should succeed him in the highest post in the Spanish Church. Mendoza advised the Queen that she should not turn over such enormous power to a *grandee* who might misuse his authority for his own ends. This, of course, fit perfectly with Isabel's policy of promoting bright, but humble, men to positions of authority, men whose loyalty would lie only to the crown. The Queen and her Cardinal discussed many names, but the conversation always returned to one man, the Franciscan Friar, Francisco Jimenez de Cisneros, the son of an ancient family that had fallen on hard times.

Joining the aristocracy entitled one to the ego-boosting pleasures of wearing his family crest, being addressed by his title and being recognized by his neighbors as a "son of somebody"—superior. Unlike the United States, where a President of General Motors is not the Duke of Detroit and a Mellon is not the Prince of Pittsburgh. When these modern titans amble among the masses, nobody knows who they are. The Spanish moguls knew exactly who they were; a special caste in the state with a mass of financial and personal privileges that reminded them of who they were every day.

The aristocrats didn't pay taxes like ordinary men. The crown might pressure them into occasional loans when the royal treasury ran dry, but these loans were secured by mortgages on the crown's income, and, for the most part, were paid back.[12] The nobles had the exclusive franchise to be tax farmers, collecting the state's revenues and skimming a percentage off the top. This commission arrangement encouraged the greedier aristocrats to milk every possible maravedis from the *pecheros* (taxpayers).

Only nobles could become knights of the military orders, which held vast estates for the benefit of their members. They were exempt from debtor's prison, and money lenders couldn't garnish their houses, arms or horses, a sort of "homestead" exemption which still exists in many American states which were part of the Spanish empire. Freed of worrying about their debts, many nobles borrowed at will, and laughed at their creditors when they came around to collect.

Nobles occupied special places of honor in church, in processions and at court. If convicted of a crime, they were locked up in special prisons where fine food and female favors were readily available. A nobleman could not be tortured or sent to the galleys, and, if sentenced to death, they were entitled to a swift beheading, rather than slowly choking to death with a hangman's noose at their throat or smothering in the smoke from the pyre. The only exception to this rule was treason against God or king, in which case a man's rank didn't protect him from the gallows or the stake. In any event, it was rare that an aristocrat was punished, since they were judged by special courts, and sentences against them required confirmation by the Royal Council of Castile. These dispensations encouraged, at worst, outright lawlessness, and, at best, high-handed arrogance.

By the late 1400s, Spain had virtually no industry or commerce, in part because of the aristocrats' scorn of bourgeois business. The nobles dominated many of the cities, where trade naturally flourishes, and ran the cities for their own benefit. Since the barons' primary concerns were land and agriculture, they were more interested in barley, olive trees and sheep than in making tools or machinery. Rainfall and the cycle of the seasons were more important than the cost of imported goods or currency fluctuations. The small amount of commerce that existed was often parceled out by the king to a single individual as an exclusive franchise. The Grand Admiral of Castile, for example, had a monopoly over maritime trade. The Admiral had his own courts, and gallows, in every major port, and shipowners paid him a tax equal to twenty percent of the value of their cargos.

Due to the medieval aristocrats' disdain of trade, the growth of a business class was stifled. "Spaniards do not dedicate themselves to business because they consider it dishonorable," an Italian visitor wrote in 1512. A bourgeois aspiring to knighthood had a high hurdle to clear if he had resorted to work, particularly manual or mechanical work. In the mid-1500s, the Spanish Parliament ordered that those men with "public shops" be barred from holding city offices, and that those already holding office be prohibited from conducting trade.[13] Augmenting the Spanish aristocrats' prejudice against businessmen was the fact that heathen

Jews and Muslims and foreigners, mostly Italians, controlled much of the nation's commerce.

Except for the few merchants who dirtied their hands in commerce, the most important source of wealth was land. Beginning in the 1200s, the Castilian kings had handed out large chunks of land, partly because they couldn't administer it all themselves, partly to buy loyalty and partly to reward faithful followers who showed valor in the Holy Crusade to conquer the Moors. Some powerful families accumulated thousands of acres and hundreds of vassals to feed their coffers. By the late 1400s, the Duke of Albuquerque could travel across Castile from Aragon in the east to the Portuguese border without setting foot off his private Dukedom.[14] These royal land grants, *senorios* (lordships), included unchecked mastery over the serfs who farmed the land or tended the livestock. In his *senorio*, a noble controlled the towns and villages located there, the administration of justice, the collection of taxes, the appointment of government officials and the raising of troops. In his feudal domain, the lord had life and death power over his vassals, and he could agree, or not, to muster his private army to support, or attack, the crown.

To keep their estates intact, many landed families followed the custom of leaving all of their property to their eldest son. Younger sons fended for themselves in the military, Church or government. On occasion, a nobleman would divide his property among brothers, or leave it to a younger or bastard son, which frequently gave rise to violent feuds. Motivated primarily by a desire to forestall fights among brothers over land, Ferdinand issued a decree in 1505 which made primogeniture the law of the land. This law, coupled with matrimonial alliances, created dynasties controlling immense portions of Spain.

With so much of Spain's wealth concentrated in so few hands, the aristocrats lived in sumptuous, extravagant splendor. Their demeanor oozed arrogance and pride, and, to provide physical evidence of their nobility and power, they put on ostentatious public displays. The Duke of the Infantado "came [to a battlefield in 1485] attended by a numerous body of cavaliers and gentlemen, as befitted so great a lord. He displayed all the luxuries which belong to a time of peace; and his tables, which were carefully served, were loaded with rich and intricately wrought silver plate, of which he had a greater profusion than any other *grandee* in the Kingdom."[15]

Ferdinand and Isabel were not immune to extravagance. In the 1480s Ferdinand invited Isabel to the town of Moclin for a war council during the War of Granada. Accompanied by her daughter and "a courtly train of damsels," she proceeded into the town through a line of Sevillian troops drawn up in full battle array. As the procession rode by, the soldiers dipped their battle flags to honor the Queen and Princess. Isabel rode a fine chestnut mule, richly caparisoned with a crimson saddle blanket and a satin bridle stitched with gold thread. The Princess wore a black velvet skirt over brocaded underskirts, a red mantilla and a black hat trimmed with gold embroidery. Mounted on his war horse, with an ornate Moorish scimitar at his waist, Ferdinand rode out to meet the Queen's party, decked out in a scarlet vest, yellow satin trousers and a brocaded cape. The royal couple bowed formally to one another. Then the King rode alongside his wife, leaned across and kissed her affectionately on the cheek.

The normally reserved Isabel indulged herself in splendor and luxury at state occasions, dressing in robes of velvet which sparkled with jewels. Her personal confessor, Hernando de Talavera, thundered against these vanities, criticizing the Queen and her courtiers for their expenditures on sumptuous attire.[16]

Apparently, the sessions in the confessional intimidated even the strong-willed Queen. "Neither I nor my ladies wore new dresses or any new clothes at all," Isabel meekly wrote after a party for the French ambassador in Aragon. "Everything that I wore there [to the party], I had worn before.., and the Frenchmen had already seen me in that costume. The only thing that was new was a silk dress that I had made for only three gold marks, the plainest thing you can imagine. That was my whole extravagance."[17]

Even though the Sovereigns enjoyed their regal pomp, the dazzling garb of the nobles became so extreme that Ferdinand and Isabel vainly passed sumptuary laws prohibiting the wearing of finery. The aristocrats observed these laws more by their nonobservance, and both men and women continued to indulge in plumage of silk, damask and velvet in striking colors, fox and sable furs, large gold chains and diamond and emerald rings. The mania of the Spanish nobles for extravagant spending was prodigious, and many foreigners commented on the Spaniards' love of luxury, status symbols of their power. Even some Spaniards felt it was too much. Listing the vices of his countrymen, one writer included "...spending inordinately on attire, much more than one's income or fortune will allow; this commonly leads to swindles and litigation...."[18]

Since the mark of a true aristocrat was his display, there was constant pressure to raise money to acquire land, buy jewels and build palaces for his aggrandizement. Nobles who entered government service received meager salaries. Facing enormous peer pressure, with little money, some government officials, as is still true in Latin America today, turned to corruption; bribes, influence peddling, favoritism. Others borrowed heavily and wound up bankrupt.[19]

In addition to their rich dress, the *grandees* surrounded themselves with armies of household servants, pages, personal bodyguards and clergy. They sent their liveried messengers dashing around the countryside carrying parchment letters in three-foot-long tubular cases made of stiff leather. A noble's messenger wore a six-inch-long metal badge bearing his lord's coat of arms to identify him for entry into other castles, and to protect him from highwaymen, who knew they would suffer if they attacked an aristocrat's man.

Because the roads were so bad, there were no carriages. Noblemen traveled by horse or mule, and servants carried ladies of rank in litters. Commoners, many of whom were bound by law to the land, had no horses and could travel only on foot. Being largely immobile, ordinary people mostly stayed at home and worked for the same family for generations. During their years in service, sometimes an unusual familiarity grew between master and servant, cutting through the barriers of rank. If the lord was generous and fair, the bonds of *personalismo* became unshakeable. When master and servant developed these strong loyalties, it was not unusual for a servant to become a confidant of his lord, sharing all the family joys and sorrows.

Because of this familiarity, the servants absorbed the "glorious prejudices" of their masters. Dignity and honor became a way of life for the casteless. One foreign visitor to Spain, noting that valets and maids in his own country stood in line with their hands out for tips, says that, when he offered Spanish servants a gratuity for their services, they were almost insulted. Beneath their dignity. Even though they might be dressed in rough, scratchy wool or garments made of the skins of cats, goats or horses, most servants didn't seem to resent the over-consumption of their lords. They reveled in their masters' pomp and majesty, in much the same way as the Argentine *desca-misados* (shirtless ones) delighted in the furs and jewels worn by Eva Peron 450 years later.[20]

Although the aristocrats pampered a few household servants, life for most of the lower class was hard. Only a year or two of bad harvests worked a desperate hardship on the serfs. They lived in feudal servitude, paying taxes to their masters and tithes to the Church. They were subject to military service when their lord was caught up in a feud or was required to furnish troops to the crown.

In peacetime, they performed grinding agricultural labor with the primitive tools then available. The peasants were under the jurisdiction of courts and judges controlled by their duke, marquis or count, not those of the king. Until 1480, the peasants were not free to sell their property or move off their masters' estates. It wasn't slavery, but close. All things, good or bad, flowed from the manorial castle. Because they were tied to the land, most serfs never saw their sovereign; the idea of a king or nation-state being only a fuzzy concept to them. The only man who had authority over them, and with whom they could identify, was their master.

While most of the serfs lived in rough hovels, their patrons lived in castles built as much for defense as for shelter. Many castles had thick walls of massive stone blocks, turrets, towers and heavy doors stout enough to resist a battering ram.

Inside, the aristocrats fitted out their castles with oak furniture covered with gilt or tooled Andalusian leather, oriental carpets and Flemish tapestries like the one owned by the Duke of Medinaceli which erotically depicts the eight loves of Mercury. On the walls they hung carved ivory crucifixes, paintings and alters to the Virgin Mary. Statues represented religious and mythological figures, or the skeleton of death mounted on a horse so scrawny its ribs showed. If the master could read, there were walnut writing desks from Germany and bookstands to hold the huge leather and metal bound books with their intricate illuminations and stylized, hand-written Latin texts.[21]

The manorial estates produced life's necessities, but Syrian, Italian and Jewish merchants imported most luxury items to sell at fairs. Linens from Holland, silver services from France, embossed with the family crest, and delicate Venetian glassware graced the aristocrats' tables. In the bedrooms, four poster beds, with curtains to be drawn against the chill, shielded the nobles from the drafts in the high-ceilinged rooms and the cold piercing the stone walls. Their private chapels had wooden wainscoting decorated with a mixture of geometric Arab swirls and the Christian symbols of the lamb, the Cross and the whips used to beat Christ.

When they entertained in their castles, the ladies and gentlemen enjoyed backgammon, dice and cards. Although Canon Law and Spain's ancient laws, the *Siete Partidas*, legislated against gambling, the nobles played games of chance regularly at parties. Some rules did apply, and a card player caught cheating three times was subject to having his fingers cut off. Chess, introduced to the barbarian Spaniards by the Moors in the 700s, was also popular. In the 1200s, the *Tratado de Ajedrez* (Treatise on Chess) was published in Spain with more than one hundred pictures detailing problems and their solutions.[22]

Outdoor entertainment revolved around the horse, then, and still, a passion with Spaniards. Although polo and horse racing were popular, tournaments, jousting and hunting were at the top of the list. The lords set aside large tracts of land as hunting preserves. If the hunting party strayed off the preserve and trampled the grain fields or vineyards of the peasants—too bad.

There were two forms of hunting; with falcons and with packs of dogs. In each, the noble sportsmen were mounted, and followed the falcons or dogs on their fine horses. When the huntsmen spotted wild geese, ducks, partridges or cranes, they unhooded the falcons to soar after their prey. In the other hunting format, packs of dogs sniffed out deer, wild goats, boar, wolves or bear, ran them into exhaustion and moved in for the kill. The hunting dogs wore iron neck collars with spikes to prevent the more savage prey from ripping out the dogs' throats. If the dogs hadn't killed the game by the time the hunters trotted up, the hunters stabbed the animals with javelins until they bled to death. In addition to this grizzly form of hunting, bullfighting was also popular, although Isabel detested the bloody spectacle. Rather than fighting bulls on foot as in modern times, during the Sovereigns' reign men on horseback jabbed at the bulls with lances in a ritual which predated the Roman conquest of Spain.

Although Spaniards enjoyed their sports, in their isolated country, cut off from the rest of Europe by the sea and the Pyrenees Mountains, they trailed their Christian cousins in art, learning and culture during the reign of Isabel and Ferdinand. The trickle of commercial contacts brought in some foreign influence. Ties to Holland and Belgium brought northern realism and the flamboyant Gothic. From Italy, the Renaissance concept of subordinating detail and decoration to unity crept across the Mediterranean Sea. In architecture, the Gothic and Renaissance influences fused with the Jewish, Islamic and Christian traditions of medieval Spain to shape the peculiarly Spanish art form—plateresque architecture. This extravagant style required rich patrons to pay hundreds of architects and artisans to build and sculpt the plateresque buildings. Cardinals Mendoza and Cisneros commissioned hospitals and universities, the Duke of the Infantado a sumptuous palace at Guadalajara and Ferdinand and Isabel chapels and public buildings. These structures still bear the coats of arms and emblems of their sponsors, a reminder of their power and authority.

Along with the foreign influence on architecture came small doses of Italian and Dutch humanism, an intellectual concept that spurred inquiry and learning based on the knowledge of Greco-Roman antiquity. Intellectually, however, Spain remained a backwash. "If there is [in Spain] a man well taught and versed in Latin, one may safely assume that he is not a Spaniard, or that he is a Spaniard raised in Italy from tenderest infancy," a foreign observer said.[23] A Spanish intellectual complained, that "there are barely two or three of us at [the University of] Salamanca who speak Latin, a larger number speak Spanish, and the rest—jargon."[24]

Ferdinand was a typical Spaniard; a man of action with very little intellectual curiosity. Even though humanism had only a precarious toehold in Spain during her reign, Isabel was a champion of the new learning. She knew Latin, and read the works of classical Roman scholars; extremely rare for a woman of her day. Isabel sensed that, if Spaniards weren't to continue being regarded as barbarians, they must assimilate the culture of ancient Greece and Rome. At her insistence, expatriate scholars were imported, including the great Milanese teacher Peter Martyr. Martyr directed the court school where he instructed the Prince, Princesses and children of nobility in Latin, history and grammar. Even Ferdinand's bastard son, Alonso de Aragon, was taught by a Sicilian professor.

The most famous Spanish-born scholar of the day was Antonio de Nebrija. After studying in Italy as a young man, Nebrija returned to his native land to fill the post of Royal Historiographer in 1473, the year printing was first introduced to Spain. He was a masterful editor of classical texts in the best Renaissance tradition, probing Greek and Roman learning and blending them into modern thinking.

Although steeped in the Greco-Roman civilizations, Nebrija's first love was his own native dialect. In 1492, he published a grammar of the Castilian language, the first grammar of a modern European tongue. At a court ceremony to present his work, Isabel asked what value this peculiar book might have. "Your Majesty, language is the perfect instrument of empire," Nebrija said. His statement was prophetic. Nebrija's organization of Castilian into a systematic whole made it the dominant language in the Iberian Peninsula, and in the lands to be discovered by Columbus across the Atlantic Ocean in that same year.

Isabel's love of learning inspired the founding of the University of Alcala to supplement the Universities at Salamanca and Valladolid. Colleges were opened at Siguenza in 1471 and Toledo in 1490. Following Isabel's lead, the Spanish aristocrats joined in sponsoring education and sending their sons to universities. One,

Don Alonso Manrique, rose to become a world class scholar. By the early 1500s, seven thousand students attended the University of Salamanca.

The Church was deeply entrenched in the schools, and many students led a monastic life, studying the sacred texts and praying with Christian devotion several times a day. The emphasis on religious studies produced the famous Polyglot Bible, published in Hebrew, Greek and Latin. This compilation of the three major Biblical languages allowed scholars to more easily compare, and debate, the exact meaning of the Holy Word. Other students delved into the more worldly subjects of mathematics, law, medicine and natural sciences. In classes and taverns, Spanish students heatedly debated the writings of the Dutch humanist Erasmus, the leading scholar of that era.

Some rambunctious students led disorderly, dissipated lives that terrorized the townspeople. The reports of trials of university students accused of mayhem and seduction of servant girls fill many pages. Another complaint against the students was that they were not motivated by intellectual pursuit, but only wanted to learn enough to line their pockets as lawyers or government bureaucrats. "They do not toil to acquire knowledge, but [they work] only with a view to profit," a Spanish scholar wrote.

Even though education was confined mostly to the aristocrats and the occasional commoner, there was an intellectual excitement brewing during the reign of Ferdinand and Isabel; a search for new knowledge, a thirst for discovery, a revival of minds numbed by the gloomy Middle Ages. In later years, somber Spanish Catholicism would isolate the nation's intellectualism from the outer world by wrapping Spain's thinking in the certitudes of the Holy Faith.

8

CHIVALRY

Chivalry saturated the minds of medieval Spaniards. Cloaked with religious trappings, the concept embodied piety, valor, dignity and honor, but carried the baggage of pride, arrogance and vanity. In the late 1400s, it permeated the entire Spanish society, shaping the character of the nation. The aristocrats accepted chivalric behavior as an immutable code of conduct, as an essential attribute of nobility. To them, it was the exclusive preserve of the high born, and the single feature that distinguished the thinking of a knight from that of ordinary men. Even though commoners were supposedly excluded, chivalric thinking trickled down into the lowest levels, and it was not uncommon for day laborers to carve one another up as bravely as would two gentlemen over some slight to their honor.

The Spanish word *pundonor*, a contraction of *punta de honor* (point of honor), sums up the country's idea of chivalry. Some critics believe that *pundonor* is an exaggeration of the human virtues pushed to the last degree of sensibility. Harsher critics see *pundonor* as a sick egotism that belches forth men's darker nature. Supporters view the cult of chivalry as the guardian of values essential to life, a positive value, the basic spring of individual and collective heroism whose daily practice is necessary for the survival of Christian civilization. *Pundonor* requires an individual to risk his life to establish or defend his honor. It glorifies the warrior, and spurs men to courageous, sometimes violent acts. These displays of honor and courage must be performed in public. Honor is something external to a Spaniard's person; it is his worth, as evaluated by other people. Witnesses are necessary to view the valiant acts.

At the siege of Illora during the War of Granada in 1486, the Duke of the Infantado, after a quarrel with other nobles for the privilege, obtained permission from Ferdinand to lead a storming party against the walls of the Moorish city. A hailstorm of stones and arrows from the town's battlements greeted the Castilians. When the Duke's men faltered, he shouted: "What, my men, do you fail me at this hour? Shall you be taunted with wearing more finery on your backs than courage in your hearts? Let us not, in God's name, be laughed at as mere holiday soldiers!" Stung by the challenge to their honor, the Duke's vassals rallied, forced a breach in the walls and took the town with the fury of their assault. On that day they fulfilled the covenant of *pundonor,* they risked their lives in the Holy Cause against the Infidels; they achieved the impossible through their physical courage and persistent effort of will.

To Spaniards in the late 1400s, honor was a watchword, a national passion. It was even codified in the ancient Spanish laws, the *Siete Partidas,* as "the reputation a man has acquired by virtue of his rank, his high deeds or his valor." A Spanish poet, in the 1400s, ranks honor above life because "the life of the reputation lasts longer and more gloriously than the physical life."[1] The titles of Spanish plays speak for themselves, *El Medico y su Honra* (The Doctor and his Honor) and *La Locura por la Honra* (The Madness for Honor). In 1513, a Florentine wrote that "The men of this nation (Spain) value honor so greatly that most will choose death rather than tarnish it."

Chivalry's gallant notions served as not only a great Spanish literary theme, they formed a basic concept of government. Honor required loyalty. In the anarchy of the 1200s, when the idea of chivalry took root in Europe, the oath of loyalty made by a vassal to his master was virtually the only form of government. Serfs were bound to obey their knights, and the knights swore allegiance to a *grandee* who, in turn, pledged himself to the king. In time of war or feud, it was a vassal's sworn duty, which could not be broken without loss of honor, to fight for his lord or king. A man gave his primary loyalty to a person, not to the nation or an idea. This personal bond, *personalismo,* bound the nation together if all loyalties flowed to the sovereign. If a *grandee* rebelled against his king, the *grandee,* and his pyramid of vassals below him, could create chaos. Many modern-day Latin American politicians would have felt perfectly at home in 1400s Spain.

The precepts of chivalry charged the ruling class with the duties of maintaining order, upholding justice and defending the Holy Catholic Church, the oppressed and the virtue of women. In practice, these ideas of the European warrior caste, the military entrepreneurs, were sometimes corrupted, and the aristocrats frequently became the oppressors and the source of social disorder. Castile was no different.

To bind the Castilian nobles to him personally, King Alphonse XI, who inherited the throne at age one amid a swirl or revolution and intrigue, created the *Orden de la Banda* (Order of the Sash) in about 1330. Before the knighting ceremony, the candidate's hair and beard were trimmed, he took a ceremonial bath and dressed in a white surcoat specially made by order of the King. The candidate was ushered into the presence of the King and at least six knights where his sword and spurs were buckled on and the scarlet sash draped around his neck. He was presented with a shield bearing his chosen coat of arms, and the King tapped him on the shoulders with a sword and said "Be thou a knight." The knight then agreed to be bound by the rules of the Order of the Sash.[2]

Among other things, the rules dealt with attending mass each day, avoiding gambling, caring for his arms and equipment and behaving honorably at tournaments. At the end of the knighting ceremony, the loyalty oath was administered. The new knight of the Order vowed "To serve the King all my life and to always be a vassal of the King or of one of his sons; but, if I leave the King's service...I shall return the sash to the King and may never ask for it to be given to me again.…[I swear] to love the knights of the sash as my brothers, and I will never challenge a knight of the sash unless it is to help my father or brother. If two knights of the sash quarrel or fight, I shall do everything possible to part them, and, if I cannot part them, I shall not help either of them."

Chivalry also dictated the rules of male-female relationships. A man defined his honor by his reputation, which he must defend at the risk of his life. For an unmarried girl, honor was tied to her virginity, and, for a wife, to her fidelity. There was little risk of a young noblewoman losing her virginity, since she was married off at an early age in a nuptial arranged by her parents for dynastic reasons. A wife's breach of fidelity shamed the honor of the whole family, and vengeance or punishment had to be sought. In a trial in the province of Navarre, the parents of an unfaithful wife denounced her, and, according to custom, the wife suffered the consequences of her adultery; beheading.[3] When it was later proven that she was innocent, her family devoted years to restoring her reputation. In another case, a lawyer in the royal service defended himself in court by testifying that he was justified in strangling his wife because her confession of infidelity sent him into a rage. The defense worked, and the court set the lawyer free.

In the 1400s in Spain, love and marriage did not go together like a horse and carriage. Love was mostly irrelevant to marriage. Marriage kept the noble line alive and provided for the enhancement, preservation and transmission of property. Uniting families was serious business, and marriage contracts and dowries were the subject of long negotiations.

In contradiction to the treatment of women as sex objects and bearers of children, medieval Castilians wildly idealized romantic, courtly love. Gallants were supposed to soften the heart of a lovely lady by speaking passionately in high flown language, by "letting their inner flame blaze forth." "They [Spaniards] are not content with declaring that these ladies are their mistresses, and that they want to serve them like slaves and to die for them. A Spanish gentlemen will tell his lady that she is his goddess and that, for him, there are no other deities in heaven or on earth; and that, if the lady died, he would wish to be, not with God, but where his lady is," the Spanish historian Pulgar wrote.[4]

The classic Spanish story, *La Celestina,* published in Burgos in 1499, describes the tragic, passionate love of a young girl who first fends off the advances of her suitor, then yields because of the erotic suggestions of the sorceress La Celestina. When her lover is killed in an accident, the maiden commits suicide in despair. Spaniards in the 1400s admired, and sought, this sublime delirium of passion. The intense love of a woman was supposed to inspire a knight to greater prowess and daring, to cause him to rise above himself with excesses of courage and valor.

Courtly love was also supposed to ennoble a man, improve him and curb his arrogance and coarseness. The rules of chivalry forbid a knight from brawling in the presence of ladies. And the rules encouraged men to keep their teeth and nails clean, their conversation void of vulgarity and their manners elegant. Although Spanish men generally treated their women as chattels, with few legal rights, the inspirational role they played gave women a higher purpose in society.[5]

While chivalry placed Spanish women on a pedestal of courtly, romantic love and demanded that they remain chaste, men were unrestrained. All levels of Spanish society accepted infidelity and whoring. Testifying in court, one Spaniard told the judges that "If

I could have all the whores I wanted in heaven, I would gladly go there. But, if there were whores only in hell, I would prefer to go there."

A Flemish nobleman tells of a visit to an "admirable bordello" in Valencia in 1501. "After dinner...[we were taken]...to the quarter of the prostitutes. It is as large as a village, and enclosed on all sides by a wall which has a single door. At the door, an official takes the visitors' weapons and cautions them that, if they wish to leave their money, it will be returned to them when they leave....The quarter has three or four streets lined with small houses, and in each are some girls richly dressed in velvet and silk. In all, there are two hundred or three hundred women. Their houses are attractively furnished and provided with fine linen. The fee is four *dineros*...of which the treasury takes ten percent...and they cannot ask any more for the night....The women sit on the threshold, each with a fine lantern above her head so that she might be better seen. There are two physicians, appointed and paid by the town, who visit the women weekly to find those who are ill with the pox or some other secret disease and remove them from this place....I have noted all these things because I never heard of such a vile place that was so well regulated."[6] If a visitor went to a "Boys Town" red light ghetto on the U.S.-Mexican border today, he would not find many differences from this five hundred-year- old description.

Chivalry, in its purest form, called up the better elements of man's nature. When corrupted, it called up the bile.

A man's honor depended not only on his bravery in battle, but on the purity of his blood *(limpieza de sangre)*. It was more noble to be born of humble but pure Christian parentage than to be a *caballero* of suspicious racial antecedents. Spaniards categorically refused to admit that Jewish or Moorish blood tinged their own Catholic blood, and popular prejudice drew a clear distinction between "old" and "new" Christians. "Old" Christians were required to prove that there was no tainted (Jewish or Moorish) blood in their lineage for at least four generations. And "new" Christians, recent converts to the Faith, were under constant scrutiny and questioning. Was the conversion a genuine religious experience, or a fraud to get ahead? Did the "new" Christian refuse to eat pork or work on Saturday?

Underscoring this deep prejudice, one wealthy Spaniard stipulated in his will that he left his fortune to his daughter "to enable her to live nobley and tranquilly, to take care of her needs, and to defend her honor." The will goes on, "My daughter and her successors shall marry only 'old' Christian men who have no stain...who have not been prosecuted or punished by the Holy Inquisition [for Judaizing]...." Spanish intolerance unashamedly expressed itself in laws forbidding persons with non-Christian blood from attending certain colleges, joining certain military orders and holding public office in some cities. Although contrary to the Christian doctrine of converting lost souls to the Holy Faith, in 1486 the Jeronymites in Spain adopted a rule excluding *conversos* (recent converts) from membership in their holy order.

Despite the prejudice, many Jews and *conversos* rose in Spanish society. One *converso,* Francisco Villalobos, the personal physician to Ferdinand and Isabel, jokingly offered the hand of his daughter to a young muleteer in Villalobos' service. The muleteer, of pure Christian blood, replied that he would marry the girl to please his master, but that he would be afraid to return to his native village with a tainted wife. "You sound like a man who is very protective of his honor," Villalobos said. "But let me assure you that...I don't know how I would defend my honor if that marriage took place."

The mystique of *pundonor* required a knight to respond with violence to any insult to his person or reputation. Among the vilest insults were impugning a man's lineage or the honor of his mother.[7] The *Siete Partidas* stressed that insults, especially if made in public, must be redressed. Since there was no law of libel or slander to provide a remedy for besmirched honor, medieval Spaniards accepted dueling as the logical solution. A man who was insulted who didn't offer a challenge, or a man who refused a duel, lost his reputation. Honor was satisfied if the duel produced some blood, no matter how slight. By the time of Isabel and Ferdinand, laws prohibited dueling, but, like most laws that defy social custom, few Castilians observed them. The code of honor was clear on that point, and the list of prisoners convicted of dueling was long. Dueling took on almost a sportive character, with noblemen as the combatants and *pundonor* as both the pretext and the justification. In one confrontation, two young nobles of the houses of Velasco and Ponce de Leon agreed to fight on horseback with lances and no armor. They squared off at each end of a narrow bridge near Madrid and charged at full speed. The necessary blood spilled that day, and honor was preserved.

The sanctioning of dueling and the glorification of war both carry with them an acceptance of the risk of death. Today, with many people living past eighty in a haze of Altzheimers, sometimes the person is glad to die. In our age of heart transplants and vaccines, it is hard to imagine the specter that was death in medieval Castile. An appalling percentage of children died, and to live past forty was considered good fortune. People died overnight of the plague, or if their "humors" were out of kilter or if the leeches couldn't suck out the disease. Death was a tragic, sudden event that must be faced bravely. Some foreigners accuse Spaniards of being obsessed with death, citing as an example the profusion of Spanish art featuring bleeding wounds, cadavers and decomposed flesh. Modern Spaniards rankle at the suggestion that they are fascinated by death, but to Spaniards in the late 1400s, death was part of *pundonor*. *Vivir bien, morir bien* (Live well, die well), Castilians said. Stories recounting executions in medieval Spain tell approvingly of a man who "remained impassive...with stony disdain" as his executioners led him to the stake, and of another another condemned man who "displayed extraordinary courage while being burned alive."

Pundonor sanctioned war and violence as the appropriate route to glory and riches, underpinning and justifying the military entrepreneur. This militarism made impatient knights more interested in conquering for gain and fame, rather than conserving or building. The reconquest of Spain from the Moors added a contempt for the farmer or tradesman who sat at home while the *hidalgos* and *caballeros* were fighting heathens, and being rewarded with titles, land and vassals for their bravery. This element of *pundonor,* together with a rich mixture of avarice and greed, inspired Pizarro to slaughter the Incas and Cortes to conquer the Aztecs.

Honor came to the man who lived for war, who won riches by force of arms, not to the man who earned his living by the sweat of manual labor. So strong was the disdain of labor, trade and commerce that one rich Spaniard decreed in his will that, if his daughter married a man who "practiced base or mechanical occupations...or trade...[they shall] lose their rights to the succession...." So much for the work ethic. In later years, Spain would pay a dear price for this scorn of business and commerce.

Like the rodeo of the American west, the supreme sport of medieval Castile grew out the knight's primary job—war. The nobles' skills in handling horses and in dexterity with lance and sword developed into the sport of tournaments. Amid pomp and pageantry, the mock wars provided the barons a stage to parade all of the prized personal characteristics of the time; gallantry, disdain for death, physical dominance and honor. Additionally, as part of the apparatus of courtly love, performing before his lady brought glory to a cavalier, and mastery on the tilting field might inspire a noblewoman to a surreptitious meeting in her chambers later that night.

The staged miniature wars started sometime in the 900s. Originally, the rules of the tournaments dealt only with the duration of the contest and whether weapons would be blunted or sharp. These early tournaments were little more than semi-organized brawls between gangs of men, sometimes numbering in the hundreds. Typically, two teams of noblemen fought with swords, maces, cudgels, axes and daggers. In these melees, which depended more on brute force and stamina than skill, the knights clanged, grunted and struggled in suits of armor until they dropped; exhausted, wounded or dead.

As the sport grew in popularity, more blood splattered the tournament fields. In one tournament in 1175, seventeen knights were killed. During the early days of the tournaments, the Church railed against them. The Church denied knights killed in tournaments burial in the rituals of the Holy Faith, and, for the more vicious warriors, the Church could levy the extreme penalty of excommunication. As the Church degenerated into corruption, tournaments became acceptable, and, in 1471, a group of knights held a tournament in front of the Vatican in St. Peter's Square in Rome.

By the time of Isabel and Ferdinand, an elaborate set of rules for these "festivals of chivalry" were in place, taken mostly from a Treatise on Tournaments written by King Rene of Naples in 1434. The new rules made skill more important than sheer strength, and the contests developed into highly refined rituals dedicated to gallantry and devotion to women. The games were an expensive hobby for the high born, partly because of the enormous cost of armor, weapons, warhorses and attendants, and partly because it was thought that only a man of noble blood could fully comprehend the chivalrous aspects of the sport.

Competitors were matched according to their skill and experience levels, while six to twelve judges kept score. In mounted combat with twelve foot lances, unhorsing an opponent was the most impressive feat, and scored the most points. Next on the scorecard was hitting the enemy's crest on his helmet, followed by squarely delivering such a stout blow to a rival's shield that the knight broke his own lance. Since this was the easiest feat, splintered lances littered the arena. The judges awarded points to the knight who fought most bravely, a subjective call. They also rewarded endurance, giving additional points to the man who stayed on the field the longest; no small feat for a man on foot on a sunny day, encased in armor, swinging a heavy broadsword. The judges deducted points from a knight who hit his opponent's saddle with a lance, and expelled a combatant with dishonor for striking a horse or using an iron glove which locked onto the lance to give a rigid grip.

Tournaments usually involved teams of six to twelve knights who rushed into a fenced arena simultaneously. Team tactics were required. Should the team, like a boxer covering himself on the ropes, save its energy until the other side exhausted itself, or should it attack with full force at the outset? Should the team attack the weak ones first, or go after the strong and then mop up the weak?

In a variation of the tournament in a fenced arena, a group of knights would issue a challenge to all comers. The challenge stated that the team, in order to win, must hold a particular place for a set period of time. In 1434, ten Spanish noblemen, led by Suero de Quinones, vowed to defend a bridge in the province of Leon for thirty days and to break three hundred lances. If he lost, Quinones said, he would wear an iron collar every Thursday for the rest of his life. Sixty-eight challengers tried, without success, to oust the defenders between July 10 and August 9, but Quinones' team broke only 177 lances. Even though the judges declared Quinones the winner, he nobley kept his losers vow and wore an iron collar every Thursday until his friends were able to persuade him otherwise some months later.

The rules established prizes. Mostly, the prizes were practical, with the loser forfeiting his horses, weapons or money. The better knights stuffed their strong boxes with their winnings, and some became wealthy. But there were more ethereal prizes. One German knight, if defeated, gave his enemy a gold ring and all his horses. If he won, the German required his foe to bow to the four corners of the earth in honor of the German's lady fair.

Jousts were *mano-a-mano* fights between only two participants, an opportunity for personal distinction and individual glory. If the two contestants were feuding privately, or settling a point of honor, the fighting could be especially vicious. For jousts on horseback, under the new rules, a wooden barrier separated the knights to avoid accidental or intentional collisions. Under the old rules, there was no fence, and the massive warhorses at full gallop, weighted down with armor and padding, frequently veered into one another with concussive force.

Over time, ballads, poems and novels (sometimes with erotic passages detailing a successful knight's amours with his chosen lady) romanticized the tournaments and jousts. The people, as in the time of the Roman gladiators, reveled in this blood sport, and tournaments drew large crowds. The sport took on an international flavor, with knights traveling all over Europe to participate.

In 1442, a Spanish knight made the long trip to England to find a worthy opponent. "I....was set the task of fighting a knight or squire especially to serve my lord the King of Aragon (who was King John II, Ferdinand's father).... I was unable to carry out this task because there were no challengers in the realm of France. So I have come to the Kingdom of England....[to find an English knight to fight him on the following terms]...We shall fight on horseback, both armed as we please with the usual weapons, namely, lances, swords and daggers, and with such equipment as either of us wish, without any trickery. He to whom God gives the victory shall have the other's sword and helmet or other head armor. If the said battle does not end in the same day, we shall complete it on foot with the armor and weapons we have left, without any repairs or replacements. Wrestling with legs and feet, arms and hands, shall be allowed."[8]

Tournaments were often staged to celebrate a wedding, knighting ceremony or coronation. The contests began on Monday and ran through Thursday, paying deference to the Church's *Treuga Dei* (Truce of God), which prohibited fighting from Friday through Sunday. Preparations for the mini-wars usually started the preceding Thursday, with the combatant's arms being put on display for inspection and admiration. Symbolism surrounded each part of the knightly trappings. The metal breastplate and helmet guarded the body as the knight safeguards the Church. The lance drove back the enemies of the Church. The two edges of the sword showed that the knight serves both God and the people, and the sword's point meant that the people must obey him.

Dressed out in a shirt of iron mail, metal plates covering most of the body, a maze of leather straps and a visored helmet with a slit for the eyes, the knight was ready for battle. These suits of armor weighed up to sixty pounds, and, on a hot, humid day, the man encased inside sweltered. The knight needed many attendants to gird him and his horse, polish the armor so that it glittered in the sun, hone the weapons to a fine edge and cinch the leather straps to tighten the metal plates. No one wanted to meet the fate of one knight whose helmet came loose during a contest, and, after a mighty blow, it twirled to face backward, blinding the helpless warrior until his attendants rushed into the arena to right the headgear.

All-male drinking bouts were a major feature of the earlier tournaments, but, later, dances and elaborate dinners with the ladies came into fashion. In romantic theory, a lady could bar a knight from the next week's events if she accused him of unchivalrous behavior. If the noblewoman claimed, and proved, that a knight repeated gossip, bought goods to sell at a profit, broke his word of honor or failed to prove his pedigree, the knight could be ejected and have his horse confiscated and his spurs cut off.

After the weekend's preparations, on Sunday the combatants took oaths to keep the peace, and the ladies selected the Knight of Honor. On Monday, after lunch, the elegantly dressed women and their noble husbands bustled into the grandstands. The judges dispatched heralds to each team to make sure the knights understood the rules. When they finished this formality, the Knight of Honor cut the ribbons barring the gates to the arena, and the games began.

Isabel and Ferdinand sponsored one such tournament to celebrate the engagement of their daughter to the heir to the Portuguese crown in April, 1490. Just outside of Seville, on the banks of the Guadalquivir River, the tournament field was set up. A stout wooden fence about 160 feet by 200 feet enclosed the arena, and there were gates at each end. The King, Queen and Princess took their seats in the gallery, hung with silk and cloth of gold richly embroidered with armorial escutcheons of the ancient houses of Castile. Some seventy noblewomen, pages from the royal household and the tournament judges joined the Sovereigns in the gallery. The combatants, who had schemed and pulled strings for the chance to win laurels before so brilliant an assemblage, readied their arms and checked their straps and buckles one last time. With pennants flapping in the spring breeze, the crowd cheered, unusually excited because Ferdinand was scheduled to participate. The Knight of Honor cut the ribbons sealing the gates to the arena and the first teams of knights rushed into battle. Later that day, Ferdinand, mounted on his warhorse, broke several lances. At sundown, with the approval of the Sovereigns, the judges ordered torches lit so the games could continue after dark. At the appointed hour, the heralds sounded retreat on their trumpets, and the noble spectators and warriors adjourned for a night of dinners, dancing and gambling.

In addition to enjoying the spectacle of chivalry's noble sport, Ferdinand and Isabel used the notions of chivalry to their political advantage, demanding loyalty from their vassals to bind Spain together as a nation, and gallantry in the fight to drive out the Moors. While the Sovereigns counted on chivalry's better notions, loyalty and gallantry, they also subscribed to its darker side; the doctrine of *limpieza de sangre* which gave moral justification to the expulsion of Jews and the cruelties of the Inquisition.

9

THE HOLY BROTHERHOOD

Nothing, not even the Inquisition, was as brutal as the rural policemen of the Holy Brotherhood.[1] The paramilitary troopers of the Brotherhood, patrolling on fast horses, kicked up clouds of dust as they raced across the countryside, relentlessly stalking the Kingdom's murderers, rapists and thieves. Because of the brutal punishments they inflicted, and their un-checked power to act as police, judge, jury and executioner, the sight of a squad of these mounted policemen approaching struck fear in suspected criminals.

The policemen were easy to identify; with their peaked green caps, forest green capes with silver piping, white ruffs at the neck, knee britches and pointed shoes. A platoon's flag bearer carried a green silk banner worked with an arrow of metallic thread and Ferdinand and Isabel's royal insignias, the golden yoke and the bunched bundle of black arrows.

When a citizen reported a crime to the Holy Brotherhood's headquarters inside a city's walls, the captain *(alcalde)* sent his runner from the police station to the nearest church to ring the alarm bell. The lieutenants and line officers hurried to the station house and saddled their ponies. The captain strapped a small tin box containing a parchment arrest warrant to his saddle, slung his leg over his horse and gave the signal to move out. Servants swung open the heavy oak doors of the police station, and the squad's flag bearer led them in the chase through rural Castile.

On their search missions, the men carried small crossbows that fired iron darts with such ferocious velocity they could penetrate all but the finest armor. They were tough, hard men, accustomed to living in the open country, pulling their dark green capes around them to sleep on the ground when necessary. These flinty policemen, calloused by a career of dealing with the scum of society, wrapped themselves in the envelope of religion that surrounded almost everything in Castile in the late 1400s. At night, around their campfires, they recited:

"Heavenly Father, help us!
Holy Mary, favor us!
St. John of Latran, favor us!
...To the Monarches, our lords,
and to all who support and sustain
the Holy Brotherhood....Amen."[2]

Like the vigilante posses of the American west, when the Brothers caught their prey, justice was harsh, relentless and swift. After a capture, the constables hauled the suspect to the Holy Brotherhood's police station in their headquarters city. In Toledo, a squad entered the town gates and clattered through the streets with their prisoner to their jail, just across the street from the cathedral where Ferdinand and Isabel had celebrated their victory after the Battle of Toro.[3] Over the iron barred window above the Gothic doorway of the jail, the suspect saw the Castilian coat of arms topped by the sinister, ratlike head of a bat with a halo around it. On command, the servants inside opened the wooden doors, and the mounted policemen guided their horses into the inner courtyard, dismounted and unsaddled. The Brothers marched the prisoner up the stone staircase to a bare white room for a formal hearing before the captain, the man who would serve as the suspect's prosecutor, judge, jury and issuer of punishment.

After a man was arrested, the town criers shouted the charges through the streets to inform the public and to solicit those with evidence to come forward. If there were only the scantiest evidence of guilt, the captain dispatched the suspect to a dank underground cell to await further proceedings. Once commenced, the proceedings could not be stopped, and appeal from the captain's judgment was almost impossible. The law required the Holy Brotherhood to complete its investigation and render a verdict within nine days of an arrest, but the captains often disregarded the law and prisoners languished in jail for months.

Once the policemen assembled what evidence they could, they dragged the accused from his subterranean cell up the stairs to the whitewashed courtroom for trial. An official read the charges, and the captain, seated behind an ornate table, heard the evidence. The captain, in his sole discretion, decided guilt or innocence. If guilty, the captain pronounced sentence. Punishment in the ordinary courts of Castile was stern, but in the Holy Brotherhood's courts it was brutal. "In the time of the Catholic Sovereigns of glorious memory, the judges [of the Brotherhood] displayed such great severity that it appeared to be cruelty," King Ferdinand's physician wrote.[4] "But it was necessary because the Kingdom (Castile) was far from peaceful, and the tyrants and proud men (renegade aristocrats) had not been been humbled. And that is why veritable butcheries of men were carried out. The executioners cut off feet and hands, shoulders and heads, neither sparing nor hiding the rigor of justice. [There were] terrifying and horrifying vivisections."

For lesser crimes, the captain confiscated property or assessed fines, which the Holy Brotherhood kept in its own strongboxes. The captain punished petty theft, under five hundred maravedis, with lashes. Grand theft, over five hundred maravedis, drew dismemberment. A leg, an arm, an ear, whatever the captain decided. For more serious crimes, the captain sentenced the prisoner to death. Statutes prohibited the Holy Brotherhood from holding executions in town. So, before dawn, the policemen loaded the condemned man in a cart for transport to a bleak field outside the city's walls.

The law stipulated in minute detail the procedures of death. "The malefactor will be tied to a straight post. This post shall not be permitted to take the form of the Cross. The culprit will be fasted to the post with a clamp of wood around his waist and his feet...; then his body shall be taken for a target and arrows will be shot at him until he dies."[5] As the morning light crept across the field, the firing squad stretched the strings of their wooden crossbows and loaded them with iron darts. The Holy Brotherhood's code required that "the convict shall receive the sacrament like a Catholic Christian, and after that he may be executed as speedily as possible, in order that his soul may pass the more securely." A priest administered the last sacraments. The captain announced the prize payable to the executioner whose dart struck true in the condemned man's heart. On the captain's signal, the crossbowmen aimed and fired. If a dart hit the heart, the man crumpled and died almost instantly. If not, he writhed until he slowly bled to death. The Brothers unhitched the wooden clamps and left the gory corpse in the open field; food for scavenging birds and packs of wild dogs. Even the Inquisition was gentler than the pitiless justice of the Holy Brotherhood. The Inquisition's executioners hung or strangled heretics, which took only a few minutes, before burning them at the stake.

By Isabel and Ferdinand's day, the Holy Brotherhood was one of the most dreaded institutions in Castile. But it originated in the mid-1200s as a private police force. City merchants organized squadrons of the Holy Brotherhood to protect their goods from the highwaymen who prowled the wild countryside of the sparsely populated Kingdom.

At the time, many Castilian cities held centuries-old royal charters granting them broad rights of independence from the power of the crown and the aristocrats. Among those jealously guarded rights was the freedom of the cities to elect the officials and captains of the local Holy Brotherhood. Unless there was a threat to the nation, the king had no authority over the rural policemen. When the threat ended, control of the Brothers reverted to the cities. The Brotherhood was also free of aristocratic control, except in those cities, like Seville, where noble families dominated the city councils and indirectly controlled the Brothers of their district.

Although the Brotherhood could operate with a fair degree of autonomy, the law sharply, and clearly, limited the perimeters of its jurisdiction. The Brothers headquartered in the cities, but they could only make arrests and try cases for crimes committed outside a city's walls in villages with less than one hundred households.[6] This restriction preserved the city court's right to handle crimes that took place within its bailiwick.

Another restriction prevented the Brothers from arresting criminals who escaped more than fifteen miles from the headquarters city. If the suspect made it past these boundaries, the constables had to stop and turn the pursuit over to the Brothers in the next district. And they could only make arrests for crimes of violence, and could not intervene in political or religious crimes; heresy and rebellion being the exclusive jurisdiction of the Church and the crown. Long-standing tradition also prohibited the Brothers from arresting a criminal who made it onto an estate of an aristocrat or from infringing on the authority of the manorial court of a nobleman. Inside the mini-kingdom of his estate, a noble's word was law. And no outsider, not even the king in most cases, could interfere in matters involving an aristocrat's vassals or crimes committed on his land.

Although law and custom restricted their activities as policemen, judges and executioners, in times of national emergency the king had the right to muster the Brothers to fight as militiamen in the royal service. But ancient custom required the king to immediately disband the Brotherhood militia after the war or rebellion ended. The townsmen and the nobles, afraid of royal power backed by a standing army, had no interest in Holy Brotherhoods from Castile's towns and cities being united under the patronage of the crown to threaten their privileges. Ferdinand and Isabel would have a different view.

When the Sovereigns ascended the throne after the weak reign of Henry IV, Castile was in chaos. For protection, many men went armed at all times. As in America's frontier period, there were few legal safeguards, and it was up to the individual to defend himself with a dagger or sword. Since a powerful bandit, aristocrat or commoner, could easily buy his way out of trouble, violence and mayhem smothered Castile's commerce.

From the Kingdom's mountains in the north, criminals attacked caravans of traveling merchants. In the south, the wild frontier along the Granadian border was a no man's land where Castilian gangs plundered Moorish villages one day and Christian hamlets the next. When the Castilians in Andalusia weren't under attack by homegrown outlaws, they had to worry about cross border raids by the Muslims. In almost all parts of Castile the greedier nobles harbored criminals on their estates, protecting them from the grasp of the Holy Brotherhood's agents. One aristocratic freebooter, Pedro de Mendana, sent his band of thieves from his stone castle to rob and pillage rich travelers, villages and hamlets. When the bandits returned from their raids to Mendana's estates, his gang split their loot with their noble patron. Mendana's thugs were so notoriously vicious that they added to their income by blackmailing several central Castilian towns into paying protection money.

The courts provided little or no protection from the rampant lawlessness. In the municipal courts, impartiality was often in question, particularly when citizens with no influence faced the powerful. In the manorial courts of the aristocrats, a man could receive a fair hearing if the lord was benevolent. If not, justice was rendered pursuant to the prejudices and whims of a single nobleman. The royal courts dispensed almost as much evil as justice, and bribes were common. Brigands and outlaw noblemen laughed at the law, and contempt for the royal judges was so great that the law "was entirely without force."

After King Alfonso of Portugal's defeat at the Battle of Toro in early March of 1476, Isabel and Ferdinand turned their attention to the anarchy in Castile. Isabel's chief political goal for all institutions in her Kingdom was to draw the threads of power into she and her husband's hands, to bunch the arrows and unite her Kingdom. Because Castile was in such a turbulent state after the struggle for succession, gaining control of the Holy Brotherhood was a first logical step. High on Isabel's list of priorities was the welding of the Brotherhood into a powerful national instrument to rid Castile of the criminal element and establish internal order. To do this, Isabel decided to centralize the police and judicial functions of the Brotherhood under her direct control, and to make the law uniform, and punishment certain, throughout the country.

Previous monarches had tried to assert control over the Holy Brotherhood. But the opposition was too strong for Isabel's incompetent predecessors. The Brothers feared that crown control might lead to a repeat of King Henry IV's dipping into the Brotherhood's private treasury and squandering the money on royal projects which didn't directly benefit the Brotherhood. The people dreaded an even stronger Holy Brotherhood, given its already existing reputation for barbarous treatment of prisoners and savage administration of justice. The cities and nobles saw royal control of the Brotherhood as a threat to their prerogatives. Despite the obstacles, Isabel was determined, certain that she would succeed where her father and half-brother had failed. Short term, the Queen wanted a national police force. Isabel also had a long term objective. She wanted the Holy Brotherhood to form the core of a standing army to fight a Holy Crusade against the hated Infidels in Granada.

Within weeks after the Battle of Toro, Isabel called Parliament *(Cortes)* into session in late March of 1476. The delegates from the three estates, nobility, clergy and townsmen, met at Madrigal, Isabel's birthplace, to consider many issues of national importance. Isabel, a cunning politician, knew there would be opposition to royal control of the Holy Brotherhood. Before the delegates arrived in Madrigal, the Queen and her scribes crafted a carefully worded document that complained about robbers, thieves and murderers, and begged that the police forces of the Holy Brotherhood be united to resolve the chaos. In addition to placing most of the emphasis on a unified police agency, the proposal insisted that new laws for the Brotherhood "must come from on high because then it will have greater vigor and force." The document was deliberately vague on the subject of the taxes needed to support the reformed Brotherhood.

The proposal dodged the issue of Isabel's long-term goal; turning the Brotherhood into a national militia. Bowing to the medieval love of form over substance, Isabel gave the document to Parliamentary representatives she could trust. They, in turn, presented it to the full Parliament to make it appear that the proposal came from the delegates. After a bit of lobbying, Isabel squeezed a resolution out of Parliament authorizing the calling of a National Assembly to draft new laws and standards for the Holy Brotherhood. The resolution didn't worry the aristocrats and churchmen in Parliament too much. The Queen's proposal didn't call for a standing army that would threaten them. They still had exclusive jurisdiction over their manorial and ecclesiastical courts. If new revenues to support a reformed Brotherhood were necessary, medieval custom exempted those elite citizens from the payment of taxes. The commoners in Parliament, who represented the cities and towns, knew who would have to pay.

The first National Assembly of the Holy Brotherhood met in the last week of July, 1476, in the small hill town of Duenas. With Isabel and Ferdinand in attendance, representatives from eight of the most important cities in northern Castile gathered in the Church of Santa Maria de Duenas to discuss the new structure of the Brotherhood. To demonstrate their interest in the Brotherhood, and to intimidate the representatives, the twenty-five-year-old King and Queen presided over the meetings from raised thrones at the front of the Church. For weeks before the National Assembly met, Isabel and her counselors spent hours pouring over the most minute details for the reorganization of the Brotherhood. Her chief advisor on the project, and the man who served as the architect of the new Brotherhood united under the Queen's patronage, was Alonso de Quintanilla, a trusted member of the Royal Council, Castile's most powerful governing body.

The delegates initially thought they were meeting to approve new procedures for the police forces of the Holy Brotherhood. As Quintanilla unfolded Isabel's proposal, it became clear that substantial tax increases would be needed to pay for the restructured Brotherhood. In its new format, the Brotherhood would provide not only a police force, but a national militia. Opposition rose to a clamor. Nobody wanted new taxes to support the additional troops for a militia and a paid staff of bureaucrats to run it. When the representatives fully understood that Isabel meant to directly control the Brotherhood police and militia branches, the debate grew ugly.

As the hostility increased, some delegates became so emotional they threatened to quit the royal presence and return home. At that point, Quintanilla stood to deliver an impassioned speech in favor of the Queen's use of the Holy Brotherhood. "Let us be free men as we should be, and not mere subjects as we are," Quintanilla said. "[We must leave behind] the *senorios* (aristocratic estates) and come into the royal liberty." By this, he meant that the townsmen would receive better and more benevolent justice if the crown controlled the Brotherhood. If, on the other hand, the sometimes corrupt city fathers, who were often dominated by equally corrupt aristocrats, continued to control the Brotherhood, justice would not be as even handed. Then Quintanilla struck a religious chord by referring to the Moorish threat to Christian Castile. He played on the representatives' patriotism by alluding to the King of Portugal's threats to mount a new invasion and seize the Castilian crown. The Kingdom needed a militia, Quintanilla said, and the sacrifices were worth it. He was not, he said, talking about the militia invading foreign countries, but he was talking about defending their own land, their own villages, their own homes.

Quintanilla then offered three important compromises. Under the new structure, control of the Holy Brotherhood would come from the bottom up. Each city would elect delegates to a provincial convention, which, in turn, would elect representatives to the National Assembly. Regarding taxes, Quintanilla said, the Brotherhood would be supported by a universal tax that all classes would pay, except for the *grandees* (the highest nobles). Finally, the militia branch of the Holy Brotherhood was only a temporary measure, and it would go out of existence after two years. When the two years were up, no one would have to pay taxes for the militia "even if demanded to do so by the King and Queen or the Royal Council." Soothingly, Quintanilla told the delegates that there would be no brusque changes, no dangerous innovations. These compromises seemed reasonable to the delegates, but Quintanilla carefully neglected to reveal all of the details.

Assured by these concessions, the National Assembly delegates and the Queen's men began bargaining the intricacies of tax law and the establishment of the delicate balance between centralized and local control of the Holy Brotherhood. Castile's medieval cities mistrusted centralized authority which, in the past, undermined their municipal powers. The city fathers, entrenched in age-old isolationism, rarely looked beyond their town's boundaries, and saw no benefit to sacrificing their local interests for some nebulous notion of a national government. To them, they owed their first loyalty to their town or province.

The Queen's lobbyists argued that, because the cities were divided and weak, despotic nobles controlled many cities and manipulated the town councils for their own selfish benefit. On the other hand, the Queen's advocates said, the delegates knew Isabel's policy. So long as there was no direct conflict between the cities' independence and the royal interest in guiding the nation as a whole, the cities would be entitled to keep their full rights. The Queen's men argued that, although Isabel was new to many of them, they knew of her integrity, fairness and love of her people. With her personal stamp *(personalismo)* on the Holy Brotherhood, it wasn't likely there would be any conflict.

The National Assembly would meet at least once each year to establish policy and adopt rules and regulations to govern the Holy Brotherhood. To make sure the National Assembly's rules were properly applied, a Royal Council of the Brotherhood would be established. The Council would keep miscreant captains in check, and would stifle the old abuses by the police. To make sure that each province and district was treated fairly, the Council of the Brotherhood would fix the amount of taxes to be raised and the quotas of men for the militia. The larger cities could establish their own local Brotherhood corporations to administer tax collection, building jails and trying cases. [7]

Under this new plan, the Queen's men argued, for the first time the cities could directly participate in the national governmental structure. By linking together under a Royal Council of the Brotherhood, the cities would have an unprecedented forum for cooperation and consultation with the Sovereigns. The Council would have Isabel's direct personal support and attention, and she planned to appoint one of her most trusted advisors, the Bishop of Cartagena, to serve as the first President of the Council. Don Alonso de Aragon, Ferdinand's brother, would be the Supreme Commander of the militia.[8] The Holy Brotherhood's champion, Quintanilla, would be the Chief Administrator. Of course, the Queen's men said, these were only recommendations to the National Assembly, which the delegates were free to accept or reject.

On the tax question, even though it might be a break with medieval custom, the *hidalgos* (the lowest rung of nobility) and the clergy would be forced to pay their fair share along with the ordinary citizens.[9] Since the Holy Brotherhood was an institution dedicated to the national good, the Queen's men said, everyone should help finance it. Of course, the delegates could understand that taxing the powerful *grandees* (the highest nobility) would be too politically risky. The basic annual tax for the militia branch of the Holy Brotherhood would be ten thousand maravedis per one hundred household. Taxes could also be levied on wine, salted and unsalted fish, bread, meat and fruit. To make the proposal even more palatable, Isabel's advisors estimated that only about three thousand men would be needed nationwide to serve in the militia.

Even though this wasn't many troops, it would form the core of an army if the Moors or some foreign power attacked Castile. Each local unit of the Holy Brotherhood would collect its own taxes and would have its own independent treasury. Isabel and Ferdinand, unlike King Henry IV, promised that they would not touch the Brotherhood's funds.

To pacify the countryside, the cities would build up the rural police force to one light horseman per one hundred households and one heavily armed man-at-arms for each 150 households. To consecrate their support, every city, town and hamlet would be required to take an oath on the Holy Cross and the New Testament to support the Brotherhood. The paramilitary police would retain their traditional jurisdiction over murder, rape of honest women, blasphemy, robbery, passing counterfeit money, harboring criminals and desecration of churches.

The police would be expected to continue, at the local level, to administer these crimes with unsparing rigor. Since Isabel wanted to expand the jurisdiction of the police branch of the Brotherhood, for the first time the constables would be permitted to arrest criminals who committed acts in the cities and fled to the countryside. In the most radical expansion of the police's jurisdiction, the Brothers would be authorized to enter on the manorial estates of the aristocrats in pursuit of criminals. Previously, the noble's estates were sacrosanct, and could not be violated by anyone without the lord's permission. The Brotherhood's jurisdiction would be further broadened to include the political crime of rebellion against the crown.[10]

After almost two weeks of negotiations, compromise and behind-the-scenes stage managing by Isabel, the delegates agreed to the Queen's proposal. On August 13, 1476, the Sovereigns signed a royal decree containing almost everything Isabel wanted. To seal their medieval agreement, most municipalities swore the required allegiance to the Holy Brotherhood. Then, the Constable of Castile, one of Isabel's stoutest supporters and one of the greatest lords in northern Castile, fell into line. He instructed all of his vassals to pay taxes for the militia, but retained his feudal tax exemption for himself personally. Many other nobles quickly followed the Constable's example.

Even though the Duke of Medina Sidonia had supported Isabel against La Beltraneja, he levied harsh criticism against the restructured Holy Brotherhood. First, the Duke said, it was too costly. Second, it was a challenge to his private army, to the manorial courts he controlled directly and to the Sevillian municipal courts he controlled indirectly through his henchmen on the town council. The proud, powerful Duke ordered Seville's city officials not to join the Brotherhood. When Isabel received news of her obstreperous subject's order, she sent two officials of the Holy Brotherhood to Seville in January, 1477, to demand compliance with the new Brotherhood laws.

The Queen's men, Pedro del Algava and Juan Reyon, took with them a letter from Isabel threatening penalties and confiscation of property if the city fathers did not obey the new law. By separate courier, Isabel sent the city fathers a letter full of *palabras dulces* (sweet words), appealing to them to join the Holy Brotherhood in order to serve God and to serve the universal good of the Kingdom. Nothing happened. After years of domination by the Duke of Medina Sidonia, the townsmen chose to face the royal wrath rather than that of the Duke.

Six months later, in June, 1477, Isabel sent a member of the Royal Council, Alonso Palencia, to step up the pressure on the Sevillians. Since the Duke of Medina Sidonia was not in Seville at the time, Palencia, Reyon and Algava met with the city fathers. The Duke's influence was so great that, not only did the city fathers refuse to comply with the Brotherhood law, they threatened to punish any citizen who did. Recalling the meeting, Palencia wrote that "[the city officials] threatened Juan Reyon with the gallows and Pedro del Algava with cutting his throat....The two [men] took refuge in the house of Pedro de Estuniga...but soon, because of cowardice, fear or his natural vacillation, [Estuniga] appeared inclined to the opinions of the Duke, with the result that [Reyon and Algava] went to the Monastery of San Pablo. This left me to take part in the negotiations alone, and I calmly resolved to confront the risk of meeting the irate Duke."[11]

The six months of relentless royal pressure worked. When Medina Sidonia returned to Seville, the city fathers, caught in the middle of the power play, argued that further resistance was useless, that Isabel would not relent or retreat. Convinced, the Duke ordered Seville to join the reconstituted Holy Brotherhood. In late July, 1477, Isabel traveled to Seville. On her arrival, the Duke of Medina Sidonia personally handed the diminutive Queen the keys to the Alcazar, Seville's fortress.

When the lesser nobility, the *hidalgos,* learned that they had lost their traditional personal exemption from taxation, they petitioned the royal couple for relief. In the petition, the *hidalgos* reminded the King and Queen that they had served them in the War of Succession. If they were needed in the future to fight the Moors or the Portuguese, the *hidalgos* said, they were prepared to perform their feudal duty to bear arms under the royal banner, and, if necessary, die in their Sovereigns' service. Recognizing their need for *hidalgo* support to govern the nation and to fight Castile's wars, Isabel and Ferdinand restored the *hidalgos* tax exemption. In addition to the lower nobility's objections, the Sovereigns sparred with the Church. At first, they decided to reduce the prelates' taxes for the Holy Brotherhood, but refused to grant a total exemption. Later, under strong pressure from the clergymen, the King and Queen reinstated the exemption.

The exemptions for the Church and nobility placed the full burden of the Brotherhood tax on the cities and the ordinary citizens. The crafty city fathers reacted by imposing an excise tax on luxury goods destined for use by "exempted persons," the aristocrats and clergy. When the "exempted persons" petitioned Ferdinand and Isabel to remove the excise tax, the young couple, still queasy about the depth of their support among these two powerful elements of society, lifted the excise tax.

Some cities chafed under the new rules and taxes for the Holy Brotherhood. When Leon, Zamora and Salamanca failed to furnish militiamen, the Sovereigns threatened them with fines of fifty thousand maravedis each. The towns raised the troops. When Ocana refused to comply, Isabel and Ferdinand went personally to the city where their powers of persuasion caused Ocana's city fathers to see the wisdom of joining the Brotherhood. In the summer of 1477, Isabel decided to go to Extremadura to whip the towns of that western province into line. Cardinal Mendoza warned against this "imprudent exposure of her person" and tried to dissuade her from going. "It [is] true that there [are] dangers and inconveniences to be encountered," the Queen said. "But [my] fate is in God's hands, and I believe that He will guide me to the right result if I pursue ends which are righteous in themselves and which I conduct resolutely."[12] The small town of Trujillo, in Extremadura, refused to buckle under and join the Brotherhood until Isabel appeared before its walls with an army and canons. The mayor surrendered without a fight.

Although the King and Queen made a few strategic retreats, they never lost site of the goal; tightening their personal and direct dominance over the Holy Brotherhood. At the National Assembly of the Brotherhood in 1477, the Sovereigns persuaded the delegates to adopt a resolution ordering that, if a city refused to contribute to the Brotherhood, citizens of other towns could not communicate with, or pay debts to, inhabitants of the defaulting city.

Another rule required that, once a city joined the Brotherhood, it could not withdraw. The delegates added a new official to the

Council of the Holy Brotherhood, an Attorney General instructed to make sure the cities and provinces carried out the Council's orders to the letter. Not fully satisfied by the appointment of an Attorney General named by the Council, the Sovereigns assigned their own man, a prosecuting judge *(juez ejecutor),* to each province. The prosecuting judge's job was to assure that all mandates were implemented by each local chapter of the Brotherhood and to report directly to the crown.

When the National Assembly of the Brotherhood met in 1478, the militia branch of the Holy Brotherhood, and the taxes to support it, were scheduled to expire. Castilians thought they would be out from under the burden of supporting the militia. Just two years before, the King and Queen had promised that under no circumstances would the Brotherhood militia stay in place for a longer term.

But, at the 1478 meeting, the Sovereigns argued that, with King Alfonso of Portugal rattling sabers in Lisbon, there was an immediate national emergency that warranted retaining a standing army. Andalusia and Extremadura threatened to pull their support for the Brotherhood militia, and there were pockets of strong opposition from other delegates. Using Portugal's militancy as their primary argument, Ferdinand and Isabel coaxed the representatives into renewing the militia branch of the Brotherhood for three more years.

In 1479, Castile and Portugal signed a peace treaty, ending the external threat to the Kingdom, and many cities stopped levying the taxes for the militia's support. In response, the royal couple issued a sharp message that it was their "deliberate and voluntary determination" that the militia arm of the Holy Brotherhood must continue. To further make their point, Isabel and Ferdinand ordered every city and town to post a decree in the public marketplace requiring the local officials of the Holy Brotherhood to punish anyone who refused to support the national army.

At the 1480 meeting of the National Assembly of the Brotherhood, the delegates adopted a new set of laws which expanded and reorganized the militia and extended the military branch until 1483. The King and Queen's plans to invade the Iberian Peninsula's last Moorish stronghold, the Kingdom of Granada, were ripening. With this sacred cause as the pretext, the Sovereigns had little trouble obtaining successive renewals of the militia. Although the earlier Brotherhood reforms reflected a tactful balance of power between the central government and the municipalities, by 1480 Ferdinand and Isabel were much more comfortable on their thrones. The new Brotherhood rules were replete with references to "Our powers," "Our orders" and "Our officials." The charade that town and crown were equal was over.

Even though support for the Brotherhood's militia held together, the citizens still feared the captains and officials of the police branch of the Holy Brotherhood. Despite the piety implied by its name, the Holy Brotherhood continued its barbarous savagery, occasional injustice, avid tax collection and confiscation of money and property that made many captains rich. The citizens petitioned the Queen that "these grievances and sentences are not remedied, as both poor persons, and those of quality, cannot complain to the captains, nor can accused persons secure justice in the courts [of the Holy Brotherhood]." Perhaps Isabel justified the Brothers' methods in her own mind, as did the American historian Prescott, who wrote in the 1840s, because "(t)his kind of wild justice is characteristic of an unsettled state of society."

To quell some of the complaints, in the Brotherhood laws of 1480, Isabel imposed stringent regulations to tighten discipline, and prohibited Brotherhood officers and their wives from wearing silk clothing, crimson cloth and gold jewelry. Despite the attempts to curb their power, the Brotherhood's constables continued to imprison suspects in Holy Brotherhood jails without charge and without releasing their names, just as the Argentine generals held political prisoners in the 1970s. Sometimes, these *desaparecidos* (disappeared ones) languished in Brotherhood cells for months, and neither their relatives nor city officials knew their where-abouts. Not until 1486 did Isabel abolish this practice. Isabel made another concession by ordering that condemned criminals be hanged or strangled to death before being shot full of arrows, but the rule was seldom followed.

When the War of Granada began in earnest, the call to arms placed enormous demands on the Brotherhood to supply men and the materiel for the Holy Cause. Brotherhood taxes almost quadrupled by the late 1480s, and the Holy Brotherhood's militia supplied twenty-five percent of the infantry under Ferdinand's command, eight thousand men in 1483 and ten thousand by 1490.

At a time when seventy-three maravedis bought a bushel of wheat and a day laborer earned seventy-five hundred maravedis a year, the militiamen were well paid. A man-at-arms earned twenty-four thousand maravedis, a light cavalryman eighteen thousand and a foot soldier fifteen thousand.[13] A commander received one thousand maravedis for each man on his roll call. Unable to resist temptation, some unscrupulous commanders faked their lists and pocketed the one thousand maravedis for each nonexistent soldier, plus the nonexistent soldier's salary.

In addition to the scandals in the militia branch of the Brotherhood, the police captains continued to be brutal, quick to judge, heedless of appeal and immediate in the execution of penalties. Even though these harsh methods successfully rid Castile of many of the "swarms of banditti," Isabel finally admitted that "the captains, archers and officials [of the Brotherhood]...have many times caused grievances and injustice to persons who appeared before them under the statutes of the Brotherhood." Although the Queen recognized that many of the citizens' complaints were justified, the Holy Brotherhood, both police and militia, were Isabel's personal pets. Isabel remained loyal to these men who fought under her flag and cleared her highways of bandits. They, in turn, reciprocated with personal loyalty to her. But, with the Moors finally defeated in 1492, Isabel could no longer justify the costly army.

Bowing to public pressure in 1498, she disbanded the militia and the national administrative structure that tied the police directly to her. The police branch, now locally controlled, remained intact for years. In fact, the Brotherhood police force continued for centuries. In its most recent reincarnation, the notorious paramilitary Civil Guard *(Guardia Civil)* patrolled the streets and enforced the laws of Spain's dictator, Generalissimo Francisco Franco.

In his 1605 novel, Miguel de Cervantes involves his hero, Don Quixote, in brushes with the Holy Brotherhood. After Don Quixote illegally frees twelve prisoners being marched in chains to serve as galley slaves, the knight errant's faithful servant, Sancho Panza, tells him that "the Holy Brotherhood do not stand in awe of your chivalry, nor do they care a straw for all the knights errant in the world. Methinks I hear their arrows whizzing around my ears."

"Thou art naturally a coward Sancho," Don Quixote says. "Nevertheless...I will take your counsel and take myself out of the reach of this dreadful Brotherhood...."

Later in the novel, the officers of the Brotherhood identify Don Quixote from the parchment arrest warrant issued against him for freeing the galley slaves. Don Quixote batters a policeman with his lance and the two engage in a brawl. When they are parted, Don Quixote shouts that "you [Brothers are the] offspring of filth and the extraction of dunghills...you...base spirited rascals....Your thoughts are too groveling and servile to understand or reach the pitch of chivalry...you are a pack of rogues indeed, and robbers on the highway of authority."

10

JUSTICE, THE ROYAL COUNCIL

"I well remember seeing her [Isabel] in the Alcazar [fortress] of Madrid, together with the Catholic King Ferdinand, that illustrious prince, her husband, sitting in judgment every Friday, dispensing justice to great and small, to all who came to seek it," wrote Gonzalo Fernandez de Oviedo. As a young man, Oviedo had served as a pageboy to the royal couple's son, John, and later had become the royal historian of the Indies.

As a mature man, Oviedo searched his boyhood memory to recall the King and Queen dispensing their personal justice to their subjects. "And on that same high platform, to which one mounted by five or six steps, in the space outside the canopy of the dais, there was on either side, to the right and left, a bench where sat twelve judges of the Royal Council of Justice and a president of said Royal Council. And in front was a clerk of the Council, named Castaneda, who read the petitions in a loud voice. And at the foot of the steps was another clerk of the chamber of the Council, who noted down the subject of each petition. And at the sides of the table where the petitions were deposited stood twelve mace bearers. And at the door of the hall of this royal court were porters who, upon order, let freely enter whoever wished to submit a petition. And the court judges were there to take whatever measures were to be taken, or to redress wrongs, or to consult with the Sovereigns. This was indeed the Golden Age of Justice, when he who was in the right obtained his due. I have observed that since God took away our saintly Queen, it is far harder to get an audience with [a minor government official's] valet than it used to be of her and her Council, and [it is now] a great deal more expensive."[1]

Before this laudatory description of royal justice could be written, Ferdinand and Isabel had to deal with a judicial system that was in total disrepute. The legacy of their predecessor, Henry IV, corruption, bribery and favoritism, discredited the courts and judges to the point that, in many cases, settlement of disputes with a dagger or sword brought a fairer result. The law itself was a jumble of ancient Roman law, Visigothic codes, the *Siete Partidas* written in the late 1200s, Church law, royal decrees, centuries' old customs and the whims of noblemen and kings. The incoherent laws provided no certainty, no predictability, even when a litigant went before the rare honest judge. Increasing the confusion, royal courts, Church courts, manorial courts, Holy Brotherhood courts, municipal courts, military order courts and commercial law courts competed for jurisdiction.[2]

If a claimant obtained a favorable result in one court, he might see his judgment removed to another court or appealed to a higher court. In addition, the royal courts followed the itinerant kings all over Castile. If the royal court agreed to hear the case, the litigant might be forced to pick up and move to the next city with the king and his judges. Despite the legal snarl, medieval Castilians seemed to have a passion for lawsuits, sometimes fighting for years through a blizzard of rehearings and appeals for only a few maravedis. In the 1400s, the Castilian legal system consumed millions of maravedis, some of which went for bribes, and enormous amounts of time.[3] The courts rendered occasional justice and fairness. Mostly, the results were erratic. At worst, they were unjust or dishonest.

To reform Castile's justice system, Ferdinand and Isabel's objective was clear—to legitimize the illegitimate legal system. Early in their reign, the Sovereigns set about the complicated tasks of eliminating the law's contradictions, streamlining the court structure and appointing competent, honest men to sit on the bench. To carry out their plan, Isabel and Ferdinand exercised their royal preeminence *(preeminencia real),* serving as the supreme judges, the "fountainhead of justice." The Sovereigns would be the ultimate redressers of wrongs, disinterested arbitrators, a court of last resort open to all citizens of Castile. Over time, by their direct personal intervention, they proved correct many Castilians' belief that "The best judge is the king."

Isabel and Ferdinand introduced many of their reforms at the

Parliament of Toledo in 1480. Most of the changes were not new, only adaptations of older laws or procedures which previous monarches tried, but failed, to implement. Although the Sovereigns were not innovators, they successfully welded a blend of old and new rules into a single royal system of justice. They also created a framework of more reliable legal institutions which "made a small number of judges suffice to maintain public peace, which [their] predecessors vainly sought to attain with soldiers."

More importantly, the royal couple established in Castilians the glimmerings of a sense of basic fairness and impartiality in the law. Pulgar, Isabel's court historian, says that "the kingdom was previously filled with bandits and malefactors of every description who committed the most diabolical crimes in open contempt of the law, [but during Isabel's reign] there was such terror impressed on the hearts of everyone, that no one dared to lift his arm against another person....The noblemen, who had before oppressed the common man, were intimidated by the fear of that justice that was sure to be executed on them....The [aristocrats'] fortresses, the strongholds of violence, were thrown open, and the whole nation, restored to tranquility and order, sought no other remedy than that afforded by the operation of the law."[4]

During their reign, Ferdinand and Isabel established permanent courts (*audencias* or *cancillerias*) in Santiago de Compostela to serve Galicia and the north, in Granada to mete out justice in the south and in Valladolid and Seville to provide forums in the central part of the Kingdom. To supervise the administration of justice, and to assure that the crown's political desires were carried out, the King and Queen strengthened the Royal Council of Justice. The Royal Council of Justice served as a supreme court, and eventually became "the essential organ of the royal power."

Traditionally, most judicial posts went to members of the aristocracy and higher clergy. In a break with the old custom, Isabel and Ferdinand began naming "men of middling condition who [owed] everything to the crown" to fill the judicial offices. Rather than appointing nobles or clergymen with little legal training, as John II and Henry IV had done during their "imbecile reigns," the royal couple designated university trained lawyers *(letrados)* to sit as judges. In a royal decree, issued in 1493, the Sovereigns required that "no *letrado* can hold any post in Our tribunals...unless he has a notarized document certifying that he has studied common or civil law for a minimum of ten years at a university."

To give the law at least a semblance of organization, Isabel instructed legal scholars to collate the laws in a more orderly fashion. This royal order resulted in the eight-volume Royal

Ordinances of Castile, published in 1485. The books containing the Ordinances, which the Queen forced all large towns and cities to purchase, were among the first publications in Spain to use the revolutionary movable type.

By 1500, Castilian presses printed and distributed five editions of the Ordinances throughout the realm, forming the basis of a national set of laws. The Ordinances were followed by a book containing the Royal Decrees, published in 1503. Although these books did not eliminate the law's confusion, they awakened in the public's mind the need for a comprehensive set of rules that would apply throughout the Kingdom. Isabel understood that the law was a necessary tool to bind her nation together, and, even on her deathbed, she worried about "how she might place at the service of her subjects an exact, concise, intelligible code of justice."

The Sovereigns instigated new procedural rules designed to speed up the wheels of justice. Under the old procedures, only blood relatives or a spouse could bring murder charges. If a powerful man committed the crime, he could easily intimidate a helpless widow or the poor relatives of a murdered man into keeping quiet. To remedy this, the new laws gave a royal prosecutor the right to bring charges. In some courts, a single judge heard all of the cases, and, particularly in smaller towns, the judge might be prejudiced against one of the litigants. To correct this abuse, the Sovereigns permitted the parties to a lawsuit to have their case reheard by the judge and a three-person jury of persons of integrity *(buenas personas)*.

The King and Queen ordered that special counsels (advocates for the poor) must defend the rights of the lower classes. As a compromise with tradition, the Sovereigns let stand the practice of allowing noblemen to be tried before special royal judges. Perhaps the single biggest failure of Isabel and Ferdinand's efforts at legal reform was their inability to gain control of the courts of the nobles and the Church. The tradition was too strong. The aristocrats and bishops were too powerful, and these private, parallel tribunals continued to operate almost unfettered by the crown.

Although the Queen was slow to intervene in cases involving noblemen and crimes against the Church, where there was a gross miscarriage of justice or her dignity was threatened, she struck with an iron fist. In the spring of 1481, Ferdinand's nephew, Federico Enriquez, the son of the powerful Admiral of Castile, engaged in a brawl with another young nobleman, Ramiro Nunez, in the antechamber of the palace at Valladolid. After the brawl, Isabel issued her personal letter of safe conduct to protect Nunez from further violence. Disregarding the Queen's safe conduct, Enriquez hired three thugs who pounded his rival with bludgeons in the streets of Valladolid. Furious, Isabel rode at night to the Admiral's castle where the young Enriquez was supposedly hiding under his father's protection. The Admiral claimed his son wasn't there. The enraged Isabel demanded the castle's keys and instructed her guards to search the castle. When the Queen's men couldn't find the boy, Isabel returned to Valladolid. Exhausted by the all night trip, the Queen stayed in bed the next day. "My body is weakened (by the all night trip)," she claimed, "and by the blows given by [Enriquez] in contempt of my safe conduct." The Admiral, frightened by the depth of Isabel's anger, turned his son over to the Queen.

Dispassionately, Isabel listened to the pleas for mercy because the high-spirited Enriquez was only a boy of twenty. Then she rendered her judgment—the young man was to be publicly humiliated by being marched through the streets as a prisoner, held in solitary confinement and, because he was related to Ferdinand, banished to Sicily rather than executed.

Insulting her dignity wasn't the only thing that drew Isabel's wrath. If the Queen's inspectors caught a judge accepting a bribe, showing favoritism or abusing his power, Isabel instantly removed him from office and strapped him with the severest penalties. Lawyers who charged exorbitant fees or brought frivolous lawsuits suffered sanctions. For the more slow-witted of her subjects, it took a while for them to understand the new ethical standards.

One rich Galician nobleman, Alvaro Yanez, must have thought he was dealing with Henry IV when he offered Isabel a huge bribe to pardon his death sentence. Some of the Queen's advisors counseled her to take the money and use it to fight the Moors. She refused, and the royal executioner carried out the sentence. Although she had the right to expropriate Yanez' property for the benefit of the crown, to avoid any taint of self-interest Isabel allowed the condemned man's possessions to pass to his heirs. With this incident, Isabel made her point—her law applied equally to rich and poor and punishment was certain. "[Isabel] was very inclined to hand out justice...rigorously," Pulgar said simply.

In addition to reforming the legal system, the Sovereigns intended to break the feudal tethers binding Castile to chaotic aristocratic control, and to outfit their Kingdom with the trappings of a centralized nation. They would do this in tandem, in the unique working partnership they formed to bring greatness to their realm. "*Tanto monta, monta tanto, Fernando como Isabel.*" To further their goal, Ferdinand and Isabel set about strengthening and reorganizing the executive branch of government—the Royal Council *(Consejo Real)*.

At the beginning of their reign, it appears that the Royal Council functioned as both a law court and as the chief administrator of Castile's business. At the outset, aristocrats and higher clergy dominated the Royal Council. In 1476, Cardinal Mendoza, the Duke of the Infantado, the Duke of Alba, the Admiral of Castile and other *grandees* sat on the Royal Council.

The royal couple took their first steps toward reform at the Parliament of Toledo in 1480. Under the new rules, a clergyman served as president of the Royal Council and the aristocrats held three seats. *Letrados,* men who earned their spurs through academic channels rather than birth or war, made up the remaining eight or nine members of the Council. But, even though three nobles and one cleric sat on the Royal Council, the bulk of the day-to-day grind of work fell to the university-trained *letrados*.

If appointed to *Nuestro Consejo* (Our Council), Isabel and Ferdinand required their Counselors to reside at either the palace with the Sovereigns or at nearby lodgings. Their work was demanding. The Royal Council held formal sessions every day during the hot months, between Easter and October, from six to ten in the morning. The rest of the year, the Council members met between nine a.m. and noon. If there was a revolt in Galicia or if Isabel demanded an immediate answer to a question, the meetings could go on for hours. In the afternoons, the Counselors dictated letters and decrees, conferred with the Sovereigns and made sure the bureaucracy carried out their orders. Sandwiched between these duties, the royal ministers listened to reports of Castilian ambassadors back from Rome or Paris, haggled with military commanders asking for more money and chastised tax farmers when revenues were too low.

As did the framers of the American Constitution, the Counselors held their deliberations in absolute secrecy to isolate themselves from public pressure or recrimination. Mace bearers guarded the door to the Council chamber to keep out the uninvited, and porters allowed entrance only to petitioners whose names appeared on the daily agenda. To eliminate time-wasting squabbles, the rules forbid the Counselors from speaking unless they had a new point to make. Simply agreeing with a previous speaker or repeating an opposition position was not permitted. If serious disagreements erupted during the Royal Council's debates, Ferdinand or Isabel made the final decision. So intent were Isabel and Ferdinand that the Royal Council pay attention to business, the Sovereigns exempted the Counselors from going through all the formalities required when the King or Queen attended a meeting.

To keep Ferdinand and Isabel abreast of the Royal Council's decisions, a clerk kept a written record of its resolutions regarding appointments, foreign policy and military and tax matters. Early in the King and Queen's reign, the Royal Council's powers were broad and ill-defined. By 1493, Ferdinand and Isabel broke through the fuzzy lines of jurisdiction and established a Council of State to handle foreign policy and political matters, a Council of Justice, a Council of Finance and a Council of the Treasury.[5]

Although new procedures and reorganization streamlined the Royal Council, the most important step Isabel and Ferdinand took was to refashion the cast of characters with "new men" to serve as Counselors. No longer would the Dukes, Counts and Admirals of Castile have the hereditary right to wield political power. In 1480, the Parliament of Toledo stated hopefully that: "Since the desire for reward is the spur to just and honorable actions, when men perceive that offices of trust are not to descend by inheritance, but to be conferred on merit, they will strive to excel in virtue, so that they may attain its reward." These "new men," the Sovereigns' men, would serve as the essential elements in the transition from medieval government to a modern state.

These men, *letrados,* were the sons of lesser nobility, wealthy merchants, converted Jews *(conversos)* and, on occasion, men from the lower class. They received their educations as lawyers at the great universities; Salamanca, Valladolid and Alcala. Like modern-day students from Harvard or Oxford, graduates of the Castilian universities formed an old-boy network within the government.

By the 1500s, over half the members of the Councils of State and Justice were graduates of these three universities. The universities fed their fresh *letrado* graduates into the lower posts of the bureaucracy, and the more diligent worked their way up to become ambassadors, judges and Counselors. Today's graduate of the University of Buenos Aires or the National University of Mexico looking for a job with the Ministry of Foreign Relations would understand the system perfectly.

By appointing and promoting educated men of merit, Ferdinand and Isabel created a new career track for ambitious young Castilians. Now, a man from the middle classes had a new outlet to achieve status and fortune, a new social mobility. Becoming a military entrepreneur or a clergyman was no longer the only route to success. Now, a bright young man could enter the university and find a job in the service of the *casa real* (royal government).

Despite the medieval idea that too much social mobility

threatened the stability of the state, the King and Queen believed that the elite should be continually regenerated by men of talent. Most important to the Sovereigns, they created a corps of government servants who owed their jobs to the royal command and whose only loyalty was to the crown. Blood and lineage remained important, but the primary criteria for advancement under the Sovereigns were intelligence, honesty and fealty. "They [Isabel and Ferdinand] took care to appoint discreet and capable officials, even though they were of the middle class, rather than important figures from the [noble] houses," a member of the Royal Council wrote.[6]

To keep up with the *letrados,* the King and Queen maintained a roster of their "new men" listing their backgrounds, qualifications and experience. So clever were the royal couple in picking good men that Ferdinand built Spain's foreign service into a grid of ambassadors and agents that was "second to none in Europe and laid the groundwork for his successes in foreign policy." In 1514, the Castilian scholar Nebrija wrote that "the power [in Europe] is held by the Spanish monarches who, masters of a large part of Italy and the Mediterranean, carry the war to Africa and send out their ships, following the course of the stars, to the Isles of the Indies and the New World."[7] It was the *letrados,* scattered throughout the government and sitting on the Royal Council, who permitted this to happen.

Although the Royal Council held great power, when issues of major importance crossed Ferdinand and Isabel's desks, the Council's authority was limited to recommending, consulting and coordinating policy—not initiating. "Ferdinand and Isabel were their own ministers," the French historian Jean Mariejol writes. "United by a rare community of sentiments and views, they personally directed foreign affairs and internal administration; they were too fond of power to relinquish it into other hands." There were a few exceptions to the Sovereigns holding on to power, most notably the extraordinary trust they placed in Cardinal Mendoza (The Third King). As the King and Queen extended their control over the Royal Council, they also began to assert their influence over the powerful Castilian military orders.

11

THE MILITARY ORDERS

By the time of Isabel and Ferdinand, the myth of Santiago Matamoros (St. James the Moor Slayer) captivated the minds and souls of Castilians. To Castilians, Santiago was both a spiritual and corporeal figure who fought beside them when they plunged into the Moorish ranks. Leading the Castilians in the Holy Crusade against the Sons of Islam, their patron saint charged into the turbaned infidels' lines of battle on his white warhorse, his flailing broadsword leaving thousands of dark-skinned corpses on the field. Castilians called their legendary comrade in arms to the battlefield with the strident cries *"Santiago! Cierre Espana!"* (St. James! Close in Spain!) and *"Dios ayuda y Santiago!"* (With the help of God and St. James!).

In Santiago's holy bones, the Castilians found an antidote to the Iberian Muslims' sacred relic, the carefully preserved arm of the Prophet Muhammad. The Arabs' *Jihad* (Holy War) almost pushed the Christians out of Iberia after the Islamic invasion in 711. The Christians believed that, with the physical presence of Santiago fighting beside them, they were invincible. So strong was the cult of Santiago that, during Cortes and Pizarro's conquest of the New World, Jesus Christ's militant cousin was supposedly seen "with his sword flashing lightening in the eyes of the Indians."[1] Between 1518 and 1892, Spaniards reported no less than thirteen miraculous appearances of Santiago.[2]

The centuries-old legend begins shortly after the Crucifixion of Christ.[3] Santiago, the son of the Virgin Mary's sister Salome and Christ's cousin, came from Jerusalem to Galicia in northwestern Castile to spread the new-found Holy Faith. Although he converted only nine barbarians during his time in Iberia, the legend credits Santiago with implanting Christianity in the peninsula. After six years of proselytizing, Santiago returned to Jerusalem where King Herod Agrippa martyred him by decapitation in 44 A.D. After his execution, Santiago's followers opened his grave to find the severed head mysteriously reattached to his body. They embalmed his remains and took them by ship back to Galicia for final burial at the site of a Roman cemetery.

Santiago's body lay hidden among the pagan Romans in Galicia for almost eight hundred years until, sometime around 814, a hermit saw a supernatural light from a bright star shining on a solitary oak tree standing on a hill. When the amazing light, accompanied by the strains of heavenly music, continued for several nights, the hermit carried the news of the celestial omen to the Christian bishop. On his arrival, the bishop found an altar and an inscription saying that Santiago, Christ's disciple, was buried at that spot. Astounded by these holy portents, the bishop summoned the Christian king to the site who, to consecrate the bones of Santiago, ordered a shrine to be built at what became the town of Santiago de Compostela (derived from the Latin *campus stellae*, the field of the star).

The legend continues with the Battle of Clavijo in 844.[4] On the first day of the battle, the Moors mauled the greatly outnumbered Christian troops. That night, the apparition of Santiago, mounted on his white charger, holding a white flag with a blood red cross, appeared to the Christian king in a dream. The warrior saint, the Christian king said, described to him the tactics that would bring certain victory. The king told his soldiers Santiago had assumed personal command of the reconquest of Iberia from the Muslims. With Santiago Matamoros' spirit leading them into the field the next day, the Christians slaughtered the Moors.

There were other miracles. One told of a groom who was riding along the beach to his wedding and was swept into the sea by a huge wave. His bride appealed to Santiago to save her lover, and the young man rose out of the sea covered with cockleshells.[5] Another legend said that Christ's cousin used the cockleshell to baptize converts. Whatever the story, the cockleshell became the emblem of Santiago.

As word of these wondrous happenings spread throughout Europe, thousands of pilgrims swarmed to Santiago de Compostela to seal their faith and ease their way into Heaven. In time, Santiago de Compostela, Rome and Jerusalem became the three holiest places in Christendom. The faithful streamed to the shrine from France, Germany, England, Holland, Norway and Sweden to pay homage to the sainted bones. Laymen came for salvation, churchmen to fulfill their vows, criminals to receive forgiveness and merchants to do business. Even Chaucer's Wife of Bath visited "Galice at Seint Jame" to venerate Santiago's remains. Most of the pilgrims began their trek in central France, walking or riding south to cross the Pyrenees Mountains and then west to Santiago de Compostela.

Cobblers along the nine hundred-mile route from Paris did a brisk business repairing or replacing the sandals many of the pilgrims wore. To warm themselves from the cold of the mountain passes, travelers donned coarse woolen cloaks. Many pilgrims wore the traditional headgear, a round, broad brimmed hat with the front brim folded up and pinned with cockleshells. For protection, they carried long wooden staffs with water gourds tied to the top. To secure their travel money, the faithful tied purses full of coins to their belts. Despite these precautions, highwaymen robbed or murdered some of the pilgrims and some died from polluted water or disease.

Even though the trip could be dangerous, travelers continued to come. To house them, inns *(posadas)* lined the road from Roncesvalles to Pamplona to Burgos to Ponferrada on in to Santiago de Compostela. Some of the Castilian inns were miserable, and one Frenchman writing during the mid-1400s, ranked them lower than French pigpens.[6] The pilgrims ate food cooked in pots the scullery maids seldom washed, gathered their own firewood, slept on beds crawling with aggressive vermin and were fleeced by innkeepers charging exorbitant prices.

Since Castilian palates were not demanding, the travelers were likely to be fed garlic seasoned with olive oil, stewed cabbages and laborers' bread. The Castilian peasants the pilgrims met "...are badly dressed. They eat poorly and drink worse. Using no spoons, they plunge their hands into the common pot and drink from the same goblet. When one sees them eat, one thinks he is seeing pigs in their gluttony; and when one hears them speak, he thinks of dogs baying. They are...disloyal, corrupted, voluptuous, expert in every violence, cruel and quarrelsome....Shamefully, they have sex with animals."[7]

After suffering dangers and discomforts on the road, if the pilgrims arrived at Santiago de Compostela during peak seasons, there were not enough lodgings, so many people slept in the streets wrapped in their heavy woolen cloaks. When they crowded into Santiago's cathedral to view the sainted relics, the stench of human body odors was so strong that priests swung a huge container of smoking incense from the ceiling to stifle the smell.

To put a stop to the rampant price gouging by the innkeepers and the violence on the holy road, a cadre of knights allied themselves with the monks of St. Lojo to form the military order of Santiago. They chose as their emblems the cockleshell and the red cross, the red on the cross symbolizing that it was stained by the blood of the infidels. In 1175, the Pope officially chartered the order of Santiago and bound its members to abide by the rules of the Augustinian religious order. The Knights of Santiago swore to help the poor, defend the traveller and carry out perpetual war on the Moors. They adopted all the elements of medieval chivalry; obedience, the saintliness of women, courage and a strict code of honor *(pundonor)*.

The Knights disdained the man who worked for a living, reserving their respect only for the man who would rather die than desert his post and who won riches and glory by the sword—the military entrepreneur. The perfect Knight, they believed, lived for war and, through sheer physical courage and constant effort of will, could achieve the impossible in the service of God. Since their charter, their legitimacy, came from the Pope, the Knights of Santiago combined their martial doctrines with those of the Church, producing a unique brand of militant Christianity. Although they believed that they were participating in a holy mission as crusading soldiers of the Faith, these high ideas didn't eliminate their desire for booty and riches.

Another band of monks and knights founded the second largest military order to defend mountain passes between Castilian and Moorish territories. The order of Calatrava, chartered in 1164 by the Pope, adopted most of the religious and chivalric underpinnings of their brothers in the order of Santiago, but with at least one difference. In addition to vows of poverty and obedience, the Knights of Calatrava swore to remain perpetually celibate, a rule that was apparently violated with frequency.

Gaining admission to the warrior fraternity was similar to the steps required to enter the clergy. A young man was sent to a convent for his novitiate where he was instructed in the aggressive Christian doctrines of the order. Upon taking the habit *(habito)* of the order of Calatrava, the young man took his vows to live a life of austere self-denial under the stern rules of the Benedictines. The Knights owned their property in common, ate only the plainest food and had meat only three times a week. At meals, in chapel and in their dormitories, the Knights of Calatrava maintained absolute silence. They wore their swords to chapel and, to symbolize their readiness for action, slept with their swords buckled on.

The third great military order of Castile, Alcantara, was a split off from the order of Calatrava. Chartered by the Pope in 1177, the Knights of Alcantara saw their role and their mission in the same way as did their brothers in the other two military orders. There were minor differences between the orders, but they were basically organized and operated in the same manner. Each order had a Grand Master and a governing counsel elected by its Knights and, in the case of Calatrava, its associated clergy. Originally, the kings of Castile only ratified an order's choice of a Grand Master by ceremonially handing over the order's flag to the new man. As the brotherhoods of Knights grew more powerful during the 1200 and 1300s the kings and the Popes began intervening in the election process. Once in office, the Grand Master appointed, as his lieutenants, commanders who directly controlled the lands and estates owned by the order. Under the commanders were the nobles of the order *(caballeros de la orden),* all of whom were granted aristocratic status.

Inspired by the crusades against the infidels in Jerusalem, the Knights of the Castilian military orders fought bravely against the Iberian Moors. At least partly because the Christian kings could not administer all of the new territories they conquered, the monarches rewarded the military orders with grants of extensive lands, fortresses, towns, villages and vassals. During the three centuries between their foundings and the accession of Ferdinand and Isabel to the throne, the Castilian military orders accumulated enormous wealth, becoming mini-kingdoms within Castile, with their own courts and absolute control over the serfs who worked their lands. They became so rich that Ferdinand estimated that the income of the three military orders exceeded that of the Kingdom of Naples.

The order of Santiago had seven hundred thousand vassals and 22.5 million maravedis in annual income, Calatrava had two hundred thousand vassals and 1.5 million maravedis and Alcantara had 100,000 vassals and 1.7 million maravedis.[8] Since the military orders had both noble and ecclesiastical status, these vast incomes were exempt from many taxes. In addition to their wealth, the military orders provided jobs as commanders and officials of the orders to some fifteen hundred second sons of the nobles and the sons of wealthy merchants anxious for their children to obtain aristocratic status. Because of their extensive income and patronage, elections to the Grand Masterships involved the most intricate plotting and bribery, frequently resulting in intimidation, violence and murder.

Medieval Castilian kings and Popes attempted to influence the military orders and their elections, but, by the time of Ferdinand and Isabel, the aristocrats controlled the warrior fraternities.[9] In the 1460s, the powerful Pacheco family maneuvered one of its members into the Grand Mastership of Calatrava, and almost succeeded in marrying him to Isabel. Later, the leader of the Pacheco's, the Marquis of Villena, resigned his marquisate in favor of his son to accept the more lucrative Grand Mastership of Santiago. From this power base, Villena, as the Grand Master of Santiago, threw his influence behind La Beltraneja's claims to the throne against Isabel's in the War of Succession.

Because of their wealth, patronage and power to threaten the crown, Isabel and Ferdinand planned to subjugate the military orders to the royal leash. Because the aristocrats dominated the orders, at first the royal couple treated them gingerly. When the Grand Mastership of Santiago fell vacant in 1476, an intense rivalry to succeed to the post developed. Isabel rode for three days on horseback from Valladolid to the convent of Ucles where the Knights of Santiago were meeting to elect a new Grand Master. At first she threatened. She told the Knights that she had applied to the Pope for the right to appoint the new Grand Master. Then, the Queen said, she would not permit the violence and disruption caused by the elections. Finally, Isabel appealed to their patriotism, saying that the order controlled too many important fortresses along the borders with Moorish Granada, raising those strongholds to the level of national importance. Only a monarch, who had the interests of the whole kingdom at heart, should control the military orders. Ferdinand, the Queen said, would be pleased to accept the vacant Grand Mastership of Santiago.

The Knights of Santiago and their backers among the *grandees* resisted. There was too much at stake. Giving up their power to name the Grand Master and the loss of loyal support from the coterie of men they appointed as commanders and Knights of the order was a direct royal threat.. Despite the hostility, Isabel refused to back down. Grudgingly, the Knights of Santiago agreed to Ferdinand's appointment. Even though the Knights consented under pressure, Isabel knew she had touched a raw nerve. It was time to compromise. Ferdinand, she said, would waive his right to the Grand Mastership if the order would accept the royal couple's faithful friend, Alonso de Cardenas, who was not a *grandee*. Under the agreement, when Cardenas died, Ferdinand would succeed him. The Knights of Santiago agreed to the compromise, and, upon Cardenas' death in 1499, Ferdinand became Grand Master of Santiago for life.

After the Grand Master of Calatrava died in 1487, Ferdinand appeared in person before the Knights and produced a Papal Bull conferring the Grand Mastership on himself. When the Knights of Calatrava resisted, Ferdinand bluntly told them that, if the Knights wouldn't accept the Pope's order, he would use force. By 1487 the Sovereigns were too firmly seated on their thrones, and the Calatravans capitulated. Then came the Order of Alcantara's turn. In 1494, Ferdinand and Isabel, in effect, bought the post by offering the Grand Master of Alcantara the Bishopric of Seville in exchange for Ferdinand's appointment. The Grand Master accepted.

To solidify their power over the warrior fraternities, the King and Queen established the Royal Council of the Military Orders in about 1489 to supervise and administer them in the name of the crown.[10] Now, if the Kingdom needed access to the orders' income, it could be pledged as collateral for loans for the good of the nation as a whole. Their new authority gave Ferdinand and Isabel yet another tool to reward loyal supporters of proven merit with jobs as commanders and Knights of the orders. Most pleasing to the Sovereigns, the usurpation of the Grand Masterships "dealt the nobility a dreadful blow."[11]

12

THE BEGINNING

Invasions and colonizations over centuries shaped and molded Ferdinand and Isabel's Spain. Stone Age hunters, Iberians, Celts, Phoenicians, Greeks, Carthagenians, Romans, Vandals, Visigoths and Arabs all left their stamp on the royal couple's kingdom. When Ferdinand and Isabel came to the throne in 1474, these cultural strains, together with feudalism and Catholicism, had blended an identifiable Spanish character, a way of thinking and doing that was different from their European cousins.

The stenciled outline of a thirteen thousand[1] year old man's hand at the Caves of Altamira marks the earliest trace of the hunters who roamed the wild Cantabrian Mountains of northern Spain. This Stone Age man placed his hand flush on the clammy cave wall and splattered red-brown paint around his hand to form an indelible personal reminder of his existence. He and his tribesmen sketched the bison, musk ox, goats and other animals they stalked for food and clothing to protect themselves from the cold northern winters. These prehistoric hunters vanished with the coming of the glaciers during the Ice Age, leaving an historical gap until the Iberians crossed from Africa in about 3,000 B.C. to occupy the southern two-thirds of the Peninsula that took their name.

Between 900 B.C. and 600 B.C., waves of Celts from Germany and France drifted into Spain. Wearing leather helmets crowned with Viking-like horns, these Celtic tribesmen settled mostly in the cold, damp northern provinces of modern-day Galicia and Asturias. Over the centuries, the Celts and Iberians melded, creating the Celtiberian culture that dominated the central areas of the

Peninsula. While the Celtiberians knitted their rough civilization in the middle of the country, the Phoenicians and Greeks rowed their galleys across the Mediterranean Sea to establish coastal trading posts at Cadiz, Malaga and other ports. These traders and merchants sailed through the straits between the Pillars of Hercules, the twin mountains facing one another at Ceuta in North Africa and Gibraltar, and may have pushed their commercial ventures to Portugal and Galicia.

Although the Phoenicians and Greeks came primarily to do business, they brought a glimpse of sophistication to the isolated Peninsula. While the Phoenicians and Greeks scouted for commerce in metals and other goods from their fortified trading posts on the eastern and southern coasts, the Celtiberians learned to cultivate the grape vines and olive trees introduced by the Greeks, and adapted Phoenician and Greek techniques in architecture, statuary and pottery to local tastes.

In about 300 B.C., the Carthagenians stormed across the Straits of Gibraltar, upsetting Iberia's trade routes to the eastern Mediterranean. The Carthagenian established major bases at Barcelona and New Carthage (later Cartagena) and captured Celtiberian hostages to be held as ransom against the possibility of rebellion. The Carthagenians soon dominated the east coast of Iberia, and began organizing their army of mercenaries, officered by Carthagenian aristocrats, for an invasion of Rome. Antiquity's great general, Hannibal, marched his men and elephants up the Iberian coast, then east through southern France and over the Alps into Italy. Although Hannibal defeated the Roman legions at Cannae in 216 B.C., the Romans had sent an army to Iberia to cut the Carthagenian's land communications through Iberia to Italy. After the Romans pushed the Carthagenians back across the Mediterranean Sea, they launched two centuries of colonization of the entire Peninsula. Unlike the Phoenicians and Greeks, the Romans were not content to establish trading posts along the coast. They meant to dominate, to exploit, to implant Roman civilization in the province they called Hispania.

Determined to incorporate Hispania into their empire, the Romans battled the wild Celtiberian tribes for control of the Peninsula for the next two hundred years. The Roman legions faced off against Celtiberians whose "bodies [are] inured to abstinence and toil, their minds composed against death....They prefer war to ease, and, if they lack foes without, [they] seek them within. Rather than betray a secret, they will often die under torture...."[2] Trained from childhood to ride horses and hit their marks with javelins and slingshots, the fierce Celtiberian guerrilla fighters struck their enemy in lightening raids and returned to the safety of their mountain strongholds. The battles were so vicious that many Roman officers refused to volunteer for Iberian service and some veteran Roman soldiers refused to march with their officers. When the Celtiberians captured Roman legionnaires, they ceremonially butchered them or dumped them off jagged cliffs to their deaths. The Romans reciprocated cruelty with cruelty, crucifying their prisoners and committing other acts of brutality that caused many Celtiberian warriors to carry a handful of poisoned leaves to swallow if they were caught alive. The Celtiberians' hit and run tactics frustrated many of Rome's greatest generals, including Julius Caesar when he was governor of Hispania in 61-60 B.C. During the reign of the Emperor Augustus, a Roman army brought the Pax Romana to the Peninsula in 19 B. C. when it finally conquered that "wild Cantabrian land which (refused to) bow to the Roman yoke."[3]

As a satellite of Rome, Hispania caught the crest of Rome's civilizing wave, and rode that wave for the next four hundred years. With peace established in the Peninsula, Hispania became the empire's wealthiest province, supplying grain, olive oil, wine, wool, fruits and fine horses. Hispania's mines produced gold, silver, iron, tin, lead and copper for their Roman masters. Even though the Romans exploited their province, they plowed back some of Hispania's wealth into bridges, aqueducts, sewage systems, amphitheaters and circuses. To move goods and Roman legions, they built a twelve thousand mile highway system, the most famous being the Via Augusta which ran from Cadiz in southernmost Hispania to the Pyrenees and on into Rome.

The roads helped make Hispania a rich marketplace for the import and export of goods. More importantly, the highways opened the Peninsula's doors to Roman culture. Sometimes by force, the Romans wrenched Hispania out of its domination by illiterate, semi-civilized tribes into the mainstream of history. The imperial Roman love of hierarchy and order offset the Celtiberian's proclivity toward tribalism and separatism. Beginning with Augustus, Rome enforced its mandate to "rule the Earth's people...to pacify, to impose the rule of law, to spare the conquered, [to] battle down the proud."[4] Their language, Latin, became the lengua franc of Hispania, eventually blotting out most dialects and languages that formed a barrier to human and mercantile commerce. Although Latin helped unify Iberia, it was not the pure, classic Latin of Rome. Hispania's "vulgar" Latin was a blend of the language of uneducated Roman soldiers and immigrants and of traders from all parts of the Roman world who spoke Latin as a second language. To this mix, the natives added an overlay of their own pronunciation and local idioms to form the roots of what developed into Castilian Spanish.

Along with a coherent language, the Romans introduced their engineering, city planning, art, philosophy, literature and legal system. While Hispanians learned from Rome, they contributed their share to the greatness of the Roman empire. Seneca the Elder, a Cordoban, wrote volumes on oratorical style and Roman law. His son, Seneca the Younger, immigrated from Cordoba to Rome and became one of the greatest stoic philosophers. Seneca's reputation as a scholar earned him the prestigious post of tutor to the emperor-to-be Nero. After Nero assumed power, he accused Seneca of plotting to assassinate him, and ordered the philosopher to commit suicide. Following the stoic doctrine of bearing life's burdens with dignity, Seneca dutifully slit his veins. Other Hispanians fared better in Rome. The Emperor Vespasian appointed the author-lawyer-educator Quintilian professor of rhetoric, and his twelve-volume work, *Institutio Oratoria*, remained a standard reference book on oratory long past the Renaissance period.

Hispania's most colorful intellectual was Martial, a witty Aragonese satirist who moved to Rome when he was twenty four. The Romans delighted in his epigrams, "Live today—tomorrow will be too late," and "The hours die and are charged against us."[5] They loved Martial's puns, parodies and graphic pornography, an art form common at the time, praising the sensuous dancing girls whose "gracefully raised arms, swirling figures, sinuous movements and dark emotions" fascinated him. Tired of the lawsuits, intrigues and violence of Rome, Martial returned to the quiet pleasures of rural life on a farm near Zaragoza. "Give me a healthy native-born servant," Martial said, "a wife who is not a prude...and my days without litigation." Writing to his friend Juvenal, he said "Here [in Hispania] we live lazily and work pleasantly...and I enjoy a vast and shameless sleep. Often I don't wake up until after 10 o'clock, and so I'm making up for all the sleep I lost in 30 years [in Rome]. You won't find togas here....That's how I like to live, and that's how I hope to die."

Although Martial was happier away from Rome's conniving politicians, four of Hispania's sons ruled as Roman emperors. Trajan, born near Seville, added England, Romania, Arabia, Iraq and Armenia to the empire during his reign from 98 to 117 A.D. Trajan's nephew and adopted son, Hadrian,[6] followed his adoptive father in office. Hadrian consolidated his father's new territories into the empire, "encouraged the arts, reformed the laws... and visited all his provinces in person."[7] His love of architecture beautified many of Hispania's cities, but his installation of the *coloni* system, which bound tenant farmers to the soil, laid the groundwork of feudalism in the province.

After Hadrian came Antoninius Pius, followed by Marcus Aurelius. As a boy, Marcus Aurelius adopted stoicism which taught him to submerge his passions with his reason and to consider virtue as the only good and vice as the only evil. Even though Marcus Aurelius was partial to philosophy, as emperor he spent much of his time in an army tent as a general. When Marcus Aurelius wasn't pouring over battle maps, he studied stoicism, and became a profound scholar who influenced his era with his brilliant writings on stoic philosophy.

While Romans debated the fine points of philosophy, the fate of Christians and Jews varied with the whims of the emperors during the Hispano-Roman period. Hadrian favored the Jews, and some fifty thousand flocked into Hispania from their desert homelands in the Middle East,[8] building synagogues and openly celebrating the Hebrew sabbath and feast days without fear. Gibbon says the Jews received such liberal treatment because, at that time, "the Jews were a nation [while] the Christians were only a sect" and it was Rome's policy to respect the "sacred institutions of their neighbors...and it was universally acknowledged that they had the right to practice their religion."

Christians enjoyed many of the same privileges under the more tolerant emperors, but the Emperor Diocletian (285 to 305 A.D.) and others persecuted rebellious Christians who refused to bow down to the galaxy of Roman gods. The Romans slaughtered eighteen Christians in Zaragoza, and martyred Saint Vincent in Valencia[9] and Saint Eulalia in Merida. Eager to die for the Faith, Saint Eulalia confronted the Roman magistrates shouting "The old [Roman] gods are worthless. The Emperor himself is nothing." To accommodate her wish for martyrdom, the Romans tied Saint Eulalia's arms behind her back and ripped the young girl's body to pieces with red hot pincers. Until the Emperor Constantine prohibited the persecutions in the early 300s, Christians intermittently suffered bones cracked, tongues ripped out and breasts cut off. In 380, the Emperor Theodosius made Christianity the state religion of the Roman Empire. As the Roman Empire began to crumble in the late 300s and early 400s, the Catholic Church took on a secular as well as a religious role, providing one of the few sources of centralization and stability in Hispania.

In addition to weaving the Catholic Church into the fabric of the state, Rome's six hundred years of rule in Hispania left an imprint that survived through the reign of Ferdinand and Isabel and beyond. Roman and Church law formed the nucleus of an organized legal system in Iberia. The language of empire, Latin, bound the country together in its early days, and created the basis for Castilian Spanish, the language that unified Spain's empire. Perhaps the most damaging legacy was to polarize political thinking between the extremes of Roman authoritarianism and hierarchy and the old Iberian traditions of tribalism and anarchy. Only during the briefest interludes in her history has Spain been able to enjoy a viable democracy, the greatest compromise between absolutism and chaos. The Romans firmly implanted these concepts and institutions, both good and bad, in the Hispano-Romans, and the institutions survived invasions of Vandals, Visigoths and Arabs.

Just as Christianity was becoming entrenched in Iberia, the Roman Empire began to crack. In 409, three Germanic tribes, who were invited into Hispania by a Roman general making a bid for personal power, over-ran the Peninsula. The most brutal of the tribes, the Vandals,[10] settled mostly in southern Hispania and named the province Vandalusia (Land of the Vandals), giving the region the root of its present name, Andalusia.[11] A few years later, in 418, the Romans offered to sign a treaty with the nomadic Visigoths which would allow them to invade Hispania on behalf of Rome and crush the Vandals and the other Germanic tribes. The partially Romanized Visigoths accepted the offer. Since Rome was already splintered by decay, the Visigoths forgot their pact with Rome and took power for themselves.[12] Unlike the Anglo-Saxons in England, the Visigoths didn't impose their Germanic language on the natives, and "vulgar" Latin remained the language of the people. In addition to the language barrier between the new rulers and their subjects, the aloof Visigoths remained an aristocratic and military elite, seldom intermarrying with the native Hispano-Romans. Although the Romans urbanized and commercialized Hispania with the five hundred towns they created, the Visigoths took the country back to agriculture and pasturing.

Even though the Visigoths were partially Romanized, they hadn't adopted the Roman version of Christianity. Their Arian strain of Christianity further separated them from the Hispano-Romans by insisting that there was a single God, not a trinity composed of the Father, Son and Holy Ghost. To the Arian Visigoths, Jesus was only a great prophet, not God come to earth. Because of the schism, the Visigoths launched a campaign of persecution against the Hispano-Roman Catholics, desecrating churches, torturing or executing the faithful and exiling the lucky ones. When the Visigoths weren't persecuting Roman Catholics, they spent much of the next two hundred years battling old

Hispano-Roman factions and pockets of Celtiberians until they achieved mastery over most of the Peninsula around 600. In 589, the Visigoth King Recared converted from Arianism to Roman Catholicism. King Recared's conversion brought further peace to Iberia and commenced an unbroken link between Church and state on the Peninsula.

With Roman Catholicism as their new state religion, the Visigoths turned with ferocity on Iberia's thousands of Jews. Many of the Peninsula's Jews were prosperous and well-educated, making them an easy mark for Christian jealousy and avarice. With the fervent ardor of the newly converted, the Visigoths codified their prejudices in the law. The *Fuero Juzco* of 654 forbid the celebration of Passover, circumcision and marriage according to Jewish rites. The *Fuero Juzco* stipulated one hundred lashes for Jews who refused to baptize their children. Other laws, which weren't heavily enforced, required Jews to become Christians or go into exile, and permitted selling Jews into slavery, except for their children under seven who were to be brought up as Christians. When the Jews rebelled, the Visigoth overlords repressed them with brutality—torture, death, slavery or confiscation of their property. Some Jews converted to Christianity to survive, others maintained their old religion and weathered the fury of Christian zeal and abuse.

While the Jews suffered, the detached Visigoth nobles in their capital at Toledo pranced and preened in their velvet slippers, elegant robes and massive gold jewelry studded with gemstones. Long gone were the scraggly long hair, leather armor and rough woolen cloaks worn by their nomadic ancestors. Now, secluded and isolated in their palaces, the Visigoth aristocrats earned the hatred of their Hispano-Roman vassals and oppressed Jews. Having lost the support of the underclass, the Visigoths further weakened the kingdom by clinging to their ancient custom of electing their rulers from the peerage. When a king died, the struggles for succession often split the nobles into rival factions whose bitter strife erupted in civil war.

One of those wars of succession proved fatal. When the Visigoth king died in 710, a group of nobles passed over the king's hand-picked successor and elected Roderick to the throne. The followers of the dead King's choice rebelled against Roderick, and Count Julian, the governor of the Visigoth's North African outpost at Ceuta, joined in the revolt against Roderick. In legend, Count Julian opposed Roderick because Roderick had raped Count Julian' beautiful daughter while she was taking a bath in the Tagus River at Toledo.[13] Poets romanticized the alleged incident:

"[Julian's daughter] was the first

Who cast off her clothes.
In the shadowy pool
Her body shone so fair
That, like the sun,
She eclipsed all others there."[14]

Roderick, unaware that Julian knew of the rape, asked the Count to send him a rare breed of falcon from Africa. Julian agreed to send King Roderick "hawks such as the King never dreamed of." Shortly thereafter, the "hawks," about seven thousand[15] Muslim warriors, united with Julian and crossed the Straits of Gibraltar to attack the amorous Roderick who had been unable to control his "love [which] with beating wings, inflamed him."

Although the legend makes a good story, it is true that a Moorish general, Tarik, ferried his army across the nine-mile-wide Straits on a reconnaissance mission and landed at the northern Pillar of Hercules, which the Arabs named Gebel al Tarik (Mountain of Tarik, later shortened to Gibraltar). The Islamic invaders met King Roderick on July 19, 711, at the Battle of Guadalete near the town of Jerez de la Frontera in the south. Before the battle began, general Tarik told his men: "Before us is the enemy; behind us the sea. We have only one choice; to win!"[16] Spurred by their fervid belief in Islam, and a healthy desire for the booty that awaited them, the Arabs crushed Roderick's army. The King was either killed or fled, the only trace of his existence being his white horse with a saddle of gilded buckskin, his cloth of gold cape and one silver shoe. In a sense, the Christian debacle was another bit of luck for Iberia. Just as the Peninsula rode the crest of Rome's wave of civilization and culture, it would follow the Moorish crescent during Islam's golden age, while Europe festered in the Dark Ages.

After Tarik won the easy victory at the Battle of Guadalete, his turbaned forces marched from town to town in more of a procession than an invasion. Tarik's superior, Musa ibn Nusair, the Arab viceroy of North Africa, joined him with more troops, and they rolled up the Peninsula, meeting little or no resistance. As the Arabs advanced, Christians took statutes of the Virgin Mary from the churches and buried them in remote places. Centuries later, when Spanish shepherds or farmers found some of the statutes, the local bishops proclaimed the discoveries were "miracles" sent from Heaven. When the Moors arrived at the Visigoth capital at Toledo a few months after the Battle of Guadalete, its citizens swung open the city's gates without a fight, and Musa placed Iberia under the sovereignty of the Caliph (Emperor) of Damascus. The Visigoths themselves made possible the "indecent ease" of the Arab conquest. The civil war over Roderick's succession divided the pleasure-loving Visigoth nobles. "Two awful years of pestilence and famine"[17] weakened them further.

The Jews, who suffered terrible persecution by the Visigothic Catholic Church, welcomed the Arabs as saviors and treated them as allies. Separated from the mass of the Hispano-Roman population by their arrogance, the Visigoth aristocrats had no support from below. In only seven years, the Moors conquered all of Iberia, except for a small slice of territory behind the Cantabrian mountains in Galicia and Asturias in the north. No nation so large fell apart so fast to an invader with so few men.

Although the internal weakness of the Visigothic kingdom provided an open invitation to the Moors, perhaps the greatest reason for the Christian collapse was the impetus provided by a part-time caravan leader and shopkeeper from Mecca—the Prophet Mohammed. Before he died in 632, Mohammed fused the teachings of Christianity and Judaism, and created his religion of Islam. Mohammed agreed with the Christians that there was a single God, that the dead could be resurrected and that a final judgment sent one to Heaven or Hell. Moses and Jesus, Mohammed said, were entitled to respect, but only as wise prophets and teachers, nothing more. The Christians claimed that Heaven was the only place of ultimate reward, but Mohammed taught his flock that fighting for Islam rewarded the true believers on earth—and in paradise.

Upon death in battle, Mohammed claimed, the faithful go directly to Heaven to enjoy an even higher level of the earthly pleasures. "The holy war (*jihad*) is the ladder to paradise,"a Saracen general said.[18] Non-believers were to be conquered, rather than converted, but the conquered must pay tribute to support the Sons of Allah. On earth, the Muslim faithful found other rewards.

> "We, Arab women, are the daughters of the morning star;
> Soft are the carpets we tread beneath our feet;
> Our necks are adorned with pearls, and our tresses areper fumed with musk.
> The brave who confront the foe we will clasp to our bosoms;
> But the dastards who flee we will spurn;
> Not for them our embraces."[19]

During the eighty years after the Prophet Mohammed's death, Muslims emerged from their nomads' tents in the Middle Eastern deserts to sweep all across North Africa. Disciplined by their five daily prayer sessions, supplied by caravans of camels, their light cavalry of desert tribesmen rode to victory after victory. Inspired by the urge to expand, the will to conquer and the spiritual flame lit by their Prophet, Muslim warriors would, in time, control an empire larger than that of Rome.

Even though Mohammed taught that dying in the service of Allah guaranteed them a special martyr's place in Heaven, when the Moors met the Christians in the craggy mountains of northwest Iberia, their advance stalled. After suffering a defeat at the hands of the Christian leader who the Moors called "[that] savage ass named Pelayo" in 718 at the Battle of Covadonga, the Muslims stopped. Although the Battle of Covadonga was probably little more than a skirmish between an Arab scouting party and a few Christians, the Muslim defeat took on a mythical, much larger significance in the Christians' minds. They had their first hero, Pelayo, the man who proved that the Moors were not invincible.

If Allah's disciples had followed the Prophet's teachings and cleaned out the nests of Christians in northwest Iberia, there might never have been a Reconquest, and Iberia might have remained perpetually Muslim. The Arab decision to leave the infidel Christians in control of the Cantabrian mountains left Jesus' followers with a staging ground from which to drive the Moors out of the Peninsula. Instead of mopping up the ragged, poorly organized Christian mountain men, the Arabs crossed the Pyrenees into France. They pushed as far north as Poitiers, where the Frankish King Charles Martel defeated them in 732, saving Europe from Muslin domination.

After Charles Martel forced them back into the Iberian Peninsula, the Moors began fighting among themselves, and Arab war lords carved their new province, Al Andalus, into petty satrapies. They were a people with "fierce character, pride, roughness and jealousy of one another, especially in political matters, [making] them the most difficult people to lead...because every Arab regards himself as worthy to rule," an Arab writer said.[20] These personal characteristics, sectarian differences between Sunnis and Shiites, family feuds, greed and ethnic rivalries, kept Muslims at each others' throats for most of the next fifty years.[21] The Moors reached a partial modus vivendi when the Arabs and Syrians settled down in the lush lands of the south and east. While those more sophisticated Muslims were busy establishing their capital at Cordoba, a contingent of dark-skinned Berber tribesmen from northwest Africa, who stamped their fiery brand of fanaticism on the Prophet's teachings, occupied the semi-arid territories of La Mancha and Extremadura in western Iberia.

Despite the ethnic separation, the Moors in Al Andalus continued their internal battles. And, in the Muslim empire's capital at Damascus, the Caliph of the Ommayad dynasty struggled to hold on to power. In 750, the rival Abbasid family revolted and massacred all of the Ommayads, except for two of the Caliph's grandchildren, Abd al Rahman and his brother. The two boys escaped, but agents of the Abbasid family captured and beheaded Rahman's brother at a river crossing. The nineteen-year-old Rahman swam to safety on the other side of the river and made his way across North Africa to Ceuta. From there Rahman crossed the Straits of Gibraltar and assembled a small army. Following Rahman's battle flag, an unwound green turban attached to a spear,[22] his troops arrived at Cordoba, defeated the emir and installed their leader in power.

Rahman I began a dynastic line of eleven emirs and caliphs who would rule Al Andalus for 250 years.[23] One of his successors, Rahman II, soothed himself with intellectual pursuits, beginning a long tradition of Arab fascination with mathematics, philosophy, science and literature. The greatest leader of the dynasty, Rahman III, came to power in 912 at the age of 21. Rahman III shared his ancestors' love of arts and sciences, and, during his reign, Cordoba became "a glittering meteor of civilization in a sky that was empty of all but a few stars."[24] Rahman III was an organizer and a warrior. He built a standing army to preserve domestic peace and a three hundred-ship navy to protect Al Andalus' commerce. With a powerful military behind him, Rahman III declared Al Andalus independent of the Middle Eastern Caliphate at Baghdad, and made himself Caliph of the new Arab empire in the west. He brought Toledo and Zaragoza under his domain. He attacked the Christians in Navarre and sacked its capital, Pamplona. Then he attacked Asturias in a "campaign of omnipotence," but the stiff Christian resistance forced him to retreat. After the defeat, Rahman III crucified several hundred of his own officers for cowardice during the rout of his army.

When Rahman III died in 961 after forty-nine years of rule, his son, a semi-invalid who lead a scholar's life, sat on the throne for fifteen ineffectual years. When Rahman III's son died in 976, he left a 12-year-old heir apparent. The Muslim nobles selected a beguiling courtier to act as regent to the boy-Caliph until he reached majority. The courtier, Almansur, came from a poor but noble family whose pedigree stretched back to an ancestor who crossed the Straits of Gibraltar with Tarik in 711. After attending the University of Cordoba, Almansur worked his way up through the government to become lord chamberlain to the old Caliph. When he assumed power as regent, Almansur quickly organized a corps of Berber troops to support him, suppressed the Arab aristocracy and set up an elaborate spy network to sniff out conspiracies and warn him of any opposition. Insecure because of his usurpation of the boy-Caliph's power, Almansur punished his enemies ruthlessly. To gain support he lavished bribes on the nobles, wooed wealthy Jews and built mosques to quiet the mullahs. To convince the mullahs of his piousness, he copied the Koran in his own hand and allowed the mullahs to burn books they believed were blasphemous.

In addition to his professed devotion to the Koran, Almansur was a strict disciplinarian. While reviewing his troops on one occasion, a soldier moved slightly, violating Almansur's orders that the troops were to stand ramrod stiff. Almansur immediately executed the soldier, hoisted his head on a spear and paraded it before the ranks of troops.

Despite two of his wives being princesses from the Christian provinces of Leon and Navarre, Almansur made himself the "scourge of Christians," decapitating some prisoners of war and torturing others. After conquering the cities of Leon, Zamora, Simanacas, Burgos and Barcelona, he rewarded his troops with the loot of war; prisoners to sell as slaves or hold for ransom and women to rape. When his army captured Santiago de Compostela, he sacked the town and demolished the cathedral dedicated to the Christians' patron saint. Before destroying the cathedral, Almansur stole its metal doors and carried them back to Cordoba to melt down to make lamps for a mosque. Even though Almansur could be brutal, he could also be sentimental, if not morbid. When he marched into battle, he carried with him a funeral shroud his daughters made for him, and instructed his officers to bury him in the shroud if he was killed. When Almansur died in 1002, the Christians claimed that he was "buried in hell."

Without Almansur's iron-fisted dictatorship to keep the nobles in line, rebellions broke out, and Al Andalus split apart into twenty-six petty states (taifas). Christians and Moors alternately razed and looted Cordoba until it became no more than a decayed remnant of the "glittering meteor of civilization" it once was. With Cordoba in ruins, the Muslims moved their capital to Seville in the early 1000s. In addition to the political and territorial struggles, the old sectarian fissures between Sunnis and Shiites further divided and weakened the Caliphate. Moors fought Moors. Moors fought Christians. Moors and Christians united in unholy alliances to fight their brothers in religion. Al Andalus was in disarray, and Muslim and Christian knights fought one day for a Christian King and the next for an Arab war lord. The military entrepreneur, El Cid Campeador (1050-1099), came into his element.

Although the Christians were not much better organized than the Moors, their capture of Toledo in 1085 marked the first great milestone in the Reconquest. The mullahs blamed the fall of Toledo on the Muslim's departure from purity and orthodoxy. Allah was displeased with the luxury of their pleasure seeking lifestyles, the wine and dancing girls in the harems and the hours spent listening to lute players and obscene poetry. The mullahs said their flirtation with Greek rationalism and scientific reasoning was a break from the blind faith required by the Prophet. Frightened by their military losses and the warnings of their holy men, the Moors rallied. They sent for fanatically pure reinforcements, the wild Berber Muslims in North Africa who ruled their emirates in the Sahara Desert.

In 1086, thousands of zealous Almoravides (those sworn to Allah) answered the call, and swarmed into Al Andalus to blunt the Christian challenge. When the Almoravides first arrived, they met all expectations, suppressing unorthodox thinking and blasphemous living. But Al Andalus' apricots and oranges, the blond slave girls and the poets and musicians enticed the Almoravides into the sybaritic lifestyle they originally came to destroy.

While the Almoravides in Al Andalus enjoyed the quiet swishing of silk garments in the harem and sipped rosewater on their couches, another, even more fanatic group of North African Muslims mobilized. The Almohades (unitarians) entered Al Andalus in 1146 to the cadence of their war drums. Respecting no other religion or culture, the Almohades persecuted Christians and Jews without mercy, forcing many to flee to the safety of the Christian north. The exodus of so much manpower, talent and wealth strengthened the Christian cause. More importantly, the zealous fundamentalism of the Almoravides and the Almohades hardened the Christians' resolve to eliminate the barbarians from the Peninsula. The Christians realized they must either band together or perish, and coalesced behind their Savior's banner. Their stunning victory at Toledo proved they could win. The spirit of Pelayo, Santiago Matamoros and El Cid would lead them to victory.

Christian clergymen prayed for the Muslims'defeat and the purification of the Peninsula under the spiritual leadership of the one true Church. The Pope granted indulgences to Christians who took up arms and fought the nonbelievers. At the Catholic Church's urging, knights from France, Germany and other European countries rallied to the holy crusade against the hated Moors. The military orders of Alcantara, Calatrava and Santiago provided armed might. Now the Christian mission was clear. It had holy sanction. It had the men with the will. Chivalric victories over the Muslims would bring them wealth and glory, as well as Christ's blessing.

The Christian forces mauled the Moors at the Battle of Navas deTolosa in 1212, signaling the beginning of the end of Al Andalus. Cordoba fell to the Christians in 1236, Valencia in 1238,[25] Jaen in 1246 and the Arab capital, Seville, in 1248. After thirty-six years of war, only the southern Kingdom of Granada remained in Muslim hands. There, the Christian advance stalled. Granada's snow capped mountains presented the same problem to the Christians as did the northern mountains of Cantabria to the Moors centuries before. Even with all the Christians energy, with all their forces, with all their crusading motivation, the mountain barriers of Granada were too formidable for a Christian assault. The Moors would hang on to the sliver of southern territory until Ferdinand and Isabel crushed them 250 years later.

The eight hundred years of Arab rule left an indelible mark on the blood and culture of Spain. "[The] Muslim influence on Spain explodes to the surface through weakened fissures....[It] is a Christian country, but one with suppressed Muslim influences that crop out at unforeseen points," James Michener says. "It is a victorious country that expelled the defeated Muslims from all places except the human heart; it is a land which tried to extirpate all memory of the Muslims, but which lived on to mourn their passing...."[26] Up through the reign of Ferdinand and Isabel, and beyond, Spaniards have argued over the degree of Arab influence on Spain.[27] Were the Muslims nothing more than infidel savages whose memory is virtually eradicated from Spain? Or did they place a lasting stamp on the Spanish mind and culture? Whatever the answer, nobody can deny that the Moors' occupation of Spain brought an element of sensuality, ornateness and elegance to the Peninsula. The Arabs preserved and transmitted much of the brilliance of ancient learning to a Europe bogged down in the intellectual desert of the Dark Ages. The Muslim presence forever distinguished Spaniards from their cousins in the rest of Europe.

The zenith of Arab culture lasted for some 250 years, from about 750 to 1000, beginning with the reign of Rahman I through that of Almansur.[28] Their first capital, Cordoba, was the most populous, most prosperous and most artistically brilliant of any city in Europe. Cordoba had nine hundred public baths, two hundred thousand houses and four hundred thousand books in its libraries while the "great and famous" library of the monastery of Ripoll in Christian Iberia had 192 volumes.[29] At a time when most European kings or nobles couldn't read or write, Arabs and Jews established many schools in Al Andalus. One caliph increased the literacy rate by establishing twenty-seven tuition-free schools for poor children, and, it was said, many beggars were functionally literate. Water flowed into the city from aqueducts and was piped to the white-washed homes, public buildings and fountains scattered throughout Cordoba. In the Arab tradition, homes had only small, iron grilled windows facing the streets; the beauty of interior patios, gardens and reflecting pools being hidden within. Islamic priests chanted *Allah akbar! Allah akbar!* (God is Great! God is Great!) from their minarets to call the faithful to prayer five times a day in the seven hundred mosques. And Cordoba's five hundred thousand citizens walked along its many paved, lighted streets, while people in other European capitals maneuvered through the filth in their streets and lived in squalid hovels.

To support their elevated lifestyle, the Moors encouraged commerce with North Africa, Europe and the Middle East. France, Italy and other nations sent ambassadors and merchants to Cordoba to negotiate alliances and make business deals. In time, the flourishing international trade produced an economic boom that made import and export taxes the largest source of government revenue. Al Andalus' ships docked at ports throughout the Mediterranean. Goods moved from Cadiz in the south over the old Roman highway, the Via Augusta, through Cordoba and north across the Pyrenees to Europeans who coveted the Iberian craftsmens' wares—pottery, silk, textiles, tooled and gilded leather, carved ivory, fine glassware and enameled weapons. To milk more profits from Al Andalus' mines, the Moors invented a system of making pure copper with a primitive process that was a precursor of electroplating. They also brought in a device, the alembic, used to distill chemicals and perfume.

While the traders negotiated in the cities, in the countryside the Arabs developed agriculture to new heights. Water, a precious commodity to the Muslims with their desert background, flowed through carefully engineered systems of irrigation ditches, windmills, pumps and waterwheels to produce abundant crops of vegetables, grains and fruits to feed the townsmen. Farmers spread fertilizer on their fields and developed new techniques of grafting grapevines and olive, mulberry, orange and apricot trees to increase production.

Greek and Byzantine artists and architects came to Al Andalus to beautify its cities, building and decorating magnificent palaces for the rulers and elegant mansions for the rich. When the Arabs first occupied Cordoba, they divided one of the principal Christian churches in half, allowing Christians to worship in their half on Sundays, while the Moors attended weekly services in their part on Fridays. Later, the Arabs bought the Christian half, tore down the structure and erected Cordoba's crowning jewel of architecture, the Great Mosque, on the site. As the population swelled, the Muslim rulers expanded the Great Mosque to a length of 600 feet and a width of 450 feet. Inside, the Arabs successfully solved the architectural problem of balancing heavy weights on slender columns.

The Great Mosque had a forest of sixteen hundred columns[30] with gilded capitals decorated by the imported artisans, arches, twenty doors, prayer niches facing Mecca, a pulpit of exotic woods and hundreds of lamps to illuminate the faithful. After Cordoba sank into decay in the first part of the 1000s, the Muslims repeated the splendor in their new capital at Seville, constructing palaces, mosques and docks and warehouses for Seville's international trade coming from the ocean up the Guadalquivir River. Later, they constructed the splendid Alhambra in Granada as an eternal monument to their presence.

The Arab builders constructed public baths (hammams), and sometimes violated the Islamic prohibition against representational art showing humans or other figures. The pictures and statutes in the baths, many pornographic, enraged the mullahs. Rabbis railed against the suspected sodomy and prostitution offered by some bath houses. Despite the religious objections, Jews and Arabs, delighted in the soothing comfort of the baths and went anyway. When the bather entered, he undressed in a vestibule and went through a series of rooms, each hotter than the last, and ended up in an unheated room where, swathed in towels, he spent an hour or so cooling off. At some baths, men went in the morning and women in the afternoon, or men and women went on alternate days. Noblewomen brought their masseuses and cosmetic specialists to prepare them for an evening's entertainment. For the men, the cool room was a sort of club where they traded gossip, discussed politics and and did business.

Christian priests saw no godliness whatsoever in the bath houses. In their diatribes against the watery temples of immorality, the priests prohibited their flocks from entering the "places of sin" where Moors and Jews allegedly indulged in sensual orgies. Bathing not only encouraged sinful practices, Christians believed, it made men soft and effeminate—unfit for battle. With this mixture of ecclesiastical and military justification for avoiding baths, medieval Castilians associated their dirtiness and pungent body odor with right religious thinking, and cleanliness by Jews and Moors came to take on a heretical significance.

Christian clergymen preached that grime and a ripe smell were tests of moral purity, and demonstrated a belief in the True Faith. If females in the confessional admitted they were too clean, their confessors denied them forgiveness unless they agreed to abstain from washing their clothes and bathing. The Mother Superior of a convent with 130 nuns proudly announced that not one of her holy women had ever washed their feet. Monks bragged that they wore the same muddy, food-stained robes for a year, and smugly called their odor the *olor de sanctidad* ("smell of holiness"). The Moors sneered that the unwashed Christians "were sprinkled with water when they were born, and were, therefore, relieved from washing for the rest of the lives."[31] By the time of Ferdinand and Isabel, Christians thought bath houses so disreputable that the Sovereigns closed them down after the conquest of Granada. "They [Ferdinand and Isabel] forbade not only the Christians, but the Moors, from using anything but holy water. Fire, not water [would become] the grand element of inquisitorial purification."[32]

Even though the Christians shunned the sanitary effects of bathing, they were keenly interested in Arab and Jewish medicine. Cordoba's doctors treated kings and nobles all over Europe, using ancient Greek and other texts to guide them in their search for cures and remedies. Since it was unthinkable for a male to see or touch a woman, female doctors specialized in gynecology and obstetrics for the rich, and midwives handled these tasks for the poor. For Jews, doctors performed circumcisions at birth, but Muslims administered the rite at the age of seven, followed by feasting and dancing at lavish parties. The physicians used the customary bleedings and herbal treatments they learned from the Greeks and Persians. They used anesthetics for difficult operations, and developed a worldwide reputation for performing successful cataract operations.[33]

Many doctors delved into philosophy and science as well as medicine, helping develop Al Andalus into the most intellectual country in medieval Europe. Scholars in Cordoba and Seville studied botany, chemistry, physics, geography and mathematics. They introduced Europe to the concept of zero, algebra, trigonometry and Arabic numerals rather than the cumbersome Roman numerals.

To supply Al Andalus' scholars with research materials, agents of the Arab rulers scoured the world to collect manuscripts on the different subjects. If a book was not for sale, the agents paid the enormous cost of hand copying the valuable document so that it could be sent back to one of the seventy libraries in Al Andalus or to the University of Cordoba. When shipments of books arrived in the Peninsula, an army of linguists translated the manuscripts from Greek, Persian and other languages into Arabic. Using techniques they learned from the Chinese to make paper, the Arabs transcribed the ancient learning on paper, rather than the thick expensive papyrus or animal skins previously used for writing. After the scribes copied the texts in flowing Arabic script, many books were translated into Latin. Once in Latin, these volumes were sold throughout Europe, establishing one of the few links between classical intellectuals and Germans and Frenchmen mired in the Dark Ages.

Al Andalus served as the filter through which ancient learning found its way into Europe, passing on the best of Greek philosophy, Roman law and government, Middle Eastern literature and Jewish and Christian theology. A Jewish scholar introduced neo-Platonism into Al Andalus. Averroes,[34] an Arab, and Maimonides,[35] a Jew, revived Artistotle's teachings. Based heavily on Averroes and Maimonides' writings, St. Thomas Aquinas harmonized Greek rationalism with the Catholic doctrine requiring blind faith in the Holy Scriptures, setting off a debate that still rages today between fundamentalist and more liberal Christians. Averroes believed in the supremacy of the human intellect, and fought against the old concept that religious interpretations should control human thought. Maimonides agreed with Averroes that, "There is no tyranny on earth like the tyranny of priests." Supporting these arguments, Maimonides, who was born in Cordoba but who left Al Andalus during a period of anti-semitic persecution, argued that there was no real conflict between reason and faith or between science and religion, and that human reason could divine religious truths.

The powerful minds of these two great philosophers, and the probing, inquiring minds of other scholars, made Al Andalus the clearinghouse of culture from the more civilized China, India, Persia and Byzantium to medieval Europe. The native Christians quickly accepted these Arab innovations, but they still clung to their old language. After their invasion in 711, only the Muslim aristocrats spoke Arabic, while the lower classes continued speaking "vulgar" Latin.[36] Over the centuries of Arab occupation, some Christians became bilingual, bringing some four thousand Arabic words into what is now modern Spanish.[37] Among intellectuals, however, Arabic became so dominate that the Christian writer Alvaro complained in 854 that, "My fellow Christians delight in the poems and romances of the Arabs. Alas! The young Christians [who have the most talent] have no knowledge of any literature or language save the Arabic."

For pleasure, the Arabs imported chess, the lute, a crude type of violin and the oval guitar. As further sensual stimulus, florid poetry became the passion of Al Andalus' Arabs, from the common people to emirs. When the Arab ruler Almansur wasn't beheading his enemies, he amused himself with the verses of his forty court poets. Supposedly, Almansur pardoned a young bard from a sentence of flogging for embezzling three thousand dinars after the young man presented Almansur with a poem that pleased him. In another story, an emir was sitting by the Guadalquivir River struggling to complete a line of poetry about the effect of the cold wind on the river. A beautiful young slave girl, who was washing her master's laundry in the river, overheard the emir and helped him complete the poem. The emir, delighted with the girl's wit, bought her out of slavery, married her and had her buried at his side after a lifetime of love.

Whether the stories are true or not, poetry was the favorite literary form in Al Andalus, and could move Arabs to emotional highs:

"The night is a sea, where the stars are the foam;
The clouds the waves, the crescent moon a ship.

or:

"The wing of darkness departs before the dawn;
Like a crow that takes wing uncovering white eggs."

or, in matters of love:

"My eyes cling to you wherever you go;
As the adjective follows the noun."[38]

So great was the Arabs' love of rhymed words that the Italian poet Petrarch said he was afraid that even "the [Moors'] cattle might begin to low in verse." Without an exact and extensive mastery of words, the Arabs thought, a man was uncivilized, his education incomplete. Perhaps because the Koran prohibited representational art, poetry filled the gap by painting word pictures that crystallized an event or thought in a few well-chosen phrases. In an age when there was no news media, poetry could be used to transmit information, propaganda or personal attacks on one's enemies. A sharp line slicing a war lord's rival might bring a bag of gold or a ruby as a reward to a clever poet. If the rival heard the poem and caught the poet, he might have his eyes put out. Despite these risks, the music of verse was so popular among all classes that many young men adopted poetry as a profession.

Apprentice poets wandered from court to court, staying in the special lodgings some nobles and emirs set aside for them, until they developed their art to a state of fluency that earned them a permanent job. One famous poet, Ammar, started life as an itinerant, drifting from the house of one noble to another, carrying all of his property in a pair of saddle bags strapped to the back of his emaciated mule. An appreciative nobleman rewarded the young Ammar's rhyming efforts with a bag of barley. Years later, an emir appointed Ammar governor of the nobleman's province, and Ammar sent him a bag of silver. If, Ammar said, the noble had given him a bag of the more valuable wheat rather than barley, the bag of silver would have been a bag of gold.

Some western critics say Arabic poetry is nothing more than dreary exaggerations, artificial metaphors and cliches in which a woman's teeth are always pearls, eyes are violets, flowers are jewels and lightening in a rainstorm is like the fire of a poet's love among his tears. "Anyone who reads Arab poets," a Dutch critic says, "...if he does not lose his senses, is misusing his leisure."[39] Others say that Arabic is a rich and flexible language which does not translate well, andthat Arabic poetry can only be appreciated in the original. Whatever the critical judgment, the florid hyperbole of Arabic poems permanently impacted the Spanish language.

Not so poetic was the slavery practiced by the Arabs. The best sources were prisoners of war and the human beings paid as tribute by Christian princes. The Moors prized blond, blue-eyed *gallegas* (Galician women) for their beauty and Catalans because they were thought to be more intelligent and better breeders. Wars and tribute alone couldn't meet the demand, and Christian, Jewish and Arab traders scoured the world to supply slaves to Al Andalus. Although Christians sometimes made slaves of Christians, Arabs of Arabs and Jews of Jews, their religious teachings prohibited them from capturing their brothers in the faith. To avoid the wrath of priests, mullahs and rabbis, the slave traders rounded up "primitives" (nonbelievers) from Africa and the wild forests of Eastern Europe.

The Moors believed that dark-skinned desert men made good farm workers, and black Nubian women had the freshest skin and sweetest temperaments. But the most desirable slaves were the Slavs (from which the Spanish word *esclavos*, slaves, is derived) who the traders herded to the great slave market in Prague to be swapped for spices,wheat and gold. After the human merchandise changed hands in Prague, their new masters marched them to smaller slave markets in France, and on to Al Andalus. In Cordoba, the slave traders sold their wares into permanent bondage to perform much of the Peninsula's menial work.

To establish value, the slave traders kept elaborate written records. If a slave would make good breeding stock, his or her family pedigree, like that of a racehorse, was part of the record. If the record reflected physical defects in a man that impaired his ability to work, or blemishes on a woman that marred her beauty, the price went down. Because falsifying a slave's records was common, inspectors patrolled the markets to prosecute the frauds. Prices varied with supply and demand, and, after a successful military campaign, a slave in poor physical condition might sell for as little as a cask of wine. One highly sought slave girl, who had "grace and vivacity, a good figure, a soft voice with perfect delivery and pureness of diction...and the most refined culture,"[40] sold for three thousand dinars at a time when a poor family could live on twenty-five dinars a year.

Most buyers put their new acquisitions to work as laborers, craftsmen, oarsmen in galleys or farm workers. Slave owners sometimes chained farm workers at night and stabled them in dank underground cellars like animals. If a slave was lucky enough to work in town in a noble's house, he was relatively well treated. A man whose owner decided he would make a good eunuch suffered another fate. After recovering from his castration, a eunuch might became a harem guard or, infrequently, a general, admiral or governor of an emir's province. The emasculations caused many deaths, but this was figured into the price of eunuches, making them as much as ten times more expensive than an ordinary slave. Although the eunuches often became obese after their surgery, their masters gave them delicate names like Hyacinth, Gaiety and Full Moon.

Plainer female slaves worked as maids or domestic servants, but a woman with both beauty and intelligence could find a place in the luxury of the harem. One advertisement by a a medical doctor who ran a school for slave girls as a sideline, read: "Know that I now have in my house four Christian girls who yesterday were dolts, but today are instructed in Logic, Philosophy, Geography, Music...Literature and Calligraphy." Additional talents, such as performing the saber dance or juggling swords and daggers, brought a premium price, and a girl with a good singing voice might be idolized like today's movie stars. If a harem concubine developed elegant manners in and out of bed, she could trade her favors for bags of gold or jewels before opening the door to her master. One story tells of a harem girl who, dressed in men's clothes, pranced around on a hobby horse fighting an imaginary battle until she collapsed in surrender to her lover. Another innovative woman swayed in a seductive courtship dance in which she played the role of a slave of passion while she proclaimed the man her master.

Eunuches guarded the harem doors to protect their master's prized possessions, the blonds, redheads and women with jet black hair to their ankles who padded on oriental carpets in Moroccan slippers. Silk tunics and pantaloons hid their bodies and veils hid their faces from all but their master. Their musk perfume, harvested from the testicles of a small deer found only in Asia, added to their allure. With their chastity secured from the eyes of rapacious, lustful men, the harem women saw life mostly through windows grilled with iron bars or observed from a roof garden.

Although the Muslim male's private preserve was designed to fulfill the Koran's promise of an earthly paradise, the harem also provided a breeding ground for the master. One prolific, and energetic, emir reveled in the forty-five sons and forty-two daughters he fathered from his stable of concubines. Despite their role as breeding stock, the harem women counted it a joyous day when they learned of their pregnancy. Under Islamic law, a slave who bore her master a child was immediately raised in status and she was emancipated upon his death. Along with the broods of children by different wives came danger. Jealous mothers, sometimes in league with favored eunuches, schemed and plotted to stake a claim to their son's succession to their father's fortune.

Although religious persecution broke out sporadically during the early years of Muslim rule in the Peninsula, for the most part Arabs, Christians and Jews lived side by side in peaceful coexistence *(conviviencia)*. Until well into the 1000s, the Muslims showed an extraordinary tolerance for Christians and Jews, leaving each religion free to follow its own rites and rituals. The Moors justified their policy of peaceful coexistence on religious grounds, because much of Islam stemmed from the Bible, and on practical grounds, because the Arabs derived substantial revenues from taxes on nonbelievers. Socially, mixed marriages were not uncommon. Arabs freely interbred with Christian women, producing a number of caliphs and emirs with blue eyes, fair skin and light hair. The son of Al Andalus' first Arab ruler married the defeated Visigoth King Roderick's widow, and even the great Pelayo's sister married a Moor.

With this intermingling and easy tolerance, Christians worshiped in their own way, governed themselves, within limits, by their own laws, held some governmental posts and served in the army. The Muslim conquerors prohibited Christians from proselytizing Arabs, approved the appointment of bishops and carefully supervised the Catholic Church's finances. The religious restrictions may have grated on some Christians, but all non-Arabs suffered under the onerous head and land taxes they paid to support their Muslim masters. Some Christians, to avoid the taxes or from religious conviction, converted to Islam. Those who clung to Christ's Word sneeringly called the converts *renegados* (renegades). Other Christians, called *mozarabs* (almost Arabs), kept the Faith but adopted Arab customs, spoke Arabic, dressed in Arab clothes and enjoyed Arab culture and poetry. A few passionate Christian zealots, whipped up by priests who feared the conversions to Islam, occasionally denounced Mohammed as a "false Prophet" or the "servant of Satan" and suffered the ecstasy of martyrdom.

Both Christians and Jews generally scorned the fanatics for stirring up trouble, which threatened all of them with retribution from their Muslim overlords. Recalling the vicious persecution of the Visigoths, the Jews felt menaced by the Christian "madmen bent on suicide" who willingly sacrificed themselves for ideology and upset the status quo that allowed followers of the three religions to mingle in salons, offices and the marketplaces.

When the Moors invaded the Peninsula in 711, the Jews welcomed them as liberators from the brutal treatment the Visigoths. Because of this early alliance, many Jews immigrated from the Middle East and, along with Hispano-Jews, moved to Cordoba, making it one of the most famous Hebrew centers of learning. Soon, the writings of Hispano-Jewish poets were well known in Europe and the Middle East, and Jewish doctors attended to Arab nobles and Christian princes throughout Europe. The Sons of Moses flourished in the Arab governments, often serving as ambassadors to European courts. The caliphs used Jews as diplomats because they felt the Christian kings would receive a neutral Jew more favorably than an Arab, and because the multilingual Jews had international contacts through their trade and financial networks. The idea that Jews were only merchants, money lenders or bankers is not correct. They played these financial roles, but they also served their Muslim rulers as prime ministers (viziers), writers, scholars, craftsmen and laborers.[41]

During those early years of *conviviencia*, Moors, Christians and Jews lived physically apart in different quarters of Cordoba. At the same time, they lived a common intellectual, political and business life. For the time being, the three groups put aside sectarian differences for a mutually beneficial commercial and cultural life that blurred racial and religious distinctions. In the late 1000s and the 1100s, the days of mutual respect, of cross culturalization, of tolerance faltered and collapsed when the fanatic Almoravides and Almohades invaded the Peninsula. Many Jews and Christians fled to Christian territory to escape the Muslim bigotry that condemned them to persecutions, executions and confiscations of property. Instead of the blurred line between the three religions, the Christian position hardened into the sharp focus of a holy crusade against anyone who refused to follow the teachings of the Catholic

Church. The Christians decided to achieve political unity "... through the banner of a dynamic religion. This concept...eventually welded nationalism and religion together...[into] a church-state. Religion...was to become a weapon, the mightiest weapon of all, in the epic struggle between two cultures."[42]

Even though Christian resolve stiffened, there were periods when Christians left Jews and Muslims in relative peace. During the reign of Alfonso the Wise, there was substantial freedom, and even Peter the Cruel had a Jewish treasurer, Samuel Levi. After Ferdinand III of Castile died in 1252, he was proclaimed "King of the Three Religions." When the Roman Church ordered Jews to wear badges marking their religion in 1215, the Castilian king and the Archbishop of Toledo joined forces to have the order rescinded in Castile. As late as 1466, a Czech traveler commented with amazement that the Count of Haro let Jews, Arabs and Christians live peaceably together in his household and celebrate their own religious rites. There was intermarriage, even though rabbis and priests frowned on mixed marriages, and almost all of the Christian aristocracy had Jewish blood.[43] Even though the ties of blood and culture were strong, many Christians envied Jews whose rose to power in government or built fortunes from ungentlemanly trade. "By incessant scheming ," one Christian said, "they [the Jews] carry off the fat of the fruits of every man's toil, enjoying power, honor, favor and riches."[44] Rumors accused Jews of crucifying Christian boys on Good Friday and Jewish doctors of poisoning Christian patients. Even their eating habits were held against them. Those prejudices led to massacres of Jews in Seville, Toledo, Valencia and other cities, forcing many members of the Jewish elite to convert to Christianity

Although the three cultures often lived in harmony in the towns, in the countryside it was frequently a different story. From the first days of the Muslim invasion of Iberia in 711, the dividing line between territory under Christian and Arab control was a vague no man's land. There was no line on a map marking the "sharp edge of sovereignty" between Arab and Christian areas. Rather, there was a frontier that constantly shifted with the fortunes of war. Safe behind the Cantabrian mountains, the Christian hill people sallied out to raid Arab farmers, travelers and settlements, and, in turn, fended off the Muslim's counterattacks. On both sides, the no man's land of the frontier was a society under arms. "Castile was born to war and suckled on war," and it was war that "forged her warrior temperament, her will to command, and her ambition to achieve a great destiny."[45]

The Christian lands in Asturias and Galicia in the north were harsh, rock-strewn wastelands that made farming almost impossible. Bandits made travel dangerous. The steep mountain passes impeded trade. About all that was left to these frugal, austere mountain men was fighting or herding animals. As warriors and shepherds not tied to a specific piece of land, they could easily drive their flocks of sheep and goats into territory newly conquered from the Arabs, and just as easily retreat to the protection of their mountains if necessary. When the Christians drove the Moors southward, recapturing their land became a territorial imperative. They established a type of homestead program to encourage settlers to occupy the new land, forming a pioneer society of wandering shepherds and small landowners who were free of dependence on great lords, free of fiefdom, "an island of free men in feudal Europe." As in the American West before 1890, the Iberian frontier created in the Christians a spirit of fierce independence, of lawlessness, a sense of taking matters into one's own hands and an unwillingness to accept authority.[46]

The transient, ever-moving frontier created an atmosphere that fostered a special type of personality—military entrepreneurs. These were the men who buckled on their armor and exploited the wealth that was there for the man bold enough to take it. To them, buying a war-horse and suit of armor was the best investment an ambitious young man could make. To them, physical stamina, willpower and audacity were more important than scholarly reasoning. To them, peacefully tending a herd of sheep didn't present near the opportunities that war did—wealth came from the booty of war, not from manual labor.[47] Each individual took precedence over institutions, each individual made his own choices and each man made his own law.[48] No surprise then, the string of military dictators in Latin America or Generalissimo Franco. The tradition is centuries old. Had these men who became military entrepreneurs in medieval Spain lived today, they would have gotten MBA's and law degrees from prestigious schools and conquered financial or real estate empires.

This frontier mentality partly explains the jigsaw puzzle of petty Christian states which were created as the Spanish pushed the Arabs southward. In the early years of the Reconquest, the Christians were motivated not so much by nationalistic or religious fervor, but by a common hatred of foreigners and a desire for land. Once they conquered new lands from the Moors, the military entrepreneurs' internecine battles split Christian territory into Castile, Navarre, Leon, Asturias, Galicia, Catalonia and Aragon. Compounding the problem, many kings followed the old custom of leaving pieces of their domains to each of their sons in the false belief that they could avoid wars of succession. Over time, however, the Kingdom of Asturias expanded to become the Kingdom of Leon, and, by the 1000s, Asturias and Leon merged into the Kingdom of Castile. With Castile spearheading the attack on Islam, the Christians pushed south, building fortresses and fortified towns as they went.

To attract immigrants to their new lands, the Castilian kings granted toleration to Jews fleeing the persecution of the Almoravides and Almohades and made mozarab serfs free men. Through the royal *fueros* (decrees), kings gave towns and cities freedoms unheard of in much of the rest of medieval Europe, including the right to rule themselves through town councils. Giving the cities and the middle class more power was not designed to foster democracy. Rather, the crown used the cities and Parliament as a check on the power of the nobles. In 1169, the Castilian king established a Parliament where bourgeois townsmen sat alongside nobles and clergymen to discuss the Kingdom's business. Although Parliament provided a sense of rudimentary democracy, it served more as a channel of communication between the king and the people.[49]

Beginning in the 1100s and 1200s, many of the freedoms faded. By the 1200s, serfdom prevailed in much of Castile. To keep the free cities and towns in line, the kings attempted to assert their power over their citizens, while, at the same time, the aristocrats schemed to control the city councils. During that period, Christianity became more aggressive and militant. The kings forced baptism on Jews and conquered Muslims. If the new converts *(conversos)* to the Catholic faith secretly reverted to their old religion, the Christians branded them *marranos* (which carried the equally vile double meanings of "pig" and "anathema").

When Ferdinand and Isabel assumed the Castilian throne in 1474, the threads of centuries of cultural and religious influences crisscrossed the character of their countrymen. Periods of prejudice and hatred had alternated with periods of tolerance. Celtiberian anarchy struggled against Roman hierarchy and authoritarianism. The fierce independence of military entrepreneurs contrasted with the servile acceptance of vassals. The pious devotion to Christ offset the militant use of the Church as an instrument of politics and the veneration of war as the path to glory. Arab intellectualism and striving for paradise on earth faced off against harsh pragmatism. When Ferdinand and Isabel came to power they dealt with these cross currents in their countrymen's natures. When they solidified their power, they used this quilt of character traits, both good and bad, to launch their next campaign—the final effort to conclude the Reconquest.

13

THE WAR OF GRANADA, THE EARLY YEARS

"Let those who are at a distance from the enemy not regard themselves as safe. They too will bow the neck beneath the yoke, be mowed down by the scimitar, unless they come forward to meet the enemy—an enemy who has sworn the extinction of Christianity. It is the moment not to talk but to fight."[1] In this stirring call to arms, Pope Sixtus IV urged Christians to fight the hated Muslims who took Constantinople in 1453, threatening Rome itself, and who still occupied the Kingdom of Granada.

Taking up the Pope's challenge, Ferdinand told his countrymen: "I intend to pick this pomegranate seed by seed." In his pun, the King referred to the fruit which appeared on the Kingdom of Granada's coat of arms and to the word from which Granada derived its name.[2] For almost two hundred years the Muslim emirs ruled from their capital in Granada. Now, Ferdinand and Isabel were ready to pick the over-ripe fruit.

As the Christian conquests faltered in the late 1200s, there were alternating periods of peace and hostility along the Spanish-Granadian frontier, but no real war. When Christians or Moors captured the others' territory, they levied heavy taxes but they normally allowed the defeated to continue to live under their customs, laws and religion. After the skirmishes, the Christian and Muslim monarches negotiated treaties providing for liberal exchanges of prisoners, free trade and the payment of tribute to the victor. With the exception of the occasional guerilla raids or rebellions by the conquered, life went on its normal course in an atmosphere of *conviviencia* (peaceful coexistence). On occasion, expediency forced Arab and Christian princes into alliances of convenience. In 1275, Granada's Arabs called for help from North Africa to fend off Christian threats.[3] When the Muslim tribesmen from across the Straits of Gibraltar tried to overthrow their hosts, the Arabs of Granada fought alongside Christians against their cousins from Africa.

In the 1450s, King Henry IV made a few ineffectual sallies against Granada. By 1463, Henry was meeting with the emir in Granada to exchange presents and pledges of mutual affection. After the meeting, a company of Muslim knights escorted King Henry back across the border with his presents — twenty horses bred from the emir's royal stud and twenty gold and jewel encrusted scimitars. Muslim and Christian knights, seeking asylum from misdeeds in their home country, often fled to the court of the king or the emir and sometimes fought against their brothers in religion. On one occasion, two Christian knights agreed to a joust in the presence of the emir in Granada. When one of the knights didn't show up to settle the point of honor, the other Christian rode around the tilting field with a portrait of his rival fastened to his horse's tail.[4]

Even though *conviviencia* marked much of the Muslim-Christian sharing of the Peninsula before 1480, mistrust and hatred still smoldered beneath the surface. The Moors dreamed of the days when they ruled the Peninsula. Christians yearned for a renewal of the glorious conquests that brought them Cordoba and Seville in the 1200s. Plucking the rich Kingdom of Granada from the Moors would not be easy. From east to west it stretched about 175 miles along the south coast of the Peninsula, and, at its widest point, poached ninety miles northward from the sea. A rampart of mountains fronted on much of its frontier with Spain, and forts guarded many of the rugged mountain passes. Arab troops garrisoned the fortified cities of Baza and Guadix in the east and Alhama, Illora and Ronda in the west. Over one thousand battle towers formed a picket fence along the solid walls surroundingthe capital city. Granada's citizens took comfort in its motto: "No conqueror but God." Although the Kingdom of Granada was geographically small, it had a large population to work its mines and well-irrigated fields.[5] The seaports of Malaga and Almeria gave the Kingdom access to goods from its flourishing trade with Genoa, Venice and other Mediterranean states. At any given time, the rulers of the pocket-sized Kingdom could muster one hundred thousand troops.[6] The Muslim force of foot soldiers, armed with deadly crossbows and light cavalrymen mounted on Arab horses, made a formidable army. Perhaps the Moors' greatest weapon was the anarchy of its turbulent Christian neighbors. Although the Muslims suffered from their own internal struggles, the Spaniards had strangled themselves in power plays pitting noble against noble and crown against aristocrats. After Ferdinand and Isabel assumed the throne in 1474, they harnessed their unruly nobles and brought a measure of unity to their nation, putting Spain in position to focus its energy on rekindling the Reconquest.

Recalling the heroic tales of Pelayo, El Cid and Santiago Matamoros, Isabel was determined to slay the Moors in a final, evangelical crusade to drive them back to Africa. The Pope and the Church ordained it. Her people ordained it. The military entrepreneurs in the nobility, the Holy Brotherhood and the military orders ordained it. Now she had a righteous cause to rally the will of her nation behind a single, clear objective. With a dramatic stroke, she would make Spain whole again, giving her personal symbol, the bundle of arrows, true meaning. She would rid the divided Peninsula of the Infidels' influence. She would divert her nobles from their clan feuds and steer their attention to the plunder she would dole out to her valiant warriors. She would finish the 780-year-old job.

At first, Ferdinand was reluctant. He hated the French, and wanted to punish them for repeatedly invading Aragon and snatching slices of its territory. Isabel argued that running the Moors out of the Peninsula would increase their royal power, enhance their prestige, make them almost invulnerable to their enemies. With a unified nation, Spain would be free of the Muslim distractions, free to send its armies storming into Italy and France, free to conquer new worlds. His wife's logic won Ferdinand over.

The Muslins furnished the pretext. On the day after Christmas, 1481, they breached a 1478 truce agreement[7] with the Sovereigns by crossing the border and attacking the fortified Christian town of Zahara, about midway between Seville and Gibraltar. After a savage battle, the Moors either killed or forced into slavery all of Zahara's men, women and children. Their leader, Abul Hacen,[8] was a fiery Christian hater, who, when Ferdinand and Isabel earlier[9] demanded that he pay them a large sum of gold as tribute, told the royal couple's ambassador: "Tell your monarches that the Kings of Granada who paid tribute are dead. The mints of Granada no longer coin gold, but steel."[10]

Abul Hacen's brutality brought quick retaliation. The Christians, led by Rodrigo Ponce de Leon, the Marquis of Cadiz, smashed into the heart of Muslim territory to attack the town of Alhama,[11] about thirty miles from Granada. Leaving his baggage train behind and marching mostly at night to avoid detection, in a three-day forced march during late February of 1482, Ponce de Leon's army arrived before dawn at Alhama. In the attack, his troops scaled the walls, threw open the gates of the lightly defended town and captured the town's fortress. While Ponce de Leon's men rested after the long march and furious battle, the Arab towns-men surrounded the fortress and threw up a log blockade in the narrow streets leading to the fortress. With a shout of "Santiago and the Virgin Mary," the Christians charged out of the fortress and engaged the townspeople in bloody house-to-house fighting.

From rooftops and balconies, the Muslim men rained down poisoned arrows, bullets and stones, while the women poured boiling oil and water on the advancing Spaniards. The Christians used their shields as a canopy to deflect the arrows and oil, and, after an all-day battle, trapped many of Alhama's townsmen in a large mosque. The Christians set the mosque on fire and, as the Moors tried to escape, slaughtered many of the fleeing Muslims. By some counts, the bodies of twenty-five percent of Alhama's citizens littered the streets.[12] After the battle, Ponce de Leon's men rampaged through the town, looting the houses of their valuables. After the orgy of blood and booty, the Spaniards freed Christian captives, and added one more body to the count—a *renegado* (a Christian convert to Islam). They executed the *renegado* as a traitor to the Faith and hung his remains from the fortress' battlements.[13]

Less than a week later, Abul Hacen marched his army from Granada to Alhama where he found the mutilated bodies of his countrymen, decomposed and gnawed by dogs and birds of prey, stacked up outside the town's walls. Furious, Abul Hacen laid siege, surrounding the town and cutting off its water supply. But the Duke of Medina Sidonia, leading an army from Andalusia, forced Abul Hacen to retreat to Granada rather than risk being hemmed in between the two Christian armies. After Abul Hacen's retreat, the Duke of Medina Sidonia and Ponce de Leon, who had fought bloody clan wars for control of Andalusia, embraced and vowed that their years of animosity were over. Despite their newfound affection, the two later squabbled over dividing the spoils from Alhama.

The Reconquest was on. At Alhama the Christians won the first victory in their glorious crusade. Ferdinand took no part in the fighting. When the fighting broke out, he and Isabel were in Medina del Campo several hundred miles to the north. After the royal couple received Ponce de Leon's dispatches from the battle at Alhama, Ferdinand set off immediately to take charge of the army. Isabel, pregnant with their fourth child, Maria, followed at a slower pace.

In the spring of 1482, the Spaniards reduced their garrison at Alhama to a few troops, and Abul Hacen again laid siege. Some of the Sovereigns' advisors argued that they should abandon the town, which was only thirty miles southwest of Granada, but Isabel counseled, "Glory [is] not to be won without danger....This was the first blow struck during the war, and honor and policy alike [forbid a retreat] which could not fail to dampen the ardor of the nation." Now at the head of the army, Ferdinand marched on Alhama and forced Abul Hacen to retire from the field without a major battle. After entering the town on May 14,1482, Ferdinand dedicated Alhama to the service of the Cross and consecrated its three principal mosques as churches. Isabel donated silver chalices, crosses and, most precious, an altar cloth she embroidered with her own hand to one of the newly endowed houses of God.

Fired by the victory at Alhama with an overdose of romantic chivalry, but still lacking a major victory in his personal column, the thirty-year-old Ferdinand immediately decided to attack Loja, thirty-five miles due west of Granada. Muslim troops mauled the poorly supplied, ill trained Spanish soldiers, killed the Grand Master of Calatrava and picked off the panicked remnants of Ferdinand's army as it fled back to Cordoba under the hot Andalusian sun in July of 1482. Even though the rout severely bruised his pride, Ferdinand learned a valuable lesson—don't wage war with inexperienced officers, raw recruits and inadequate supplies.

While Ferdinand and Isabel planned their next move against the Moors, intrigue and schemes hatched in Abul Hacen's harem provided the Spaniards a powerful weapon. When the aging Abul Hacen fell in love with a beautiful Greek harem girl, his former favorite, Saroya,[14] began plotting against the young girl in order to protect the succession for her own son, Boabdil.[15] Abul Hacen learned of the plot and promptly imprisoned the jealous Saroya and Boabdil in the Alhambra. The ambitious mother and her son escaped and, because of Abul Hacen's oppressive rule, rallied enough support to drive Abul Hacen out of the city of Granada. Abul Hacen and his brother, El Zagal,[16] Granada's finest soldier, slipped out of the city to link up with loyal forces in the seaport of Malaga and the cities of Baza and Guadix in the eastern part of the Kingdom.

With his nation divided, Boabdil decided to enhance his popularity and prestige by launching a campaign against the Spaniards.[17] Boabdil mustered an army of infantry and cavalry and crossed the border into Spain in April, 1483, headed north toward the fortified Christian town of Lucena. Outside Lucena, two wings of the Spanish army caught the Muslims in a pincers maneuver and broke the Muslim lines of battle. Panicked and loaded down with the loot they stole from Christian villages and farms, Boabdil's troops fled in confusion to the Genil River. [18] Trapped at the river swollen by spring rains, the Spaniards slaughtered the Moors. With fifty of his personal bodyguards dead, Boabdil failed in his attempt to swim the swift-running river. Stranded, Boabdil hid in the reedy thickets along the riverbank until three Spanish infantrymen captured him and turned him over to their commander, the Count of Cabra.

At their court in northern Spain, Ferdinand and Isabel received the news of the triumph at Lucena. Ferdinand rushed south to Cordoba to meet with his generals and to determine Boabdil's fate. Some Spanish commanders wanted to keep Boabdil in humiliating captivity. The Count of Cabra and others argued that releasing Boabdil would continue the divisive rivalry between him and Abul Hacen, making the Reconquest even easier. When the squabbling Spaniards couldn't reach agreement, Ferdinand put the issue to the Queen. Knowing that the Arabs' internecine feuds would eventually cripple the Moors, Isabel decided on release, but only on certain conditions. Boabdil agreed to a two-year truce, to surrender his Christian prisoners without ransom and to pay annual tribute of twelve thousand gold doblas. He also agreed to allow the Spaniards to freely cross his territory to fight Abul Hacen and El Zagal, and to surrender himself and his son to the Sovereigns upon request. The Spaniards achieved total submission. Now Boabdil was nothing more than a puppet of the Spanish Sovereigns. In a letter dated 1483, Ferdinand summed up the decision "to put Granada in division and destroy it. We have decided to free him [Boabdil]. He must make war on his father."[19] With Boabdil neutralized, the monarches were free to attack Abul Hacen and El Zagal.

When the War of Granada began, Ferdinand, thirty-one, was in the prime of his life. His swarthy skin, deeply tanned from days in the saddle hunting or riding with his army, contrasted with Isabel's fair skin and auburn hair. His dark hair began falling out at an early age, and, with a touch of vanity, he brushed it forward to cover his receding hairline. Although he was short, about Isabel's height, his body was muscular and well proportioned. As a young man, Isabel's private chaplain described Ferdinand as "possessed of a comely, symmetrical figure."[20] His heavy jowls and sensual lips could bend in a smile of delight at the antics of his children or snarl in rage at a disloyal or rebellious nobleman. Even though he had a high-pitched, squeaky voice, he could be eloquent and persuasive with an ambassador from the Pope or a foreign king when he needed a favor.

His eating habits were moderate, but his love of games and the boudoir were not. He fathered five children by Isabel and at least five illegitimate children by his mistresses. His pious wife disapproved of the liaisons, and broke them up whenever she could. Isabel apparently didn't harbor lasting resentment of the dalliances, and seemed to accept them as typical behavior of the men of her time. His other worldly pleasures included gambling, hunting and breaking a lance or two on the tilting field. At times, Isabel complained of his frivolity, particularly the women and gambling, for personal reasons, but also because she was afraid it detracted from his royal dignity. A calm, relaxed man, he probably took the criticism of his personal lifestyle with a slight air of bemusement and proceeded to do what he wanted.

Ferdinand's formal schooling was almost nil. He received a smattering of religious training, and shared all medieval men's inborn respect for the Church and a lively fear of eternal damnation, but never to the same extent as his devout wife. Before he was ten, his father, King John of Aragon, took him off to war to fight the French and the rebels in Catalonia. What little education he had, he got in an army camp, not at the knee of a black-robed pedagogue. Brought up in a world that extolled all the chivalrous virtues of a medieval knight, he learned every trait of the military entrepreneur. He could pick out a good warhorse or judge the strength of the steel in a sword. He knew little, and cared less, about Cicero's stoic view of the world. If Isabel wanted to discuss whether the famous Hispano-Roman Quintilian's treatises on education would apply to the tutelage of the Prince and Princesses, Ferdinand could not read the Latin.[21] Even though he was barely literate, his dark eyes danced with an innate intelligence. Behind his lively, expressive eyes and placid exterior lay a calculating mind as skeptical and materialistic as that of Machiavelli.

Ferdinand's natural intelligence opened his inquisitive mind to new ideas. He would listen to Columbus' arguments about how easy it would be to find a new route to Japan and China across the Ocean Sea. He would discuss new military tactics with the Swiss mercenaries in his army. He would probe the German artillerymen Isabel brought to Spain regarding the techniques of turning a city's walls into powder. Although his receptive mind was far from parochial, his basic mentality was conservative. He rolled over new ideas in his mind carefully, calculating the nuances of every move before making a decision. Because he was not a radical reformer, preferring to make changes deliberately and slowly, it took him almost twenty years to gain complete control of the military orders. Along with Isabel, Ferdinand spent years manipulating the Parliament, aristocrats and Holy Brotherhood to bring them under his and Isabel's sway. Even though he seldom made hasty decisions, he learned from his mistakes, as he did from his disastrous attack on Loja with raw troops and few supplies. Perhaps his reluctance to act fast and his cautious weighing of the issues stemmed from an insecurity based on his flawed education. More likely, it grew out of his basic mistrust of almost everyone.

Even though Ferdinand trusted few men's judgment, he trusted Isabel's judgment implicitly. The military was his bailiwick, but he consulted the Queen constantly on major strategic decisions during the Wars of Succession and Granada. If his commanders advised retreat, Isabel's *palabras dulces* (sweet words) and superior logic were always there to spur them on. If an ambassador proposed a dynastic marriage with the King of Portugal or the King of England, Ferdinand sought Isabel's analysis of the potential effect on the House of Trastamara. Even though the King thought his wife paid too much attention to her religious advisors, during their thirty-five-year marriage they always worked in tandem, their minds acting as one in a true marriage partnership. *Tanto monta, Monta Tanto, Isabel como Fernando.* (The one as much as the other, Isabel and Ferdinand are equal).

At the outset of their marriage partnership, Ferdinand chafed at Isabel's superior claim to the throne. Ferdinand's back bridled at the terms of their marriage contract which gave Isabel the right to approve the making of war or alliances. This was no way to harness a man. Women, in his medieval mind, were almost chattels or somebody to tumble with in bed. It rankled him that Isabel was a Castilian, supported by her people. No matter that they had the same grandfather and were second cousins and that his mother was a Castilian. He was a foreigner, an Aragonese, who had to tread lightly in his dealings with the Castilians.

"Ferdinand was not an agreeable person," Samuel Morison says, reflecting the traditional view that Ferdinand was not as great as Isabel. It must have been difficult for the proud king, schooled in *pundonor's* macho teachings, to listen to such praise of his wife as that of Peter Martyr: "[Isabel is] an incomparable woman who far transcends all human excellence, the mirror of every virtue, the shield of the innocent and an avenging sword to the wicked." Isabel was shrewd. She handled her husband with the utmost grace, never twitting him, never treating him as an inferior, never rubbing his nose in her superior position. Despite the burrs that nettled Ferdinand at the beginning, as their partnership grew, he came to trust, love and respect her beyond all others. The King and Queen might be different in many ways, but they both had the good sense to make compromises when necessary, and to draw on the other's best qualities. If the Sovereigns had differing strengths and weaknesses, they were both survivors who shared common goals.

Although he was skeptical of most men, Ferdinand placed great stock in the advice of Cardinal Mendoza and a few others. For the King, the litmus test for *un hombre de confianza* (a man you could trust) was a man's usefulness to the Sovereigns. He was a keen judge of men and their motives, and he had a well-deserved reputation for astuteness in picking the best man for a particular job. With his thorough understanding of human nature, he could quickly read a man's character and, sometimes, predict what a man would do before he did it. When he did admit a man into his confidence, he demanded absolute loyalty and devotion. If Ferdinand sensed the slightest resistance or disloyalty in one of his subordinates, the man would suffer.

Ferdinand took pleasure in the work of government, paying attention to even the smallest details, insisting that even the most trivial matters be brought to his attention. Because of his suspicious, methodical nature, he never accepted blindly the advice of his ministers. When a royal commission gave him their report, he subjected them to a rigorous cross examination into their reasons and rationale for making the recommendation. He was jealous of his prerogatives and reluctant to delegate authority to his officials on major issues. He dispensed information to his advisors only on a "need to know" basis, dribbling out bits of his plans to three of four people, but keeping the overall plan to himself. To Ferdinand, secrecy in matters of state was an article of faith. "To pursue a course of action, the motives of which were secret, was almost second nature to him, habitual."[22] He believed that the skilled ruler was the one who could most completely hide his thoughts and motives, and the one who was the most convincing liar and the most unscrupulous deceiver. These traits sometimes slowed the wheels of government, but, more important to Ferdinand, they kept him in control of everything.

Politically, Ferdinand believed in absolute monarchy. Born into the anarchy of Aragon when he was a boy, and brought up in the chaos in Castile after he married Isabel, he shared his wife's conviction that all authority must be concentrated in their hands. All groups and institutions must, in the Sovereigns' view, submit to their will, to their goal of unifying their nation. To achieve that goal, Ferdinand acted as a true medieval tribal chieftain, fighting for the throne and staying there by deceit, cunning and, if necessary, cruelty. When his subjects looked into his bemused eyes, they always knew that violation of the King's trust would meet with an iron fist. But he could also act with delicacy and diplomacy. At the beginning of his reign, he successfully gained the confidence of the Castilian nobles who treated him as a foreigner who might try to usurp the powers of their Queen. With the greatest deftness, he could flatter and charm when necessary.

In his foreign policy Ferdinand was a complete pragmatist, unscrupulous, but ever adroit. He and Isabel negotiated marriages of their children to Henry VIII of England, the heir apparent to the Portuguese throne and Philip of Austria, building an international network of friends, or, at least, neutrals. He recovered the provinces of Cerdana and Roussillon from France, and expanded Spanish territory in Italy. Ferdinand was willing to fight when necessary, but only if diplomacy failed, and only if his calculations led him to believe he was certain to win. He was a master at playing off one enemy against another, and used his considerable skills at cajolery and lying to disarm his adversaries. When he heard a story that King Louis XI of France complained that Ferdinand lied to him on two occasions, Ferdinand laughed, saying: "[King Louis] is the liar. I lied to him not twice, but ten times." Because of the wars between France and his father, King John of Aragon, Ferdinand was violently anti-French, viewing France as his single greatest enemy. More than once during the War of Granada, Ferdinand urged Isabel to break off the war with the Moors and attack France.

For all his maneuvering against the French, and others, in *The Prince* Niccolo Machiavelli[23] writes a paean:

> "Among the Princes of our time Ferdinand of Aragon, the present King of Spain, may almost be accounted a new Prince, since from one of the weakest he has become, for fame and glory, the foremost King in Christendom. And, if you consider his achievements, you will find them all great and some extraordinary.
>
> "In the beginning of his reign he made war on Granada, which enterprise was the foundation of his power. (He) kept the attention and thoughts of the Barons of Castile so completely occupied with it, that they had no time to think of changes at home. Meanwhile, he acquired a reputation among them and authority over them. With the money of the Church and of his subjects he was able to maintain his armies, and, during the prolonged contest [the War of Granada], to lay the foundations of that military discipline which afterwards he made so famous."

Between 1483 and 1487, the War of Granada degenerated into the spasmodic violence of a series of *cavalgadas* (raids or skirmishes). In surprise guerilla attacks into Muslim territory, marauding Spaniards trampled crops, demolished farm houses and uprooted vines. The Spaniards "[swept] away herds and flocks... leaving the land of the infidel in smoking desolation...[and pursued their] slow and destructive course like a stream of lava from a volcano."[24] The Spanish army chipped away at the Kingdom of Granada's outer ring of defensive forts and garrison towns, but fought no decisive battles. The Spanish navy harassed ships headed for Granadian ports, interdicting the Arabs' Mediterranean supply lines. While the Christians attacked their perimeter, the Moors blitzed Spanish supply trains and villages in cross-border incursions, but did no major damage.

During the four-year hiatus, Ferdinand and Isabel organized, trained and provisioned their army, and developed their grand strategy for the final Reconquest. As one of their major strategic decisions, the royal couple decided to squeeze the Kingdom of Granada in a vise, methodically nipping off territory in the west and then the east, isolating the capital in a war of attrition. There would be no set piece battles on open plains, and no frontal assault on the city of Granada until it was surrounded, its seaports blockaded and its subordinate towns crushed and turned into Christian settlements. This step-by-step approach would require the Sovereigns' patience, their ability to pick away at the Moors until the infidels realized that their cause was hopeless. There would be no gluttony, only small bites.

Ferdinand and Isabel's second decision was to divide and conquer. Inside the Kingdom of Granada, civil war between Boabdil and Abul Hacen ripened the pomegranate to the point of bursting into rot. The heavy taxes Abul Hacen levied, about three times greater than those paid by Castilians, and his despotic rule made him a hated man.[25] Boabdil's agreement to become a Spanish vassal after his defeat at Lucena, caused his people to think of him as a weakling and a traitor to Islam. The Kingdom of Granada was poised like the legendary scorpion to sting itself to death when surrounded by a ring of fire.

During much of 1483-1487, Boabdil controlled the city of Granada in the center of the Kingdom, and Abul Hacen and El Zagal held power in the seaport of Malaga in the west and Guadix, Baza and Almeria in the east. With the Kingdom of Granada split, and its rulers in disrepute, the Sovereigns knew that a few gestures of friendship and liberal sprinkling of gold would keep Boabdil in line. At the same time, the Sovereigns did their best to bribe Abul

Hacen and El Zagal into continuing their struggle against Boabdil.

The royal couple decided to mount siege campaigns, encircling one Arab city and town after another with trenches until famine and fear forced them to surrender. Since the Moors were weaker in number, the Sovereigns reasoned, they probably wouldn't come out of their walled towns to fight anyway. The Kingdom of Granada's mountainous terrain didn't lend itself to the fast-moving tactics of cavalry in open plains. It would be a war for the infantry to surround and seal off a town from water and food while heavy artillery battered away at the a town's walls. Siege warfare would require massive amounts of stores to feed the Spanish armies while they camped outside a town's battlements waiting for the Moors to surrender. It would require skilled engineers and sappers to plan the trenching, mining and placement of cannons to pinpoint the targets. It would require disciplined troops to battle the Muslim horsemen who sallied out of a town's gates to harass the Christians. When the time came, the Spanish soldiers would need to be prepared to scale the walls and not break ranks under the hail of arrows and stones and the boiling oil and water being dumped on them.

Ferdinand and Isabel primed their army's morale with a masterful propaganda campaign. The royal couple wrapped the War of Granada in the robes of the Catholic Church, claiming that they were fighting the Prophet's minions to expand Christ's dominions, not to enhance their own territory. "We have not been moved to this war by any desire to enlarge our realms, nor by greed for greater revenues," Ferdinand said somewhat disingenuously. Their objective, the Sovereigns claimed, was "to expel from all of Spain the enemies of the Catholic faith and dedicate Spain to the service of God." Armies of clergymen, including Cardinal Mendoza, mingled with the troops to hold masses and celebrate victories with religious processions. In the psychological war against Islam, it was the priests' duty to arouse and sustain the fervor of the Christians—to impress on them their divinely appointed mission to free Spain from the Moors, to imbue in the soldiers a militant Christianity that motivated them to fight and die for Jesus Christ.

On the orders of the Sovereigns, Spanish songwriters composed *romances fronterizos* (frontier ballads), one of which expressed the hope that Ferdinand and Isabel would conquer "as far as Jerusalem" and another of which, titled *Sobre Baza* (Onward to Baza) encouraged persistence in the war. The priests called Ponce de Leon "another El Cid born in our time."[26] They called on Santiago Matamoros, not as some ethereal saint to worship from afar, but as a real, earthly figure to spur the troops into battle. When the clergymen weren't busy implanting a sense of participating in a holy mission as soldiers of the faith, they sometimes took up swords and strapped on armor to fight alongside the common soldiers. "Praying for God's grace, and thumping with the mace," *(A Dios rogando y con la maza dando)* the saying went.[27]

The Sovereign's friend in Rome, Pope Sixtus IV, issued a Bull of Crusade in 1482 sanctifying the war and making it the duty of the international community of Christendom to join in the battle.[28] This alliance between Church and state served the royal couple well. "One of the advantages your neighboring rulers envy you for," the Queen's historian Pulgar told her, "is having within your frontiers people against whom you can wage not merely a just war, but a holy war, to occupy and exercise the chivalry of your kingdom. You Highness should not think of it as a small convenience."[29] The Sovereigns kept the Pope closely advised of their progress. Sixtus IV honored them with a gift of a huge silver cross which the Sovereigns always displayed at the highest point of a conquered Arab town's walls.

When the Spaniards occupied a town, they converted mosques into churches with special purification rites, making the point that Jesus was on the ascendency and Mohammed was on the decline. In moving ceremonies that stirred Spanish emotions, the priests removed the manacles and chains that bound Christian captives and slaves and hung them on the walls of newly consecrated churches to remind the faithful of Moorish brutality. When Ferdinand returned from the field, priests escorted him in solemn pomp to a mass where he offered prayers of thanksgiving.

Isabel clearly understood the dramatic appeal of the holy war. The Queen's self-confidence as she visited the troops in their camps boosted their flagging spirits. One royal official told the King that "[Isabel] fights no less with her many alms and devout prayers than you [Ferdinand] do with your lance in hand."[30] She brought the pomp and circumstance of her unflappable, feminine majesty to the battlefield to awe and inspire her soldiers. Riding among their tents and campfires on a man's warhorse, she made herself the "soul of the war."

"Her presence seemed at once to gladden and regenerate our spirits, which were drooping after long vigils, dangers and fatigue," Peter Martyr says. During one siege, the Moors watched from their battlements while Isabel, surrounded by her ladies in waiting, rode through the camp.

"Isabella's psychology confounded the Moorish mind. Her self-assurance hinted at infinite resources. Her serenity brought fresh confidence to her own forces," historian Alan Lloyd says. Isabel understood her countrymen's fascination with gallantry, and their romantic notions that placed women on a chivalrous pedestal, and, with "inspired virtuosity," she played her femininity to the hilt. She wrote gracious letters to compliment her soldiers on their valor. With money in short supply, the royal couple understood Napoleon's maxim, three hundred years before the French Emperor said it, that a few titles or badges of honor bought more loyalty and desire than gold could. The Sovereigns lavished honors on men whose chivalry led them to glorious acts, creating five new dukedoms during the war. [31] When the Count of Cabra delivered them Boabdil as a captive after the battle of Lucena, Ferdinand and Isabel did the Count the unusual honor of rising to meet him, seating him next to them and telling the Count that "the conqueror of kings should sit with kings."

As part of the propaganda campaign, the Sovereigns didn't hesitate to publicize Muslim atrocities. When El Zagal captured a squad of Knights of Calatrava, he cut off the Knights heads, slung them from his saddle and paraded the grizzly trophies before the citizens of Granada. Ferdinand and Isabel made sure that story was broadcast to their subjects. To further unify her subjects behind the common goal, Isabel appealed to their patriotism, calling on them to give their all for the War of Granada. Her appeal helped her to achieve her most cherished objectives—to solidify Spain under the Church's banner, to bring an end to the aristocratic feuds, to break her countrymen's traditional isolationism and to make Spain politically, culturally and geographically whole.

Ferdinand and Isabel knew that propaganda could work equally well to soften up the enemy. They let it be known that they were prepared to treat captured Muslim towns with generosity, leaving the Arabs free to keep their property and continue to worship Islam. They wouldn't raise taxes beyond those exacted by Boabdil or Abul Hacen. They would punish Spanish troops if they vandalized or brutalized the Moors. All this gentle treatment awaited the Moors if they would surrender. If a town refused to surrender or a conquered town revolted, the royal couple would show no mercy. To make their point, when the Muslim citizens of one defeated village rebelled, Ferdinand hung 110 men from the village's walls, razed the town and sold all of the rest of its men, women and children into slavery.

To implement their strategic decisions, Ferdinand and Isabel used the 1483-1487 lull to build up their army. During this period of relative peace, Isabel gave birth to their last child on December

5, 1485, Princess Catherine of Aragon, who later married Henry VIII of England. While Ferdinand was the commander in chief, Isabel was the quartermaster general in charge of planning and arranging the logistics to cart ammunition, clothing, food and armaments to the war zone.

To apply their siege strategy, the army would need heavy artillery to blast a town's walls into rubble. Although cannons varied in size and caliber, the largest and most terrifying were the lombards. The cannons heaved their 175 pound balls about two thousand yards and could fire only once an hour.[32] Even though their gunners could fire only a few shots in a day of fighting, "The conquest of Granada was due less to feudal chivalry than to these fearful engines of destruction," the French historian Jean Mariejol says. "No wall, however massive, could withstand a sustained fire. Without artillery, the war might have dragged on forever." Crude, bulky weapons, the lombards were about twelve feet long, weighed several tons and hurled fourteen inch balls that would eventually bash down even the strongest ramparts. Most of the cannon balls were rock, dug out of quarries located near the battlefield and handcrafted into smooth spheres by stone cutters.

The Spaniards developed an even more terrible weapon to pound the enemy. By heating their few iron cannon balls almost to the melting point before firing, the incendiary shells exploded in a shower of sparks when they hit the target, killing Moors and setting fire to houses. At the beginning of the war, in 1482, there were only sixty-five skilled artillerymen in the royal service, and foreigners had to be imported. Although many skilled foreigners served as gunners, Francisco Ramirez, the father of the Spanish artillery, had overall command of the artillery. One official document lauded his efforts for "casting down and leveling to the ground the greater part of the fortress of Alhabar."[33] Isabel herself observed with pleasure the smoke and fire from Ramirez' ordnance as it obliterated large segments of the walls of the town of Moclin, and set off a gigantic explosion when a heated iron cannon ball ignited a Muslim gunpowder cache. Later in the war, Ferdinand personally commended Ramirez for his role "In the conquest of the...Moors of Granada for the holy Catholic faith, Senor Francisco Ramirez...[who], moved by zeal for the Holy Faith...exposed his person to great dangers and labored in the combats and the taking of all the cities, towns and fortresses that their Majesties gained in this war."[34]

To support Ramirez' artillery, Isabel recruited blacksmiths and engineers from Italy, France, Belgium and Germany. She mustered carpenters, harness makers and stone workers. She imported large quantities of gunpowder from Sicily, Belgium and Portugal, and Spanish laborers dug underground pits to store the precious powder. The Queen set up factories and forges to make cannon balls and guns, and, by 1489, the army had two hundred pieces of heavy artillery and some thirteen hundred other cannons. She rounded up hundreds of drivers and carts to haul the cannons and equipment. With little money, she forced Castilian towns to herd together fourteen thousand horses, donkeys, mules and oxen to pull the lumbering carts and gun carriages. So that the dray animals could move the army's baggage, Isabel ordered bridges to be built and goat trails to be turned into roads. The Queen's engineers repaired existing roads, filling in ruts with rocks and cork trees so the oxen could pull the cannons through the mud. The transportation problems were enormous, requiring the beasts of burden to pull wagons up the craggy slopes of the Andalusian mountains. "He who had not seen the [mountain] passes by which those monstrous lombards...made their way would have deemed it an incredible thing," Pulgar said.[35]

The grand army Ferdinand and Isabel assembled was a national and international force. Lured by the Pope's call to arms to fight the Muslim crescent, military entrepreneurs from all over Europe flocked into Spain to have at the Moors. Swiss, Italian, Belgian, German and English knights and mercenaries fought in Christ's service. The most famous Englishman was the Earl of Rivers, who held himself out as a wealthy, highborn man allegedly related to the British royal family. Whether or not Rivers carried royal blood, he brought three hundred Englishmen armed with long bows and battle axes to the Sovereigns' army. When he mounted a scaling ladder during the battle of Loja, a stone smashed Rivers square in the face, knocked out two of his teeth and sent him sprawling to the ground unconscious. After the battle, Ferdinand and Isabel paid Rivers a personal visit and rewarded his valor with twelve Andalusian horses and an elegant tent to lie in while he nursed his wounds.

The foreigners only supplemented the Spaniards from Andalusia and the tough mountaineers from Galicia and Asturias. Aragonese troopers kicked up clouds of dust as they marched up and down the drill fields. Able bodied men from Castile and Leon learned to fire crossbows and harquebuses with deadly precision. "Who would have believed," Peter Martyr wrote, "that the Galician, the fierce Asturian and the rude inhabitant of the Pyrenees, men accustomed to deeds of atrocious violence, and to brawl and battle on the slightest occasion at home, should mingle amicably, not only with one another, but with the Toledans, the La Manchans and the wily and jealous Andalusians; all living together in harmonious subordination to authority, speaking one language, and subject to one common discipline...."[36]

The Holy Brotherhoods, the military orders and the *grandees, caballeros* and *hidalgos* supplied men and materiel for the cause. The nobles and the military orders furnished forces made up of about sixty percent horsemen. Cardinal Mendoza brought one thousand foot and one thousand mounted soldiers to the field. The troops from the cities and the Holy Brotherhood were mostly infantry who wore red crusaders crosses stitched to their uniforms.[37] Ferdinand assumed direct command of the Holy Brotherhood's ten thousand foot soldiers, turning the Brotherhood primarily into a military, rather than a police, organization.[38] With its of crime fighting mission suspended, the Holy Brotherhood supplied seventeen thousand dray animals and eight thousand men as drovers.[39] Ferdinand and Isabel raised troops from their royal lands, and Ferdinand fielded a personal bodyguard of one thousand knights, half light cavalry and half heavy cavalry. To swell the ranks, the Sovereigns granted pardons to some one thousand criminals who agreed to serve.[40] Some men fought for noble reasons, loyalty to their lord or the crown or a burning desire to defeat the Moors. Others were interested only in the thrill of battle and the booty and glory it would bring. Whatever their reasons, this mixing of men from throughout the Peninsula helped forge unity. Where these men had once lived in isolation in their communities, hating foreigners and intruders from other parts of Spain, now they came together to serve the common national purpose. Now they served in the vanguard of their country's holy mission to drive out the Infidels. Now they redirected their mistrust of their brother Spaniards to a passionate hatred of the Moors.

Even though Ferdinand and Isabel clearly focused the soldiers' mission, when the War of Granada began the army was mostly a rag-tag band of poorly trained militia. In the ancient feudal tradition, the Spanish noblemen conscripted their peasants, laborers and tradesmen, put pikes or swords in their hands and marched them off to war, usually only for short enlistment periods. The soldiers' primary loyalty, their duty of *personalismo,* was to the aristocrat who recruited them, and they fought as the bondsmen of their master. When Ferdinand tried to assume command over the Duke of Medina Celi's men, the Duke protested: "Tell the King, my lord, that I came to serve him with the men of my household, and that I shall not serve in the war unless accompanied by my men. It is not reasonable for them to serve without me at their head."[41]

This *personalismo,* loyalty to one's immediate superior, created erratic groupings of soldiers based on where they came from or who their master was.[42] One duke might have sixty percent cavalry, another ten percent. One marquis might have one hundred crossbowmen, another twenty five. One count might have ten artillery pieces, another only two. Ferdinand had no organized battalions, regiments or companies with equally distributed forces and arms, making his job as commander in chief a nightmare of trying to figure out whether a particular duke had enough cavalry or cannon to perform the job at hand.

If one wing of the army needed a large force of calvary, the horsemen might be concentrated on the other wing. If Ferdinand wanted to mass his bowmen and pikemen for an assault on a town's walls, they might be tied up fighting somewhere else. In their reforming zeal, Ferdinand and Isabel required longer enlistment periods and began reorganizing their unwieldy army into battalions of five hundred troops with roughly equivalent numbers of infantry, harquebusers and cavalry. Over time, the Spanish soldiers developed a loyalty to their military unit, not to the man who brought them to the front. They learned to fight, not in the old medieval way where individual bravery carried a premium, but as a unified fighting force commanded by trained professional soldiers who guided their men through intricate tactical maneuvers. With these basic reforms, the Sovereigns crafted the pattern for a standing army that would dominate Europe for the next one hundred years.

"Spanish towns poured [into the army] their noblest and vilest elements, the most high minded and the most infamous, the most generous and the greediest—the honor and the refuse of the Spanish people."[43] Although this comment on Spanish soldiers refers to a period shortly after the end of the War of Granada, it was also true of the men who faced off against the Moors. If their pay didn't arrive on time, they might threaten their officers with mutiny. It was not unusual for them to execute or rape prisoners. Dice rolled and cards clicked in the gambling around campfires, sometimes erupting into brawls and murder. If the urge struck a trooper bored with days of besieging a Muslim town, one of the horde of whores would accommodate him behind a nearby thicket. In what was probably a vain attempt to discipline the men, the pious Isabel instituted a ban on gambling, blasphemy and prostitution, and instructed her army chaplains to enforce the moral tone she set.

Although her warriors didn't like her curbs on their more earthy instincts, they worshiped their Queen. Rather than leaving the wounded to die in the field, the usual custom of the day, out of her own purse Isabel set up field hospitals to tend the broken limbs and gashes inflicted by Muslim scimtars. "It is well worth while," Peter Martyr wrote to the Archbishop of Milan, "to see the four large hospital tents....Such is the number of doctors, chemists, surgeons and their assistants...that they are in no way inferior to your Hospital of the Holy Ghost...in Milan."[44] Isabel made regular visits to the camps to pass out clothes and money, and to lift her soldiers' spirits by encouraging them to endure the hardships. During battle, she set up a command post and received hourly reports of the course of the fighting, sending food and ammunition where it was most needed.

To finance the enormous cost of the War of Granada,[45] Isabel coerced wealthy individuals and religious orders into lending money, and she mortgaged the revenues from her royal lands to back up the loans. If the merchants or nobles balked at her requests for loans, the Sovereigns' chosen "lenders" were subject to having their property confiscated and the offender's goods sold. When she ran out of royal land to mortgage, she pawned her jewels to raise money, pledging her crown and a ruby necklace to the city of Valencia for a sizeable loan. She persuaded the Pope to issue Bulls of Crusade which granted indulgences to redeem the sins of those who contributed to the cause.

Pope Innocent VIII's bull in 1485 dedicated one-tenth of the Spanish Church's considerable revenues to defeat the infidels. The Holy Brotherhood raised three hundred million maravedis during the critical years of the war. Special taxes on Jews and Moors living in Spain brought in almost as many millions as the Sovereigns raised from the sale of Arab captives as slaves. The army consumed money in huge gulps, and, at the height of the war in 1490, Isabel sometimes levied taxes every twenty days. The Sovereigns taxed imports and exports, consumption and commercial transactions, and the royal tax collector stood guard at mountain passes to collect duties on the migratory flocks of sheep. The historian Bernaldez says there were *muchas murmuraciones* (much muttering), but the taxes were paid. The crown's monopoly on mines and salt production added to their coffers.

Since almost all the money went for the war, there was nothing extra for a petitioner like the lanky Christopher Columbus, who stalked the Queen from siege to siege to ask for financing for his fanciful scheme to cross the Atlantic Ocean. Single minded, the Sovereigns dedicated everything, their time, money and effort, to their goal—purging Spain of the Sons of Islam.

14

THE WAR OF GRANADA, THE FINAL PUSH

By 1487, the holy crusade's surge had pinned the Moors into a few strongholds; the seaport of Malaga in the southwest, the towns of Almeria, Guadix and Baza in the east and the city of Granada in the center.

Inside these fortified towns, the Muslims prostrated themselves on their prayer rugs in the quiet of their mosques while the clatter of Christ's armored horsemen and Spanish trumpet blasts interrupted their communion with Allah. When the Muslim reconnaissance parties scouted their enemy's siege camps they reported back to their turbaned leaders an awesome show of men and materiel. Perhaps their arabesque poetry, the sensuous guitar music, the perfume of the harem or the soothing warmth of their baths may have calmed the Moors. But even these pleasures couldn't disguise the fact that a resolute pair of Catholic Sovereigns meant to destroy them.

In Isabel and Ferdinand's siege camps outside the thick stone walls, the Sovereigns' forces kicked up clouds of dust as they tramped across the drill field and moved cannons into position for the next day's barrage. Smoke billowed from the campfires as cooks labored to feed the army. The smell of roasting meat blended with the *olor de sanctidad* (smell of holiness) of the unwashed soldiers. Every day, squads of foragers rode out of the Christian camp to requisition sheep, cattle, chickens, grain and fruit from Muslim shepherds and farmers.

If the food or water poisoned their stomachs, or if Moorish swords gashed their limbs, their captains sent them to the Queen's field hospital where, with luck, Isabel herself might pay a visit. Blacksmiths sweated over forges, stoking the charcoal that heated the metal the smiths shaped into swords, shields and daggers. The blacksmiths' assistants, their faces and hands blackened, burned wood to make the charcoal and stacked it in piles outside their masters' tents. Sutlers haggled over the inflated prices they charged the troopers for a bit of honey, extra salt or new boots. For a small tip, camp followers washed away the *olor de sanctidad* clinging to the mens' underwear and uniforms when the smell and grime became unbearable.

Drovers and muleteers tended thousands of dray animals that deposited tons of manure in their roped off corrals, producing a ripe odor that attracted millions of flies. Aided by the hot Andalusian sun, latrines full of human waste added to the stench. To feed their animals, the Spaniards scavenged the countryside for the mountains of hay and other feed they needed. Sappers sharpened their picks and shovels to dig tunnels up to, and under, the Moors' walls. Carpenters repaired the fleet of wagons and carts which hauled food and supplies. Woodworkers fashioned rough lumber into scaling ladders and battering rams, and made tall wooden towers on rollers with drawbridges at the same height as the walls for the Spaniards to leap out and attack the enemy.

Tailors stitched clothing and shoemakers tapped hobnails to outfit the troops. Armed guards patrolled underground pits full of precious gunpowder. The soldiers herded Muslim captives into holding pens until they could be sold as slaves or exchanged for ransom. Knowing that the Koran teaches that the ringing of bells is the sound of blasphemy, the Spaniards organized platoons of men to sit outside the Infidels' walls and conduct psychological warfare by clanging bells.

Off duty, the soldiers sat around their fires and told stories of their women back home in the mountains of Galicia or the hard scrabble of Extremadura, or fantasized a chivalrous encounter with one of Isabel's "choir of nymphs," the silk clad young ladies in waiting who attended the Queen at the battlefield. When the daily routine became too boring, and if they were out of sight of the Queen and her priests, the troopers played cards and dice or snuck off with a tantalizing whore. If caught by the moral policemen, the clergy, a soldier violating Isabel's strict rules would be tied to a flogging post to receive the required number of lashes to pay for his sins. A few men, homesick or unhappy with late pay or a brutal officer, deserted and returned to their homes in Seville or Toledo.

While the Sovereigns trained their army during the four-year lull in the War of Granada, the Moors' internal strife met Ferdinand and Isabel's every expectation. Boabdil intrigued and fought against Abul Hacen and his brother El Zagal for control of what was left of the kingdom. In 1486, El Zagal deposed his aging, despotic brother. When the Sovereigns put their plans into gear, the intericene struggle between Boabdil and El Zagal's supporters had left the Kingdom of Granada weak and divided. To implement their grand strategy of enveloping Granada from the east and west, the Sovereign's launched their first major campaign in the spring of 1487.

Taking advantage of Granada's disarray, Ferdinand and Isabel marched their army of twelve thousand horsemen and forty thousand foot soldiers out of Cordoba's gates to the cheers of a huge crowd, including a tall Genoese mariner, toward their objective—the seaport of Malaga.[1] In a hard march, mules and oxen strained in their harnesses to pull the heavy carts and cannons over the rough mountain passes. The Spanish troops struggled to ford rivers rushing with the spring runoff. Although the army met little opposition, the Muslim light cavalry occasionally picked off Christian stragglers and staged a few ambushes. After a ten-day march, the Spaniards met their first major resistance a few miles from Malaga at the small town of Velez.[2]

When Ferdinand's heavy artillery arrived, he surrounded the town and ordered his cannoneers to batter down Velez' walls. While the Spaniards pounded away at the town's ramparts, El Zagal sent troops from the city of Granada to relieve Velez. El Zagal knew when he left Granada that he was gambling that Boabdil's followers in the city wouldn't rise against him and take the capital. He also knew that losing Velez and Malaga might be an even bigger gamble.

When the Moors' relieving force arrived at Velez, El Zagal deployed his men for a surprise night attack on the Spaniards besieging the town. But the Spaniards captured a messenger carrying the Moors' battle plan, and met the Muslim assault with unexpected ferocity, chasing El Zagal from the field. While El Zagal was away from the city of Granada, he lost on another front. Boabdil's supporters revolted and turned the capital over to the young ruler. When El Zagal returned to the city of Granada, news of the disaster preceded him. Boabdil closed the city's gates, forcing El Zagal to seek refuge in his eastern stronghold at Guadix.

In later fighting during the siege at Velez, the Moors almost killed Ferdinand while the King was rallying his troops to beat back a Muslim sortie. The Marquis of Cadiz rescued the King, and the Spaniards finally drove off the Muslim army. After Velez surrendered, Isabel granted her new city of Velez the right to place on its escutcheon a figure of Ferdinand on horseback running a Moor through with his lance.[3]

Ferdinand chose Malaga as his next target. This ancient city had been an old Carthagenian and Roman port, and was the second city and major deep water seaport of the Kingdom of Granada. Because Malaga handled the bulk of the Kingdom of Granada's import and export trade, it was a rich city with spectacular Moorish buildings, beautiful gardens and sparkling fountains. At its back was the sea, and in front were orchards and vineyards.

Knowing the Spaniards were on the march, Malaga's citizens stocked the city with ample supplies of food and arms to stand off the expected siege. They worked feverishly to put its walls and towers in perfect repair. The Moors were sure that Malaga's fortress, the Gibralforo, was impregnable. Even though Malaga had only fifteen thousand citizens, escaping Arabs from the countryside and a contingent of African mercenaries swelled its ranks. The Muslim general, Hamet Zeli,[4] was known to be brilliant, fearless soldier.

Malaga was daunting, but there was little threat from Boabdil, who was busy consolidating his power in the city of Granada, and was neutralized by his pledge to the Sovereigns not to fight. El Zagal nursed his wounds far away in Guadix, and, the Spanish thought, there was little chance he would send a relieving force to squeeze the Spaniards from the rear. Ferdinand knew he had a superior force of ground troops, and Isabel had organized a fleet of galleys and caravels to close the trap, blockading Malaga's harbor.[5] Still, the Sovereigns opened surrender negotiations with General Zeli. Ferdinand sent the Marquis of Cadiz to offer liberal terms and a fat bribe if Zeli would lay down his arms. The fiery Muslim told the Marquis that he would fight to the last man, and that there wasn't a payoff large enough to make him betray his countrymen.

Rebuffed, Ferdinand ordered his troops to encircle the city. With picks and shovels, they dug trenches and piled up mounds of earthen breastworks. It was hard, hot work in the May sun of 1487. The cannon fire from Malaga's walls increased the danger, forcing the Spanish to dig the close-in trenches at night. With the earthworks sealing off the city by land and Isabel's ships cutting off access to the harbor, the noose around Malaga was in place.

Spanish officers shouted at their troops as they cut roads to haul the ponderous lombards from Velez to Malaga. When the heavy artillery arrived, the Spanish artilleryman Ramirez ordered the German gunners to swing the cannons into position for the siege. Still cautious, Ferdinand made a second attempt to negotiate a surrender. This time he sent the Arabs a warning—if the defenders wouldn't give up "[I will] make them all slaves." General Zeli, strongly supported by black African troops and *renegados* (Christians converted to Islam), answered with a volley of murderous fire from the cannons mounted on Malaga's walls, and sent a raiding party of light cavalry to harass the Spanish camp.

To further hearten the Moors, signal fires in the mountains told that El Zagal was sending a column of cavalry to relieve Malaga. In the Spanish siege camp, only inconsequential skirmishes broke the boredom. During that summer of 1487, the idle Spanish soldiers began hearing rumors of outbreaks of plague in nearby villages. Another rumor claimed that Isabel, who was holding court in Cordoba, wrote to Ferdinand pleading with him to withdraw from Malaga.

When Ferdinand heard the rumors, he sent his army of priests to boost morale by reminding the soldiers that they were fulfilling Santiago's holy mission. The King summoned Isabel to the camp to dispel any notion that the Sovereigns were thinking about retreat. The Queen, accompanied by Cardinal Mendoza, her teenaged daughter Princess Isabel, her ladies in waiting and a personal bodyguard, rode into the camp to the cheers of her soldiers and to the roar of Spanish cannons firing at Malaga. "Hope now brightened every countenance. A grace seemed to be shed over the rugged features of war...," Prescott says.[6]

While Isabel's presence buoyed her army's spirits, inside Malaga morale was fast deteriorating. The once hopeful signal fires now told the Moors that the duplicitous Boabdil had sent a large force from Granada which destroyed El Zagal's relieving army. The Christian army swelled to sixty thousand men.[7] The lombards and lighter cannons pounded Malaga incessantly, hurling stone and molten cannon balls through the fog of choking gun smoke created by the cannons. Muslim scouting parties brought back reports that the Christians were building wooden assault vehicles on rollers, catapults and battering rams. After three months of blockade, Malaga was almost out of food, its citizens reduced to eating dogs, cats, horses and the boiled hides of animals. They put cooking oil on grape leaves to make them more palatable and made a type of bread from palm leaves. People starved to death. Many deserted, telling the Spanish of the city's plight.

Still, the Moorish soldiers slipped out of Malaga's gates day and night to skirmish with the Christians. During one foray, the Spaniards captured a turbaned warrior who told them that he had secret information that would unlock Malaga's gates. The Moor said he could only disclose this valuable information to the King and Queen.[8] The Marquis of Cadiz sent the Moor to Ferdinand's tent, but the King was sleeping and Isabel refused to talk with him without her husband. The Spanish guards took the Moor to an adjoining tent where Isabel's old friend, Beatriz de Bobadilla, and Isabel's cousin, a Portuguese Duke, were playing chess. The Moor, who spoke no Spanish, mistook Beatriz and the Duke for the Sovereigns, pulled a knife out of his robes and slashed the Duke across the head. He lunged at Beatriz, but her heavy dress deflected the thrusts. Bodyguards heard the screams from Beatriz' tent, rushed in and hacked the would-be assassin to a bloody pulp, inflicting over one hundred wounds.

Enraged, Ferdinand instructed his men to put the Moor's mangled body in a catapult and hurl it over Malaga's walls. The Muslims retaliated with their own brutality. They executed a Christian prisoner, tied his body to a mule, popped the mule's backside and sent the corpse wobbling into the Spanish camp.

After the assassination attempt, Ferdinand decided to press the attack. Sappers dug a tunnel, mined it with gunpowder and blew a battle tower to smithereens. The Christians, their steel helmets gleaming in the sun, stormed through the breach and forced General Zeli's army to retreat into Malaga's fortress, the Gibralforo. With their fighting forces pinned inside the Gibralforo, Malaga's citizens sent a delegation to Ferdinand to sue for peace on liberal terms which guaranteed the safety of their lives and property. The victorious King refused to meet with the Moors and demanded unconditional surrender on his terms. Through one of his commanders, Ferdinand sent the Malagans a message: "Since hunger and not good will prompts you to surrender your city, either defend yourselves or submit to whatever punishment shall be pleasing to the King and Queen—to wit, death to those for whom it is destined, slavery to those for whom slavery [is destined]."[9]

The Moors sent a second delegation offering to give up all their property in exchange for their lives. If Ferdinand refused, the Moors said, they would hang their six hundred Christian captives and fight to the last man. Unmoved, Ferdinand replied that, if the Muslims killed even one Christian prisoner, he would slaughter every man, woman and child. Surrounded, starving, their army immobilized in the Gibralforo, the townsmen surrendered Malaga on August 18, 1487. The next day, General Zeli surrendered his army and the Gibralforo fortress. Even though the Moors went down to defeat, the court historian Pulgar lauded their bravery: "Who does not marvel at the bold heart of these Infidels in battle, their obedience to their leaders, their dexterity in the wiles of war, their patience under privation, and undaunted perseverance in their purpose."[10]

The triumphant Spanish army marched into Malaga, tore down the Muslim battle flags and raised their own banners and the huge silver cross given to the Sovereigns by Pope Sixtus IV. The priests consecrated Malaga's principal mosque to the eternal service of Christ, and rang the holy bells of Christendom. "The celestial music of their chimes," Pulgar wrote, "sounding at every hour of the day and night, caused perpetual torment to the ears of the infidel."

In a dramatic ceremony, the Spanish paraded the emaciated Christian prisoners before Ferdinand and Isabel where their chains were cut off and the Sovereigns gave them food and gifts. Isabel, and many others, were moved to tears at the sight of their haggard brothers in Christ. In a more gruesome ceremony, the Spaniards tied twelve *renegados* to posts, and horsemen at full gallop stabbed them with lances until they crumpled to the ground. Then the Spaniards turned on the Jews who converted to Mohammed's teachings, burning them at the stake or releasing them in return for ransom. "These were the fetes and illuminations most grateful to the Catholic piety of our Sovereigns," a priest wrote.[11]

After the Sovereigns dealt with the heretics, they pronounced the fate of the heathen Malagans. To set an example for other Muslim towns that refused to surrender, the royal couple ordered that a third of Malaga's citizens be sold into slavery to raise more money to finish the war. They distributed another third as slaves to Spanish noblemen, the Pope and the Queens of Naples and Portugal. They exchanged the remainder for Christian prisoners being held in North Africa.

Before his orders were carried out, Ferdinand told the Malagans that he would release them if they paid thirty doblas per person as ransom. In order for him to decide whether there was enough money to pay the ransom, Ferdinand required the Malagans to provide a complete list of all their property. Believing the King, many Malagans gave the Spaniards a list of all their property and told where it was hidden. With deceit Machiavelli would have lauded, Ferdinand confiscated the property and sent the Moors into slavery. Ferdinand's message[12] was clear—defeat was inevitable. Surrender or suffer.

With Malaga's surrender, the Moors lost the western part of their kingdom and major seaport. As winter approached, Ferdinand and Isabel returned north to Aragon and Castile in the fall of 1487 to attend to long-neglected domestic affairs and foreign policy negotiations. While in the north, the Sovereigns began planning a sweep through eastern Granada to cut off El Zagal's key towns of Almeria, Guadix and Baza.

In the summer of 1488, with a small force of about twenty thousand men, Ferdinand entered the Kingdom of Granada. In a pitched battle, El Zagal mauled the Christians and drove them back into Spain. The defeat, and a plague epidemic and famine caused by a bad harvest, forced the royal couple to wait for a better time. By late May, 1489, they were ready to renew the assault. At the head of fifteen thousand cavalry and eighty thousand infantry,[13] Ferdinand invaded. The names of Spain's greatest families, Ponce de Leon, Guzman, Manrique, Pacheco and Zuniga, sprinkled the army's rolls. The artilleryman, Ramirez, the Grand Masters of Calatrava, Alcantara and Santiago and the Great Captain, Gonzalo Fernandez de Cordoba,[14] rode alongside the King toward their target—Baza.

Famed for its silk manufacturing and mining in the snow capped Alpujarras mountains, Baza lay in a valley twenty-five miles long and nine miles wide. A thick forest screened the town from the valley's plains and the mountains rose up to shelter it from behind. Twenty thousand Muslim soldiers garrisoned the town, and their commander, Cid Hiaya,[15] provisioned it for the expected siege with over a year's supply of food.

The Spanish columns crossed the mountains into the valley and took up positions just outside the forest. Because the trails and paths through the forest acted as a sieve for the Moors to come out and skirmish with the attackers and to smuggle in supplies, Ferdinand ordered an assault to clear them out of the woods. It was a bad decision. The Moors knew their ground, and the trees nullified the Spaniards' superiority in artillery. The heavy foliage made the Spanish cavalry useless, forcing the horsemen to dismount and fight on foot. Brambles and undergrowth snared fourteen-foot-long pikes and lances. Squads and companies lost touch with their officers, turning them into disorganized bands fighting off the swarming Saracens who attacked from every angle. The hand-to-hand combat at close quarters went on for twelve hours until the Spanish finally retreated.

Ferdinand called his generals to his tent for a war council. They could never blockade Baza, some said. With mountains at its back, and the forest protecting its front, it was impossible. Winter came early in the mountains, they argued, and the freezing rains, snow and mud would cut their supply lines over the passes, making life in the siege camp miserable. Even the stalwart Marquis of Cadiz agreed that, if they set up camp for a prolonged siege, El Zagal, who was headquartered twenty miles to the west at Guadix, might outflank them from the rear. If El Zagal achieved even the slightest success, this might cause Boabdil to arrange a truce with his uncle and join in the attack. Instead of being the besiegers, they would be the besieged—on two fronts.

As Ferdinand always did when he had a hard decision to make, he sent a dispatch rider plunging north over the mountains to Jaen, where his partner and most trusted counselor was requisitioning dray animals, food and men for the army. After Isabel read the King's letter, she drafted a carefully worded response. Beginning with *palabras dulces* (sweet words), she made it clear that she would not meddle in her husband's military bailiwick.

However, the Queen said, the Almighty had always been on their side. God had guided them through many difficult days in pursuit of their goals. God wouldn't forget them now. Not when they were so close to the final defeat of the heathens. Although the decision was Ferdinand's, Isabel said, he should remember that the Moors were at their lowest ebb. The Queen advised that he should consider that they had already spent millions of maravedis, and that they might not be able to assemble such a large force again. She ended her letter with a spirited promise that, if the soldiers would do their duty, as quartermaster general, she would do hers. Once again Isabel inspired her army to fight.

After reading the Queen's letter, the Spanish commanders devised a new battle plan. Ferdinand set up camp at one end of the three-mile-long forest, and the Marquis of Cadiz positioned his forces at the other end. Some 4,000 Spanish troops exchanged their weapons for axes and began chopping down the dense woods, while their brothers in arms fought off Muslim cavalry attacks. The work took seven weeks, and, when they leveled the trees, the Spanish began digging trenches and building earthworks where the forest once stood. Then the soldiers completed the loop by digging a trench and building stone walls around the side of Baza facing the mountains.

With the Christians camped at Baza, it would have been relatively easy for El Zagal to move his forces the twenty miles from Guadix to attack the besiegers. One of Ferdinand and Isabel's strategic weapons, diplomatic maneuvering to keep El Zagal and Boabdil at each other's throats, quashed the threat. El Zagal sat in his well-fortified Guadix—neutralized by fear that

Boabdil would march against his undefended rear if he came out to fight the Spanish.

With El Zagal immobilized in Guadix, at Baza Spanish and Arab cannons exchanged barrages. Knights clashed in chivalric cavalry charges and platoons of infantry fought with swords and crossbows. Although the skirmishes brought individual glory to Muslims and Christians alike, they had little effect on the overall siege effort.

Because the Spaniards spent weeks chopping down the forest and digging trenches, winter became an enemy. When the Spanish understood the Muslim strategy, to harass the Christians with hit and run guerilla tactics until winter forced a withdrawal, Ferdinand countered. He ordered his men to build earthen huts and wooden lean-tos. As the Moors watched from their battlements, in only four days the Spaniards constructed a town of some one thousand crude structures to house themselves during the cold months. Not quite home, but more comfortable than sleeping on the ground or in leaky tents.

From her headquarters at Jaen, Isabel kept a steady flow of supplies coming into the siege camp. Sutlers from Castile and Aragon peddled luxury items to the troops, and the Queen's hospitals made camp life more bearable for the sick and wounded. Despite these comforts, heavy mountain rains that autumn of 1489 brought misery. Rivers and streams over-flowed, washing away many of the mud huts and lean-tos, and turning the siege camp into a swamp. The deluges made quagmires of supply roads, bogging down mules and oxen and sucking at wagon wheels. In their soggy clothes, the soldiers fought off Muslim sorties almost daily. Morale plummeted.

Ferdinand sent for Isabel. Accompanied by her most trusted advisor, Cardinal Mendoza, her best friend, Beatriz de Bobadilla, and a tall Genoan, Christopher Columbus,[16] the Queen rode into the siege camp on November 7, 1489. Her appearance was magic. "[W]hen...the hearts of the soldiers were fainting under long-protracted sufferings, she appeared among them...to cheer their faltering spirits and inspire them with her own energy."[17]

Word spread among the troops that Isabel was in the camp, and, three days after her arrival, she and Ferdinand reviewed their troops. "[F]rom the moment of her appearance, a change seemed to come over the scene," a writer present at the Spanish camp said.[18] The Moors, looking on from their battlements, correctly interpreted the Spaniards' psychological ploy as a sign of resolution—the enemy was there to stay.

Baza's commander, Cid Hiaya, dispatched a messenger to

Guadix to tell El Zagal that, even though the garrison's strength was reduced and ammunition was low, he would continue to hold out, but only if El Zagal promised to send an army to break the siege. Still looking over his shoulder at Boabdil in the city of Granada, El Zagal instructed Cid Hiaya to negotiate the best terms he could. Cid Hiaya surrendered, ending the seven-month siege. Ferdinand and Isabel entered Baza on December 4, 1489.

Because El Zagal, the Muslims' best general, still held Guadix and the port of Almeria, Ferdinand didn't insist on the harsh surrender terms he demanded two years earlier at Malaga. Baza's citizens could keep their property and either go to North Africa or stay in Spain and live under their own religion and laws. At the surrender ceremony, the Sovereigns heaped gifts and flattery on the Muslim commander. "Isabel's compliments were repaid in substantial coin," an Arab historian wrote.[19] Cid Hiaya agreed to join Ferdinand's household and to be baptized a Christian in return for being treated as "a great *caballero*," retaining his property and being exempted from taxes.[20] The Sovereigns asked one more favor. If Cid Hiaya could convince El Zagal to give up Guadix and Almeria, the royal couple would reward him with more chests of gold.

After riding the twenty miles from Baza to Guadix, Cid Hiaya presented El Zagal with Ferdinand and Isabel's proposal, a title, land, lucrative salt mines and a large income if he capitulated. As El Zagal analyzed his situation, he calculated that the fall of Baza cut his dominions in two, threatening him with a two-front war—Ferdinand to his east and Boabdil to his west. Cid Hiaya told him the Spanish had superior forces, and it would only be a matter of time until the Christians ground down El Zagal's army. Faced with the choice of submitting to the Christians, who offered generous terms, or his hated nephew Boabdil, Ferdinand and Isabel's offer seemed the lesser evil.

To El Zagal it was better to negotiate now, while he still had bargaining chips, than to wait for inevitable defeat and suffer the same treatment as the Malagans. "What Allah wills, He brings to pass in His own way," El Zagal said. "[Let] His will be done." The Sovereigns' bribes, Allah's apparent will and the hopelessness of his situation convinced the fierce old warrior to surrender. Peter Martyr witnessed the scene: "His (El Zagal's) appearance touched my soul with compassion. For, even though he was a lawless barbarian, he was a king, and he had shown his heroism countless times." Ferdinand and Isabel's army marched into Guadix and Almeria in late December, 1489.

With the defeat of the Moors' most talented military commander, the noose was tight, but it hadn't snapped the enemy's neck. The Sovereigns still needed one more victory to complete the 781-year struggle to exterminate the Infidel presence from the Peninsula. All that was left of the Arabs' Iberian empire was a dried husk, a small area around the city of Granada.

With the city's population swelled by Muslims fleeing from their defeated provinces, clearly it couldn't sustain a long siege. Many of the two hundred thousand Moors crowded behind Granada's walls hated their discredited leader, Boabdil, whom they saw as a puppet of the Spanish. Divided by factionalism, depressed by Ferdinand and Isabel's pincers strategy which snipped off supply and escape routes, Granada seemed ready to implode. To add to the pressure, Ferdinand instituted a scorched earth policy in the spring of 1490, sending his troops on search and destroy missions to seize livestock and to confiscate or burn crops.

With their enemy's situation hopeless, Ferdinand and Isabel sent a deputation from their court at Seville to Boabdil to remind him of the promises he made after his capture at the battle of Lucena in 1483.[21] Now, the Spanish ambassadors said, was the time to surrender, to pay homage to the royal couple, to become their vassal. If the Granadians didn't surrender, they would suffer the fate of the Malagans—death or slavery and loss of their property.

Granada's wealthy merchants argued for a surrender. But the ruined and desperate Muslims who had lost all of their property to the Christians, and the Moorish knights who hated the Christians, wanted to continue the fight. One Muslim nobleman roused the Granadians with a cry akin to "Give me liberty or give me death."[22] Vacillating as usual, Boabdil told the Sovereigns' ambassadors that, although he was disposed to surrender, he was no longer his own master and that the citizens of Granada wouldn't let him comply. After peace negotiations collapsed, Boabdil sent raiding parties on the attack. The spurt of militancy boosted Muslim spirits, encouraging Baza, Guadix and Almeria to revolt. Ferdinand quickly crushed the rebellions in the east, and, with "unsparing rigor," stepped up his efforts to devastate Granada's grainfields and pastures.

With the Crescent waning, in the spring of 1491 Ferdinand marched his eighty thousand-man army[23] through burnt out fields and orchards, and drew up on a wide plain a few miles outside Granada's walls. The Genil River and stout walls and battle towers covered the side of Granada facing the plains, and, like Baza, mountains covered its rear. The snow-capped Sierra

Nevada mountains framed Granada and its royal palace, the red-walled Alhambra, looming on a hill overlooking the city. Inside the Alhambra, Boabdil and his strong-willed mother, Saroya, strolled through the arcaded galleries and elegant pillars to plan their defense. Outside the city's walls, Ferdinand and Isabel prepared for a siege.

Up until the War of Granada, the Spanish mounted knights were the elite of the Spanish army. But gray granules of gunpowder shook the centuries-old assumptions about war, and its philosophical underpinning, chivalry. The slow, cumbersome armored men could be blown away, and their armor pierced, with one shot from a gun. The technology of gunpowder made the knight, and his entire chivalric value system, obsolete. Even though poets and balladeers praised their boldness and valor, these warriors, clad in burnished steel suits and mounted on massive armored war-horses, no longer played a major role in the Sovereigns' battle plans. In addition to being cumbersome, it cost about eight thousand maravedis to outfit a cavalryman and took four attendants to see to his needs. Like bulky tanks, they clanked through the Spanish siege camp outside Granada and occasionally fought the Moors in ineffectual *mano-a-mano* jousts. In the reorganized Spanish army, these feudal warriors would be reduced to secondary roles. Highly mobile light cavalry and infantry would take their place.

The Spanish army's new elite, foot soldiers dressed in helmets and breastplates, went into battle with shields, pikes, crossbows, swords or harquebuses. In 1488, Ferdinand and Isabel issued a law organizing the royal infantry into brigades of eight hundred men and companies of fifty.[24] Each brigade had a captain, a lieutenant, a standard bearer and trumpeters, fifers and drummers to signal attacks or changes in formation during battle.

Before the institution of uniforms, the troops wore whatever clothes they had, making it impossible to distinguish one regiment from another or friend from foe. To cure this problem, the Sovereigns ordered the Holy Brotherhood's soldiers to dress in red trousers, a pointed helmet and a loose white jacket with a blood red cross symbolizing the Holy Crusade. The new rules standardized the length of pikes at fourteen feet. Although the crossbows' arrows could pierce light armor, over time gunpowder muskets with more power and range would replace the crossbow.[25] The light cavalry *(jinetes)* wore visored helmets and metal plates over their chests, arms and legs. With their feet planted in short stirrups, they carried lances to gore the enemy in lightening charges.

As part of the reforms, the Sovereigns extended the enlistment periods from a few weeks or months to a time frame consistent with their overall military plans. They set aside the old custom of disbanding the army at the end of a battle or when winter began. No longer would the troops pack up their arms and go home at first frost. No longer would it be necessary to spend millions of maravedis bringing the soldiers back for the spring campaign, and weeks regrouping them into a coherent force.[26] Now the soldiers signed on for the duration. Based on Ferdinand and Isabel's reforms, the Great Captain, Fernandez de Cordoba, formulated his military tactics and strategy which led him to victory in Spain's Italian wars several years later. [27]

Despite these reforms, during the War of Granada, the old feudal system of dukes and counts bringing their irregular militiamen to the field hung on. But modern technology, in the form of gunpowder, required new techniques, new organization. Ferdinand assumed command of the Holy Brotherhood, the military orders and the mercenary forces, using them as an experimental laboratory to weld together the backbone of a professional, national army unified under the royal flag. [28]

As the Spanish enlisted men at Granada practiced new maneuvers to the cadence of drums and memorized fife and trumpet signals, the nobles pranced through the siege camp like a "peacock train of high fashion." Knowing that it was only a matter of time until Granada fell, the siege camp had more the air of a prolonged festival or carnival than a war zone. The historian Oviedo describes the Duke of the Infantado's arrival at a battle camp with all the pomp of a court pageant: "[The Duke] came attended by a large body of knights and gentlemen, as befitted so great a lord. He displayed all the luxuries which belong to a time of peace; and his tables, which were carefully served, were loaded with rich and curiously wrought silver plate...."[29]

The "large body of knights and gentlemen" Oviedo referred to included the Duke of the Infantado's fifty men who rode horses blanketed with gold embroidered cloth, his pack mules with silk harnesses and his retinue of five hundred men with plumes and silk vests.[30] So great was the aristocrats' penchant for ostentation that Isabel privately criticized the noblemen's' lavish indulgence in clothes, jewelry and food. Their tents, striped with vivid colors, bore their brocaded coats of arms. Pennants and battle flags flapped in the breezes sweeping down from the Sierra Nevada mountains. The summer sun turned the knights' armor into gleaming points of light. At night, the nobles' elegantly liveried pages carried torches to light their way through the camp. Draped in blue, red, green and white cloth, the aristocrats' war-horses, bred to carry hundreds of pounds of armor, strutted and snorted. Bishops in red and gold robes wandered among the men to bless their cause, while hooded priests stalked gamblers and prostitutes. The noblemen's wives paraded in their jewelry and brocaded robes.

When Prince John was in the camp, he and his ten companions, selected from the sons of the nobility, rough housed. When they weren't playing, the Prince and his friends studied with the Italian schoolmasters Isabel imported as tutors.[31] In the siege camp, Germans, Swiss, Englishmen, French and Italians struggled with their rudimentary Spanish to buy religious trinkets and luxury items from the sutlers. Religious zealots, opportunists and astrologers with glowing forecasts of Christian fortunes milled around the tents of their patrons. Inside the tents, the noblemen sat at tables set with elaborate candelabra and scooped their food off of gold and silver encrusted dishes.

Riding his chestnut warhorse, the stocky, swarthy Ferdinand appeared "surrounded by his courtiers, with their stately retinues, glittering in gorgeous panoply, and proudly displaying the armorial bearings of their ancient houses."[32] Many admired the King's guile and deviousness that kept Boabdil and El Zagal divided. Others praised his military prowess and bravery that brought them to Granada's walls. All looked on with respect when the royal pages paraded the ensign of Santiago and the banner of the Sovereigns, bearing the lions and castles of Leon and Castile and the black eagles of Aragon.

While Ferdinand and Isabel's royal guard of one thousand horsemen patrolled the royal couple's compound, Isabel rode among her troops on a white charger, accompanied by one of her children[33] and her silk-gowned ladies in waiting. The soldiers responded to her graciousness, her resolution, her femininity, her gritty self-assurance. On sunny days, a wide-brimmed black hat covered the Queen's auburn hair and shaded her blue-green eyes as she went to her hospitals to encourage the wounded or sick. Each day at sunrise, she and a select group of nobles assigned to protect the royal personage celebrated mass. During those final days at Granada, Ferdinand and Isabel were already the supreme lords of Castile, Aragon, León, Sicily and a long list of other territories. Now their troops were massed to add another jewel to their crowns.

By July 1491 the Spaniards had effectively blockaded Granada, but there was little sign from inside the walls that the Moors were ready to surrender. The Arabs grabbed at rumors that Muslim forces from North Africa would relieve them. They told themselves that nobody could defeat the two hundred thousand people crammed inside the walls. They called on Allah. They sent their infantry and cavalry bursting out of Granada's gates to harry the Spanish. Meanwhile, the Spanish, remembering the psychological impact of the village they built outside Baza, decided to build a town in front of Granada.

In addition to playing a mental game with the Moors, Ferdinand and Isabel worried that "general winter" might demoralize their army if Boabdil held out much longer. On the Sovereigns' orders, the camp began to echo with the sounds of stonemasons chipping at rocks and carpenters sawing logs. In just three months, the Spanish built solid stone houses and stables along streets that channeled into two broad avenues laid out in the shape of a cross. Many soldiers wanted to name the new town after their Queen, but Isabel christened it Santa Fe "in token of the unshaken trust in Divine Providence manifested by her people throughout this war."[34]

As the town of Santa Fe took shape, the siege's squeeze began to take effect. Some Muslims rioted as Granada began to run low on food and supplies. Others plotted to overthrow Boabdil or organized factions to intrigue against their brother Arabs. A small band of sixteen Spaniards further demoralized the Moors by sneaking into Granada and tacking a parchment document bearing the words "Ave Maria" on the door of the principal mosque.[35] Boabdil's pleas to emirs in Morocco, Egypt and other North African provinces fell on deaf ears. There would be no Almoravides or Almohades to save them. In fact, North African Muslims sold wheat to feed the Spanish army. And the Sovereigns' lavish bribes convinced some of Boabdil's advisors to work in secret for the Spanish.

Convinced of the Sovereigns' iron determination, in October 1491, Boabdil flinched, and sent his prime minister (vizier) to open secret negotiations with the Sovereigns. Since a large block of Granadians still wanted to hold out, the Muslim and Spanish representatives met at night, sometimes in Granada and sometimes on Christian territory. After almost a month of bargaining, the two sides reached a final agreement on November 25, 1491. Reflecting the ancient tradition of *conviviencia* (peaceful coexistence), the surrender terms permitted the Moors to freely practice their religion, to be judged under their own laws by their own magistrates[36] and to keep their property. The treaty called for an exchange of prisoners and exempted the Arabs from tax increases for three years. Boabdil would reign over a small principality, but as a vassal of Ferdinand and Isabel. The pact set January 24, 1492, as the day Boabdil would formally turn over Granada and lay down his arms.

When word of the surrender treaty leaked to Granada's citizens, angry mobs rioted, screaming for Boabdil's head. "If you think," one Muslim warrior said, "that the Christians will remain faithful to what they have promised, or that their Sovereigns will prove as generous a conqueror as they have been a valiant enemy, you deceive yourselves."[37] With the turmoil in Granada and the threat to his person, Boabdil sent an urgent plea to Ferdinand and Isabel to occupy the city sooner, on January 2, 1492.

The Sovereigns acted quickly, and, during the night of January 1, Ferdinand and Isabel sent a squad of men to the Alhambra to protect Boabdil and escort him out of the city the next morning.[38] Dressed in a full suit of armor, with trumpets blaring and flags flying, Cardinal Mendoza led a large detachment of Spanish soldiers over a road built to haul artillery from Santa Fe to Granada. Granada's gates opened, and Boabdil, his mother and his family, accompanied by a squad of fifty Muslim knights, exited. Cardinal Mendoza sent Boabdil and his party through the Spanish lines, and continued his slow march to the city's walls. Entering through the gate of Los Molinos, he took possession of the Alhambra. There, on the walls of the palace's halls and courtyards, the Cardinal saw the Arabic script spelling out Granada's motto: "There is no conqueror but Allah."

When Cardinal Mendoza's men raised Pope Sixtus' huge silver cross and the flags of Castile, Aragon and Santiago over Granada's walls, in the Spanish camp a court herald shouted: "Santiago, Santiago, Santiago. Castile, Castile, Castile. Granada, Granada, Granada. For the very High and Mighty lords, Don Ferdinand and Dona Isabel...who have won the city of Granada and its whole kingdom by force of arms from the infidel Moors."[39]

Cannons fired in salute and the royal choir thundered out a Te Deum. The Spanish troops fell to their knees to give thanks to the Almighty for leading them through 781 years of struggle against the Sons of Allah. After almost eight centuries, the Christian King Roderick's defeat by seven thousand Moors in 711 was avenged.

As the army prayed, Spanish officers conducted Boabdil and his party to their forty-year-old Sovereigns. The ceremonies were brief, an anticlimax to the ten year War of Granada. Boabdil handed Ferdinand the keys to Granada, paid homage to his new masters and rode off toward his principality in the Alpujarras mountains.

As he ascended a mountain pass, Boabdil stopped to take a last look at his lost city, and burst into tears. "You do well to weep like a woman for what you could not defend like a man," his mother Saroya sneered. The spot where Boabdil supposedly wept is still called the place of *El ultimo suspiro del Moro* (The last gasp of the Moor).[40] A year later, Boabdil sold his principality back to Ferdinand and Isabel, left Spain and went to North Africa where he died fighting in the service of a Muslim emir. "Wretched man who could lose his life in another's cause, though he did not dare to die in his own cause," an Arab historian wrotebitterly .[41]

While the Moors took their last gasp, some forty thousand [42] Christian peasants immigrated to lay claim to farm and pasture lands abandoned by Moors who chose exile in North Africa rather than a life under Christian rule. Ferdinand and Isabel appointed governors to administer royal justice in the conquered province. And the royal couple assigned the Count of Tendilla[43] and Isabel's confessor, Hernando de Talavera, to implement their policy of *conviviencia*. The Sovereigns instructed Tendilla and Talavera to set up the necessary governmental machinery to preserve public order and to consolidate their grip on their new territory under the liberal terms of the surrender agreement.

Isabel and Ferdinand assigned Talavera the task of converting the Moors to the Holy Faith. Talavera, who the royal couple later appointed Bishop of Granada, was a tolerant man with an intense interest in Arabic studies. He encouraged conversion to Catholicism by "charitable persuasion," even though more militant Christians urged a policy of forced adherence to Christianity. To carry out Talavera's policy that assimilation into Christ's fold must be voluntary, by preaching and instruction, the clergyman instructed his priests to learn to speak Arabic, to conduct mass in the language of the Infidels and to try their best to understand the Muslim customs. Although Talavera's gentle approach brought many Moors to the Cross, it was not fast enough for the zealots.

The defeat of the Moors in a Holy Crusade engendered a fierce conviction that the Christian God watched over the Spanish race, that their God chose them to perform a sacred mission, that Spaniards must purge the nation of heresy. Isabel, encouraged by her religious advisors, believed all of this—and more. Now, as a Queen flushed with victory, her girlish piety had hardened into an unshakeable belief that only unity under the One Faith would bring about the complete moral and material redemption of Spain.[44]

In her steely view of Christianity, God, through His earthly agents in the Catholic Church, ordained she and Ferdinand's accession to the throne. God compelled victory in the Wars of Succession and Granada. God allowed her to tame the unruly aristocrats and bring her nation out of chaos. God instilled in her a burning faith that He sat on her shoulder, directing and controlling her destiny. But the pragmatic Ferdinand counseled moderation toward Moors and Jews. Let the nation settle down. Consolidate their power. Enjoy the enormous prestige the victory brought them. She tempered her views for a while, but, in time, her ardent fundamentalism would dominate.

While the Sovereigns savored their conquest at home, Christians all over the world celebrated the triumph. The French credited the Spanish with finishing Charles Martel's work at the Battle of Poitiers. When the Pope received Ferdinand and Isabel's letter saying that "this kingdom of Granada which [the Pope's predecessors] so much labored to obtain... has been secured [for Christ]," the Pope personally held a high mass at St. Peter's Cathedral and ordered several days of public rejoicing.

In London, King Henry VII, who was negotiating to marry his son Prince Arthur to Princess Catherine of Aragon, ordered the Cardinal of England to read a proclamation lauding Ferdinand and Isabel from the pulpit of St. Paul's Church. In his tribute, the English Cardinal credited the recovery of the Kingdom of Granada to "the help of God Almighty and the glorious Virgin and the virtuous apostle St. James (Santiago)."

The gains, though, were not all heavenly. The victory ended a long and costly war and the centuries-old threat of Saracen invasions from North Africa. Ferdinand and Isabel had new lands to tax and riches to pass out to their favored subjects. Spain was a nation with common desires, a sense of unity, a sense of patriotism. Now Spain could devote its time, energy and money to expand its glory beyond its borders. It could channel its resources to support the dreams of a very Christian gentleman from Genoa—Christopher Columbus.

15

COLUMBUS, THE SOVEREIGNS CONSENT

With his overweening self-confidence, Columbus refused to quit, to give up, to crumple under the scorn. After his experiences with the royal committees in Portugal and Spain, Columbus knew the arena he was entering. On one side, he confronted minds soaked in medievalism's blind faith in Scripture and devotion to dogma. On the other, he faced off against the Renaissance's scientific probing and wide-ranging inquiry. Like knights in a tournament, in the late 1400s these philosophical systems charged one another with concussive force. In order to avoid being trampled, Columbus understood that he must arm himself to fend off the barbs he knew would be hurled at him by these opposing forces.

During the last few years of the War of Granada, Isabel and Ferdinand marched steadily toward an inevitable, glorious victory over the Moors. During those same years, Christopher Columbus suffered the derision and mockery of doubting academics and courtiers. Even though his vision and imagination appealed to Isabel, to his "harsh critics" on the royal committee, they meant nothing, and, in fact, were detrimental. While his mind worked at the conceptual level, the scholars, lawyers and clerics he would confront, with their minds trained in intricate Roman logic, demanded hard scientific proof on the one hand, and Biblical evidence on the other. He knew that he must carry the burden of proof, and that his self-taught mind must out-think the classically trained academics who subjected his theories to the tests of precise rhetorical arguments.

With medieval and Renaissance audiences to please, he launched a feverish campaign of study. "[I sought the advice of] learned men, priests and laymen, Latins, Greeks, Jews and Moors, and many other sects," Columbus wrote "[And I read] all that has been written on geography, history, philosophy and other sciences."[1] Columbus put together a substantial private library of books to use as research tools, and completely covered the margins of some pages with his written observations. In five of his most favored books he wrote some 2,500 margin notes in Latin, Castilian and Italian.[2] Along with his brother Bartholomew, who joined him in Cordoba, Columbus plumbed classical, medieval and Biblical wisdom.

The much respected ancients, Ptolemy and Aristotle, confirmed that the earth was round. "Not only does the earth have the form of a sphere," Aristotle wrote, "but...this sphere is not large." The Hispano-Roman author Seneca asked in his writings: "How much is that space between the last beaches of Spain and India?" and answered, "[T]he space of a very few days if the ship is driven by favoring wind."

With pen and ink, Christopher and Bartholomew Columbus noted in the margins of the French Cardinal Pierre d'Ailly's world geography: "Pierre d'Ailly agrees that the sea is entirely navigable," and "He agrees that water does not cover three quarters of the earth." Beside a passage in d'Ailly's book, *Imago Mundi*, describing countless islands in the Orient full of precious gems, Christopher drew a pointed forefinger to mark its importance. Columbus also scoured the *Historia Rerum*, written by Aeneas Sylvius Piccolomini, who later became Pope Pius II. Piccolomini quoted classical writers who told of trips to the Arabian Sea and India, and Columbus noted that: "If the distance had been considerable, it would have been impossible to face it happily: This proves that it was short." In the works of d'Ailly and Piccolomini, published in the 1400s, Columbus found not only modern scientific support, but backup from two great churchmen.

Because Marco Polo's estimate of how far the land mass of China extended to the east disagreed with the great Ptolemy's teachings, many medieval sages discounted the Venetian's stories. Even though some scholars treated Polo's tales as wild exaggerations, Columbus seized on Polo's book, *Il Milione*, as a major resource. To Columbus, Polo's claims that almost 7,500 islands dotted the great ocean east of China, and that Japan lay 1,500 miles off the coast of China, only proved that Toscanelli was right. Polo's descriptions in *Il Milione* of the riches of the Orient, the amber, pearls, silk, spices and golden roofs, inspired Columbus to write 366 margin notes in the Venetian's book.[3]

While combing through Sir John Mandeville's travel book, Columbus read the tales of oriental monsters, Sciapodes who walked on one foot and Monoculars who had a single eye in the middle of their forehead. Even though these stories of distorted freaks must have disheartened Columbus, Sir John also talked of the wonders of India and of five thousand islands sprinkled across the ocean to the east. For Scriptural backup, Columbus used the Books of Kings and the Books of Chronicles which discuss the eastern journeys of Solomon and Jehoshaphat. As authority for the proposition that land, not water, covered most of the earth, Columbus quoted the Biblical Prophet Esdras who said: "You [God] commanded that the water be gathered in one-seventh of the earth, and the other six parts You kept dry so that some of these, being sown...and cultivated, could serve You."

Piece by piece Columbus assembled his data, twisting and turning the scraps of evidence to form a quilt of scientific and Biblical sources to prove his case. To back up his dreams and vision, he constructed what, to him, were logical, coherent arguments. He collated, read and reread, checked and cross-checked, until he could present a prospectus setting forth his plan of action. The more he studied, Columbus merely reinforced the conclusion he began with; that his great enterprise could—must—be achieved.

He collected maps, and, with his brother Bartholomew, drew his own version of the world's geography. He tested his arguments with his friends Fathers Marchena and Perez. He lobbied his acquaintances in the high clergy. He button-holed counts, dukes and other noble patrons to tell them of his latest findings. Even though he asserted his arguments with force, when he confronted the artifice of Roman dialectics, Columbus may have been self-conscious about the gaps in his education. In a letter written to Isabel and Ferdinand in 1501, Columbus admitted, "It could happen that Your Highnesses...might reproach me...as a person of scant culture, an ignorant seaman, an ordinary man."

Perhaps the intellectual batterings he received from Spanish and Portuguese scholars cowed him somewhat. "Professionalism is a harsh critic." More likely, with his invincible conviction that he was right, the haughty Genoan's 1501 letter to the Sovereigns was false modesty, and Columbus wrote off the scholar's broadsides as academic snobbishness. Or, as the historian Granzotto argues, because Columbus was self-taught, he stubbornly insisted on the correctness of his mistakes, blindly believing in the things he thought he discovered. Perhaps it was his courage that led him to greatness, the courage to stick by his great enterprise when the sharpshooters took aim at his arguments.

Columbus' antagonists conjured up an image of the Atlantic Ocean as a vast sea of infinite nothingness, an impenetrable "Sea of Darkness" which God intended to be inviolable by man. Sniping at his "proofs," they reasoned that, if the Atlantic had no end, how could anyone expect to reach the end of something infinite, something that the Divine will ordained to be unknown.

With their medieval frame of reference, a few scholars clung to the discredited belief that the earth was flat. By sailing west, a ship would plunge off of the earth's edge into the abyss of space. But many princes and bishops had globes in their libraries. Christian, Jewish and Arab scientists taught that the earth was round.[4] Ptolemy's *Geography*, written in the 100s and a standard reference work by the 1400s, clearly refuted the flat-earth argument. No lettered man thought the earth was flat.

Some, however, argued that the earth was shaped like a pear, with Europe at the top of the smallest part of the pear. Therefore, the argument went, if Columbus sailed downhill, it would be impossible to return by sailing back uphill to Spain, even with favorable winds. To beat back this theory, Columbus cited Ptolemy, Aristotle and many other scientists and thinkers who described the world as a sphere. A few doubters dredged up the old argument that, in the "torrid zone" near the Equator, nothing could survive in the brutal heat. From his own experience in Ghana with the Portuguese, Columbus could give personal testimony of the falsity of that proposition.

In most academic minds, the east was a fuzzy concept, a hazy land somewhere beyond Persia, described only by suspected charlatans like Marco Polo and Sir John Mandeville. They referred to it interchangeably as the Orient, the Indies, the Spice Islands, India, Cathay, Japan, Cipango and China.[5] Like modern myths of people from outer space, rumors circulated of people in the Orient who might be men of a completely different race or men from Hell.

Perhaps these devils from Hell would enslave Christians, or the children of lustful amazons would prove invincible. At the very least, horribly disfigured monsters with eyes in their bellies, long tails or their heads upside down on their shoulders lived somewhere "out there." In the sea, fiendish devilfish and other hideous creatures lurked, just waiting to devour a boatload of Spaniards. Hadn't Jonah been swallowed by a gigantic fish, and, only with the help of God, been disgorged? What if God didn't look so favorably on an expedition captained by a vain foreigner from Genoa? In these and other arguments Columbus confronted the medieval man's fear of the unknown "[which was] always ready to spring to the surface like a latent disease."[6]

Orthodox clerics argued that Columbus' great enterprise might be blasphemous, perhaps even heresy. The Bible taught that God drowned all mankind in the Great Flood, and that all men descended from Noah. If, Columbus' assailants said, God wanted men to penetrate the western sea, as part of His divine mission He would have sent men to the west long before now. If this was true, and the revered St. Augustine said it was true, then there could be no men in these parts.

Relying on the medieval conviction that Scripture and truth were inseparable, it made no sense to these conservative clergymen that God, who promised salvation to all, would permit men to live in a place where the Gospel was unknown. To these clerics there was no difference between an opinion and an article of the Holy Faith. Because religion enveloped almost every issue, and because the judges of the Holy Inquisition lay in wait for heretics, Columbus carefully crafted his ecclesiastical arguments. He reminded the churchmen of Jehoshaphat and Solomon's journeys to the Orient and the Prophet Esdra's assertion that six-sevenths of the earth was land where men could easily migrate.

Taking a risk, Columbus rebutted Scripture with scientific evidence, pointing to the Nordic sagas of Eric the Red and the hand-carved wood and oriental bodies that washed ashore on Atlantic islands. Surely, these facts proved that, if God hadn't wanted men to live in lands to the west, why were they there? To cap his theological case, Columbus told his critics of his heart-felt belief that somehow God predestined him to carry out His divine mission to bring Christ's word to the Orient's heathens.

After debating the theological arguments, Columbus' attackers turned to more earthly questions. Suppose, just suppose, some argued, that even if men existed in unknown lands, Columbus might find nothing of value; no spices, no gemstones, no gold. Columbus responded that Polo and Sir John were so specific in their descriptions. Yes, they may have tampered with the facts a bit and some of their details varied, but, despite the exaggerations, there were many similarities, and why would they have reason to lie?

Other nay-sayers doubted the existence of Antilia, the Antipodes, St. Brendan's Island and the Seven Cities. Perhaps these were nothing more than products of lively imaginations or wishful thinking. But, Columbus said, look at all the maps which placed these mystical lands to the west. Yes, the maps put them in different locations on the globe, but they were there. Could all those chartmakers from Genoa, Venice, Portugal and Germany be wrong?

While Columbus and his adversaries fired volleys back and forth, in the end the issue turned on the practical question of whether a fleet could sail west to the Indies and return safely. To answer that question, both sides refined their cases with scientific facts. The easiest part of the argument for the Renaissance part of Columbus' mind was whether sufficient favoring winds would power his fleet to and from the Indies. From his visits to the Azores and the Canaries, he could certify from personal experience that the winds in the Canary Islands blew from east to west, and, at the latitude of the Azores, the winds flew from west to east. When his critics asked "Do the winds blow to the west forever, or do they peter out somewhere in the middle of the Sea of Darkness?" there was no answer. It was anybody's guess.

The hardest questions were strictly geographic. How far is it between the Canary Islands and Japan and China? How large is the earth's land mass? Most medieval geographers agreed that 360 degrees divided the globe. But it was an open question as to how long a degree was. Even though some ancient geographers, including Aristotle, correctly computed the length of each degree as about sixty miles[7] at the Equator, Columbus seized on the computation of a degree by an Arab scholar, Alfragan, who calculated that each degree equalled 56.66 miles. Although Alfragan calculated in Arabic miles, Columbus, knowingly or unknowingly, assumed that Alfragan meant Italian miles, which were forty-five miles long at the Equator. With this bit of tinkering, Columbus shrank the globe twenty-five percent from its actual size.

On the issue of how far it would be from the Canaries to the Orient, Columbus whittled down Ptolemy's estimate. Ptolemy, who many medieval scholars accepted as the supreme authority on geography, said that land covered fifty percent of the earth's surface. Columbus, relying on the Prophet Esdras, Marco Polo and Marinus of Tyre, stretched the land mass even farther.[8] Marinus claimed that land covered almost sixty-five percent of the earth.

Still not satisfied, Columbus carefully juggled the combination of figures to fit his theories. He added more land because of Polo's claims about how far east China went. By spotting Japan 1,500 miles off the coast of China, and the Canary Islands some 350 miles west of Europe, Columbus lopped off another 1,850 miles. To carve off even more distance, Columbus made one final adjustment. Since the Canaries lay at latitude twenty-eight north, at that latitude it wouldn't be as far around the earth as it would be at its full Equatorial girth. Instead of a degree being forty-five miles at latitude twenty-eight north, Columbus calculated a degree to be only forty miles, chopping off another eleven percent. When Columbus added up his figures, the voyage was well within the range of then-available ships and technology.

On a straight line, the true distance from the Canary Islands to Japan is about 10,600 miles and 11,000 miles to China. By beginning his reasoning process with the answer he wanted, and then plugging in the evidence which fit his preconceived conclusion, Columbus reduced the distance by some seventy-five percent. When he finished his intricate arithmetic, Japan lay only 2,400 miles to the west of the Canaries and China 2,800 miles. With any luck, if Toscanelli's prediction was right, he could use the mythical Antilia as a way station.

Even if Toscanelli was wrong or Columbus sailed past Antilia, a swift caravel averaging four miles per hour would put him on Japanese soil in about twenty-five days. Yes, the trip would be a longer voyage than anyone had yet made, but, ever the optimist, he knew it could be done. If Isabel's experts threw the medieval version of "Numbers don't lie, but liars use numbers" at him, he could answer with a fusillade of Renaissance reasoning from d'Ailly, Piccolomini and his other authorities.[9]

Although Columbus could cite chapter and verse of his "proofs," he continued to meet with delays and rejection in Spain. Like any good business strategist, he kept his options open. As backup to the Spanish option, Columbus sent his brother Bartholomew to Lisbon in the autumn of 1487 to renew negotiations with King John of Portugal. Bartholomew arrived in Lisbon just a few months after a Portuguese sea captain, Bartholomew Diaz, set sail on an expedition to find the tip of Africa. No doubt Bartholomew reported to his older brother on Diaz' voyage, and on the rumors he heard in Lisbon of a westerly voyage King John authorized two Portuguese merchants to make to find the Orient.[10]

With this news of Portugal's two-pronged effort to find the Indies, Columbus may have panicked, seeing "his" glory slipping away into the hands of others. In early 1488, Columbus wrote a personal letter to King John. The Portuguese King replied on March 20, 1488:

> "To Cristobal Colon, our special friend, in Seville.
>
> Cristobal Colon. We, John, by the grace of God. King of Portugal...[and] either side of the sea on Africa...send you many greetings. We have seen the letter that you wrote us and we highly value the good will and affection with which you show your wish to serve us. As to you coming here,

both for what you mention and for the other things for which your activity and your keen mind will be necessary to us, we desire it and it will be a pleasure for us to see you, because the matter that means so much to you can be carried out in such a way as to satisfy you. And, inasmuch as you might harbor some distrust of our justice because of some obligation you might have, We, with this letter, guarantee you that, during your arrival, stay and return, you will not be arrested, held, accused, tried or considered responsible for anything, civil or penal, of any kind."[11]

Whether Columbus accepted King John's invitation to return to Portugal is not known.[12] In any event, Bartholomew Diaz returned from his discovery of the Cape of Good Hope in December of 1488, unlocking Portugal's door to India. Somewhat pessimistically, Diaz named Africa's southern tip the Cape of Storms, but King John exuberantly renamed it the Cape of Good Hope. With Portugal's discovery of a viable route to the Orient, King John, excited by Diaz' discovery, apparently showed no further interest in Columbus' questionable proposal.

Exercising his other options, Columbus had sent Bartholomew to England.[13] There, Columbus' brother showed King Henry VII a map of the world depicting the lands to the west they would discover.[14] Since the English showed little interest in the venture, Columbus continued his networking in Spain, receiving warm receptions from his patrons.

The Count of Medina Celi took him into his household, and the monks at La Rabida encouraged him. Even though he still had powerful support from Father Marchena, Cardinal Mendoza and other important men, there was still nothing definitive from the King and Queen during 1488. In early 1489, however, the Sovereigns' attitude became more positive. Perhaps the dramatic news of Diaz' discovery spurred Isabel and Ferdinand. Or the royal couple got wind of Columbus' flirtations with England and Portugal. In the spring of 1489 they issued a royal order:

> "...to the members of the Councils, ministers of justice,.. knights, squires and honest men in all cities... Christopher Columbus must come to this court...to concern himself with some affairs to be concluded in our service; whereby we command you that, when he should pass through said cities and villages, he be given hospitality and food...And you must not quarrel with him...And you must do nothing to hinder him any way under pain of our justice...Given in the city of Cordoba on 12 May 1489. I the King. I the Queen."[15]

It was the first piece of good news Columbus had received in years. In the summer of 1489 Isabel granted him an audience at Jaen where she was busy raising supplies for the troops at the front. Ferdinand was at Baza preparing for the siege that the royal couple hoped would be the last battle in the War of Granada. With soothing *palabras dulces*, Isabel told Columbus that, when the Sovereigns eradicated the Moors, she would be prepared to support his great enterprise. It would only be a matter of time until El Zagal surrendered Baza, Almeria and Guadix, she explained. Then, all of eastern Granada would be under Spanish control. Under their agreement with Boabdil, the Moor agreed to capitulate whenever the Sovereigns commanded it. Just wait. Just be patient. Meanwhile, Isabel said, Columbus could live at court, and, when she went to visit the siege camp at Baza, she expected him to accompany her to witness the defeat of the Infidels. She understood his grand design, she said, and its importance to Spain. It would only be a matter of a few months.

Ecstasy. From the Queen's own lips, a promise to support his voyage. Had she not treated him with her renowned grace? Had she not encouraged him? Had she not granted him a place at court and asked him to go with her to Baza? Despite all the nay-sayers, the mystical attraction between these two people, so similar in many ways, worked.

In the late autumn of 1489, Columbus made the one-hundred-mile trip over the rugged supply roads Isabel's engineers carved through the mountain passes from Jaen to Baza. Trailing behind the Queen's entourage on the muddy roads, Columbus' mule would have threaded through trains of oxen straining to pull heavy cannons and supply wagons loaded with the food and clothes Isabel requisitioned for her troops. Along the way, he would have seen the sutlers carting merchandise to sell to the men and the camp followers eager to peddle their services to the soldiers.

When he arrived at Baza on November 7, the rains had turned the camp into a quagmire, and the soldier's morale was low. As he slogged through the mud behind the Queen while she reviewed her troops, Columbus saw first-hand that the mystical attraction that existed between the two of them also existed between Isabel and her army. Inspired by her presence, the Spanish intensified their efforts to root the Muslims out of their stronghold. Less than a month after her arrival, Baza surrendered.

Now, only one barrier stood between Columbus and the achievement of his dream. Boabdil must surrender the city of Granada. The wily Muslim had given Isabel and Ferdinand his solemn promise that, on their orders, he would become their vassal. Under pressure from the Arab mobs who fled to the safety of

Granada's walls, Boabdil reneged. To the King and Queen, Boabdil's determination to hold out meant more lives lost, more taxes for their already strained nation, more time until they unified Spain. To Columbus, Boabdil's broken promise risked his life's ambition, his dream. Isabel gave him her promise of support, but, he knew, minds change with circumstance.

For the next two years, 1490-1491, Columbus followed the court from place to place, taking time out to visit his friends at La Rabida, the Count of Medina Celi and his mistress, Beatriz Enriquez de Harana. After toying with the idea of approaching the French King, Columbus sent his brother Bartholomew to France to see if he could muster support for the venture. Although Bartholomew made important contacts at the French court, King Charles VIII refused to back the great enterprise.[16]

Columbus, after wandering around Spain for two years, went to La Rabida in the fall of 1491. La Rabida, his spiritual home in Spain, was the place where his legitimate son Diego was housed and schooled, the place where friends believed in him and gave him consolation and unquestioning loyalty. There, in the monastery's cloisters, Columbus told his old friend, Father Juan Perez, that, after almost seven years of frustration and scorn, he was leaving Spain for France. The War of Granada kept dragging on, Columbus said, diverting the Sovereigns' attention from his plan.

He was forty years old and had two young sons to support and educate. And, because he sacrificed financial security for his dream, he was tired of living in near poverty, dressing in threadbare clothes and humiliating himself by begging patrons for money. After listening to Columbus' woes, Father Perez mounted his mule and rode to the Spanish siege camp at Santa Fe in front of Granada. Still convinced of the viability of the great enterprise, the Queen's former confessor persuaded Isabel to summon the disheartened Genoan to Santa Fe.

After receiving a letter from the Queen and twenty thousand maravedis to buy a mule and new clothes, Columbus arrived in time to watch Cardinal Mendoza, dressed in a full suit of armor, enter Granada on January 2, 1492, and raise the Sovereigns' huge silver cross over the city's red walls. Columbus heard the court herald shout, "Santiago, Santiago, Santiago. Castile, Castile, Castile," and saw Boabdil ride by with his escort of fifty turbaned knights before uttering *El ultimo suspiro del Moro* (The last gasp of the Moors). A few months later, Columbus wrote: "I saw the royal banners of Your Highnesses placed by force of arms on the towers of the Alhambra, which is the fortress of the city. And I saw the Moorish King come from the gate of the city and kiss the hands of Your Highnesses and of the Prince."[17]

With the final crushing of the Moors, the atmosphere in Spain was heady, triumphant. Even though Isabel promised to support his venture two years earlier, Columbus' critics must have gotten the Queen's ear. After a fresh study of the great enterprise, Isabel's royal commission said no.[18] Too many contradictions, too many disputed facts and theories. When he received this final word, Columbus stuffed his precious books and maps in his saddlebags, and, with Father Perez, left Santa Fe, headed for France.

Later in the day, the keeper of the royal treasury, Luis de Santangel, heard that the Genoan had left Santa Fe. Santangel, a constant friend of Columbus, obtained an immediate audience with the Queen that same day. At their meeting, Santangel summoned every ounce of his eloquence to convince Isabel to overrule the royal commission.[19] Regarding Columbus' scientific evidence, Santangel said, some of it might be wrong, but most of it had not been rebutted. Nobody could prove or disprove for sure that Japan lay 2,400 or 10,000 miles away. Anyway, these arguments concerned only the technocrats of the royal commission.

After brushing over the academic arguments, Santangel turned to what he knew would tweak Isabel's interest—the broader political and policy issues of statecraft, the issues that affected the Sovereigns' power and prestige. With their conquest of the Moors, Santangel said, the King and Queen achieved their first goal; unifying the nation. Now it was time to turn to another goal; to make Spain preeminent in Europe. If Columbus was lucky enough to find the western route to the Indies, the payoff for Spain would be enormous, making Isabel and Ferdinand the most powerful rulers in Europe. Wealth would flood into Spain, just as it had when Portugal exploited its colonies in Africa. Even if Columbus got rich, there would be plenty to go around, and the royal treasury would get the lion's share. He knew, Santangel said, that the crown was short of money just then, but, he said, he and his friends would be pleased to underwrite the voyage.

Politically, Santangel said, it would be a disaster for Spain if this energetic man took his project to another monarch. If the French or English kings gained control of the possible mountains of gold and spices from the Orient, Santangel argued, they would squash the Sovereigns and their successors. Santangel also reminded Isabel that the Portuguese had rounded the Cape of Good Hope and were pushing ever closer to India. If Spain's neighbor to the west captured this enormous prize, the wily King John might use his new wealth to finance wars against Spain.

And, Santangel said, if Columbus could form an alliance with the Oriental potentates, the strategy the King and Queen used against the Moors in Granada could be applied on an even grander scale. With the kings of the east moving against the Muslims in Baghdad and Constantinople, and the Christians invading from the west, the same giant pincers maneuver the Sovereigns used in the War of Granada would work again.

Finally, even though the Reconquest made Spain whole from a religious standpoint, there were still many powerful nobles who might challenge the crown. If Columbus discovered a new source of land and riches, it would focus the nation's attention on exploiting them, rather than cutting up the limited pie in Spain. It would open new realms for the military entrepreneurs in her kingdom to exploit.

Yes, Columbus' demands for titles and riches were somewhat high, Santangel said, but the man wasn't asking for anything up front. It was all on the come. Only if he succeeded would he become Admiral of the Ocean Sea. In other words, the risk warranted the gamble.

Isabel agreed. She immediately despatched a royal messenger, who caught up with Columbus and Father Perez a few miles outside of Santa Fe at a bridge. The Queen, the messenger said, ordered Columbus back to court "at once [because] Her Highness is ready to conclude the affair."

It is not difficult to imagine the joy that must have filled Columbus as he rode back to Santa Fe. For fourteen years his emotions skyrocketed and plummeted on the whims of monarches and the happenstance of events. For fourteen years the great enterprise occupied every tissue in his brain. Now it would happen.

Even in this moment of exhilaration, Columbus' pragmatic businessman's mind turned to the delicate issue of his compensation for services rendered. Assisted by Father Juan Perez in the negotiations, Columbus demanded the titles of Admiral of the Ocean Sea and Viceroy and Governor of all the islands and lands he discovered, for himself and his heirs in perpetuity.

He wanted ten percent, tax free, of all gold, silver, pearls, gems and other goods mined, produced or acquired in his new domains. In addition, he would have the right to invest twelve and a half percent in each voyage and to keep twelve and a half percent of the profits. To govern the new provinces, Columbus would give Ferdinand and Isabel a list of three candidates for each royal appointment to chose from, and Columbus would be the supreme judge of all commercial disputes in his lands. He made it clear that there would be no dickering, no bargaining. That was it.

Some of Columbus' critics called his requests exorbitant.

Talavera said that "such demands savored of the highest degree of arrogance, and [it] would be unbecoming of their Highnesses to grant [so much] to a needy foreigner."[20] To Columbus' detractors, these non-negotiable demands only confirmed that he was swollen with pride and vanity, that his arrogant conceit was unlimited. How, they may have asked, could this man who lived on handouts, this shabby dreamer, have the audacity to confront the Sovereigns with such ultimatums.

Columbus never budged. To him, it was just, fair, his due. Isabel and Ferdinand agreed. On April 17, 1492, the King and Queen signed the Capitulations which granted Columbus his every request. Two weeks later, the Sovereigns confirmed the Capitulations in a Royal Patent which read:

> "Inasmuch as you, Cristobal Colon, are setting forth at our command...to discover and conquer certain islands and mainlands in the ocean sea...it is just and reasonable that, since you are exposing yourself to risk in our service, you be rewarded for it...[and that after the discoveries you shall be] authorized to call and entitle yourself Don Cristobal Colon...."[21]

These documents gave Columbus the right to create a viceregal dynasty and granted him almost full sovereign power over the new dominions, but only if he found them.

Since nobody had any idea which Oriental potentates Columbus might meet, Isabel and Ferdinand signed three copies of a letter of introduction, undated, with a blank space for Columbus to fill in the name of a khan or king or, perhaps, Prester John:

> "To the most serene prince __________, our very dear friend, Ferdinand and Isabel, King and Queen of Castile, Aragon, Leon, etc., greetings.....We have learned with joy of your esteem and high regard for us and our nation and of your great eagerness to receive information concerning our successes. Wherefore, we have resolved to dispatch our noble captain Christopherus Colon to you...."

With a full set of documents authorizing the voyage in his briefcase, Columbus left Granada and set out for Palos in May of 1492 to muster ships and crews. Before he left, he arranged for Isabel to appoint his legitimate son Diego to join the court as a page to the heir apparent, Prince John.[22] The first task was to raise the $700,000 (in 1985 U.S. Dollars) needed to pay for the voyage.[23] Luis de Santangel, who was not only the royal treasurer but a co-treasurer of the Holy Brotherhood, borrowed some of the money from the national police force. Columbus raised a much smaller amount from his friends, and the crown may have advanced a portion of the funds.[24] It is almost certain that Isabel did not pawn the crown jewels to pay for the trip because the Queen mortgaged most, if not all, of her gems to pay for the War of Granada.

To ease the cash needs for the expedition, the royal couple ordered the citizens of Palos to make good a fine levied on the town for some long-forgotten offense against the monarchy. In a letter addressed to the citizens of Palos, and read to them in the Church of St. George, a former mosque, the Sovereigns commanded: "Know ye that, whereas for certain things done and committed by you to our disservice you were condemned and obligated by our Council to provide us for twelve months with two equipped caravels at your own proper charge and expense ...within ten days of receiving this our letter...."[25]

The fine, furnishing two fully outfitted caravels, netted the Nina and the Pinta. For the third ship, Columbus negotiated with a friend he met in Palos during one of his visits to La Rabida. Juan de la Cosa chartered the Gallega, renamed the Santa Maria, to Columbus to serve as the fleet's flagship. To aid in recruiting sailors, the Sovereigns agreed to pardon persons accused of crimes if they signed on for the voyage.

Still, Columbus found it almost impossible to recruit the officers and men he needed. The old epithets of "madman" and "dreamer" followed Columbus to Palos. Palos' citizens resented being forced to supply and outfit the Pinta and the Nina. "[M]any persons mocked the said Admiral for the enterprise he wanted to carry out, going to discover the Indies," a Spaniard testified in a lawsuit some twenty years later. "[A]nd they taunted the Admiral in public and considered his enterprise foolish...."

Another man testified that "all mocked him for pursuing such a plan and teased him and considered him mad." Because he was a foreigner, "no person was acquainted with him...nor knew who he was...."[26] Another fear the mariners of Palos may have had was that this tall, aging man from Genoa had few credentials as a navigator or seaman.

Columbus, branded a fool, an unknown quantity and an inexperienced sailor, called on his old friend Father Marchena. Marchena advised him that there was one man whose reputation in the Palos area would help. Marchena told Columbus that the highly respected sea captain he had in mind had sailed the Mediterranean for some thirty years, and had ventured as far as the Canary Islands and the west coast of Africa. This man knew the Ocean Sea, and would be fully capable of understanding Columbus' theories about a voyage to the west. Although this grizzled old mariner built a modest fortune during his years at sea, Marchena thought the lure of the Orient's riches might entice him to sign on. The man, Martin Alonso Pinzon, was away in Rome delivering a load of sardines during the early summer of 1492.

When Pinzon returned to Palos, Marchena arranged a meeting with Columbus. Marchena was right. After Columbus presented his nautical arguments and made it clear that Isabel and Ferdinand had given him broad power to pass out rewards, Pinzon agreed to lend his prestige to the great enterprise. Even though Pinzon eagerly agreed to help, for some reason, Columbus, ever suspicious, mistrusted his second in command. Despite the tension between the two men, Pinzon recruited his younger brother, Vicente, and immediately began a search for officers and men.

"[T]he aforesaid Martin Pinzon," Hernando Janes said years later, "[went] in search of people, saying: 'friends, come along, make this voyage with us; why do you live here pinching pennies? Make this voyage. We shall discover lands with the help of God, and...we shall find houses with roofs of gold and all riches and good fortune.' And for this and the faith they had in Martin Alonso, many people were found in the city of Palos and the cities of Huelva and Moguer."[27] Although the Pinzon brothers would captain the Nina and the Pinta, some mariners still refused to go because the voyage was "a vain thing...and would not find land" and because "the thing was too uncertain."

After calling on his many relatives and friends in the area, Martin Alonso Pinzon mustered full complements of pilots, navigators, able bodied seamen and ordinary seamen. "[I]f Martin Alonso had not decided to make this voyage and had not taken part in it personally," Francisco Medel testified, "no one would have dared go, for many of those who went thought they were going to their death and that they had little hope of coming back, but they had decided [to go], on seeing Martin Alonso go in person."

Columbus spent the hot months of June and July, 1492, getting to know his officers, pilots and navigators. In Andalusia's summer heat, Columbus and his captains discussed the rigging for their three ships, the course they would take and the supplies they would need. They agreed on their departure date, August 3, 1492, one day after the deadline Isabel and Ferdinand set for all Jews to get out of Spain or convert to Christianity.

16

COLUMBUS, PALOS TO THE CANARIES

August 2, 1492, was the day set by the Sovereigns for all Jews to convert to the Holy Faith or be expelled from Spain. On the Jewish calendar it was the ninth day of Av, the day of the destruction of the Temple.

About three hundred thousand Jews chose to leave, and, doubtless, Columbus saw many of them on the docks at Palos trying to escape the Peninsula before the deadline. "They looked like ghosts, pale and emaciated with staring eyes," a Genoese chronicler wrote. "I would have said they were dead had they not occasionally moved. Many died there on the pier." Remorsefully, he says, "Their suffering appeared just, according to our religion, but very cruel if one considered them not animals but human beings created by God in His image."

Ignoring the inauspicious misery, in the morning darkness of August 3 Columbus went to the church of St. George in Palos to confess his sins and take communion. He knelt before the ornate, candlelit alter, made the sign of the cross, rose and walked to the wharf to be rowed to his flagship, the Santa Maria. Shortly before sunup at 5:15, he ordered the anchors raised to catch the outbound tide. The hemp ropes strained in the hardwood pulleys until the anchors were aboard. The odyssey began.

As the sun's rays crept over the houses of Palos, a ship's boy chanted a religious ditty:

"Blessed be the light of day
and the Holy Cross we say;
and the Lord of Veritie

and the Holy Trinity.
Blessed be the immortal soul
and the Lord who keeps it whole.
Blessed be the light of day
and He who sends the night away."[1]

The sailors threw hawsers to the towboats which would pull the fleet down river on that calm August day. The rhythmic splashing of the ash oars didn't drown out the Franciscan friars' morning hymns drifting over the whitewashed walls of La Rabida, about a mile and a half below Palos. The religious music, coming from the place which first gave him and his small son shelter when they arrived in Spain eight years before, comforted the pious Captain General of the Fleet.

To those on shore, the two caravels and the merchant ship wouldn't have attracted much attention, except that they flew the royal banner of the the Spanish Sovereigns, red and gold, quartered with the solid castles of Castile, the charging lions of Leon and the black eagles of Aragon. The fleet also ran up a flag specially designed by Columbus. It bore a green cross on a white field. Over one arm of the cross was a crown with the letter "F" above it, for Ferdinand. Over the other was a crown and the initial "Y", for Isabel.[2]

The crewmen rearranged the cargo for proper balance, shoving and pulling the barrels of pigs feet packed in lard, wine and water casks and deer skin sacks filled with gunpowder. The fleet eased down river at a speed of about two miles per hour, and rode the high tide over the bar of Saltes at the mouth of the Odiel and Tinto rivers at eight o'clock that morning. They were in the open sea. Columbus set the course for the eight-hundred-mile trip southwest to the Canary Islands. He sent the barefoot men scrambling up the masts to unfurl the sails to catch the strong but variable wind. In the sharp ocean breeze, the white canvas sails with huge red crosses painted on them billowed their pregnant bellies from the spars. Then, the crewmen lowered the royal ensign and Columbus' green crossed flag so they wouldn't shred in the ocean winds.

At the end of the day, Columbus made his first entry in what was to become the most famous, and most debated, ship's log ever written. Some scholars acclaim it as the most complete and accurate ship's journal produced up to that time, while others say that Columbus' two contemporary biographers, his illegitimate son Ferdinand and his friend Las Casas, edited the real log into self-serving distortions of the truth.

The debunkers, a small group of revisionist historians in the

1800s, perhaps too anxious to boost their academic reputations by making a "new discovery," accuse Ferdinand Columbus and Las Casas of deliberately falsifying and embellishing the log to glorify their father and friend. It is not disputed that Ferdinand, Columbus and Las Casas saw, and relied on, the original log or that their writings favor Columbus. But to say that their versions of the journal were a hoax appears unwarranted. There is too much accuracy, the descriptions of flora and fauna are too vivid and there is too much of Columbus, and only Columbus, in the the log. There are errors and incorrect assumptions, but no more than would have been made by any man who sailed uncharted waters and saw things no European had seen before.

The furor over the log's accuracy arose because the original, which Columbus presented to Isabel in Barcelona when he returned, disappeared after her death. Isabel had ordered the court scribes to make an exact copy for Columbus. This document, known as the Barcelona copy, was inherited by Columbus' legitimate son Diego, and finally passed into the hands of Columbus' grandson Luis. Like many descendents of great men, Luis Columbus was a wastrel, "Devoid of morality," one historian puts it. While jailed for bigamous marriages to three wives, Luis Columbus bribed his jailers for overnight passes and bedded a fourth wife. To support his mushrooming families, and his otherwise libertine lifestyle, Luis sold off family assets, including the Barcelona copy of the the log. It was last seen in 1554.

Shortly after Columbus set sail for the Canaries, he wrote a preamble to the log, addressing it to Ferdinand and Isabel. "Most Christian, exalted, excellent and powerful princes, King and Queen of the Spains and of the islands of the sea, our Sovereigns: It was in this year of 1492 that your Highnesses concluded the war with the Moors who reigned in Europe. Afterwards...based on the information that I had given Your Highnesses about the land of India and about a prince who is called the Great Khan, which in our language means 'King of Kings,' Your Highnesses decided to send me, Christopher Columbus, to the regions of India, to see the princes there and the peoples and the lands, and to learn of their dispositions, and of everything, and the measures which could be taken for their conversion to our Holy Faith."[3]

In the preamble Columbus then reminded the Sovereigns that he told them that ambassadors from the Orient had visited the Pope, asking that missionaries be sent to spread Christianity, and that the Pope did nothing. As a result, Columbus said, "many people [who believe] in idolatries...were lost [souls]. Your Highnesses, as Catholic Christians and princes devoted to the

Holy Christian Faith and to the spreading of it, and as enemies of the Muslim sect and of all idolatries and heresies, ordered that I should go to the east, but not by land as is customary. I was to go by way of the west, whence until today we do not know with certainty that anyone has gone."

In the first part of the preamble, Columbus paid obeisance to his patrons and set the high moral tone of his mission—to save heathen souls from eternal perdition. No mention here of gold and riches. Unusual for the acquisitive Italian. He intended this introduction to touch only on the noblest themes. But he couldn't resist reconfirming his new-found rights: "Therefore, after having banished all the Jews from Your kingdoms and realms, during (the) month of January Your Highnesses ordered me to go with a sufficient fleet to the said regions of India. For that purpose I was granted great favors and ennobled; from then henceforward I might entitle myself 'Don' and be High Admiral of the Ocean Sea and Viceroy and Perpetual Governor of all the islands and continental land that I might discover and acquire, as well as any other future discoveries in the Ocean Sea. Further, my eldest son shall succeed to the same position, and so on from generation to generation forever after."

Next, Columbus told the King and Queen how he organized his fleet, and assured them that he would be diligent in their service. "...I decided to write down very carefully everything I might do and see and experience on this voyage, from day to day. Also, Sovereign Princes, besides describing each night what takes place during the day, and during the day the sailings of the night, I propose to make a new chart for navigation, on which I will set down all the sea and lands of the the Ocean Sea, in their correct locations, and with their correct bearings. Further, I shall compile a book and shall map everything by latitude and longitude. And, above all, it is fitting that I forget about sleeping and devote much attention to navigation in order to accomplish this. And these things will be a great task."[4] Columbus was well aware that many Europeans had visited the east. But only one, Marco Polo, was famous all over Christendom. Polo's book, *Il Milione*, which Columbus scoured for years, made the Venetian famous. Columbus would write a book too.

On August 4 and 5 the fleet steered a steady course southwest by south toward the Canary Islands. Since the Spanish had recently conquered the Canary Island natives, the Guanches, and had set up a colony, the way from Spain to the the Canaries was familiar. Columbus chose the Canaries as his departure point for two other reasons.

Many of the world maps he poured over showed Japan to be on the same latitude as the Canaries. And, from his many sea voyages as a younger man, Columbus had learned about the winds at different latitudes, which convinced him that the favorable easterlies gusting across the Canaries would transport him quickly across the Atlantic.

During the shakedown phase of the voyage in familiar waters, everyone was at ease. The men got to know each other's capabilities, and the officers and crewmen learned the peculiarities of their ships. How fast they sailed. Which type of rigging brought out their best. Whether the sails, rudder and lines were in good repair. The smaller ships in the fleet, the Nina and the Pinta, were caravels that could easily outrun the bulky merchantman, the Santa Maria. Because of their speed and maneuverability, caravels were often used for war or piracy. Now, they were to take on the new task of exploration. Isabel and Ferdinand's expropriating the Nina and the Pinta from the citizens of Palos not only provided the Captain General with two fine ships, it cut the cost of the voyage. The flagship, the Santa Maria, was chartered from its owner, Juan de la Cosa.

The Nina, the smallest ship in the fleet, was Columbus' favorite because, he says, she was so "staunch and well made." Although not much larger than many modern day pleasure yachts, the sixty-seven-foot long, twenty-one-foot wide craft would sail more than twenty-five thousand miles under Columbus' command during three voyages to the New World.[5] On this first voyage, the Nina carried a complement of twenty-four men. During the Palos-Canaries leg, the Nina was rigged with triangular lateen sails. With a stout wind, the Nina could dart through the sea at speeds up to ten or eleven miles per hour. After being captured by pirates in 1497 off Sardinia, and being recaptured by her master and crew, the Nina disappeared from history in 1499. Her official religious name was the Santa Clara, but, following Spanish custom of the time, she was nicknamed Nina, probably after her owner, Juan Nino of Palos.

The Pinta (which literally means "the Painted One," but which was the Spanish sailors' slang for whore) was slightly larger than the Nina, seventy feet long and twenty-two feet at the beam. Twenty-six men were stacked aboard the square rigged three master. As the smartest sailer in the fleet, she could scud through the water at a clip, leaving a wide trail of phosphorescent foam on a moonlit night. The Pinta made several cross-Atlantic voyages until she was caught in a hurricane in July of 1500 and went down in the vicinity of the Turks and Caicos Islands in the Caribbean.

Columbus' least favorite ship was his flagship, the Santa Maria. She was a clumsy cargo ship which waddled through the water, never able to keep up with her two sleek caravel sisters. She had a length of seventy-seven feet, a beam of twenty-six feet, and she carried forty men.

On the mainmast and the foremast, square sails caught the trade winds for speed, and, to the rear, a triangular sail was used for maneuvering. The tiller of the rudder entered the hull between the main deck and the raised quarterdeck. As a result, the helmsman, who stood on the main deck, had to steer blind. At the stern, on the quarterdeck, there was a small stateroom for the Captain General. Forward was a low forecastle which housed spare ropes and sails. Galician shipwrights built the chunky merchantman of hewn planks four inches thick, held together by iron bolts and wooden pegs. Because of her origin, she was sometimes called "La Gallega" (girl from Galicia), or, to the prudish Columbus' chagrin, "Mariagalante" (Naughty Mary).

The Santa Maria, designed to sit low in the waters of the stormy North Atlantic, carried sand and rock ballast for further stability. This, and a large store of provisions, made her even more sluggish. As Columbus says in the log, she was "very cumbersome and not suited to the work of discovery." In that same log entry, the Captain General complains that he was forced to charter the dull-sailing Santa Maria from Juan de la Cosa because "The people of Palos...did not fulfill to me what they had promised to the King and Queen. I should have been given ships suitable for this journey, and the people of Palos did not do that." Even though Columbus disliked the Santa Maria, he proclaimed that, overall, his fleet was "*muy apto para semejante hecho*" (well suited for the job).

Columbus outfitted and manned his fleet primarily for discovery, but it was still necessary to be prepared for pirates and privateers. The Nina carried ten breech loading swivel cannons called "bombardas;" 4.5 centimeter guns which used shards of jagged metal as ammunition to fend off boarders. The vessels were also armed with cast iron lombards, calibered at four inches. The lombards, mounted on gun carriages, were designed to throw stone cannon balls into the rigging of enemy ships. Crossbows and espingardas, akin to a shotgun, rounded out the weaponry.

To keep the fleet together and to send signals, off the stern of each ship hung an iron firepot. At night, the flames could be seen from a goodly distance, and, during the day, plumes of smoke told their location. As a signaling device, the crewmen covered and uncovered the firepots the required number of times with a wet canvass blanket to create puffs of smoke during the day and flashes of light in the dark.

The wooden ships leaked, despite the gooey pitch used as a sealant, and the morning watch had the daily task of pumping out the bilge water sloshing in the hold. Pump as they might, it was never possible to completely dry the ships' innards. The rotting wood and ships' stores, combined with the slops the men frequently deposited in the hold, produced a horrible stench, particularly on a hot, humid day. These foul conditions, accepted as a matter of course in medieval Europe, created breeding grounds for cockroaches, lice, fleas and rats.

Aboard the three ships, the longest of which was only twenty-five yards, ninety men were squeezed into cramped quarters. There were twenty-two able seamen with specific duties, nineteen ordinary seamen and sixteen cabin boys. The remaining thirty-three were officers and passengers.[6]

In the 1400s Castilians had little sense of nationalism, but they maintained an intense loyalty to family, hometown and region, in that order. The manifests of the three vessels show that the crew's makeup was very much a family affair, an old boy network. There were four Pinzons, three Ninos, two Quinteros (who were related to the Ninos), two Perezes, two Arraezes and two Medels. It was a Spanish, and, more specifically, an Andalusian affair. Seventy-four came from southern Spain, ten from the Basque provinces or Galicia in the north and one from Murcia. The fleet's crew included five foreigners; a Portuguese, a Genoan, a Calabrian, a Venetian and the tall Captain General with his pronounced Italian accent.

Columbus carried the dual titles of Captain General of the Fleet and captain of the Santa Maria. Only after he returned to Spain would he assume his title of Admiral of the Ocean Sea. Vicente Pinzon, about thirty, commanded the Nina. Vicente's grizzled older brother, Martin Alonso Pinzon, about forty-eight, captained the swift Pinta.

Martin Alonso Pinzon was a skilled, experienced mariner from a seafaring family of Palos, and his stature as a seaman was largely responsible for Columbus being able to recruit a full complement of men to embark on this voyage of "dubious safety and improbable success."

Legend has it that, while on a trip to Rome, Martin Alonso saw a Papal document which piqued his interest in a voyage to discover a westerly route to the Orient. This document, which has never been found, supposedly told of a transatlantic voyage by the Queen of Sheba to Japan. In addition to having a substantial dose of Columbus' curiosity and sense of adventure, Martin Alonso Pinzon possessed some of the Captain General's other traits; tenacity (some called it stubbornness), pride verging on arrogance and fierce ambition. With the two top men so alike, friction between them was inevitable.

Although the captains had dictatorial command of everything aboard their ships, it wasn't necessary for them to be expert mariners or navigators.[7] The masters (akin to today's first mates) controlled day-to-day operations, and the pilots were in charge of calculating the distances traveled and plotting the course. Juan Nino, Columbus' favorite shipmate, served as the master of the Nina. Francisco Pinzon, a cousin of Vicente and Martin Alonso Pinzon, filled the master's post on the Pinta, as did Juan de la Cosa on the Santa Maria. The pilots were Peralonso Nino on the Nina, Cristobal Garcia Sarmiento on the Pinta and Sancho Ruiz on the Santa Maria.

The chief petty officer, with direct control over the red-capped seamen, was the boatswain, or bosun. He shouted the master's or the pilot's orders to the men on calm days, or, with his bosun's whistle, piped signals when the wind or sea was up. In addition to handling the men, the bosun was in charge of inspecting for damage, repairing worn bilge pumps and rigging and making sure the rats didn't chew the sails or gnaw into their food.

The ordinary seamen and cabin boys were a tough, coarse lot. Hard and dangerous work made hard men. The sailors all carried knives for use in their work and for eating, but, if someone insulted a man's treasured honor or dignity, they drew the well-honed blades in anger to satisfy their injured *pundonor*. Even though they bristled quickly at a slight, they could laugh at a finger sliced off by an errant knife blade, and their rough humor took the form of friendly profanity and tacking crude nicknames on one another. Mostly illiterate, they could be persuaded by *palabras dulces* (sweet words) or intimidated by threats. When words didn't quell their more brutish instincts, iron discipline and harsh punishment did.

A step up from ordinary seamen and cabin boys were the men with a particular skill; stewards in charge of the food, water and wine, surgeons to tend cuts and breaks, carpenters to make repairs and tailors to stitch split sails. Even though the fleet was headed for parts unknown which might be populated with hostile forces, there were no professional soldiers. Although Columbus used the conversion of Infidel souls to the Holy Faith as a major selling point with Isabel, there were no priests. The Captain General manned and equipped his fleet for only one purpose—discovery.

Conquest and conversion would come later.

Passengers included Luis de Torres, a converted Jew who spoke Hebrew and Arabic.[8] Many people at that time thought that Arabic was the mother tongue of all languages, so it was assumed that Torres would be able to communicate with the Oriental potentates. For one of the most important jobs, Columbus brought along someone he knew he could trust, Diego de Harana, the cousin of his Spanish mistress. Arana served as the marshall of the fleet; the enforcer, the man who would superintend keel hauling and ducking if a crewman became insubordinate. Or he could apply another common punishment; tieing a man to the mast with a bucket of iron slung around his neck and leaving him there for hours or days, depending on the severity of the offense.

Ferdinand and Isabel posted their own men aboard to guard their interests. Pedro Gutierrez was the Sovereigns' official representative, and Rodrigo Sanchez was the comptroller, whose job was to see that the King and Queen were allocated their just due. Rodrigo Escobedo acted as secretary of the fleet to record all possessions taken in the name of the Sovereigns.

Among the more colorful crewmen were a convicted murderer from Palos, Bartolome de Torres, and three of his friends who had staged a jailbreak to free Torres. When word circulated in the Palos area that the Sovereigns promised to pardon any criminals who agreed to go on Columbus' voyage, the four turned themselves in, signed on as crewmen on the Santa Maria and received the royal pardon.[9]

Thus outfitted and crewed, when the fleet was three days out it ran into its first problem on August 6. The wooden rudder on the Pinta slipped out of its sockets in heavy seas after receiving a battering from the rear by waves whipped up by a robust wind. The Pinta's crew jerry-rigged the rudder, and continued the voyage, but with difficulty. The suspicious Columbus blamed the mishap on two men from Palos who, he claimed, didn't want "to make the voyage, and even before we left Palos they attempted to delay or prevent the enterprise. They complained all the time and concocted excuses for not sailing." In one of his few favorable comments on the Pinta's captain, he wrote "I was relieved to learn what a resourceful captain I had in Martin Alonso Pinzon, who is an experienced and ingenious man. He has been able to temporarily repair the rudder with some ropes in order that we might proceed."

Columbus ordered Pinzon to steer for Grand Canary Island to fix the rudder at the rudimentary repair facilities there, while he sailed the Santa Maria and the Nina west to Gomera Island to look for a substitute for the Pinta. Calm winds and the sea put the two ships in the doldrums for three days. When he arrived at Gomera on August 12 he sent the ship's boat ashore to see if a spare ship was available. The shore party returned with the bad news that there was no ship at Gomera capable of making the long voyage to the Indies. The shore party did report, however, that the governess of the island, Dona Beatriz de Peraza y Bobadilla, was expected to return home soon from the Island of Lanzarote on a forty ton vessel which the Captain General thought "would be perfect for my needs."[10] Columbus decided to wait at Gomera for Dona Beatriz, and he sent a messenger on an inter-island brig to Grand Canary to tell Martin Alonso Pinzon to repair the Pinta's rudder and come to Gomera as soon a possible.

The Nina and the Santa Maria rocked at anchor for twelve days in Gomera, with no sight of Dona Beatriz or the Pinta. Columbus, sensing that his men were "restive and uneasy" due to the delay, weighed anchor on Friday, August 24, and sailed east back to Grand Canary. That night, as they sailed past Tenerife Island, a twelve thousand-foot volcano erupted in a fiery shower of molten rocks and flames. "Many members of the crew were astonished and frightened [by this bad omen] for they had never seen such an occurrence," Columbus wrote.

Perhaps the superstitious crew remembered the chapter in Genesis when "...the Lord rained upon Sodom and Gomorrah brimstone and fire from the sky. He...destroyed...those cities... and all that grew on the ground." A few crewmen may have seen paintings in church illustrating the Biblical story of Lot's wife running from heavenly flames, glancing back with a terrified look at the ruined cities and the smashed ships in the harbor, just before God turned her into a pillar of salt. "I calmed them," Columbus said, "by telling them about Mount Etna in Sicily and other volcanos that I have seen, and I explained to them the cause of this great fire."

At nine o'clock the next morning, August 25, the two ships made port at Grand Canary to find that almost nothing had been done to repair the Pinta's rudder. Columbus laced into the Pinta's captain and crew: "Martin Alonso and his men have no good excuse for making such little progress with the Pinta. I am aware that there are few facilities [to make repairs] on Grand Canary, but sometimes one must make do with what is at hand."

Although he was mad because the Pinta's rudder hadn't been repaired, Columbus noted approvingly that, while he was in Gomera, the Pinta's crew recaulked the caravel, which leaked badly during the cruise from Palos. The sailors hauled the Pinta on skids up the beach and careened her on her side. They scraped off the barnacles and moss, which create friction and slow a ship in the water, and applied a thick sticky mixture of tallow and pine tar to prevent worms from burrowing into the hull, causing rotting. After they caulked one side of the hull, the crew turned the Pinta to the other side and repeated the process.

Columbus, always quick tempered when his subordinates didn't follow his orders, must have used his most strident voice of command to upbraid the men. In just five days, the Santa Maria's bosun and the fleet's best carpenters, working with the local blacksmiths, repaired the Pinta's rudder. During that time, the Nina's sailors switched her triangular lateen sails to square rigging. Because square rigged ships sail faster when there is a wind at their back, Columbus said, "These winds [of the Canaries] blow steadily from the east or northeast every day of the year, and a square rigged ship has every advantage in these latitudes."

On the afternoon of August 31 he set sail for Gomera, and arrived on the morning of September 2. There he met the thirty-year-old enchantress, Dona Beatriz de Peraza. As a young girl, Beatriz, a descendant of one of Castile's oldest noble families, had served as maid of honor to Queen Isabel. When King Ferdinand's ever roving eye fell on the sprightly young woman, she became his lover. The puritanical Isabel never agreed with the accepted Spanish custom of husbands having mistresses, particularly when Ferdinand was involved.

Fortunately for Isabel, Don Hernando Peraza, the despotic Governor of Gomera, was brought to court in Spain to answer murder charges. Isabel, a schemer when need be, engineered a plea bargain. In return for a pardon, Peraza agreed to marry Beatriz and take her, immediately, back to Gomera. Several years later, the native Guanches killed Peraza for raping a native girl. When Columbus arrived on Gomera, Dona Beatriz de Peraza was acting as Governess of the island on behalf of her minor son. Knowing that the Captain General was on a royal mission, she entertained him in her stone castle as lavishly as the primitive island permitted. It is almost certain that the lusty widow and the forty-one-year-old Columbus had an affair.

While his crew sweated during the next four days to reprovision the fleet with wine, molasses, dried meat and salted fish, Columbus spent much of his time in the arms of his new lover. A modern novelist pictures Dona Beatriz as a stunningly beautiful, sadomasochistic love goddess who was violently attracted to men of strong character and great power, and men who were risk takers. Columbus was all of these. The novelist, Abel Posse, imagines Dona Beatriz as having "Tremendous hips. Tiny waist. Planetary, Picassoesque thighs, but fine ankles as delicate as the wrists of a Viennese organist...[Dressed] in a kind of gauzy Hellenic tunic. Sandals of gilded leather. Thick black hair loose on her shoulders. Large green eyes, closer to the stalking panther than the fleeting gazelle."[11] Perhaps a bit dramatic, but even if she weren't a man eater, she turned the head of a king and an admiral. She must have been an erotic beauty, and, as a friend of Columbus wrote, the Captain General was "fired with love" for the seductress.

In between trips to Dona Beatriz' bedchamber, Columbus talked with the Spanish conquerors of the island. "These Spaniards swear under oath that every year they see land to the west, where the sun sets," he wrote. These tales reminded Columbus of similar stories he had heard years before from the Portuguese colonists on Madeira and the Azores. The stories he heard on Gomera only corroborated his belief that the mythical St. Brendan's Island, or some other lands, existed not too far to the west.

Even the charms of an amorous noblewoman couldn't divert the determined Captain General from his mission for long. With wooden barrels of fresh water and firewood lashed to the decks of the Nina, Pinta and Santa Maria, and their holds filled with provisions, Columbus left his lover and set sail for the Indies on September 6, 1492. No doubt, Dona Beatriz watched from the square tower of her castle while the crewmen hoisted the white sails bearing their red crosses to begin the epic trip to the Orient.

17

COLUMBUS, THE CANARIES TO NEW WORLD

During the morning of September 6, 1492, a Spanish sea captain told Columbus that a Portuguese squadron was looking for him. "There could be some truth in this because King John [of Portugal] must be angry that I went over to Castile," the Captain General said. He immediately ordered the fleet to haul anchors and, before noon, they were under sail. The weather wouldn't cooperate. In calm winds, the sails hung slack for two days until a stiff northeast breeze picked up, and the pilots set the course due west along latitude twenty-nine.

At sunrise on Sunday, September 9, they were out of sight of land. "[M]any men... wept for fear they would not see it again for a long time. I soothed them with great promises of lands and riches." Columbus' September 9 comment on the crews' morale was the first of many during the Canaries-New World leg of the trip, because, during the voyage, the mens' emotions gyrated wildly. Anger, joy. Fear, exhilaration. Superstition, appeals to the Almighty.

Columbus clearly recognized the psychological problem, the bundle of human emotions which boil over when men venture into the unknown and dangerous. He dealt with their swings of mood with a blend of threats, strict discipline, *palabras dulces*, lies when he thought it necessary and promises of rewards. More importantly, he never lost his serene calm, and never took his eye off the objective. Keeping his head about him and subduing the sailors' volatile fear would test every ounce of the Captain General's nerve.

Like all great commanders, Columbus spent considerable time anticipating and manipulating his mens' morale. The living conditions aboard ships compounded his problem. The Nina, Pinta and Santa Maria were designed for two or three day trips in the Mediterranean Sea, or the short hops between Spain and France, England or Italy, rarely out of sight of land for more than a day or two. To outfit the fleet for the voyage, their holds were stuffed with ballast, water and wine barrels, pottery jars of olive oil and other ship's stores. There was little room for the ninety men. The captains had small cabins on the sterncastles, and there may have been bunks for the other officers. Since hammocks were unknown, the men slept anywhere they could. In fair weather, on the deck, and, in foul, below deck in the malodorous hold—with the vermin.

Their food was frequently bad, and always monotonous. Breakfast might be cheese, garlic cloves and pickled sardines. The crew ate one hot meal a day, the cooking being done in an open firebox, screened to cut the wind. After a few days at sea, the only fresh meat was an occasional fish the men harpooned or caught on a trolling line. Drinks were water and wine, which sometimes soured. The sailors ate out of a common bowl, or, with their knives, carved a chunk of stringy salted meat until the bones were "clean as ivory." The ships carried chickpeas, beans, lentils, rice, honey, almonds and raisins. Sea biscuits, baked ashore from wheat, were kept in the driest part of the hold. A modern-day backpacker would have felt at home.

Each sailor furnished his own clothing; a shirt, pants, hooded parka and red woolen stocking cap. Since the men lived and slept in their one suit of clothes, there was no need to wake the men early for their watches. Washing their clothes and bathing were accomplished at the same time, by jumping into the sea on a calm day. Each crewman let his beard grow, fresh water being too precious to waste on shaving. As the stubble grew longer, it protected their faces from the chafing of wind and sun. When the hold was not used as a toilet, the men used the *jardin* (garden), a seat hung over the rail. Much used, no doubt, if the crew ate spoiled food or drank soured wine. One Spanish author wrote poetically of the lovely views of the moon and stars from the *jardin*, and the impromptu baths from the waves on a stormy day. Another, a serious Spanish bishop, complained of the indecency of exposing oneself to the rest of the crew, and of the frazzled rope end coated with tar he used to rasp himself clean.[1]

The captains divided the seamen into two groups to serve four-hour watches beginning at three, seven and eleven o'clock of each day and night. At the change of each watch, to avoid error, the helmsman, standing on the main deck shouted his course up to the officer on the quarterdeck, who repeated it to the new officer who repeated it to the new helmsman. Every morning, the seven o'clock watch swabbed the decks with sea water and worked the bilge pump to void the hold of the prior day's leakage. The morning watch tightened or loosened the lines so that the section of rope that rubbed all night in the wooden blocks wouldn't wear and snap. During the day, the crew scrubbed equipment, spliced ropes and repaired rigging; a grinding routine, broken only when the bosun ordered the horny-handed men into the rigging to raise or lower sails.

The same boring food, the same boring drink, the same boring work spiced the emotional stew aboard ship, particularly on this voyage, which would be longer than any European had ever made. In these conditions, grousing starts. The men form cliques, faces become surly, tempers spark.

Harking back to his younger days when he jiggered the compass on the voyage to Tunis, Columbus wrote on September 9: "To sustain [the crews'] hope and dispel their fears on a long voyage, I decided to reckon fewer leagues than we actually made."[2] In other words, he "cooked the books," faked the distances traveled. He did this, he rationalized, so the men would think they weren't too far from home, and so they would believe they had enough supplies to make it back to Spain. The Captain General knew it would be only a matter of time until the men began clamoring to return. Ironically, the faked distances he showed the crew were closer to correct than were the supposedly "true" distances. On September 10 he told his first lie: "Today I made 180 miles at a speed of 7.5 knots. I recorded only 144 miles in order not to alarm the sailors if the voyage is lengthy." The next day he said: "Tonight I made another 60 miles, but only recorded 48 miles." The deception continued almost daily.

Before sunup on Saturday, September 15, "I saw a marvelous meteorite fall into the sea 12 or 15 miles away to the southwest. This was taken by some people to be a bad omen, but I calmed them by telling of the numerous occasions that I have witnessed such events." Was this another lie? We don't know, but it frightened Columbus. "I have to confess that this is the closest that a falling star has ever come to my ship."

Explaining away natural phenomena five hundred years ago wasn't easy. Going to sea was a risky business, and mariners were very superstitious and very religious. They attributed unusual events either to evil spirits or the invisible hand of God. To summon the Lord, each evening the crewmen held vespers, offered prayers to the Holy Spirit begging protection and sang the Benedictine chant, Salve Regina, to salute the Blessed Virgin. At the daily services, the sailors recited the Pater Noster and Ave Maria. Throughout the day, sometimes as often as every half hour, the ship's boys chanted prayers. "God give us good days, a good voyage, good passage to the ship..; many good days may God grant His graces to the men fore and aft. Amen."[3]

Three times a day, the devout Captain General retired to the privacy of his cabin to pray and read religious texts. The 107th Psalm must have consoled him:

> "Some go down to the sea and travel over it in ships, to do business in the great waters;.. For He commands and raises the stormy wind, which lifts up the waves of the sea... Their [those aboard] courage melts away because of their plight. They reel to and fro, and stagger like a drunken man... He hushes the storm to a calm and to a gentle whisper, so that the waves are still."

In an age when all but a few were certain of Divine intervention in every phase of life, these words from the Bible must have cheered Columbus and his men. Just have faith, the Bible said, and God will tame the seas to a whisper. Even though the Holy Scriptures had explanations for almost everything in that era of little learning, little experimentation and little inquiry, ordinary men still feared the unknown. Often, they rationalized the inexplicable with dark superstition.

On September 16, 1492, Columbus estimated a sail of 117 miles, but told the men they only made 108 miles. During that day, amidst storm clouds and drizzle, the three ships plowed through patches of strange yellow-green weeds. The next day they saw "a great deal of weed...weed from rocks that lie to the west. I take this to mean that we are near land. The weed resembles stargrass, except that it has long stalks and shoots and is loaded with fruit like the mastic tree. Some of this weed looks like river grass, and the crew found a live crab in a patch of it. This is a sure sign of land, for crabs are not found more than 240 miles from shore."

Columbus was wrong. There was no mother lode of the valuable mastic, which he saw on the Isle of Chios eighteen years earlier, and he wasn't near land.[4] He was entering the Sargasso Sea, a huge oval shaped meadow of seaweed in the middle of the Atlantic Ocean. Excited, because he thought weeds only grew in shallow water, he ordered a sounding to be taken with six hundred feet of line. Nothing. The ocean floor was closer to twelve thousand feet under the solitary sea, and the fleet was actually closer to the Canaries than to the Bahamas.

After sighting what they believed were weeds indicating they were near land and a few land-based birds: "Everyone is cheerful, and the Pinta, the fastest sailing vessel, went ahead as fast as it could in order to sight land. All the indications of land come from the west, where I trust Almighty God, in whose hands are all victories, will soon deliver us to land. This morning I also saw another ringtail...a bird that is not accustomed to sleeping on the sea." Ever the wishful thinker, Columbus followed his old habit, developed while he was gathering proof that a voyage west to the Indies was feasible, of grasping at the smallest shreds of evidence to confirm his unshakeable preconceptions.

On September 18 and 19, Columbus and Martin Alonso Pinzon argued over the course the fleet should follow. The swift Pinta sailed far ahead of the paunchy Santa Maria, and, at sundown on the 18th, Pinzon heeled about and drew the Pinta alongside the Santa Maria. Pinzon shouted that he spotted land about forty-five miles to the north. The Captain General's suspicion of the salty old mariner was growing. "He is a fine captain and very resourceful, but his independence disturbs me somewhat. I trust that this tendency to strike out on his own does not continue, for we can ill afford to become separated this far from home."

After Pinzon's report of land to the north, Columbus' officers urged him to break off his westerly course. "But," the stubborn Captain General said, "my calculations do not indicate that land is in that direction, and I am not going to waste time with it. I have sailed for 11 days under a full sail, running ever before the wind, but tonight the wind freshened to the point that I ordered the topsails taken in."

On September 19 Martin Alonso again pressed Columbus to steer north to find the land Pinzon was sure he saw. Columbus thought, yes, the fleet might very well be sailing between islands to the north and south, but a few inconsequential islands weren't the primary objective. In the log Columbus wrote: "It is my desire to go directly to the Indies, and not get sidetracked with islands that I shall see on the return passage, God willing. The weather is good."

Because of the alleged sightings, and a dispute over where they were, the Captain General signaled with puffs of smoke for all captains and pilots to board the Santa Maria for a conference. Juan Nino of the Nina reckoned they were 1320 miles west of the Canaries. Sancho Ruiz, Columbus' own pilot, calculated 1200 miles. The trade winds had actually pushed them about 1260 miles west.

During his trip to Ghana years before, Columbus experienced firsthand the winds blowing steadily from the east and northeast at the tropical latitudes. From his extensive reading and his talks with well-traveled sailors, he knew of the winds that seldom vary from their westerly course along the Tropic of Cancer. He couldn't have known how far west they blew or whether they blew continuously. Would the breezes peter out after a few days' sailing? When he had sailed two thousand miles, would they switch to the north or south? By this time in his life, it was second nature for Columbus to grasp the slightest evidence to bolster his arguments. His willingness to take a risk and to trust his intuition led him to the fortunate conclusion that the trade winds would carry him safely to the Indies.[5]

With the trade winds providing the power, medieval mariners plotted their course through the seas. In the late 1400s there were two ways of navigating, neither very precise. Celestial navigation ("shooting the stars") with today's instruments is very accurate. But the only tool Columbus worked with, a primitive quadrant, was useless on a cloudy night, and, when the Santa Maria yawed and rolled in the Atlantic's swells, it was almost impossible to get a true reading. On the few occasions Columbus used his quadrant, he pointed the hardwood device at a star. A silk cord with a small weight at its end swung along a quarter circle marked with degrees to determine latitude. Knowing of the chance for error, Columbus didn't trust the quadrant, and kept it stowed in his cabin for most of the voyage.

What he did trust was his years of experience in dead reckoning navigation. Columbus kept careful account of his direction and speed. To this data, he factored in the effect of the currents and the direction and strength of the wind. The key instrument for his computations was the compass. Columbus' faith in the compass was almost slavish, because, he said, the needle "always seeks the truth." The compass card had thirty-two points, a fleurs-de-lis marked north and the magnetized needle rested on a post in the center. The Captain General brought spare needles and extra lodestones.[6] If the magnetized needle grew weak, he recharged it with a precious lodestone, which he kept under lock and key in his cabin.

On the raised quarterdeck at the rear of each ship, where the officer of the watch stood, a rectangular box with the compass inside was fixed to the heavy deck planks. A wooden hood protected the compass box from the weather, and a copper olive oil lamp illuminated the compass at night. Doubling up, the pilots installed another compass on the main deck, close to the tiller where the helmsman guided the ship. The officer of the watch shouted steering instructions through an open hatch down to the helmsman, and the helmsman reconfirmed the orders by checking his compass and yelling the ship's direction back to his officer.

Every half hour, the officer marked the course steered and his estimate of the speed on a slate hanging on the bulkhead next to him. At the end of each four-hour watch, the officer totaled the half hourly notes in the log book. Every twelve hours, he made summaries of the calculations. Because keeping accurate records and steering a true course were crucial to dead reckoning navigation, a fresh helmsman took over every hour. If the helmsmen let the Santa Maria stray off her westerly course, Columbus chewed them out. "I reprimanded them several times for this," he said.

As an experienced navigator, Columbus could estimate his speed by "feel." If he wanted more precision, he dropped a piece of wood overboard from the bow and timed the passage from bow to stern. He could estimate short time periods by reciting a well-known rhyme or chant or by counting his pulse beats. He could measure longer time periods with sand clocks.

Venetians made the most accurate sand clocks of delicate glass. The craftsmen filled half of the clock with enough sand to run through its pinched waist every half hour. Aboard ship, the officer of the watch assigned a crewman the duty of turning the clock when the sand drained out of the top section.

Because exact time keeping was so important to dead reckoning, the crewman was subject to punishment if he failed to make the turns. In addition to the risk of a dozing crewman missing a turn, the fragile sand clocks could be thrown off by the ship's lurching through the water during storms, or by the sun warming and expanding the glass neck between the two chambers. To make up for these defects, the pilot recalculated the exact hour with a device he knew was right; the sun at high noon, sunrise or sunset. On a clear night, he estimated the time by sighting on the position of the Little Dipper or other constellations as they moved across the sky.

When Columbus assembled the time, course and speed data, he plotted his location on a sheepskin chart. For the former mapmaker, using his ruler and dividers was the easiest part of the process. Scholars dispute many details surrounding Columbus' life and character. Almost all agree that he was a master seaman, the finest sailor of his time and, perhaps, the greatest dead reckoning navigator who ever lived.

A French sailor, explorer and scholar, Charcot, describes Columbus as "a seaman who had '*le sens marin,*' that intangible and unteachable God-given gift of knowing how to direct and plot the way of a ship in the middle of the ocean...."[7] God blessed the Captain General with excellent hearing, eyesight and sense of smell. The brackish scent of the sea or a glance at the clouds or a star told him things ordinary men couldn't divine. With the crude navigational methods and tools he had to work with, Columbus missed the total distance traveled on the first voyage by only nine percent. His men, who doubted him on many occasions, must have sensed that their Captain General was the only man who could guide them safely and surely to and from the Indies.

Like the waves in the watery desert of the Atlantic, the crews' spirits rose and fell. After spotting three songbirds early in the morning of September 20, Columbus wrote: "This was a comforting thought, for, unlike the large water birds, these little birds could not have come from far off [land]."

As the fleet nudged farther into the Sargasso Sea, with its thick mat of yellow-green weeds, the crews' reaction was mixed. "In a way, this weed comforted the men, since they have concluded that it must come from nearby land. But, at the same time, it caused some of them great apprehension because, in some places, it was so thick that it actually held back the ships. Since fear evokes imaginary terrors, the men thought that the weed might become so thick and matted that there might happen to them what is supposed to have happened to St. Amador, when he was trapped in a frozen sèa that held his ship fast."

After sixteen days at sea, the Captain General noted on September 22 that the wind changed, blowing in his face from the west and southwest. Although this slowed his progress, "[T]hese contrary winds are very helpful because the crew is agitated, thinking that no winds blow in these parts that will return them to Spain."

What he anticipated, that fear of the endless space around the sailors would eventually grip them, was happening. As the solitude of the lonely ocean worked its way inside the men, tension mounted, and, on the next day, Columbus reported that: "The crew is grumbling about the wind. When I get a wind from the SW or west it is inconstant, and that, along with the flat sea, has led the men to believe that we will never get home."

He tried to sooth them by telling them that the sea was flat because they were near land. Quixotically, a few hours later the sea made up without any wind (probably because of a hurricane several hundred miles away), and, later that day, the wind blew smartly from the west northwest. Certain that this was a sign of Divine intervention, Columbus wrote that: "Such a sign has not appeared since Moses led the Jews out of Egypt... As with Moses when he led his people out of captivity, my people were humbled by this act of the Almighty....The crew was relieved. The men tried to catch some fish, but could not get any to bite at the hooks. Eventually they harpooned several." Comforted by his somewhat presumptuous comparison of himself to the Old Testament prophet, Columbus rested easy that night, sure that the hand of providence was on his shoulder.

The keen student of his crews' temperament misread their bent. The sailors' tottering morale plunged into open threats of mutiny. The men had been squinting into the red sun glowering in the western sky for days—with no sight of land. Even on a voyage to a known destination, it was hard to control a crew of illiterate sailors. On this trip to the unknown, the problem was exponential.

Day after day, the crewmen were jammed into the small ships, eating bad food and being shouted at by officers with dictatorial power. No privacy, no place to escape someone you grew to hate. The same faces and the same voices. A foreigner's accent grated on the nerves. Men from the south against men from the north. Minor mistakes blown out of proportion. Rumors. Motives questioned. Sullen looks, sidelong glances. Curses. *Hijo de puta* (Son of a whore). Cliques knotted on the forecastle to bitch. And their accusations centered on one man—their Genoese Captain General.

"All day long and all night long those who are awake and able to get together never cease talking to each other in circles, complaining that they will never be able to return home," Columbus wrote on September 24. "They have said that it is insanity and suicidal on their part to risk their lives following the madness of a foreigner. They have said that, not only am I willing to risk my life just to become a great lord, but that I have deceived them to further my ambition. They have also said that, because my proposition [to go west to the Indies] has been contradicted by so many wise and lettered men who considered it vain and foolish, they may be excused for whatever might be done in the matter. Some feel that they are not obligated to go to the end of the world, especially if they are delayed any more and will not have sufficient provisions to return."

Some of the crew threatened murder. "I am told by a few trusted men, and these are few in number, that if I persist in going onward, the best course of action will be to throw me into the sea some night. They will say that I fell overboard while taking the position of the North Star with my quadrant. Since I am a foreigner, little or no account will be asked of the matter, but, rather, there will be a great many who will swear that God has given me my just desserts on account of my rashness."[8]

The crews' menacing actions upset Columbus, and he was shocked that the men couldn't see that God was on their side. "I am having serious trouble with the crew, despite the signs of land that we have [seen] and those given to us by Almighty God. In fact, the more God shows the men manifest signs that we are near land, the more their impatience and inconstancy increases, and the more indignant they become against me."

Ever suspicious, quick to blame others, Columbus lashed back: "I know that the men are taking these complaints to the Pinzons, and that the Pinzons have sided with them. Since most of these people are from Palos and the surrounding area, they stick together, and I know that Martin Alonso cannot be trusted. He is a skilled mariner, but he wants the rewards and honors of this enterprise for himself. He is always running ahead of the fleet, seeking to be the first to sight land." Distrustful though he was, Columbus was still cold bloodedly practical: "I am fully aware that I must use him [Pinzon], because his support is too great among the men."

While his crew was almost in panic, Columbus remained calm, in charge. His grey eyes never flinched in fear or doubt. His self-confidence, which some called arrogance, never deserted him. "I am...sure that, if I lose command, the fleet will never reach the Indies and will probably never get back to Spain. With God's help, I shall persevere."

Whatever Columbus did or said, whether threats or *palabras dulces*, the crew submitted to the unswerving will of their Captain General. Although he was a skilled manipulator of men, he needed what every leader must have—a great deal of luck.

On September 25, the day after the threatened revolt, at sunset Martin Alonso Pinzon pulled alongside and shouted from the quarterdeck of the Pinta: "Land, Land. I claim the reward [a prize of ten thousand maravedis promised by Isabel and Ferdinand to the first man who saw land]." Columbus wrote that: "When I heard this stated so positively, I fell to my knees to give thanks to Our Lord, and Martin said Gloria in Excelsis Deo with his people. My people did the same thing, and the Nina's crew all climbed the mast and rigging, and all claimed that it was land. At that moment, I myself was sure that it was land, and reckoned that it was about 75 miles to the SW....All told, we had gone about 65 miles, but I told the people that we had made 39 miles. The sea is very smooth and some of the men went swimming."

The upbeat mood lasted only until sunrise the next day, September 26, when Columbus determined that what they were sure was land was nothing more than a mirage created by storm clouds and wishful thinking. Despite the bad news, the sailors remained relatively calm, and, for the next eleven days, Columbus kept the prows of his fleet headed due west. During that period, the Captain General reported sightings of frigate birds, terns, petrels and ringtails. As an avid student of the Bible, Columbus knew that Noah learned he was near land from a dove. From his discussions with Portuguese navigators, he knew that they often followed the flights of birds to land.

Despite the favorable sightings of land birds, a sudden declination by the compass needle caused alarm. "[T]he compass needle declined to the NW by a point, but at dawn it was right on the North Star. This is because the needle points true, but the star rotates. For some reason my pilots do not understand this phenomenon, and it makes them agitated and confused. These variations make them quite apprehensive, especially on a voyage of this length into strange regions. My explanation has only partly allayed their fears."

During a driving rainstorm on October 1, Columbus and the Santa Maria's pilot calculated the total distance traveled. The figure he gave to the men, 1752 miles, was 369 miles shorter than what he believed to be the truth. "I did not reveal this ['true'] figure to the men because they would become frightened, finding themselves so far from home, or at least thinking they were that far."

All day, October 3, he saw no birds, and he assumed that he left behind a group of islands in the middle of the ocean. "I could have visited those islands last week, but I did not want to delay by beating windward because they were not my objective. My goal is the Indies, and it would make no sense to waste time with offshore islands."

After sailing all night under a full moon, on Saturday, October 6, Martin Alonso Pinzon challenged Columbus again, demanding that the course be altered to the southwest. The Captain General responded with a decisive no. This decision wasn't popular, and Columbus notes that the men started to "murmur and complain," but "despite their grumblings, I held fast to the west."

Luck struck again. On October 7 some of the men thought they saw land ahead, "but it was not very distinct." Columbus knew that the soft wooly clouds, when tinted purple, orange and pink, could play tricks on the eyes of a man craving to find land. This time no one shouted "land" because, after the first false sighting, Columbus ordered that any man who claimed he saw land, which was not discovered in three days' sailing, would forfeit the ten thousand maravedis prize money offered by Ferdinand and Isabel.

Columbus sent a crewman to the firepot swinging from the stern to signal, with the proper number of puffs of smoke, for the fleet to assemble. After the ships rendezvoused at sunrise and the captains decided to press on for a few more days, the excited captain of the Nina ordered full sail and shot ahead of the Pinta and the Santa Maria.

Shortly, Vicente Pinzon ran up a signal flag on the Nina's mast and fired a cannon to trumpet a positive sighting. "Joy turned to dismay as the day progressed, for, by evening, we had found no land, and had to face the reality that it was only an illusion. God did offer us, however, a small token of comfort: many large flocks of birds flew over, coming from the north and flying to the SW... and they were land birds...either going to sleep ashore or fleeing the winter in the lands from whence they came. I know that most of the islands discovered by the Portuguese have been found because of birds." With this log entry, Columbus was the first European to report on the great fall migration of ducks and geese from North America along the Atlantic flyway to South America. They were close, due north of Puerto Rico, but still some 375 miles from landfall.

On October 7, under pressure from Martin Alonso Pinzon, Columbus changed his course from due west to southwest, where the flocks of birds were headed. If Columbus hadn't shifted course to the southwest, he might have landed between Florida and Virginia, depending on the effect of the Gulf Stream, making North America a Spanish colony.

October 10 was the most critical day of the voyage. The crew had last seen land thirty-one days before, double the previous record for open sea navigation. Rations were getting short. The pilots and the men wanted to turn back. Mutiny was brewing again. In understatement, Columbus said the men "grumbled and complained of the long voyage." This time, the northerners, Basques and Galicians, stirred up most of the trouble. The Captain General exploded with a tongue lashing: "I reproached them for lack of spirit, telling them that, for better or worse, they had to complete the enterprise on which the Catholic Sovereigns had sent them." He probably told them of Martin Alonso's threat to "Hang half a dozen...or throw them overboard. If you [Columbus] dare not, my brothers and I will do it."[9]

Columbus followed up his tongue lashing with *palabras dulces*, reminding them of the riches and rewards awaiting them if they would just stay the course for a few more days. Possibly he pointed out the practical problem that most of the food and water was gone, and they didn't have sufficient supplies to make the sail back to Spain. Then, his stubborn, unyielding nature flashed: "I...told the men that it was pointless to complain. No point at all. I am going to the Indies and I shall sail on until, with the help of Our Lord, I find them."

Thursday, October 11, started out nasty. In rough seas, the Santa Maria took on more water than at any other time during the voyage. Despite the squalls and crashing waves, the men were "cheerful" and "breathed easier" because they saw large flocks of birds, reeds, other land plants and a stick that looked as if it was carved by a man. In the late afternoon, the sky cleared and the sun glared on the white canvas sails with their huge red crosses. The men gathered for vespers, fervently sang the Salve Regina and gave a special thanksgiving to God for giving "us renewed hope through the many signs of land He provided."

On that clear night, the sky was vivid with brilliant stars. Orion. The Milky Way. But sailing at night is dangerous. Reefs and shoals lurk unseeable beneath the sea. Columbus' grace period with the crew was running out, and, despite the risk, he decided to proceed at full speed. With a good wind blowing, the Captain General wanted to cover as much distance as he could. From the deck of the Santa Maria, Columbus could see the full sails of the Nina and the Pinta silhouetted in the moonlight. The stout oak masts creaked and the lines strained as the ships plunged ahead, throwing spray.

Confident, and, no doubt, excited, he promised to give the first man to sight land a silk vest to go along with the Sovereigns' ten thousand maravedis prize. After urging the crew to be "ever vigilant," he doubled the lookouts to watch for reefs and to spot land. He posted a man high up in the crow's nest and another on the forecastle. To keep fresh men on the job, the lookouts switched off every hour. Every half hour, when the ship's boy turned the sand clock, he sang out a ditty, and the lookouts responded with a shout to show that they were awake.

At about ten p.m., while Columbus paced the quarterdeck, he thought he saw a little wax candle bobbing up and down. "It had the appearance of a light or torch belonging to fishermen or travellers who alternately raised or lowered it, or perhaps were going from house to house." After three false alarms, and afraid of his over anxiousness to find land, Columbus questioned his own extraordinary eyesight. He called two of the Sovereigns' representatives up to the quarterdeck to take a look. One thought he saw the light, the other didn't. Columbus passed it off as "such an uncertain thing that I did not feel it was adequate proof of land."[10]

With the three ships sprinting through the swells at about ten miles per hour, at two a.m. on October 12, 1492, Rodrigo de Triana, a sailor aboard the Pinta, strained his eyes westward, blinked and spotted white sand beaches gleaming under the three-quarter moon. "*Tierra. Lumbre.*" (Land. Light.), Triana yelled.

Martin Alonso Pinzon verified the sighting and fired the signal cannon. "I now believe that the light I saw earlier was a sign from God," Columbus said. "And that it was truly the first positive indication of land.... I hauled in all sails but the mainsail and lay-to until daylight. The land is about six miles to the west." With the fore and mizzen sails furled, the fleet tacked lazily offshore during the rest of the night. At sunup, all hands were on the main deck, still damp with the night's dew. The air smelled fresh, and it was "a great pleasure... [to] taste the morning." As fingers of light broke the Caribbean dark, the fleet edged along the reefs on the south side of the island until they found a safe spot to anchor. Shortly after dawn, crewmen rowed Columbus ashore in the Santa Maria's dinghy.

When Columbus stepped ashore that morning, in Europe it was early afternoon. Perhaps, on that same day, the forty-year-old Leonardo da Vinci was designing a statue for his patron in Italy, the twenty-seven-year-old Erasmus was pouring over Roman classics on a rainy day in Holland and the twenty-three-year-old Machiavelli was scheming to obtain a bureaucratic post in Florence. Those Renaissance men were changing the way Europeans thought and acted.

Not until Neil Armstrong's boots first stirred the moondust almost half a millennium later, was there as dramatic an event as Columbus wading through the water to set foot on a white sand beach in the Bahamas. Many writers have attempted to characterize the momentousness and magnitude of the discovery. "It was the achievement of Columbus to convert conjecture into certainty, to substitute knowledge for hypothesis and to open a way across the Atlantic which has never since been closed," one writer says. "The first footfall of Columbus on the shore of the New World echoed like a thunderclap down the centuries, and its reverberations have not died away," says another.[11]

Superlatives aside, the riches found in the New World made Spain the dominant power in Europe for two centuries, and Spanish culture, language and religion spread from Northern California to the southernmost tip of South America. Intellectually, Columbus' discovery stimulated more important and longer lasting changes. Although the waves of the Renaissance were already churning in Europe, the new sense of optimism, opportunity, speculation and inquiry created by the discovery helped shatter the superstition and ignorance of the Middle Ages.

Columbus delivered up to Western Europe a truly "New World," a place for its military entrepreneurs to conquer and exploit, a place where daring, an adventurous spirit and practical experience were more important than blind adherence to accepted dogmas, a place to build a new society.

For Columbus personally, it was triumph. In thirty-three days he covered 3200 uncharted miles. As to his fourteen years of poverty and humiliation—over; of begging and wheedling—over; of rejection and scorn—over. Now he was Admiral of the Ocean Sea, Don Christopher Columbus.

18

COLUMBUS, THE CARIBBEAN

As the sun rose on October 12, 1492, bewildered natives gaped at the three enormous "houses on water" bobbing off their shore. They squinted in the morning light in astonishment at the trees sticking up from the middle of the "houses on water" and the white sheets hanging from the trees, flapping in the humid morning breeze.

What was this apparition? Who were these strange men, with hair on their faces and pale skin, aboard the "houses on water?" Perhaps they were "men from the sky." Were they friend or foe? The natives knew that cannibals lived somewhere to the south. Were these unwelcome visitors preparing to butcher them and serve them up in ritual meals?[1]

As the startled natives gazed in amazement, from the sterncastle of the Santa Maria Columbus stared back at the men standing on the beach of his new domain. "At dawn we saw naked people, and I went ashore in the ship's boat, armed," Columbus wrote.[2] Just after sunrise, crewmen from the Nina and the Pinta rowed the Pinzon brothers and the Sovereigns' representatives to the beach.

When the rest of the advance party splashed ashore, Columbus gathered them together: "I unfurled the royal banner...which displayed a large green cross with the letters F and Y at the left and right side of the cross. Over each letter was the appropriate crown of that Sovereign." Tending to religious matters first, the Spaniards knelt in the gritty sand to give thanks to the Almighty for guiding them to the Indies. Then, turning to temporal matters, Columbus ordered the captains and the royal officials "to bear faith and witness that I was taking possession of this island for the King and Queen. I made all the necessary declarations and had these testimonies carefully written down....To this island I gave the name San Salvador (Our Savior), in honor of our Blessed Lord."[3]

Despite their initial fear, some of the curious natives came out of the island's dense foliage to examine these aliens who planted sticks in the sand; sticks with pieces of cloth attached to them that bore mysterious symbols these men seemed to worship. What, the natives wondered, were these things that appeared to be weapons, these long metal poles that glinted in the sun? What was this unintelligible tongue these strangers babbled as they went down on their knees, put their hands together and bowed their heads? Wouldn't their white skin burn under the bright Caribbean sun? Perhaps that's why these foreigners covered their arms and legs with vividly colored material and their chests and heads with metal clothes and put animal skins on their feet. Wouldn't they swelter in the tropical heat? As the natives edged closer, they got their answer; the bodies of these strangers, with their treasured *olor de sanctidad,* stank.

At first, the natives, Taino Indians, approached the Spaniards timidly.[4] Columbus wrote: "In order that we might win good friendship, because I knew that they were a people who could better be freed and converted to our Holy Faith, I gave to some of them red caps and to some glass beads, which they hung on their necks, and many other things of slight value, in which they took much pleasure."

Then, somewhat shocked, Columbus continued: "[All were] as naked as their mothers bore them, and the women also, although I did not see more than one very young girl. They are very well-built people, with handsome bodies and very fine faces, though their appearance is marred somewhat by very broad heads and foreheads....Their eyes are large and very pretty...." [5]

In a letter written later to Isabel and Ferdinand, Columbus commented that: "[The Indians] are so guileless and so generous with all they have, that no one would believe it who has not seen it. They never refuse..., to give up anything they possess; on the contrary, they invite you to share it and show as much love as if their hearts went with it...."[6]

This letter, copies of which circulated widely throughout Europe, began the myth of the "noble savage" who lived in a "state of nature." Later, in the 1700s, philosophers of the Enlightenment developed a political concept that, in a "state of nature," men have the inalienable right to life, liberty and the pursuit of happiness.[7]

Thus, unwittingly, and indirectly, Columbus' view of "virtuous and noble savages" sprouted over the centuries into the most fundamental principle set forth in the American Declaration of Independence.

Expecting to find Negroes because he was on the same latitude with Africa, Columbus said with surprise that "[the Tainos'] skin is the color of Canary Islanders or of sunburned peasants, not at all black as would be expected....These are tall people...and they do not have bellies, but very good figures....Their hair is not kinky, but straight and coarse, like horsehair....Many of the natives paint their faces; others paint their whole bodies; some, only their eyes or nose. Some are painted black, some white, some red; others are of different colors."[8]

"They are friendly and well-dispositioned people who bear no arms, except for small spears, which are certain reeds, without iron, and some of these have a fish tooth at the end, while others are pointed in various ways. They have no iron. I showed one my sword, and, through ignorance, he grabbed it by the blade and cut himself....Many of the men have wounds on their bodies, and when I made signs to them to find out how this happened, they indicated that people from other nearby islands come to San Salvador to capture them, and that they defended themselves....I believe that people from the mainland come here to make them slaves." Assuming that, like the Portuguese did with the Africans, the natives would be valuable as slaves, Columbus added: "They ought to make good and skilled servants of quick intelligence....I think they can easily be made Christians...."

After coming to the ominous conclusion that the natives would make good slaves, Columbus explored San Salvador and traded with the Tainos. In exchange for the Spaniards' red caps, hawk's bells, beads and other trinkets, the Indians bartered parrots, balls of cotton thread and "dry leaves which they hold in great esteem," tobacco. Dry leaves were of no interest to Columbus. "I have been very attentive, and have tried very hard to find out if there is any gold here. I have seen a few natives who wear a little piece of gold hanging from a hole made in the nose. By signs, if I interpret them correctly, I have learned that by going to the south...I can find a *cacique* (chief) who possesses a lot of gold and has great containers of it."

Disappointed to find amiable, but impoverished, barbarians with little gold, Columbus set sail on October 14 to find the mother lode.[9] With six Tainos aboard to serve as guides, for several days he carefully picked his way through the maze of islands, reefs and shoals in the Bahamas chain. He landed on several small islands, which he named Santa Maria de la Concepcion, Fernandina, Isabela and Isla de Arena (Sand Islands).[10] On Fernandina he saw "houses that looked like Moorish tents, very tall, with good chimneys." In the houses, he found beds that were "like nets of cotton," hammocks, which became the standard bedding on ships for centuries thereafter.[11]

Everywhere he went, he asked about gold, and the exact location of China, Japan and India.[12] Although he frequently complained of his inability to communicate with the natives, one Indian word he learned was *nucay*, the Taino word for gold. When he asked where the *nucay* was, the naked Indians pointed south, sometimes mentioning a place that sounded to Columbus like *colba* or *cuba*. On Saturday, October 27, Columbus wrote: "I hauled up the anchor at sunrise and departed for Cuba, which I am told is magnificent, with gold and pearls. I am now certain that Cuba is the Indian name for Japan." The next day, Sunday, he anchored off the northeast coast of Cuba.[13]

The fleet cruised Cuba's north coast for several fruitless days until, in early November, he sent an embassy inland to find the Great Khan of Cuba. Naively, he sent his interpreter, a converted Jew who spoke Hebrew and Arabic, and another crewman, whose only claim was that he once met an African king during a voyage to West Africa. They found nothing of value.[14] No golden roofs. No cities of ivory and alabaster. No khans in gold brocade.

On November 4, Columbus himself went ashore to inspect. After showing the Indians samples of pepper and cinnamon he had brought from Spain, they gave him the good news that, farther south, he would find the precious spices, along with gold and pearls, and "I further understood them to say that there were large ships and merchandise."

Marco Polo and Sir John Mandeville were right. Somewhere to the south lay harbors forested with ship's masts. With this bit of information, and an abundance of wishful thinking, Columbus convinced himself that he had found China, or, at least, was very close. Although the Cuban Indians raised his spirits, Columbus also got the bad news: "I also understand that, a long distance from here, there are men with one eye and others with dogs' snouts who eat men. On taking a man, they behead him and drink his blood and cut off his genitals." Perhaps, he thought, the myths and legends he brushed off so lightly during his arguments with his critics in Spain were true.

During stops at bays along Cuba's coast, Columbus found many strange new vegetables; maize, beans and sweet potatoes, which he described as looking like carrots and tasting like chestnuts. The Indians ate sweet nuts which, Columbus mistakenly thought, were the coconuts Marco Polo described.[15] The natives puffed on rolled tubes of plant leaves "which gave a soothing effect and almost intoxication and relieved them from weariness."[16] To smoke the rolled up leaves, which they called *tobaco*, the Indians inserted one end of the tube into a nostril, inhaled a few times and passed it on to a friend. In addition to discovering cigars, crewmen foraging inland ran across a gooey substance they incorrectly thought was valuable mastic. Columbus confirmed the specious find: "I knew that it was mastic....there is enough in this vicinity to produce fifty tons a year. An Indian told me by signs that mastic is good for the stomachache. I also found a great deal of aloe."

No spices or gold yet, but he remembered Genoa's merchants who made fortunes in the mastic trade with Chios. Even though the gooey substance was a false find, while the Nina and Pinta were beached for recaulking, two sailors came across geese and the first four-footed animals they saw in the islands; dogs that didn't bark, which the Indians raised and roasted for food.

Although Columbus focused most of his attention on riches during his first three weeks in the Caribbean, on November 6 he addressed his other obsession. In the log, he wrote a note directly to the Sovereigns: "I have to say, Most Serene Princes, that if devout religious persons knew the Indian language well, all these people would soon become Christians. Thus I pray to Our Lord that Your Highnesses will appoint persons of great diligence in order to bring the Church such great numbers of people, and that they will convert these peoples...."

As always, his businessman's mind returned to profit, this time to slaves: "Today there came to the side of the ship a canoe with six youths in it, and five came aboard. These I ordered held and am bringing them with me. Afterwards I sent some of my men to a house...and they brought seven head of women....I did this so that the men I had taken would conduct themselves better in Spain than they might have otherwise, because of having women from their own country with them. On many occasions in the past I have taken men from Guinea (West Africa) to Portugal...."

Columbus never mentions whether his sailors consorted with the naked Indian women, but it is hard to imagine that the tough sailors, who had been away from home for months, remained chaste. Since Columubs well knew of Isabel's piety and distaste for adultery, he may have deliberately suppressed any references to cohabitation.

Although the fresh, nude females may have tantalized the

crewmen, what intrigued Columbus and his captains were the places where, the Indians told them, riches abounded; Babeque to the east and Bohio to the southeast.[17] Tempted by the natives' tales of gold and pearls, and tired of Columbus' fumbling around in Cuba, on November 21 Martin Alonso Pinzon broke away from the fleet, headed due east to Babeque. "I could see him for a long time, until he was 12 miles away," Columbus wrote. "Martin Alonso Pinzon sailed away with the caravel Pinta, without my will or command. It was through disloyalty. I think he believes that an Indian I had placed on the Pinta could lead him to much gold, so he departed....He has done and said many other things to me." Scholars speculate as to why Martin Alonso pulled away from the fleet, but Morison has it right: "He'd be damned if he'd follow that Genoese upstart any longer. The proper thing to do...was to go after the gold."

Although the insubordinate Pinzon deserted, Columbus continued tacking along Cuba's north coast, asking the Indians for more details about the land they called Bohio. They told him that a people called the Canibs lived there, and insisted the Canibs ate human flesh, had only one eye and faces of dogs. "I do not believe any of this," Columbus said. "I feel that the Indians (of Bohio) belong to the domain of the Great Khan."

In search of Bohio and the Great Khan, during the night of December 5-6 the Santa Maria and the Nina crossed the sixty-mile wide Windward Passage from Cuba to the Island of Hispaniola, modern-day Haiti and the Dominican Republic. On the northwest tip of Hispaniola, Columbus found a harbor he thought was as grand as the Bay of Cadiz.[18]

After sailing for almost two months through the Bahamas and along Cuba's coast, all he picked up were a few glittering trinkets. Now, in Hispaniola he could almost smell Japan or China. He wasn't sure which, but he was convinced he was nearing the Orient's real riches. As he navigated along Haiti's north coast, his enthusiasm rose. Consumed by Renaissance acquisitiveness and intense medieval religiosity, Columbus peppered the log with references to his twin obsessions—gold and God.

The white haired Genoan was certain that the Indians could be easily tamed by Christianity and made to work the fields of this rich land; harvesting pepper, medicinal rhubarb, nutmeg and mastic. His expansive imagination convinced him that he and his Sovereigns would soon be richer and more powerful that even God himself conceived. Once he cracked the language barrier, armies of priests would bring the submissive natives to the Holy Faith. "I hope in Our Lord that the Indians I am carrying will learn my language and I will learn theirs," he wrote. "Then I can return and talk with these people. I hope to God that I can have some good trade in gold before I return to Spain."

Although gold was number one, Columbus never forgot his God. As was his custom, "I raised a large cross at the entrance to the harbor (the Bay of Mosquitos in Haiti), on a little rise on the western side.[19] This is a sign that Your Highnesses possess this land as your own and especially as an emblem of Jesus Christ, Our Lord, and in honor of Christianity."

All along the Haitian north coast he saw fine, deep harbors that would protect Spain's merchant vessels from storms while they loaded cargoes of goods to take back to the mother country. His notes on the port he named St. Nicholas reflected his exuberance:[20] "As I approached the entrance of this harbor, I marveled at its beauty and excellence. Although I have praised the harbors of Cuba, this one is even superior....[and on the shore is] a grove of trees of a thousand kinds, all loaded with fruit. I think these are spices and nutmegs, but, since they are not ripe, I do not recognize the kind."

Another harbor, he declared "is very beautiful, and all the ships in Christendom could be contained herein....it is 12 fathoms deep inside. [And a] ship can be secured with any kind of line against any winds....Once in, there is no fear from any storm in the world."[21] He noted that the native houses and canoes were bigger, shoring up his belief that he was indeed approaching a more sophisticated, wealthier nation. He sent a scouting party to examine a town of "more than 1,000 houses and [which] must have had a population of over 3,000." Another village had only a few huts, but "some very wide roads, and places where many fires had been built....[and] some of the best land in the world...."

Playing to his audience back home, the Sovereigns and the colonists he hoped to attract, he constantly drew comparisons to Spain. He saw cultivated fields with "crops [that] look like wheat in the month of May in the vicinity of Cordoba...evergreens, oaks and arbutus, the same as in Castile...[and] extensive valleys and planted fields and mountains, all like those in Castile." His sailors caught "mullets and soles and other fish like those in Castile....[and] I heard nightingales sing...like those of Castile." The sly salesman never missed a chance to assure his Spanish patrons that they would feel completely at home in this new land. Just like his mentor Marco Polo, he would dazzle the home folks with tales of a land rich beyond imagination, but so similar to Spain that they wouldn't miss a thing.

Even though, in Columbus' eyes, everything resembled Spain,

he grew restless with the Indians' conflicting stories. Some natives said there was gold farther to the east in Hispaniola or on Babeque. "[Others] indicate that there is continental land behind La Isla Hispaniola, which they call 'Caritaba," he wrote on December 11. "They say that it is of infinite extent, which supports my belief that these lands (Hispaniola) may be harassed by a more astute people, because the inhabitants of all these islands live in great fear of the people of Caniba. So, I repeat what I have said before, that the Caniba are none other than the people of the Great Khan."

As the Nina and Santa Maria navigated along Haiti's north coast, at night Columbus saw the Indian signal fires warning their brothers of the strangers in the area. When the two ships put in to port, the natives abandoned their villages, fearing the worst from these "men from the sky" in their "houses on water." To abate the Indians' fear, during a storm on December 16, Columbus rescued a single Indian floundering in an almost swamped canoe. "I wondered how he was able to keep himself afloat when there was such a high wind. I brought him and his canoe on board and pleased him greatly by giving him glass beads, hawks' bells and brass rings....I let the Indian go ashore in his canoe and trusted that he would spread the word that we Christians are good people."

Columbus' diplomatic policy, kindness rather than brutality, paid off. When the Santa Maria and the Nina anchored close to shore later that day, about five hundred natives came out of the trees to the beach. "The *cacique* and all the others went about as naked as they were born, and the women too, without any shyness, and they are the handsomest men and women I have found up until now," Columbus wrote. "

They are exceedingly white, and, if they wore any clothing and were protected from the sun and the air, they would be almost as white as the people in Spain." Here, Columbus wasn't spouting racial prejudice. Rather, he expressed the Spanish belief that Spanish aristocrats weren't supposed to sweat in the sun, and therefore, that tanned skin was undignified. In the same way that ancient Chinese nobles grew long fingernails to prove they didn't work with their hands, in Spain pure white skin was an outward sign of nobility.

Even though he was initially kind to the Indians, Columbus harbored darker notions regarding the Indians' future. "Your Highnesses should know that this island, and all the others, belong to you as much as Castile does. To rule here, one need only get settled and assert authority over the natives, who will carry out whatever they are ordered to do....The Indians always run away;

they have no arms, nor the warring spirit. They are naked and defenseless, hence ready to be given orders and to be put to work."[22] With this foreboding comment, Columbus expressed the European assumption that the natives were good for little else but slavery.

As the Indians milled about, Columbus spotted one young man, about twenty-one, who the natives treated with deference. From his days at the Portuguese and Spanish courts, Columbus learned to pick out men of importance. To him, this young man appeared to be a *cacique*. Columbus sent the supposed *cacique* a gift, and, late in the afternoon, the young man came aboard the Santa Maria.

Through his Indian interpreters, Columbus told the *cacique* that Ferdinand and Isabel were the greatest Sovereigns in the world. "[But] the King did not believe this. [He] believed that we are from the sky (Heaven) and that the realms of the Sovereigns of Castile are in the sky and not in this world." Columbus provided the *cacique* with a Sunday dinner of Castilian food and rough Spanish wine, but the *cacique*, not liking the European delicacies, politely ate only one mouthful and sipped the wine before giving the rest of the food and drink to his servants.

The *cacique's* tribesmen had a few bits of gold to whet the Spaniards' appetites, but the next day, Monday, December 17, a shore party met a man who had a piece of gold "as big as your hand." Columbus knew he hadn't found the Seven Cities of Gold yet, but, with his lively imagination, he could almost feel handsful of the soft, malleable metal between his fingers. On December 18, an old Indian man told him that another island, some three hundred miles away, had "so much gold that the whole island was gold. On other [islands] they gather it and sift it with sieves and melt it to make bars...." With this news, he left his Indian friends, and headed east along Haiti's north coast.

When a storm blew up on December 22, Columbus anchored the Santa Maria and the Nina about three miles offshore, and sent the ships' boats out with nets to haul in fresh fish. During the day, a large canoe pulled alongside the flagship, and the Indians gave Columbus a belt. Hanging from the belt was a mask of a human face made of hammered gold. Leaning over the gunwales of the Santa Maria, his Taino interpreters struggled to communicate with the Indians in the canoe who spoke a different language. After fighting through the language barrier with hand signals, Columbus understood that the Indians brought him an invitation to visit the realms of a *cacique* who lived nearby.

Even though Columbus thought the greatest *cacique*, the Great Khan, was much farther east, since there was no wind he remained at anchor. While the Santa Maria and the Nina bobbed offshore, on December 23 Columbus sent an embassy of six men ashore to find the minor *cacique's* nearby village. During that Sunday, the Indians paddled more than 120 canoes out to the Spanish ships with fresh water and food, and some one thousand Indians swarmed over the Santa Maria and the Nina to trade with the Spaniards.[23] One Indian told Columbus of a land called "Cibao." Because the word Cibao was so close to Marco Polo's word for Japan, Cipango, Columbus knew, without doubt, that he was closing in on Japan.

There in Cibao, the Indian said, the "*cacique* carries gold banners of hammered gold." While Columbus listened to the stories of golden flags, the Indians and Spaniards bartered until late at night. And, during the middle of the night of December 23-24, the six-man embassy returned with a report of a large village about nine miles away. The six Spainards told Columbus that a *cacique* lived in a village "[that] is larger and with better arranged streets than any others we have passed and discovered up to now....[A]nd all the people of the village, more than 2,000 of them, came together in the plaza, which was very clean. The *cacique* paid great honors to the men, giving them food and drink. Then the *cacique* gave each one some cotton clothes, such as the women wear, and parrots for me, and some gold."[24] Excited by the reports of golden flags and real cities, before sunrise on December 24 Columbus ordered the crews to man the capstans and haul in anchors.

The Santa Maria and the Nina tacked along Haiti's north coast during the day, headed east. With a gentle breeze and a dead calm sea, on the eve of the Savior's birth Columbus made the dangerous decision to continue sailing at night. Because the Indians had swarmed over the ships until late at night on December 23-24, and because of the excitement caused by the glowing report of a city with two thousand people, Columbus had been awake for almost forty-eight hours.

At 11 o'clock on Christmas Eve, "I decided to lie down to sleep because I had not slept for two days and one night. Since it was calm, the sailor who was steering the ship also decided to catch a few winks and left the steering to a young ship's boy, a thing which I have always expressly prohibited throughout the voyage. It made no difference whether there was a wind or calm; the ships were not to be steered by young boys."

In the dim light of a quarter moon, just after the sand clock ran dry to indicate midnight on Christmas Day, 1492, the current edged the nose of the Santa Maria gently onto a coral reef.[25]

Feeling the slight jar of the ship's prow, and hearing the rudder grinding on the sea bottom, the dozing ship's boy at the helm "gave tongue" (shouted). Bolting out of his cabin, the Admiral of the Fleet was the first on deck. Shouts. Curses. Columbus immediately ordered the anchor rope lashed to the capstan and told Juan de la Cosa to lower the ship's boat and take the anchor out to sea. When the anchor was firmly attached to the sea bottom, the Santa Maria's crew would winch the Santa Maria free by turning the capstan, pulling the flagship backward off the coral reef. Instead of following his commander's orders, de la Cosa instructed the oarsmen to row the one and a half miles to the Nina, leaving the Santa Maria stranded. "Treachery," Columbus said.

Vicente Pinzon, the Nina's captain, refused to allow de la Cosa aboard, forcing de la Cosa to turn back to his ship. Vicente Pinzon lowered his own ship's boat, and reached the lurching Santa Maria first. By then, it was too late. The undertow and the waves had edged the Santa Maria's prow further up on the coral reef.

Finally, the flagship pivoted until it lay broadside to the reef. Each surge of the sea bashed the crippled Santa Maria's hull against the coral's teeth. To lighten the Santa Maria and float it off the reef, Columbus ordered his sailors to cut the heavy mainmast and dump it overboard. But the grinding of the wooden hull on the coral's rugged surface opened seams in the helpless Santa Maria's bottom, and water flooded into the hold. Columbus passed the word to abandon ship.

When the sun came up on the Spaniards' first Christmas Day in the New World, it was not greeted by masses, carols and thanksgiving. But by sweating, cursing men straining to save as much of the Santa Maria's stores as possible.

Columbus sent the fleet's marshall, Diego de Harana, the cousin of his lover Beatriz de Harana, and a royal official to ask the local *cacique* for help. "I instructed them to beg the *cacique* to come to this harbor with his boats. The village of the *cacique* is about five miles beyond this reef. My men told me that the *cacique* wept when he heard of the disaster. He sent all his people from the village with many large canoes to help us unload the ship. The *cacique* displayed great haste and diligence, and everything was unloaded in a very brief space of time. He personally assisted in the unloading...and guarded what was taken ashore in order that everything might be completely secure." Amazed by the Indians' honesty, Columbus wrote: "I certify to Your Highnesses that in no part of Castile could things be so secure; not even a shoe lace or a breadcrumb was lost."

Working hand-in-hand, the "men from the sky" and the Indians saved most of the Santa Maria's supplies. With this close working relationship, Columbus felt he now understood the natives' true nature. Grateful for the Indians' help, Columbus wrote: "They are an affectionate people, free from avarice and agreeable to everything. I certify to Your Highnesses that, in all the world, I do not believe there is a better people or a better country. They love their neighbors as themselves....They may go naked, but Your Highnesses may be assured that they have good customs among themselves...."

On December 26, the Spaniards and Indians continued the salvage operation on the Santa Maria. While the men worked, Columbus and the *cacique*, Guacanagari, had lunch aboard the Nina. That evening, Columbus joined the *cacique* ashore for an Indian feast of manioc, shrimp, game and bread. At dinner, the otherwise naked *cacique* wore a shirt and a pair of gloves Columbus gave him. "[H]e was more excited about the gloves than anything else that had been given him," Columbus said. "By his manner of eating, his decent behavior and his exceptional cleanliness, he showed himself to be of good birth."

During dinner, Guacanagari told Columbus of his fear of the vicious Canib people who made periodic raids with bows and arrows and seized his people as slaves.[26] To ingratiate himself with Guacanagri, Columbus "told the *cacique* by signs that the Sovereigns of Castile would order the destruction of the Canibs, commanding the Canibs to be brought before them with their hands tied."

Partly to demonstrate to Guacanagri how the Spaniards would crush the Canibs, and partly to impress the *cacique* with the power of Spanish arms, Columbus ordered a display of firepower. One of the crew's most skilled archers fired a quiver of arrows which "impressed him (the *cacique*) very much." To press the point, Columbus "ordered that a lombard and a musket be fired, and the *cacique* was spellbound when he saw the effect of their force and what they penetrated."

To reinforce the psychological impact of his superior weapons on Guacanagari, a few days later[27] "[I] showed him the force of the lombards and their effect. For this purpose, I ordered one loaded and fired at the side of the Santa Maria, which was aground....The *cacique* saw how far the lombard shot reached and how it passed through the side of the ship. I also had the people from the ship fight a mock battle with their arms, telling the *cacique* not to fear the Canibs if they came. I did all this so that the *cacique* would consider [the Spaniards] as friends and also that he might fear them."

After intimidating the Indians with the lombard blasts, many crewmen, pointing out that they could not all return home on the Nina, pleaded with Columbus to let them stay on the tropical island. Agreeing with the request, Columbus designated thirty-nine men to remain in Hispaniola to form a colony in the New World.[28] He named it La Navidad (Christmas). He placed his mistress' cousin, Diego de Harana, in charge with "all of the powers I have received from the Sovereigns, in full."[29] Using timbers from the Santa Maria, he set the men to work building a tower and fortress surrounded by a large moat. "This is not because I believe this to be necessary with these Indians, for I am sure that I could subjugate the entire island—which I believe is larger than Portugal and with twice the population....These Indians are naked, unarmed and cowardly beyond help. But...since these Indians are so far from Your Highnesses, it is necessary that the [Indians know the Spanish] and what they can do, in order that the Indians may obey Your Highnesses with love and fear."

Having arranged for the establishment of a settlement, in the log entry for December 26 Columbus rationalized the reasons for the wreck of the Santa Maria. "All this was the will of God; the ship's running aground so easily that it could not be felt, with neither wind nor wave; the cowardice of the ship's master (de la Cosa)...the discovery of this country."

Satisfied that his misfortune was the result of the Divine will, Columbus took swipes at the citizens of Palos and his unwieldy flagship: "[T]he Santa Maria was very cumbersome and not suited to the work of discovery. The reason I took that ship in the first place was due to the people of Palos, who did not fulfill to me what they had promised the King and Queen. I should have been given ships suitable for this journey, and the people of Palos did not do that."

Concluding his December 26 report, he wove together his twin goals: "I hope to God that, when I come back here from Castile...I will find a barrel of gold...[and a] gold mine, and spices [so that] the Sovereigns will prepare for and undertake the conquest of the Holy Land. I have already petitioned Your Highnesses to see that all the profits of this, my enterprise, should be spent on the conquest of Jerusalem."

Although he was mad at the citizens of Palos, between December 26, 1492, and January 4, 1493, Columbus and Guacanagari exchanged gifts and held chummy meetings. As they chatted at their banquets, they came to know and trust one another. During that period, an Indian messenger brought word of the sighting of another "house on water," perhaps the missing Pinta, in a harbor about twenty miles away. Columbus sent a Spaniard in an Indian canoe to investigate, but he found nothing. Meanwhile, Columbus prepared for the voyage home. He would prefer, he said, to remain in the New World to collect more gold.

But, fearing that further exploration of the treacherous coasts might result in another shipwreck, he loaded the Nina with water, wood and foodstuffs. "I have only one ship remaining, and it does not appear reasonable to expose myself to [further] danger," he wrote.[30] "If I had the Pinta with me, I would certainly have obtained a cask of gold....I do not want anything to befall me and prevent my returning to Castile and informing the Sovereigns of everything I have found. If I were certain that the Pinta would reach Spain in safety with Martin Alonso Pinzon, I would not hesitate to continue the exploration. But...since Pinzon would be able to lie to the Sovereigns to avoid the punishment he deserves...I feel confident that Our Lord will give me good weather and everything will be remedied."

Despite his anger towards Martin Alonso, Columbus was comfortable that his ambassadorial work with Guacanagri resulted in a diplomatic alliance that would permit the colony of La Navidad to prosper until his return. Before leaving the thirty-nine Spanish colonists, he gathered them in a circle and charged them to pray to God, to obey Diego de Harana's orders and to not rape the Indian women or attack the men. Then, "I promised them that I would petition the Sovereigns to grant them special favors, which they truly merit...."[31]

At sunrise on January 4, 1493, Columbus weighed anchor and planned his course to pick up the trade winds that he knew blew from the west to the east at the latitude of the Azores Islands. Two days later, shortly after noon, he sent a lookout scrambling up the Nina's mainmast to watch for shoals and sandbars. From the crow's nest high above the Nina's deck, the lookout saw the billowing sails of the Pinta. As the errant Pinta drew alongside the Nina, Columbus shouted orders to Martin Alonso Pinzon to return with him to a safe harbor, about thirty miles away.

When the two ships anchored off Hispaniola's north coast, Martin Alonso Pinzon came aboard the Nina to apologize. Lamely, Pinzon mumbled out the feeble excuse that he became separated against his will. Columbus would have none of it: "He gave many reasons for his departure, but they are all false," Columbus snapped. Furious at his mutinous second in command, in the log, but not directly to Pinzon, Columbus hurled vitriolic thunderbolts: "Pinzon acted with greed and arrogance that night when he sailed off and left me, and I do not know why he has been so disloyal and untrustworthy."

Later, Columbus discovered that Martin Alonso forced his crewmen to give him half the gold they found, and required them to take an oath to lie about Pinzon's activities. In writing, but not orally, Columbus exploded: "[Martin Alonso's] wickedness is so well known that he cannot hide what happened. Martin Alonso Pinzon and Vicente Yanez Pinzon and their followers are greedy and untrustworthy. They do not respect the honor I have shown them, and they have not, and do not, obey my commands. Rather, they have done and said many unjust things against me. And Martin Alonso left me from 22 November to 6 January, without cause or reason, but from disobedience."

Even though he was enraged, Columbus looked at his cards. Martin Alonso's brother Vicente captained the Nina. During the threatened mutinies on the trip over, many of the crewmen from the Palos area had sided with the Pinzons. Martin Alonso, Columbus knew, could count on the sailors' loyalty and he could not.

Bitter, but ever practical, Columbus wrote: "I am going to ignore these actions in order to prevent Satan from hindering this voyage, as he has done up to now. All this (disobedience) I have endured in silence, in order to finish my voyage successfully. On account of this, in order to escape such bad company, which I have to ignore, I have decided to return....Now is not the time to think about punishment....Besides, I want to return as soon as possible to bring the news and to rid myself of the bad companions I have. [When I return home] I will not suffer from the evil actions of persons devoid of virtue, who, with little regard, presume to follow their own wills in opposition to those who did them honor."[32]

Despite the bad blood between the grizzled old mariner and the forty-one-year-old Admiral, they established a truce based solely on necessity. Knowing they would have a better chance of making it back to Spain by sailing together, each decided to cooperate during the voyage home. The rivals instructed their helmsmen to sail east along Hispaniola's north coast.

On January 13 the Nina and the Pinta reached the tip of what is now the Dominican Republic. Before heading into the open sea, they put into port to take on supplies. While the two caravels stood offshore, an Indian canoed out to the Nina to speak with the Admiral. From the first, Columbus didn't like the looks of the Indian: "[H]e is much uglier in the face than any of the other Indians I have seen; it was all smeared with charcoal....He wears his hair very long, drawn back and tied in a pony tail, then gathered in a net of parrot feathers. He was naked like all the others. I assume he is one of the Canibs who eat men...."

More importantly, from the Nina's quarterdeck Columbus saw that these Indians had bows and arrows, the first natives he had seen with these weapons. In addition to having four-foot long arrows with tips of fish teeth, some smeared with poison, these warriors carried heavy wooden clubs to bludgeon their enemies. Despite these ominous signs, Columbus sent a reconnaissance party ashore to trade with this new, fiercer tribe. When the Spaniards reached the beach, the Indians prepared for an attack.

In the first of many battles between Europeans and native Americans, "They (the Indians) ran to get their bows and arrows where they had laid them, and returned with ropes in their hands to tie up the men. The sailors were ready, since I always advised my men to be on guard. When the Indians approached, the sailors attacked. They gave one Indian a great cut on the buttocks and wounded another in the chest with an arrow. When the Indians saw that they could gain little, although there were only seven Spaniards and more than 50 of them, they took flight....In one way it troubled me and in another it did not, i.e., in the sense that now they might be afraid of us."

The day after the first European-Indian clash, and the opening of the first wound in many centuries of bloodshed, Columbus wrote a rambling, bitter discourse attacking the people of Palos and his critics in Spain:[33] "The caravels are leaking badly at the keel, largely because they were badly caulked in Palos....His Divine Majesty well knows how much controversy I had before starting from Castile, and no one else was supportive of me except God...and, after God, Your Highnesses supported me, but everyone else opposed me without any reason whatsoever. And they are the reason why the Royal Crown of Your Highnesses does not have 100,000,000 more in revenue than it has....But Almighty God will take care of everything." In this parting shot before leaving for Spain, Columbus verbally thumbed his nose at those who doubted his genius or courage, those who said he was a mad dreamer and those who questioned his great enterprise. If the gesture had existed at the time, one can imagine Columbus standing on the sterncastle of the Nina popping the eternal Italian sign for "up yours."

"With the greatest geographical secret of all time locked in his breast," Morison says, the two-ship fleet left Hispaniola on January 16, 1493, loaded with captive Indians, a few gold ornaments, parrots and other trinkets from the Indies. The two caravels cruised generally north and east to pick up the trade winds blowing to the east.

They crossed through the weed beds of the Sargasso Sea, and, on January 23, Columbus noted in the log that the Pinta sailed badly because of unsound main and mizzen masts. Sarcastically, he wrote: "If her captain, Martin Alonso Pinzon, had taken as much trouble to provide himself with a good mast in the Indies...as he did to separate himself from me with the intention of filling his ship with gold, he would have been better off."

After almost three weeks of following a northeasterly course, at the latitude of Bermuda Columbus found winds blowing predominantly to the west. By chance, he discovered the trade winds that became the established Atlantic sea lanes for centuries to come, until the age of steam. Satisfied that he was on the same latitude as Cape St. Vincent in Portugal, the Admiral pointed his fleet's prows due east on February 5, 1493. Strong winds scudded the two caravels through the sea, sometimes at speeds of ten knots per hour. Making good headway, the pilots and captains huddled from time to time to check their position and calculate how much farther they had to go until they reached Europe. The weather was generally good, until, on February 12, the two ships ran into a vicious arctic storm pushing down to collide with the warm tropic air.

For the next four days huge pyramid-shaped waves battered the Nina and Pinta. "I experienced great difficulty with the wind, high waves and a stormy sea. There has been lightning three times toward the NNE, which is a sure sign that a great storm is coming.... I went with bare masts most of the night.... The wind... increased and the sea became terrible, with the waves crossing each other and pounding the ships.... [A]nd the waves were frightful, coming in opposite directions. They crossed each other and trapped the ships, which could not go forward nor get out from between them, and they broke over us.... Then the caravel Pinta, on which was Martin Alonso, began to run also and eventually disappeared from sight...."

Separated from the Pinta, pitching and rolling during most of the days and nights, the tiny caravels creaked and groaned through freezing showers and squalls. Although his legs were cramped from exposure to the cold and water, and he became exhausted from lack of sleep, Columbus took every precaution. He hauled in sails, letting the Nina run before the wind, and filled empty wine and water barrels with sea water for additional ballast to stabilize his ship.

Because the hurricane refused to abate, he called on the ultimate resort—God. On February 14, as the icy foam and spray crashed over the decks, Columbus assembled the drenched crewmen three times to draw lots from a red sailor's cap to see which man would make pilgrimages of thanks if the Almighty would deliver them from their misery. Columbus won two of the lotteries, obligating himself to carry a five pound candle to a shrine to the Virgin Mary in Extremadura and to the church of Santa Clara in Moguer, near Palos. [34]

Terrified, Columbus wrote: "I...feel great anxiety, because of the two sons I have in Cordoba at school, if I leave them orphaned of father and mother in a foreign land. And I am concerned because the Sovereigns do not know the service I have rendered on this voyage and the very important news I am carrying to them, which would move them to help my sons."[35] Although confident that God would see him through, but fearful that his epic voyage would sink with him in silence, Columbus resorted to the ancient maritime act of desperation. "I have written on a parchment everything I can concerning what I have found....I sealed the parchment in a waxed cloth, tied it very securely, took a large wooden barrel, and placed the parchment in the barrel...and [threw] it into the sea."[36]

Sure that God heard his prayers, Columbus noted in the log that, during the night of February 14-15, the sky began to clear. At sunrise on February 15, the Nina's lookouts spotted land. Some crewmen thought it was the Madeira Islands, and others the Rock of Sintra near Lisbon or the shores of Castile. But, after checking his navigation charts, Columbus correctly said that it was the Portuguese Azores Islands.

Because of the heavy seas stirred up by the hurricane's aftermath, it took the Nina three days to reach the Azorian island of Santa Maria. "The inhabitants...said that they had never seen such a storm as that which prevailed for the past 15 days, and they wondered how we had escaped....My navigation has been very accurate, and I have steered well, for which many thanks should be given to Our Lord."

Even though the island's inhabitants initially received him cordially, Santa Maria's governor accused Columbus of illegally trafficking in Portugal's Africa trade. After squabbling with the Portuguese governor for several days, the Admiral finally convinced the governor to permit him to repair the battered Nina and reprovision her for the eight-hundred-mile trip to Europe. With a stout wind blowing to the east, the Nina left the Azores on February 23. The favorable winds powered the little ship and its crewmen and captive Indians towards home, until, on March 3, they ran into a "squall [which] split all the sails and I found myself in great danger, but God willed that I be delivered from it....[W]e experienced a terrible storm and thought we would be lost because the waves came from two directions, and the wind appeared to lift the ships in the air...."

As the hurricane force winds howled, the crew again drew lots to see who would make a pilgrimage of thanksgiving, and vowed to fast on bread and water on the first Saturday after their safe return. Later that evening, "We saw indications of being near land...." By Columbus' reckoning, he was close to the craggy Portuguese coast. Having unpacked his last sail from the forecastle, and with mountainous waves crashing on the Nina's planks, even though they were so close to land, they were still in extreme danger. Rather than heading for shore in the dark, Columbus ordered the Nina to beat back and forth during the night, well away from the rocky Portuguese coast he knew so well.

"When the sun came up [on March 4], I recognized the land, which was the Rock of Sintra, near the river at Lisbon....At 9 o'clock in the morning I stopped at Rastelo, inside the [Tagus] river at Lisbon, where I learned from the seafaring people that there never has been a winter with so many storms; 25 ships had been lost in Flanders, and there were other [ships] here that had not been able to depart for four months."

Just after he docked at the village of Rastelo in the mouth of the Tagus River, Columbus wrote to King John of Portugal asking permission to sail further upriver to Lisbon. He wrote the letter, Columbus said, because he was afraid that the villagers at Rastelo might think the Nina's hold was filled with gold and "might undertake some crime against me." Also, he wanted to make it clear to King John that he did not violate the Portuguese-Spanish treaty by going to Portugal's colonies in Africa and that he went only to new lands, the Indies.

On that same day, March 4, 1493, Columbus dispatched a letter overland to Ferdinand and Isabel. He was worried, he said, that Martin Alonso Pinzon, who disappeared in the hurricane three weeks before, might have beaten him back home and stolen all his glory. He wanted the Sovereigns to know that his landing in Portugal was no cause for suspicion and that he had not deserted to King John.

The next morning, March 5, the two greatest discoverers in the world at that time met.[37] Also tied up at Rastelo was the pride of King John's navy, a Portuguese man-o-war equipped with cannons that could blast the sixty-seven-foot long Nina out of the water. Its master, Bartholomew Diaz, who had rounded the Cape of Good Hope only four years before, approached the Nina in a small, armed boat.

When Diaz' boat drew alongside the Nina, the great Portuguese explorer ordered Columbus to come aboard the boat. Indignant at Diaz' effrontery, Columbus replied: "I...am the Admiral of the Sovereigns of Castile, and...[I will not] leave my ship unless compelled to do so by force of arms....[And that] it was the custom of the Admirals of the Sovereigns of Castile to die rather than surrender....[Diaz] moderated his demands...but requested to see the letters from the Sovereigns of Castile....I was happy to show them to him."[38]

After reading Columbus' letters of authorization from the Spanish monarches, Diaz backed off. Not wanting to create an international incident, later that day the Portuguese sent a welcoming party, complete with drummers, trumpeters and pipers, who "with great ceremony...offered to do everything that I ordered them to do."

As word of the discovery spread, for the next two days people crowded aboard the Nina to gawk at the cargo of Indians, parrots and other exotica Columbus brought from the Indies. On Friday, March 8, the Admiral received an invitation from King John to visit him at Valle do Paraiso, several miles outside of Lisbon where the King had fled to escape a plague in the capital.

Columbus and his small entourage, including a few of his ten captive Indians, wove through the narrow Lisbon streets he knew so well. Surely he visited the convent where he first met his wife Felipa in 1479 and prayed at her tomb for Almighty God to bless her immortal soul. The Admiral may have paid other visits; to the Genoese quarter to see old friends and to the map store where he worked with his brother Bartholomew on their plans for the great enterprise so many years before. Wandering along the familiar streets of Lisbon, perhaps Columbus mused contentedly on those times when, as a bridegroom, he struggled to make a name, and a fortune, for himself.

Although Columbus was comfortable in his old home city, the Indians, after experiencing two horrible storms at sea and being pawed and poked at by the curious Portuguese for two days, must have been terrified. The Admiral makes no mention of the Indians' state of mind, but the exposure to cold weather for the first time in their lives, the pungent stink of Lisbon's streets, the cries of plague victims and the sight of the largest beasts they had ever seen, horses and mules, must have convinced the Indians that they were indeed in the home of the "men from the skies."

After a heavy downpour, Columbus and his party slogged over muddy roads to Valle do Paraiso. There, the weaver's son sat down with a king. "[King John] himself received me with great honor and showed me much respect, asking me to sit down, and talked very openly with me." After a few pleasantries, the Portuguese monarch got to the point. He accused Columbus of poaching on Portugal's African territories. Even if the Admiral hadn't poached, King John said, under his treaty with Isabel and Ferdinand the new discoveries belonged to Portugal.[39]

Although King John's blunt statements increased the tension, Columbus diplomatically replied that he had not seen the treaty, and assured the Portuguese King that his instructions from the Spanish Sovereigns clearly prohibited him from going to Portugal's African colonies. Then Columbus produced the peculiar artifacts from the Indies and the bronze-skinned, straight-haired Indians. When King John saw that Columbus' captives were not like the black, kinky-haired Negroes of Africa, he seemed to accept the Admiral's explanation. Although Columbus knew that King John had murdered his own brother-in-law, and that the King's violent temper made him dangerous, he also knew that King John probably had no interest in risking a war with the newly unified Spain. Since the War of Granada no longer diverted Isabel and Ferdinand's attention, Columbus calculated that there was little chance King John would do him harm.

Columbus was right. After the Admiral made his case, the atmosphere's electricity abated, and the King treated him "graciously," Columbus said. But, recalling King John's rejection of his great enterprise, the proud Admiral of the Ocean Sea apparently couldn't resist the temptation to say "I told you so." Although the wily King John continued to respond to Columbus "graciously," a Portuguese court historian wrote that the King was inwardly furious at the Admiral's arrogance and his exaggerated tales of enormous gold and riches.[40] And, the historian says, some of King John's counselors advised him to murder Columbus and blame it on the boastful Admiral's "discourteous shortcomings."

Even though the Portuguese King was capable of murder, he brushed aside his advisors' urgings. After mass on Sunday, March 10, King John again received Columbus. Still suspicious that the Admiral had somehow tricked him, the doubting King put the Indians to the test.

King John dumped a bowl of beans on a table and asked the Indians to make a map of the lands Columbus discovered. When the Indians arranged the beans to form a rough map of Cuba, Hispaniola and other islands, King John finally admitted that he was beaten. "[T]he King," John's court historian recorded, "clearly understanding the extent of the lands discovered...could no longer conceal his great chagrin...over the loss of things so valuable, which, by his own fault, he let slip from his hands; and, in a wave of passion, smote his breast and cried in a loud voice, 'O man of little comprehension! Why did I let slip an enterprise of so great an importance.'—these or similar words."

After breakfast on March 11, 1493, Columbus and his party left Valle do Paraiso and arrived in Lisbon the next day. During the Admiral's absence, by King John's order the Portuguese made the Nina seaworthy and provisioned it for the short trip to Spain. With a strong wind from the north northwest behind her, the Nina left Lisbon at eight in the morning on March 13. The caravel rounded Cape St. Vincent, where her Admiral swam ashore seventeen years before, and arrived off the coast from Palos before dawn two days later.

Columbus waited for the noon tide to sweep the Nina up the Saltes River, past the whitewashed walls of La Rabida to Palos. His 224-day voyage was complete. With the greatest irony, that same noon tide powered Martin Alonso Pinzon and the Pinta to Palos' docks a few hours later.

After the two caravels had separated on that stormy night in mid-February, Martin Alonso Pinzon had navigated to a small Spanish port in Galicia, just north of the Portuguese border.[41] Morison describes the scene when Pinzon sailed into port and saw that the Admiral beat him home: "That finished poor old Martin Alonso. Already a sick man from the hardships and exposure of the voyage...he could bear no more. Without waiting for the Pinta's sails to be furled, without reporting to the flagship, or so much as hailing [his brother] Vicente Yanez, Martin Alonso Pinzon had himself rowed ashore, went to his country house near Palos, crawled into bed, and died."[42]

With his rival dead, in the log's last entry on March 15, Columbus wrote of his seven and one-half-month odyssey: "[God] does all good things...and nothing can be imagined or planned without His consent. This voyage has miraculously proven this to be so...by the remarkable miracles which have occurred during this voyage...." Taking one last swipe at his critics, Columbus wrote that he achieved his mission despite the "opposition and against the advice of so many of the principal persons of your [the Sovereigns] household, who were all against me and treated this undertaking as folly." He concluded the log simply: "[T]he writing is now completed."

Almost immediately, Columbus dispatched letters to his sons in Cordoba and to Isabel and Ferdinand, who were holding court in Barcelona.[43] Columbus spent two weeks at his spiritual home, La Rabida, with his old friend and supporter, Father Juan Perez.

After a series of parties and banquets in and around Palos, and many trips to church to fulfill the vows made aboard ship, Columbus and his Indian captives, dressed in loincloths and carrying their short spears, traveled to Seville. They arrived on Palm Sunday and spent Holy Week in Seville. Just after Easter he received a letter addressed to:

> "Don Cristobal Colon, Our Admiral of the Ocean Sea, Viceroy and Governor of the islands that he has discovered in the Indies. We have seen your letters and we have taken much pleasure in learning whereof you write, and that God gave so good a result to your labors....It will please God that...you should receive from us many favors....And we desire that you come here forthwith...so that you may be quickly provided with everything you need...and because, as you can see, the summer has begun, and you must not delay in going back there [the Indies], see if something can be prepared in Seville or in other districts for your returning to the land which you have discovered....From Barcelona on the 30th day of March, 1493. I the King. I the Queen."

In Andalusia's fair spring weather, Columbus set off for Barcelona with a few attendants, six Indians, parrots and gold. He paused a few days in Cordoba for a reunion with his two sons and his mistress, Beatriz de Harana. When the Admiral told Beatriz that he left her cousin, Diego de Harana, in charge of the new colony at La Navidad she was pleased at the confidence her lover showed in her family. After a round of banquets in Cordoba, and accolades proclaiming him a "great man," Columbus and his entourage traveled in an almost regal procession through cheering Spaniards lining the roads to see him and his exotic Indians.

Las Casas described the triumph: "The news had begun to spread all over Castile that new lands had been discovered.... [And] the man who had discovered them was coming by such-and-such a road, and he was bringing with him men from [the Indies] ....Everywhere the towns and villages were emptied and the roads were crowded so that people could see him and welcome him."[44]

Ebullient after receiving the acclaim of thousands of Spaniards who gathered to applaud their new hero, Columbus and his party arrived in Barcelona. On April 20, 1493, he presented himself to Isabel and Ferdinand at the palace. There, within the gray stone walls of the royal residence, the Sovereigns paid him the highest possible honor by rising from their thrones to greet him. When he knelt before them, the royal couple paid Columbus further tribute by bidding him to stand and take a seat beside them and Prince John. Don Christopher Columbus, who medieval custom destined for a life hunched over a weaver's loom, sat down beside the King and Queen of Spain.

Then, Isabel and Ferdinand bestowed a coat of arms on their Admiral of the Ocean Sea; an escutcheon quartered with Castile's castle, Leon's lion, golden islands dotting the sea and five anchors. After the welcoming ceremonies, royal pages carried the gold, parrots and other strange artifacts from the Indies around the audience chamber for the assembly of noblemen and bishops to examine and admire.

In the palace chapel, clergymen lined up the mystified Indians before a statue of Christ bleeding on the cross, and performed the ritual of baptism. With Isabel, Ferdinand and Prince John acting as godparents to the new converts, the ornately robed churchmen sprinkled the Indians with holy water and bestowed proper Christian names on them. They named one Diego Columbus, after the man who captured him. With the formalities and sacraments completed, the Sovereigns asked questions for more than an hour. As Columbus and Isabel's blue eyes met, the magnetism, the mystical attraction between the Queen and her Admiral, worked its charm. This tall Genoan had proved her instinct and her judgment correct.

Chatting in the throne room in Barcelona, neither Isabel, Ferdinand nor Columbus could possibly understand the magnitude of the voyage's importance. To the Sovereigns and their Admiral, the discovery signified gold, power and service to God. Over the years, to Europeans the voyage opened vistas of a brave new world, inspiring a spirit of discovery, adventure, avarice and plunder. In time, it would destroy centuries of parochial, narrow thinking, and would serve as a primary triggering event that forced Europe out of the Middle Ages into the expansive Renaissance.

19

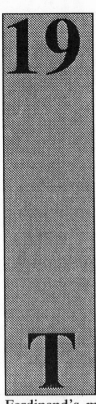

THE CHURCH, THE INQUISITION

The Roman Catholic Church intruded into every facet of medieval Spain; its thinking, its economy, its politics. Cardinal Mendoza, *El Tercer Rey* (The Third King), acted as Isabel and Ferdinand's most trusted advisor until he died in 1495, and Cardinal Cisneros played the same role during the latter part of the Sovereigns' reign.[1] In addition to the power wielded publicly by Cardinals Mendoza and Cisneros, in the privacy of the confessional the Queen's confessors instructed her not only of the Lord's grace, but also whispered through the confessional screen their advice on the handling of affairs of state.

Christianity, transplanted to the Iberian Peninsula by the Romans some fifteen hundred years before, was Spain's oldest institution, surviving through centuries of rebellions by its military entrepreneurs, wars with the Moors and fierce persecutions by the Romans. In the beginning, Christianity was only an inconsequential semitic cult whose faithful minority suffered physical torture in orgies of martyrdom. By the late 1400s, Castilians treated these martyrs as national heros, and the Holy Church became, next to the nobles, the richest, most powerful force in Castilian society.

During Isabel and Ferdinand's reign, Castile and Aragon's seven archbishops and thirty-three bishops supported their extravagances with an annual income of 178 million maravedis.[2] The higher clergymen's revenues varied, but the Primate of Spain, the Archbishop of Toledo, lived in the grand manner on thirty million maravedis. The multitude of nunneries and monasteries of the Franciscans, Dominicans and Benedictines raked in another one and a half million maravedis per year. Together, the ecclesiastical revenues accounted for abut one-third of the national income.[3]

Because the jobs in the higher clergy were so lucrative, nobles conspired to place their second sons in the pulpit. Even Ferdinand couldn't resist the temptation, nominating his nine-year-old illegitimate son Alfonso to the Bishopric of Zaragoza.[4] By the Sovereigns' time, the intertwining of aristocrats and clergymen was so ingrained in Castilian society that the prelates actively participated in almost all phases of political life, cooperating with the government at all levels.

With this influence, and the enormous wealth amassed over the centuries, the Church's power seeped into all of Castile's institutions. Much of the wealth came from donations by devout kings and nobles who instructed their lawyers to write clauses in their wills passing title to the Church of lands, vassals and villages upon their deaths. To further build up their incomes, the clergymen rented their lands to serfs who sweated in the fields to pay their clerical masters. Although excommunication was supposed to be used only as penalty for crimes against God, the priests abused the punishment by applying it to secular nonpayment of rent, excommunicating some recalcitrant peasants as many as ten or twenty times during their lives.

Ordinary citizens contributed another large chunk of income to the Church's coffers through tithes, which, in effect were a religious tax. In medieval Spain, tithes were mandatory, not voluntary as they are today. Again abusing their powers, the clergymen threatened excommunication if a parishioner did not pay his tithe on time. To further enhance their income, the priests peddled indulgences to their flocks which supposedly pardoned a man or woman's violations of God's laws and paved their way into heaven. While the ignorant poor bought the indulgences to relieve them of their sins, some bishops openly took bribes in return for appointments to lucrative posts in the Church hierarchy.

In addition to the Church's directly owned wealth, its close alliance with the quasi-religious military orders and the aristocrats added to its power and influence. Just like their cousins in the aristocracy, custom totally exempted the priests from the crown's taxes. Even though clergymen and nobles were subject to some city taxes, the churchmen often used the sanctity of their holy offices as an excuse to escape the city tax collector's bite, skillfully evading taxes that even the nobles had to pay. Not only did the churchmen enjoy the benefits of a tax haven, the priests were subject only to the jurisdiction of the Church's courts. If a cleric committed a crime, he could easily escape the justice of the secular courts by appealing his case to the Church courts where he could expect a more favorable ruling.[5] "Most men say that no one dares to commit a crime unless he is [a priest]," one writer noted.[6]

Escaping the harsh justice of the secular courts and the greedy clutches of the tax farmers was so attractive that many laymen finagled to obtain a semi-phony clerical status. Some laymen paid their priests to turn them into instant clerics, nominally dedicating themselves to the service of Christ in ordination ceremonies, but continuing to live a secular life. For the more flagrant, their only sign of alliance with the Church was to have the town barber cut their hair in the clerical tonsure, bald on top, and to don clerical robes on appropriate occasions.

With its privileges, and its hand on the levers of power, the Church dominated the intellectual life of Castile. Religious literature with titles such as *The Imitation of Christ, Exercises in the Spiritual Life* and *Life of Christ,* a mystical novel of the Passion, filled the bookstores. Churches presented religious drama focusing on Christ's suffering and the Nativity. Although most of the theatrical productions portrayed the Church as the people's shield against Satan, in some cases the plays drew the ire of the more pious clerics by presenting plays containing nudity and obscenity.

While books and plays spread Christ's message, the Church exerted its greatest influence over Castile's thinking through its dominance of the universities. The prelates established faculties of theology at Valladolid, Barcelona, Lerida, Perpignan and, the greatest of all, at Salamanca. Salamanca, founded in 1401, produced an old-boy network which supplied Castile with most of the leading archbishops, bishops and other higher clergy. Because the clergymen constituted much of Castile's educated class, they infiltrated the government, holding important posts at court and serving as political advisers to the kings.

Although many of Castile's educated men came from the clergy, the majority of the priests couldn't read or write the Church's mother tongue, Latin, and others neglected their preaching. Finding a good preacher "is rarer among the...prelates than finding a white crow," Peter Martyr said. Regarding their ignorance, a medieval Spaniard wrote that "many priests who have charge of souls are not only ignorant...but...some do not know or understand the Scriptures."[7]

Reaching farther down into the society, in the cities and towns the Church actively supported laymen in the formation of fraternities to help build churches and hospitals for the poor and to give aid to orphans.[8] In addition to these brotherhoods of laymen, cults dedicated to particular saints or the Virgin Mary drew enthusiastic support. All Castilians were devoted to their militant Christian hero, Santiago Matamoros. Almost anyone who had sufficient means made the pilgrimage to the sainted warrior's tomb in Santiago de Compostela or to other churches which supposedly possessed holy relics that produced miracles. The most fervent believers, the flagellants, whipped away their sins until blood splattered the floors of churches and monasteries.[9] In one Benedictine monastery at Valladolid, the devout monks took turns whipping themselves every day during Advent and Lent.

Although these acts of blind faith were common, much of the Castilian Catholic Church showed little semblance of holiness. Some clergymen performed their duties out of true piety, serving as the people's direct interface with God. But, generally, the Church was corrupt. The corruption began at the top of the hierarchic chain, in Rome, where Pope Sixtus IV presided over the Vatican in regal pomp.[10]

Beneath Sixtus' bejeweled robes of office dwelt a hard, imperious man of lascivious tastes. His minions slipped his whores through the back corridors of the Vatican to parties where "none of the allurements of love was lacking...[and] lust was unrestrained." At one of these orgies, Sixtus' cooks outdid themselves by serving a whole roasted bear, stags reconstructed in their skins and peacocks in their feathers. When Sixtus wasn't dallying with prostitutes, he attended to business by packing the College of Cardinals with his favorites and relatives. The Pope appointed two of his nephews, who, though only in their twenties, already had notorious reputations as profligates. "[Sixtus] raised nepotism to a new level," Barbara Tuchman says. Although he devoted portions of the Church's vast revenues to restoring the Vatican Library and building the Sistine Chapel, Sixtus diverted substantial amounts of God's money to his own pockets and to those of his relatives.

In Spain, the church was equally dissolute. Although Cardinal Mendoza served as an extraordinary counselor to Isabel and Ferdinand, he also loved his extravagant lifestyle and whores. His three bastard sons each founded powerful aristocratic families under their father's loving tutelage. "Your costly dishes and lavish gifts seem a great virtue to worldly men, but in heaven they are vices," a contemporary satirist wrote.[11]

Emulating Cardinal Mendoza, many churchmen led licentious lives in the shadows of the sanctuary. The priests and monks frequently disregarded the Church's official rules requiring them to learn Latin, preach sermons regularly and ban carnivals in the churches. Disregard of their vow of celibacy was almost universal. Many members of the clergy proudly recognized their bastard sons and built castles for their mistresses. So rampant was the practice of the tonsured prelates keeping mistresses that, under Castilian law, an illegitimate son of a priest or abbot could inherit from his father if he died without a will.

With widespread abuses, attempts at reform in Seville in 1478 prohibited priests from "being ruffians and from having public women to sell at a profit (whoremasters)." Having mistresses was so common that few complained of the illicit affairs, but directed their anger at the ostentatious lifestyles in which the priests and monks' kept their women. Writing about a village priest near Valencia, a devout member of the clergy said: "His parishioners found him a wife....There is not one in the village as well dressed and adorned as she."[12] Since large segments of the clergy lived in open violation of their vows of celibacy, their sins went largely unpunished.

When the Castilian Parliament issued decrees prohibiting the flagrant deviances from God's prescriptions, the churchmen hid behind ancient tradition which held that they could be prosecuted only in the Church's courts. Some of the higher clergy tried to enforce disciplinary measures to tone down the scandals and debauchery in the cathedrals and monasteries. But many bishops ignored the vices and others never visited their dioceses, preferring the more sumptuous life at court where they could curry royal favor.

While absenteeism was not uncommon, necessity forced some bishops to remain in their dioceses to protect their turf from rapacious noblemen. If needed, the Archbishop of Santiago could raise a private army of three hundred knights on horseback and three thousand foot soldiers to fend off attempts by aristocrats to seize any portion of his wealth. In 1477, the Bishop of Segovia sent his troops into the streets and incited mobs to attack the royal governor of Segovia, requiring Isabel to ride to the city to put down the violence.

Although many clerics followed the Church's dogma to the letter, some prelates adopted with equal fervor the doctrines of the military entrepreneurs, strapping on burnished suits of armor to fight for or against the kings. In the War of Succession, Cardinal Mendoza eagerly entered the temporal life by fighting at Isabel and Ferdinand's side, while the Archbishop of Toledo and his army of one thousand men joined La Beltraneja's rebels.[13] Later, Cardinal Mendoza and his private army played a major role in the War of Granada. When Cardinal Cisneros, who served as Isabel's personal confessor beginning in 1492, became the Archbishop of Toledo after Mendoza died in 1495, he led two armies in holy crusades against the Moors in North Africa. "The smell of gunpowder is sweeter than the perfumes of Arabia," Cardinal Cisneros said. Inspired by the myth of their warrior-saint, Santiago Matamoros, these bellicose clergymen spent almost as much time studying new military techniques as they did reading the Scriptures.

The ordinary clergy, sated with their tax-free wealth, were often undisciplined, lax in their observance of rituals, ignorant and illiterate. The monks in some monasteries took part in violence and banditry along with the nobles. The friars, one reformer wrote, "sin gravely in sumptuous buildings. They study not for love of God but so as to rise in the world. They are absorbed in secular affairs....They go through the streets with their eyes raised to look at the ladies....They can only talk of money and women."[14]

Early in their reign, Isabel and Ferdinand saw the corruption and confusion in the Church and summoned the prelates to Seville for a synod to adopt reforms.[15] Merely purifying these brown and black robed warriors against Lucifer was not the only purpose of the synod. As with every Spanish institution, Isabel and Ferdinand wanted control. During Seville's hot days of July, 1478, the churchmen at the synod agreed to cooperate with the Sovereigns in their drive to achieve national unity, to resist Papal influence and to make certain reforms, including requiring bishops to reside in their dioceses and giving the royal courts jurisdiction over crimes committed on lands owned by the Church. Because many Church fortresses faced the Muslim frontier, the Sovereigns argued that the castles were part of the national defense and pushed through a measure which allowed them to place royal officials in charge of Church fortresses.

In 1482, Isabel and Ferdinand launched their first attack on the Pope's right to name higher clergy in Castile. When Sixtus IV, with his penchant for nepotism, attempted to appoint his nephew to the Bishopric of Cuenca, the Sovereigns protested. Sixtus answered that "he was head of the Church, and, as such, possessed unlimited power [to make appointments] and that he was not bound to consult...any potentate on earth."[16] His Holiness touched the Sovereigns' rawest nerve; a direct assault on their power in Spain. Isabel and Ferdinand immediately counterattacked with orders to all their subjects to vacate the Papal dominions at Cuenca, and called for a general council to investigate ecclesiastical corruption in the nation. Then they called in their most trusted advisor, Cardinal Mendoza, to iron out the problem. Mendoza, an able diplomat, successfully negotiated an agreement with the Pope which permitted Isabel to appoint her candidate to the Bishopric of Cuenca. Even though the Sovereigns disputed many issues with the Church, they did agree on one fundamental point; that society should be organized around a framework of hierarchy.

Over the years Isabel and Ferdinand gradually asserted their control over the Castilian Church. During the early days of their reign, the Sovereigns' hold on the throne was still too shakey for them to press for their major goal, gaining absolute mastery over the Spanish Church, including the right to appoint all archbishops, bishops and other important Church officials.

Up until their reign, with few exceptions, the Roman Pope made these appointments, sometimes naming foreigners to govern the Church's domains in Spain.[17] But, during their tenure, the Sovereigns picked away at the Papal power of appointment and, by the time they died, the Spanish monarches had the exclusive right to dole out ecclesiastical patronage. In addition to the power of appointment, in 1494 Isabel and Ferdinand pressured the Pope into granting them the right, in perpetuity, to one-third of all tithes received by the Church.[18] When Pope Innocent VIII died in 1492, Isabel and Ferdinand used all their power and influence to successfully obtain the election of a Spaniard to aid them in their struggle to control the Castilian Church. In return, the new Pope, Alexander VI, rewarded the Sovereigns with the title of "The Catholic Kings" and the right to designate Church officials.

To curb the aristocrats from intriguing to have their candidates appointed to the higher clergy, Isabel and Ferdinand followed the same policy they used in making government and judicial appointments. Isabel insisted that the morals and education of a candidate for a high Church post were the most important criteria in his selection. High birth, Isabel said, would no longer be an essential passport to the appointment of a bishop or archbishop. Instead of promoting churchmen because of their family connections, the Sovereigns nominated pious, university trained men from the lower nobility and middle class; men who owed their loyalty to the Sovereigns, not to a foreign Pope or an aristocratic family.

As Isabel and Ferdinand's appointees exerted their influence over the Church, they cooperated with the Sovereigns in an attempt to enforced strict discipline over the priests and monks.[19] In 1480, the Sovereigns decreed that a clergyman who overtly kept a concubine would be banished from his parish for one year for a first offense and flogged for a second offense. Although the royal laws went unheeded for the most part, when Cardinal

Cisneros, the Archbishop of Seville, Diego de Deza, and the Archbishop of Granada, Hernando de Talavera, all appointees of the Sovereigns, rose to power in the 1490s, they sent their agents to the cathedrals and monasteries to enforce the reforms.[20] Despite the pressure from above to throw out their mistresses, many prelates resisted. When one of Cardinal Cisnero's agents informed him in 1499 that twenty-five of his priests in Toledo had committed sodomy or kept mistresses, he apparently thought it useless to discipline them, and took no action. In Andalusia, rather than abide by the strict rule of celibacy, some four hundred priests converted to Islam and moved to North Africa with their female companions.

Although Isabel and Ferdinand's prescriptions to cure the Church's vices did not totally succeed, the Sovereigns introduced sufficient reforms to shield Spain from the Reformation's radical reaction to the corruption, keeping Spain perpetually in the fold of the Faith. As a result, Martin Luther's thunder had no effect in the Iberian Peninsula. "Here, as in so many of their governmental activities, Ferdinand and Isabella displayed an uncanny ability to take the initiative and give viable shape to their subjects' ill-defined aspirations," Professor Elliott says.[21]

Following the precepts of *personalismo,* which required that the masters listen to the concerns and prejudices of their vassals, in 1492 the Sovereigns capitulated to the fever-pitched bigotry stirred up by their successful Holy Crusade against the Moors. Ferdinand and Isabel believed that, not only were they charged with cleansing the Church of its internal evils, they were duty bound to exterminate "all sources of pollution, the most noxious [being] universally agreed to be the Jews." On March 31, 1492, scarcely three months after the Moors' defeat at Granada, the Sovereigns issued a decree giving Jews two choices; prior to August 2, 1492, they must either convert to Christianity or be banished from Spain. The court historian Bernaldez described the exodus:

> "They [Jews] went out from the lands of their birth, boys and adults, old men and children, on foot, and riding on donkeys....They went by the roads and fields with much labor and ill fortune, some collapsing, others getting up, some dying, others giving birth, others falling ill, so that there was no Christian who was not sorry for them...the rabbis were encouraging them ....And so they went out of Castile."[22]

The expulsion of the Jews from Spain had the same effect as did Fidel Castro's expulsion of political undesirables from Cuba centuries later. This act by Ferdinand and Isabel eliminated a large portion of the commercial and professional classes; the educated, trained men Spain needed to run its government and its economy. In the next centuries Spain would pay the price for its embrace of the racist doctrine of *limpieza de sangre* (purity of blood). The execution, imprisonment and exile of the men who knew how to create wealth, to finance important projects and to organize the government contributed in large measure to Spain's squandering of the wealth it amassed from the New World. Instead of remaining the most potent empire in the world, controlling all of Latin America, most of the Western United States, Florida, the Philippines and other colonies, Spain's decline began only one hundred years after Christopher Columbus opened the door to conquest, power and riches.

Although many European nations had already expelled the Jews, Spain's ancient tradition of *conviviencia* (peaceful co-existence), inherited from the centuries during which the Moors controlled most of the Iberian Peninsula, continued until the early 1300s.[23] Inside the cities and towns, Jews often lived in separate sections, governed by their own officials. The law exempted Jews many from municipal taxes, and made them liable only for crown taxes. During the 1300s, Catholic priests intensified the popular hatred of Jews by blaming the plagues, famines and chaos in society on the Sons of David. Although Jews played an important part in Castile's financial community, anti-semitic propagandists exaggerated the Jews' roles as tax collectors and financiers. As did Hitler five hundred years later, the propagandists took half truths, repeated them over and over, blew them out of proportion and perpetrated the "big lie."[24] Fanned by lies, a wave of anti-semitic massacres broke out in 1391 in all parts of the Iberian Peninsula. Thereafter, the intolerance, always just under the surface, continued to erupt in violence in many Castilian communities.

Toledo's citizens rioted in a particularly savage outburst in 1449 against the *converso* (Jews converted to Christianity) tax farmers working for Alvaro de Luna, and waves of anti-semitic violence again broke out during the early years of the Sovereigns' reign in 1468 and 1473. Despite the pogroms, about half of the Jews remained faithful to the Old Testament, but the other half converted to Christianity to save their lives and property.[25] The vast majority of the converts only submitted to Christianity to escape death, and remained Jews at heart, continuing to secretly practice their ancient Hebrew rites. Castilians called these converts *conversos* or, more pungently, *marranos,* which carried the dual meaning of convert and pig. Christians then subdivided themselves into "Old Christians," who could trace the purity of their blood for at least four generations, and "New Christians," who could not.

Old Christians made the New Christians the constant subject of suspicion, charging that they made false conversions, that they were not bonded brothers of the Faith and that they secretly continued "Judiazing" practices. This, outwardly professing belief in Christ's message while maintaining their Hebrew faith, constituted a capital crime—heresy.

The propaganda campaign against Jews drew results during Ferdinand and Isabel's reign. Laws prohibiting usury made it possible for Old Christians to refuse to pay their debts to Jewish money lenders. In Trujillo, Christians stoned Jewish houses. In Vitoria, they attacked Jews in the streets and broke into the synagogue to beat and spit on praying Jews. The Old Christians accused Jews of atrocities, including one widely circulated rumor of a ritual murder where Jews crucified and cut out the heart of a Christian child in an attempt of create a magic spell to destroy Christians. The malevolence toward Jews lapped over to their *converso* cousins. The *conversos'* wealth, their intermarriages into the nobility and their rising power in the Church and the bureaucracy only added to the jealousy and resentment.[26] Churchmen hated the New Christians because of their dubious conversions, aristocrats because of their dependence on *converso* loans and the people because the *marranos* skimmed off fat percentages of the taxes they collected as tax farmers.

The odium extended not only to converted Jews who secretly practiced their old religion, but to Moors and converted Moors.[27] Although the purges began with Jews, the campaign to stamp out religious heterodoxy was also applied to *moriscos* (Moorish converts). After Granada fell on January 2, 1492, the Archbishop of Granada, Hernando de Talavera, instituted a program of "charitable persuasion" to convert the Muslims. Talavera urged his priests to learn Arabic so they could explain the word of the true God to the Arabs and permitted them to maintain most of their Islamic customs. Talavera's tolerant approach came in for criticism by the fundamentalists. Disgusted with Talavera's mild success at bringing Moors into the fold, Cardinal Cisneros persuaded Isabel to adopt a policy of compulsory conversion. Riots broke out in the Muslim quarter of Granada and, in Andalusia's mountains, the Moors openly revolted.

With the rebellions as a pretext, Cisneros declared that the Moors forfeited all their rights, granted in the treaty signed after the War of Granada, to continue to follow the Prophet's teachings.

"They (the Moors) should convert and be enslaved, because as slaves they will be better Christians," Cisneros said. Ferdinand and Isabel agreed. In 1501, by royal decree Christians made a huge bonfire in Granada with Arabic books, and, in 1502, another decree ordered all Arabs to submit to baptism or leave. Most Moors elected to kneel before the priests and receive the sprinkles of holy water, ending eight hundred years of Arabic presence in Spain.[28]

Today, religious toleration is a supreme virtue in our secular society, but in medieval Spain toleration was the supreme vice. Not only was religious impurity thought to poison the essential elements of society, it violated Isabel and Ferdinand's primary political goal; unity, homogeneity. To destroy this deadly virus, rigid, unforgiving, fundamentalist Christianity turned to the ultimate weapon—the Inquisition.

In the early years of their reign, Isabel and Ferdinand appeared almost as protectors of the Jews. They employed Jews as their personal physicians and financial advisors, and repeatedly intervened to stop cities from restricting Jewish commercial activities. Taking a direct personal interest in her Jewish subjects, Isabel wrote in 1477: "All the Jews in my realms are mine and under my care and protection and it belongs to me to defend and aid them and keep justice."[29] Despite the royal protection, the Castilian Parliament passed laws requiring Jews to wear distinctive symbols, and some cities forced Jews to live in *aljamas* (ghettos). The cities added to the anti-semitism by prohibiting Jews from selling food and shutting them up in the *aljamas* on Christian feast days. The religious frenzy stirred up by the War of Granada only increased the hatred of non-Christians and *converso* heretics.

Faced with mounting public pressure, the Sovereigns bowed to their subjects' wishes and, in 1480, issued a decree establishing the Holy Office of the Inquisition.[30] In 1483, Isabel and Ferdinand raised the Inquisition's prestige and importance by making it one of the five Castilian Councils of State, an integral part of the government. In that year the Sovereigns established the *Consejo de la Suprema y General Inquisicion* (Royal Council of the Supreme and General Inquisition), and appointed a Dominican fanatic, Tomas de Torquemada, as the Inquisitor General.[31]

The Inquisition addressed itself to rooting out heretic *conversos* who still secretly continued Judiazing practices, but the Inquisition never brought charges against Jews who had not been baptized. While the Inquisition attempted to uncover Castile's crypto-Christians during the 1480s, popular pressure caused the Sovereigns to expel Jews from Seville, Cordoba and Cadiz. Isabel and Ferdinand also sanctioned expulsions in other areas, and some towns and cities began throwing out their Jews. Finally, in 1492, the Inquisitor General, Torquemada, and others convinced the pious Queen to issue a decree completely banishing the Jews from Spain.[32] As the primary justification for the expulsion, the royal decree cited "the great harm suffered by Christians from the contact, intercourse and communication which they have with the Jews, who always attempt in various ways to seduce faithful Christians from our Holy Catholic Faith."

After the Sovereigns published the decree of expulsion, a deputation of Jews approached Ferdinand and offered a large sum of money for him to reconsider. When Torquemada heard of the proposed bribe, he supposedly burst into the Sovereigns' chambers, hurled thirty pieces of silver on the table and demanded to "know for what price Christ was to be sold again to the Jews."[33] Ferdinand rejected the bribe, but pinned the blame for the expulsion on Torquemada: "The Holy Office of the Inquisition...has provided that the Jews be expelled from all our realms...and has persuaded us to give our support and agreement to this....," Ferdinand wrote.

The Sovereigns and Cardinal Mendoza acted as sponsors to many prominent Jews who converted and welcomed them into the glories of the Faith. Other Jews chose exodus. Rich Jews paid the travel expenses of poor Jews. They sold their property at deep discounts to raise money. Some traded their house for a donkey, and others their vineyards for cloth or other goods they could carry out of the country. In the diaspora, Jews fled to Portugal, the Netherlands, Italy and North Africa. However, when they arrived in what they thought would be safe havens, many met with death. "Some of them [Jews] the Turks killed to take out the gold which they had swallowed to hide it;...and some of them were sold for men servants and maid servants in Genoa...and some of them were cast into the sea."[34]

Although Spanish Christians believed that the expulsion would purify Spain and make it a stronger, unified nation, forcing the Jews to chose between exile or conversion only drove many Jews who elected to convert underground. Instead of openly practicing Judiaism, many *conversos* continued their Old Testament ways in secret.[35] After attending Mass they returned to their homes to hold Jewish services, and after a baptism they washed away the Christian holy water. With so many heretics in their midst, the Inquisition's mission to prosecute the illicit religion took on a new importance.

Like McCarthyism and its red baiters, anti-semitism in medieval Castile took on a life and a momentum of its own. Anti-semites accused the *conversos* of infiltrating the Church and threatening to destroy it from within. Fanatics railed that Jews and *conversos* were traitors, homosexuals, blasphemers, child murders and assassins. Jew baiters claimed that rabbis administered the Jewish rights to the *conversos* in secret. They accused *conversos* of such vicious crimes as refusing to eat pork or work on Saturdays, circumcising their male babies, slaughtering animals and fowl in ritual ways to make their meat kosher and cooking with olive oil rather than Christian lard or fat.

To cleanse Spain from those who made dubious conversions, the Inquisition began its work in earnest in 1483. The Sovereigns appointed four members to the new Royal Council of the Inquisition, headed by the austere Inquisitor General Torquemada, who served under Isabel and Ferdinand's direct control and supervision.[36] To commence its business in the city of Valencia the Inquisition published an Edict of Grace and Faith commanding persons guilty of heresy to come forward and confess their sins and denounce others within a period of thirty days.[37] The Inquisition addressed its Edict:

> "To all faithful Christians, both men and women...of every condition, quality and degree...whose attention to [this Edict] will result in salvation in our Lord Jesus Christ...[to] declare and manifest the things which they have seen, known and heard tell of any person or persons, either alive or dead, who has said or done anything against the Holy Catholic Faith; cultivated and observed the law of Moses or the Mohammedan sect, or the rites and ceremonies of the same; or perpetrated diverse crimes of heresy; ...changing into clean personal linen on Saturdays...; preparing on Fridays the food for Saturdays...; who do not work on Friday evenings and Saturdays...; celebrate the festival of unleavened bread, eat unleavened bread and celery and bitter herbs; ...who say prayers according to the law of Moses, standing before the wall, swaying back and forth...; who slaughter poultry according to the Judaic law ...; who do not wish to eat salt pork, hares, rabbits, snails or fish which do not have scales; who bath the bodies of their dead and bury them in virgin soil according to the Jewish custom; ...who become, or know of others who become, circumcised; who invoke demons...; who say that our Lord Jesus Christ was not the true Messiah promised in Scripture, not the true God nor son of God; ...[who] say that our Lady the Virgin Mary was

not the mother of God or a virgin before the nativity and after; [who say and believe] that the law of Mahomet and its rites and ceremonies are good and can bring about their salvation;...."[38]

The Edict concluded with an order to all people to "state all that you know, have seen, heard or heard tell in any manner whatsoever ...and to appear before us personally." If a repentant *converso* confessed to washing away the *olor de sanctidad* (smell of holiness) or making blasphemous statements within the thirty-day grace period, he could expect merciful treatment. If he denounced another for the heinous practices of burying the dead according to Jewish rites or eating unleavened bread, he might send the guilty man to the stake. If a sinner held back his barbarous crimes of cooking with olive oil or changing his underwear on Saturdays he could expect the full wrath of the the Inquisition. Confused by the broad, all-encompassing list of crimes and terrified of the Inquisition's brutal punishment, thousands flocked to the Inquisition's courtrooms to confess or denounce. After the publication of Edicts of Grace and Faith, in Seville the Inquisition filled the prisons, in Toledo twenty-four hundred penitents rushed to save their souls and skins and in Valencia twenty-seven hundred converted Muslims admitted their wickedness.

The Edicts of Grace and Faith created a religious police state that Joseph Stalin would have approved. In effect, it made every individual an agent of the Inquisition, and made every man and woman conscious that his or her slightest word or act might subject him or her to prosecution.

Children accused their parents, relatives their kin and neighbors their friends. Household servants were particularly eager to testify against their masters. In many cases they swore that their masters ate meat during Lent or sent chickens and goats to be ritually slaughtered by rabbis. To ferret out even more information, the Inquisition paid professional informants and spies blood money for turning in their neighbors. In their sermons, Christian priests made denunciation a moral duty owed to Jesus Christ and God. Before the expulsion of the Jews in 1492, the inquisitors pressured rabbis to expose *conversos* who read the Torah. To settle family feuds or a point of honor, Christians sometimes accused other Christians of such trivial crimes as urinating on church walls.

Out of spite or jealousy, many people levied charges that were pure conjecture, guesses or hearsay, often designed to curry favor with, or immunity from, the Inquisition in the event somebody else denounced them. Fear gripped everyone. "Preachers do not dare to preach...for their lives and honor are in the mouths of two ignoramuses [who might testify against them], and nobody in this life is without his policeman....[M]any rich people leave the country...in order not to live all their lives in fear and trembling every time an officer of the Inquisition enters their house; for continual fear is a worse death than a sudden demise."[39]

When the officers of the Inquisition received a complaint, their rules required them to present the charges to a panel of priests for review. In many cases zealous inquisitors sent their policemen to make arrests before they drew up any formal charges. At the same time the religious police took the accused into custody, they seized all his property. After making an inventory of the victim's goods, the inquisitors sold them off to pay for the expenses of jailing him. Since the plodding course of Inquisitorial justice sometimes took years, a man acquitted later would leave jail with all his assets, pots, pans, spoons and clothes, sold at auction to pay the salaries of jailers and other officials. The accused's family, deprived of their property and their bread winner, often wound up begging, living on public charity or, in some cases, dying of hunger.

Contrary to the procedures followed in the ordinary courts, the Inquisition's procedures protected the accusers with a veil of secrecy. The witnesses' names were never published and the accused were not confronted by the persons who denounced them. When the police hauled a defendant before the Inquisition's tribunals he was not even told the nature of his crime. The judges merely demanded that the accused confess to unnamed crimes alleged by unnamed witnesses.

Although the Inquisition grew into a vast bureaucracy over the years, during the Sovereigns' reign the staffs were small. Two inquisitors made up the tribunal, which acted as judge, jury and issuer of sentences.[40] The tribunal appointed its own prosecutor and a few other officials. To supplement its personnel, the Inquisition named "familiars," laymen who performed duties assigned to them by the Inquisitorial court.[41] One of the "familiar's" duties was to act as spies, and many men sought the prestige of serving as God's informer. Being a "familiar" was a high honor, carrying with it a number of privileges, and some noblemen maneuvered to gain the appointments. "Familiars" had the right to bear arms to protect the inquisitors, were exempt from some taxes and could have their crimes tried in the Inquisition's court. If a "familiar" committed murder, rape or any other crime he could be assured of a friendly hearing by the Inquisition's courts. So attractive and prestigious was the office of "familiar" that it was up for sale, and many Inquisition officials lined their pockets with the sales proceeds.

Once accused, the Inquisition's victim was presumed guilty, and carried the burden or proving his innocence. The Inquisition's duty was to obtain a confession and attempt to persuade the guilty to rededicate their lives to Christ. After an arrest, the judges gave an accused three warnings over a period of several weeks to confess to the unstipulated crimes. "The effect of this enforced ignorance was to depress and break down a prisoner," Kamen says.[42] "If innocent, he remained bewildered about what to confess, or else confessed crimes the Inquisition was not accusing him of; if guilty, he was left to wonder how much of the truth the Inquisition really knew, and whether it was a trick to force him to confess ....[After] the three warnings, the prosecutor...read out the articles of accusation, [and] the accused was required to answer the charges on the spot, with no time or advocate to help him think out his defense." The charges could include invoking demons, making favorable comments about the laws of Mohammed or Moses, eating fish and hard boiled eggs during periods of mourning or pretending to go into a trance and claiming an ascension into heaven.

Only after the accusation was read did the defendant have the right to counsel. In the early years, prisoners could select their own lawyer, but, over time, the paranoia of the Inquisition required the accused to use lawyers selected by the Inquisition. Even though the victim now had a lawyer, he or she still didn't have the names of the accusers, and all evidence which might identify the accusers was suppressed.

Without a list of witnesses, and with important evidence concealed, mounting a defense was difficult, sometimes impossible. The most successful defense was for the defendant to give the tribunal a list of persons who might be attacking him out of personal hatred, a vendetta or to gain some advantage in business or politics. To assert this defense, the accused named every person he could think of who might bear false witness against him, and, if successful in including the persons on the Inquisition's secret list of accusers, the defendant might be acquitted or given a light sentence. Another defense permitted the accused to provide his own witnesses who would swear that he was a good Christian and that he had never committed any heretical acts against the One True Faith.

To mitigate the sentences, a defendant could plead drunkenness, insanity, extreme youth or excessive grief. If a man or woman could prove that he or she denied the Resurrection or "perpetrated diverse crimes of heresy" while drunk, the accused received a sentence of banishment rather than the stake. Occasionally, accused persons asserted as a defense that they were practicing Jews who had never been baptized and, therefore, were not subject to the Inquisition's jurisdiction.

There was no trial in the formal sense. Instead, over a period of months, and sometimes years, the jailers dragged the accused before the Inquisitorial tribunal in a series of audiences where evidence was presented and the defendant was interrogated. Since the witnesses against the accused were anonymous, there was no cross examination. On some occasions the defendant was held in prison for up to seven years before sentence was pronounced, and, not infrequently, an accused heretic died in jail. Despite his death, if found guilty posthumously, the Inquisition burned his effigy or his corpse.

Prison deaths were not uncommon. Living with fleas and other vermin in tiny, unheated cells for months, and cut off from all contact with the outside world, the prisoners lived in miserable conditions.[43] If they complained of the conditions, the warders gagged them, shackled them with chains or placed an iron fork under their necks to keep their heads forcibly upright for days. When the accused entered prison, the jailers warned them to remain silent and to not converse with any other prisoner, and led them down dank corridors to a small cell with brick floors and stone walls. No light or fresh air penetrated the cell, except that coming through the grate in the thick wooden door. Peep holes allowed the prison guards to spy on the prisoners. As part of the psychological effort to break down an accused, the jailers sometimes left human skulls in the the cells.

The prisoner slept on a straw mattress on the floor and relieved himself in an iron pot which he emptied only once a week. "The place was...very cold in winter," one prisoner wrote. "[A]nd so damp that very frequently the grates were covered with drops of water like dew; and my clothes during the winter were in a state of perpetual moisture. Such was my abode for the period of nearly three years."[44]

If the harsh, unhealthy conditions didn't crack a defendant's will and lead him to confess his sins, the Inquisitors resorted to torture. Since the Inquisition's mission was two-fold, to punish religious crimes and to save the criminal's soul, if the accused refused to confess his guilt voluntarily, the "art of torture" was justified. In the torture chambers, the inquisitors and a representative of the local bishop assembled to question the accused. Off to the side, a secretary dutifully recorded the questions and answers. Because the objective was not to kill the prisoner, but to obtain a confession, a doctor usually attended the sessions to revive the accused or call off the proceedings if it appeared he or she was about to die.

Merely bringing the accused into the torture chamber was often sufficient to obtain a confession. If this failed, the officials began their manipulation of the instruments of torture. First, the officials stripped the prisoner to his or her underwear. If the officials selected the *garrucha,* they strapped the prisoner's hands behind his back, tied the strap to a rope suspended from a pulley on the ceiling and attached heavy weights to the accused's feet. Then the officials slowly hoisted the victim in the air, suddenly released the rope and caught it with a sharp jerk that wrenched arms and legs.

If the *garrucha* didn't extract a confession, and if the almost naked prisoner was still conscious, the officials applied a water torture called the *toca*. In this procedure, the officials clamped the prisoner on a rack, forced his mouth open and stuffed a linen rag down his throat. Water was then poured on the cloth to create a simulation of drowning or suffocation. Another favorite was the *potro* (the rack). The officials laid the accused on a wooden frame, bound his body with ropes and tightened the ropes until they bit into the victim's flesh. In another procedure, the officials laid the victim on the ground with his feet facing an open fire. The officials then rubbed combustible oils on the prisoner's feet and "the heat penetrating into those parts (the feet) [caused the victim to suffer] pains worse than death itself."[45]

While the torturing went on, a secretary of the Inquisition calmly took notes of the the proceedings. One detailed account of the torture of Elvira del Campo in the mid-1500s in Toledo starkly recounts her ordeal:

> "She was carried to the torture chamber, and told to tell the truth, when she said she had nothing to say. She was ordered to be stripped and again admonished, but was silent.... The tying of the arms commenced.... One cord was applied to the arms and twisted and she was admonished to tell the truth, but she said she had nothing to tell. Then she screamed and said, 'Tell me what you want [me to say] for I don't know what to say.' She was told to tell what she had done...and another turn of the cord was ordered. She cried, 'Loosen me, Senores, and tell me what I have to say: I do not know what I have done, O Lord have mercy on me, a sinner!' Another turn was given and she said, 'Loosen me a little that I may remember what I have to tell; I don't know what I have done; I did not eat pork for it made me sick; ...loosen me and I will tell the truth.'...

> The cords were separated and counted, and there were sixteen turns, and in giving the last turn the cord broke.... Then the [cloth] was placed in her throat and she said, 'Take it away, I am strangling and am sick in the stomach.' A jar of water was then poured down, after which she was told to tell the truth....but though she was questioned repeatedly she remained silent. Then the inquisitor, seeing her exhausted by the torture, ordered it to be suspended."[46]

This matter-of-fact telling of a horrible brutality parallels the same cold-blooded detail in which the Nazis kept minute records of their atrocities almost five hundred years later. It reflects the terror of a victim who didn't know what to confess to. Unless she confessed to something specific, the torture continued. If she confessed to a specific crime, this might not be the one that interested the Inquisition, and the torture continued.

Whether the accused confessed or not, after months or years of interrogation and torture the Inquisitorial tribunal would meet to decide guilt or innocence. Acquittal was possible, but rare because an acquittal was taken as a mistake made by the Inquisition.[47] More likely, if the Inquisitorial court didn't have sufficient evidence it "suspended" the case, meaning that the case could be reopened if new evidence warranted.

The majority of cases resulted in reconciliation with the Catholic Faith. For minor offenses, the convicted person swore to abide by the Church's laws and to do penance. For more serious crimes, the guilty took the same oath but were condemned to prison, flogging, exile, the galleys and confiscation of property.[48] One convicted man, Pero Amigo, who admitted that he said that Christianity was a hoax, received a relatively light sentence. After Amigo swore to remain perpetually faithful to Christ, the Inquisition sentenced him to house arrest and to wearing a penitential cape to Mass on Sundays and feast days.

To subject the guilty to public shame and scorn, the Inquisition required convicted persons to wear the *sanbenito;* a yellow cape with one or two crosses across the breast. The length of time the man or woman was required to wear the *sanbenito* depended on the gravity of the crime, but many were condemned to wear the *sanbenito* for life when he or she appeared in public, making him or her a pariah in society. So great was the popular fear of touching the *sanbenito* that when a person condemned to wear it walked the streets, the terrified faithful scattered in all directions to avoid the contamination of its touch. When the guilty persons died, their *sanbenitos* with their names on them were hung in the parish church to remind their neighbors and relatives of the convicted persons' perpetual guilt and humiliation. Until Spain abolished the practice in the 1800s, *sanbenitos* hung in churches for centuries.[49]

For persons who committed serious crimes, refused to repent their heretical sins or had previously been convicted but relapsed into heretical practices, there was the stake. In 1490 the Toledo Inquisition burned one woman who "said publicly that in the Law of Moses she wished to die." In Aragon, the Inquisition condemned another woman "in absentia" after she fled because she admitted eating kosher meat, giving alms to Jews and fasting on Yom Kippur. Because ancient custom and law prohibited the Inquisition from taking a person's life, the Inquisition handed over those condemned to the pyre to the civil authorities.[50] If, after conviction, but before the execution, the condemned person repented his sins, he was "mercifully" strangled before the executioner lit the fire. If he did not repent, he lived to feel the flames licking at his body.[51]

To carry out the sentences the Inquisition staged an *auto de fe* (act of faith); a public ceremony held "partly...to stress the serious nature of the crime, partly to spread the glories and terrors of the Holy Catholic Faith, partly to provide the famished populace with a spectacle...."[52] The inquisitors announced the *auto de fe* two or three weeks in advance to allow the Old Christians time to make arrangements to attend. A few days before the *auto de fe*, carpenters erected seating galleries in the Plaza Mayor for the officials of the Inquisition and other dignitaries.

People flocked into the city where the *auto de fe* was to be held to witness the public atonements for sins committed against their Holy Faith. The night before the *auto de fe* the sinners condemned to the stake learned their fate, and jailers dressed the prisoners in black *sanbenitos* with flames and demons painted on them, and fitted them with tall dunce caps to further mark their infamy. Before dawn on the day of the *auto de fe,* the jailers served breakfast to the guilty. As the sun came up, church bells clanged and the crowds streamed into the Plaza Mayor. Bearing the official flag of the Inquisition, a herald led a procession of the city's priests and the convicted criminals into the Plaza Mayor. As the heretics made their way through the crowd, some of the pious Old Christians pelted them with rotten food and fruit, cursed them and shouted derision. Armed guards pushed the crowds back so that the condemned could be herded in front of the galleries for the formal ceremonies.

The crowd quieted when the secretary of the Inquisition held up a cross over the black draped pulpit and altar. The people raised their hands and swore an oath to defend the Catholic faith and its protector, the Inquisition. After this formality, a churchman stood to preach a sermon. These "sermons" were usually not religious in nature, but rather a stream of invectives and insults directed at the guilty to increase their humiliation. The persons condemned to lesser penalties marched one by one before to pulpit to learn, for the first time, the severity of the sentences. Because the Inquisition's rules required that every detail of each charge be read aloud, if there were a large number of penitents the ceremonies could last for more than a day. After the Inquisitorial official read the charges, each convicted person was given the opportunity to publicly repent; to swear on the cross that he believed in the Catholic faith, to say that he detested every form of heresy and to willingly accept his punishment.[53]

After the ceremonies of the *auto de fe,* the Inquisition turned the persons condemned to the stake over to the civil authorities, together with the effigies and disinterred corpses of those who died in prison or bribed their jailers and escaped. A confessor attended each man or woman, marching with them in the procession to the *quemadero* (place of burning) in a last minute attempt to extract a repentance. A squad of soldiers surrounded the prisoners to protect them from the fury of the crowd. Since showing sympathy for the condemned was also a crime, onlookers spurred by religious zeal made sure they demonstrated sufficient hatred to assure that they would not wind up as an accused.

Some enraged Old Christians set fire to the condemned mens' beards, a custom know as the "shaving the New Christians," to give them a foretaste of what was to come. "To make these holocausts of human beings more ghastly, the pageant was enhanced by processions of exhumed corpses and heretics in effigy. Artificial dolls and decomposed bodies with grinning lips and mouldy foreheads, were hauled to the huge bonfire, side by side with living men, women and children," an observer wrote.[54] "All of them alike...were enveloped in the same grotesquely ghastly San Benito, with the same hideous yellow [dunce caps]....The procession presented an artistically loathsome dissonance of red and yellow hues, as it defiled, to the infernal music of growled psalms and screams and moanings, beneath the torrid blaze of Spanish sunlight."

When they reached the *quemadero* outside the city's walls, the executioners led the condemned up a scaffold, tied ropes around the prisoners' necks to hold them upright at the stake and fitted leather sheaths over the mens' penises. The executioners strangled those who repented at the *auto de fe* or during the procession to the *quemadero.* A distinguished person, or royalty if they attended, lit the first fire. Then the executioners "set fire at the four corners of the pyre to the brushwood and charcoal that had been piled up.... [I]t began to burn on all sides, the flames rising swiftly up the platform and burning the wood and clothing. When the cords binding the criminal had been burnt off he fell through the open trap door into the pyre and his whole body was reduced to ashes."[55] With ghoulish curiosity, the wealthy paid high prices for good seats and thousands of spectators in fanatic festival mood cheered as the flames charred the victims of the religious orgy. "Pious cruelty," Machiavelli called it.

The phenomena of the Inquisition can perhaps be explained in the context of its times, but never excused. Its effect, sealing off Spain from the burgeoning humanism in Europe and the Renaissance's probing curiosity, stultified Spain, isolating it from the new scientific investigation, the new economic theories and the new liberal view that rational men could control their own destiny. Instead, Spain locked itself in a straight jacket of orthodoxy and conservatism. Politically, the nation bound itself to the Catholic Church's view that society could only be organized by a system of hierarchy, with an all-powerful, absolutist Pope or a king at the top.

Ironically, Isabel's imposition of the Inquisition denied the pious Queen a status she would have done almost anything to attain; sainthood. During the centuries after her death, several attempts have been made to canonize the devout daughter of the Church whose policies kept her nation and all of Latin America firmly under the influence of the Catholic Church. But this one act, sponsoring and promoting the Inquisition, has kept her out of the domains of the blessed saints who sit at the knee of Christ. With her fervent devotion to the Faith, nothing could have been as important to her as having the opportunity to serve as a perpetual handmaiden of the Deity. But an act which she believed was so right, so politically correct, lowered a barrier that will probably never be raised.

EPILOGUE

After the War of Granada ended in 1492, Isabel and Ferdinand turned their attention to foreign policy. They arranged their childrens' marriages to foreign princes and princesses to form a grid of alliances designed to enhance Spain's power. Princess Isabel married Prince Alfonso of Portugal. When Alfonso died, Princess Isabel married his brother, King Manuel of Portugal. Princess Catherine of Aragon first married Prince Arthur of England, and, when Arthur died, King Henry VIII. From that union, the Sovereigns' blood line continued with Mary Tudor (Bloody Mary) who struggled with Queen Elizabeth for the English throne. Isabel and Ferdinand double hitched their fortunes to the Holy Roman Empire by marrying Prince John to Princess Margaret of Hapsburg and Princess Joan to Prince Philip of Hapsburg.

Despite the Sovereigns' wedding plans, a rash of deaths shredded the carefully created network of dynastic matches. Prince John died in 1497, leaving his widow pregnant. Later that year, Prince John's posthumous son, was stillborn. The Sovereigns' favorite daughter, Princess Isabel, died in 1498 and her son, the heir to the Portuguese crown, died in 1500. After Princess Isabel's death, the Sovereigns again cemented their ties with Portugal by the betrothal of their youngest daughter, Princess Maria, to King Manuel of Portugal in 1501.

Grief from the deaths of her children and grandchildren and her age finally brought down the diminutive Queen. About six weeks before her death in 1504, Peter Martyr wrote to the Count of

Tendilla: "Her whole system is pervaded by a consuming fever. She loathes food of every kind, and is tormented with incessant thirst...." As Isabel's condition worsened, Martyr wrote a week later: "We sit sorrowful in the palace all day long, tremblingly waiting [for] the hour when religion and virtue shall quit the earth with her....She can hardly be said to die, but to pass into a nobler existence, which should rather excite our envy than our sorrow. She leaves the world filled with her renown, and she goes to enjoy life eternal with her God in heaven. I write this, between hope and fear, while the breath is still fluttering within her."[1]

In her will Isabel stipulated that her body be transported to Granada to be buried in a Franciscan monastery in the Alhambra, in the shadows of the Moorish battlements she conquered twelve years before. "But," she wrote, "should the king my lord prefer a sepulchre in some other place, then my will is that my body be there transported, and laid by his side; that the union we have enjoyed in this world [may be enjoyed in heaven]."[2]

She ordered a simple funeral, the money saved to be distributed as alms to the poor. She made specific bequests to her lifelong friend, Beatriz de Bobadilla, and other favorites. To Ferdinand she left a substantial sum of money and beseeched "the king my lord that he will accept all my jewels...so that, seeing them, he may be reminded of the singular love I always bore him while living, and [be reminded] that I am now waiting for him in a better world...."

After providing for the distribution of her worldly goods, she issued her last orders as Queen. From her deathbed, Isabel instructed her ministers to form a commission to codify the laws, and enjoined her successors to treat the Indians in the New World with kindness and convert them to the Holy Faith. Even as she lay dying, Isabel couldn't shake her habit of tending to the smallest details; she issued orders to clear up nagging tax issues which were still pending.

Because her two oldest children, John and Isabel, were dead, the Queen mandated that her grandson Charles, the infant son of Joan and Philip of Hapsburg, would succeed to the crown of Castile when he came of age. During the interim, Isabel's will said, Joan would be the "queen proprietor" and Philip "as her husband" would receive obedience from her subjects. At the time Isabel wrote her will, Joan and Philip were living in the Low Countries, and Joan had shown definite signs of mental instability. Addressing these issues in her testament, Isabel stipulated that, if Joan was outside of Spain or, if inside Spain "does not desire, or is not able to engage in its government," Ferdinand would act as regent of

Castile until Prince Charles reached majority.

As her friends and courtiers gathered at her bedside to witness the last rites of extreme unction, Isabel told them: "Do not weep for me, nor waste your time in fruitless prayers for my recovery, but pray rather for the salvation of my soul." Just before noon on November 26, 1504, the fifty-three-year-old Queen closed her blue eyes and died.

Her death cast a pall over the nation she and her marriage partner had created. Her subjects remembered her triumphs; the Wars of Succession and Granada, and her opening of the New World to Spain's military entrepreneurs. Most of all they remembered her personality; her love of her people demonstrated through her *personalismo*, her devotion to the one true God and her intelligent, always active, mind. Politically, her vassals applauded the Queen's unification of the Spanish kingdoms, her establishment of the crown's preeminence and her reform of Spain's institutions. The Old Christians lauded her decisions to expel Jews and Moors and to stalk heresy with the Inquisition's vengeance.

Many Spaniards, and perhaps the Queen herself, thought she qualified for sainthood. Despite her accomplishments, which created the framework for Spain to become Europe's most powerful nation, her religious fundamentalism, her unyielding orthodoxy discredited her memory. Isabel's apologists say that it is difficult to condemn her because she was a woman of her times, and her decisions to expel minorities and hunt down heretics were not only excused, but were extolled, by her contemporaries. But one of her greatest admirers, Professor Prescott, quotes the Queen's own words to condemn her, "[T]he prevalence of a bad custom cannot constitute its apology."[3]

With Isabel in her tomb at Granada, the cords holding her bundle of arrows together snapped. Pro-Ferdinand and pro-Joan-Philip factions quickly formed. The clerics and nobles supporting Joan and Philip remembered Ferdinand's flashes of cruelty, his devious manipulations and the yoke he applied to their necks. He was, they said, almost a foreigner, an Aragonese, and would probably pack the government with his cronies from Barcelona and Zaragoza.[4] Many merchants and townsmen resented Ferdinand for the heavy taxes he levied to support his Italian wars. Powerful Spaniards who profited from the extensive wool trade with the Low Countries feared that the dispute between Ferdinand and Philip would interfere with their monopoly.[5]

Joan (known later as *Juana la Loca*, Joan the Demented) had apparently inherited the gene of madness from her grandmother, Queen Isabella. Philip (known as "the Handsome") was a flagrant womanizer; more devoted to his whores and mistresses than to affairs of state. In Philip, his Spanish supporters calculated, they had another compliant weakling like King Henry IV who they could dominate. Without their counsel, the aristocrats and prelates believed, neither Joan nor Philip could run the country. These rebels, Ferdinand's loyal supporter Bernaldez wrote, "acted more out of greed for the royal patrimony than for the good of the kingdom."

The possibility of civil war faced the nation, but Ferdinand was "determined to reign and govern this kingdom of Castile for the rest of his life," the King's personal secretary told the English ambassador. The men who owed their positions in the government and Church hierarchy to Ferdinand continued to support him as regent of Castile until Prince Charles was old enough to become King. Ferdinand's advocates noted that, even though the King was from Aragon, he spent most of his life in Castile fighting for its interests, and he was the husband of their cherished Isabel. By comparison, Philip spoke no Spanish, and sneered at the Spaniards' lack of sophistication and crude customs. Their politically astute Queen, Ferdinand's clique argued, suspected Joan's madness, and clearly provided in her will for Ferdinand to remain as regent of Castile. Since it was Isabel's desire that Ferdinand retain power, the rules of *personalismo* required them to back the King. Further, Ferdinand's supporters said, Isabel had always resented Philip's parading his whores in front of Joan and otherwise abusing the young woman during her moments of insanity.

In Spain, the scheming, the plots and the divided loyalties threatened to split the nation, to plunge it back into the chaos that existed when the Sovereigns came to power thirty years before. "The nobles sharpen their teeth like wild boars with the hope of a great change," Peter Martyr wrote. In the Low Countries, where Joan and Philip lived, Spanish nobles and secret agents flocked to their court to pledge allegiance.[6] "Every shoemaker in the Spanish court was sending his allegiance," one of Ferdinand's loyalists sneered.[7]

Joan, unbalanced in her mind and torn by divided loyalty to her father and her husband, struggled in the awkward trap. Philip connived with the Pope to remove Cardinal Cisneros as Primate of Spain. As part of his propaganda campaign, Philip issued a public statement accusing Ferdinand, the "old Catalan" his enemies called him, of saying that Joan was insane. Philip conspired with France, the country Ferdinand had hated since boyhood, to dominate Spain. He entered into secret negotiations with the powerful Duke of Medina Sidonia and other Castilian magnates. When the

Marquis of Villena (who was "nursed to faction from the cradle") saw the way the political winds were blowing, he followed his family's tradition of disloyalty and allied himself with Philip.

Ferdinand countered. He called Parliament into session to ratify his position as the lawful ruler of Castile.[8] Ferdinand remembered the success of his and Isabel's propaganda campaigns in the past and spread rumors that Philip had imprisoned Joan, and that Philip was attempting to quash the Holy Inquisition in an unholy effort to gain the support of heretic *conversos*. He nipped Philip's attempted French alliance by compromising with his lifelong enemy. Ferdinand married Germaine de Foix, the niece of the French King Louis XII, and signed a treaty with France which made it impossible for Philip to invade Castile by land. Although Ferdinand cut off Philip's French connection, the King's marriage to a foreigner, a usurper of Isabel's bed, further inflamed many Castilians against the King.

Although Ferdinand was a master at political connivance, his Castilian support crumbled. Philip organized an army of three thousand Flemings and Germans and sailed for Spain, landing at La Coruna in Galicia in April, 1506. The mounting opposition forced Ferdinand to sign a truce with Philip in June. In the agreement, Ferdinand abandoned his claims to govern Castile. Later that same June day, the duplicitous King renounced the treaty. Then he quit Castile for Aragon and sailed for his possessions in Italy. Philip's rule lasted for only one discontented summer. The twenty-eight-year-old playboy died in September, 1506.

Even though his rival was dead, Ferdinand remained in Naples. During that time, Bernaldez wrote, "some [aristocrats and churchmen] thought that it was the end of the world and [that] the time of King Henry IV had returned....[H]e who could take most, did so...." The Duke of Medina Sidonia snatched Gibraltar, part of his family's patrimony which the crown took from him in 1502. The Count of Lemos retook his family's domains at Ponferrada. It appeared that the Sovereigns' thirty years of discipline and unity were wasted.

Joan refused to govern, and referred all matters of state to Ferdinand for decision. In her confused state, Joan the Demented believed the prophecy of a Carthusian cleric, that Philip would rise from the dead, and kept her husband's embalmed body in her chambers at all times. During her fits of lunacy, Joan refused to wash, change clothes or eat. With her husband's corpse always nearby, Joan lived the deranged life of a recluse until she died almost fifty years later. Still leery of his Castilian enemies, Ferdinand sent emissaries from Naples to Spain to weld together a coalition. Finally, in the summer of 1507 he returned to Castile with a small army, sacked the castles of disloyal nobles and invaded rebellious cities. Adroitly applying his political skills, Ferdinand came to terms with most of the rebels, forgiving their transgressions and allowing them to keep their titles and property. By 1510, the leading aristocrats and clergymen had sworn fealty to the King as regent of Castile.

Ferdinand the warrior sent his armies to conquer Navarre, bringing most of that independent kingdom, of which his father John II of Aragon had once been king, under the Spanish flag.[9] He sent military expeditions, led by Cardinal Cisneros, to North Africa to conquer port cities and seal off invasion routes which the Arabs might exploit. He dreamed of invading Egypt and reconquering Jerusalem for Christianity. The King continued to send his armies to Italy under the command of Spain's Great Captain, Gonzalo de Cordoba, who received his basic training during the War of Granada.[10] As a result of these campaigns, Spain developed a professional standing army, the fear of which extended Spain's influence throughout Europe for centuries. Ferdinand the diplomat nurtured Spain's ties to the Papacy, Portugal and England. He formed the rudiments of Spain's foreign service by establishing permanent embassies in Rome, Venice, London, Brussels and at the migratory Austrian court.[11]

Even though Ferdinand kept the diplomatic channels with the Hapsburgs open, like his counterpart Henry VIII of England, the King never gave up hope of siring a male heir. To deny the Hapsburg succession through his grandson Charles, Ferdinand, then an old man of fifty-eight, fathered a son by Germaine de Foix. But the baby, Prince John of Aragon, died a few hours after his birth. Even though disappointed by this loss, Ferdinand kept up his efforts to secure his Trastamara dynasty through the male line. Court gossips claimed that the King took heavy doses of aphrodisiacs to increase his potency, but they didn't work.

The wily old man died just after midnight on January 23, 1516, in a small village in Extremadura without a male heir. Ferdinand "died embittered and resentful, cheated not by his opponents, all of whom he had outwitted, but by a malignant fate which had placed his masterwork (Spain) in the hands of alien descendants," Professor Elliott says. Ferdinand's sixteen-year-old grandson, a Hapsburg, succeeded to the throne as Charles V to pilot Spain through the beginning of its Golden Age of imperialism and mastery over colonies around the globe.[12]

While the Sovereigns suffered grief and savoured glory during their final years, Christopher Columbus had only brief moments of joy after his epic first voyage. Jealous courtiers and back stabbing subordinates tormented the Admiral of the Ocean Sea. Crippling arthritis and bouts with malaria weakened his body. More importantly, the Admiral never fulfilled his dream of finding the passage to the Orient. When Columbus died, his holy mission to convert the Indians to Christianity was a mockery of slavery and brutality. He found only negligible amounts of gold, not enough to pay the expenses of his expeditions. Despite the setbacks and disappointments he would meet during his last years, the iron-willed visionary tried three more times to unravel the geographic puzzle that would provide him a breakthrough to the riches of the East.

The second and third voyages were disasters. Ferdinand and Isabel made one of their rare errors in their judgment of human nature; they assigned the wrong man to the wrong job. Exploration and discovery would only be secondary objectives of the next two voyages. Columbus' royal patrons designed the second and third expeditions primarily for colonization, for creating a society out of whole cloth and for bringing the Indians to Christ. Successfully completing these tasks required a man who could organize, pay attention to details and diplomatically handle men in difficult situations. For the most part, these talents escaped Columbus. His mind scanned only the big picture, and, for Columbus, discovery and gold were the only goals of his grand design.

To Columbus, only lesser men, technocrats and detail-oriented bureaucrats, attended to the intricacies of logistics and shuffled papers. Others might have the patience to deal with the petty complaints of scheming officers and greedy noblemen, but the proud, arrogant Admiral had no time for such trivia. He was a stubborn man of action, and his monomania indelibly focused his thoughts on achieving his great enterprise. He was a navigator and a discoverer, nothing more. He was like the thousands of promoters and scientists who have a brilliant idea and found a new business to exploit it, but are incompetent to run the organization.

Isabel, the shrewd judge of men and their flaws, came to understand the failings of her Admiral and Viceroy as an administrator. But, in the heady atmosphere of triumph and optimism after the first voyage, she kept the promises given to Columbus in the Capitulations in 1492. In the spring and summer of 1493 Columbus, who only a few months before had been the butt of cruel jokes and scathing criticism, reached the pinnacle of his glory.

Almost immediately after Columbus' triumphant meeting with the Sovereigns in Barcelona in April, 1493, Ferdinand and Isabel instructed their Admiral to prepare for a second voyage. Isabel appointed one of her trusted servants, Juan de Fonseca,[13] to serve as quartermaster to marshall men and supplies for the second voyage.

Fonseca haggled with the wine merchants and horse traders, and bought wheat, crossbows and muskets to outfit the fleet that would carry twelve hundred men to reinforce Spain's first colony in America. With the excitement generated by the discovery, hundreds of noblemen and commoners clambered to be included on the manifest of the seventeen ships. On board were Diego Columbus, the Admiral's youngest brother, Juan Ponce de Leon, who later discovered Florida, and Juan de la Cosa, who drew the first map of the New World. Twelve priests, including the Benedictine monk Bernardo Buil, signed on to begin God's work in the Indies, but there were no women and no Pinzons.

While sail makers and ships chandlers readied the armada, Fonseca and Columbus quarrelled. With his new status, the Admiral and Viceroy insisted on a full complement of body servants. When Fonseca objected, Columbus went behind his back and got the Sovereigns' approval for him to take five. Columbus complained that the ships Fonseca chartered were inadequate, the crews deficient and the provisions of second quality. In this, the Admiral was right; many of the horses were broken down nags, and swindling merchants put wine in cheap casks that would burst in the tropical heat.

Despite the bickering, the fleet set sail from the old Phoenician and Roman port city of Cadiz in September, 1493, only six months after Columbus' return from the first voyage. After a fast run to Gomera in the Canary Islands, the now-distinguished conqueror of the Ocean Sea spent a few days in the arms of his mistress, Beatriz de Peraza, "with whom our Admiral in other times had fallen in love."[14]

After taking on fresh water and provisions at Gomera, Columbus pointed his prows south and west, making landfall at the Island of Dominica in three weeks, just before dawn on November 3, 1493. Realizing that he was south of Hispaniola, the Admiral set his course to the northwest, discovering Guadeloupe, the Virgin Islands and Puerto Rico. Pausing in Guadeloupe, a shore party found a deserted village whose inhabitants fled from the "houses on water," leaving behind "large cuts and joints of human flesh, shin bones set aside to make arrows of, caponized [castrated] Arawak boy captives who were being fattened [to be roasted for food], and girl captives who were mainly used to produce babies...."[15] From the Indian tribe's name, Canibs, came a new word, cannibal.[16]

During this part of the voyage, the priests went ashore to celebrate the first funeral mass in the New World for a crewman killed in an earlier skirmish with the natives. Another first, the New World's first recorded rape, took place in the Virgin Islands. One European, Michele da Cuneo, carefully wrote down the details of his assault: "Having taken her into my cabin, she being naked according to their custom, I wanted to have my pleasure of her. I wanted to put my desire into execution, but she did not want it and scratched me with her finger nails....I took a rope and thrashed her well....Finally, we came to an agreement...[and] I don't mind telling you that she seemed to have been raised in a school for whores."[17]

The brutality was reciprocal. Before reaching the settlement at La Navidad, the fleet put into port on Hispaniola's north coast. There they found two decomposed corpses, identifiable as Europeans only by the stubble of beard on the face of one of the dead men. The ships weighed anchor on November 27, 1493, and, by sundown, were bobbing offshore from La Navidad. The crews lit flares and fired cannons. No answer. Only the cries of birds and the sound of waves punctuated the total silence.

The next morning the Admiral sent a reconnaissance party ashore. Columbus' Indian friend, Guacanagari, told him what happened. After the Admiral left in January, the Spaniards went on a rampage of greed and lust. Emulating the delights of the Moorish harems, the colonists each captured three or four women to use as slaves and concubines. Remembering El Cid's legacy of military entrepreneurship, they strapped on metal breastplates and took up arms to pillage for gold.

Even though they were better armed, the Spaniards made themselves vulnerable by splitting up into marauding gangs which scoured the countryside, and by brawling among themselves over women and gold. Inland, they met a formidable foe, the *cacique* Caonabo. In retaliation against the Spaniards' atrocities, Caonabo ambushed the roving bands of Spaniards in the thick jungle, picking them off one-by-one. With only eleven men left to garrison the fort at La Navidad, Caonabo attacked and wiped out the last remaining Spaniards, including the brother of the Admiral's Cordoban lover, Diego de Harana.

After the massacre at La Navidad, the myth of the kind, noble savage ended, and the myth of the indestructible white man was gone forever. To the generally peaceful Indians of Hispaniola, the Spaniards were no longer white gods sent from heaven. They were as beastial as the Canibs who hunted them for meat. To the

Spaniards, their Genoese Admiral was a liar. Columbus had led them to believe that the natives were gentle, timid people waiting to deliver themselves into the arms of the Holy Church and to placidly agree to work for their new masters. Instead, the Spaniards found a world not unlike the one they had just left. This wild new world would require them to employ European war-making techniques to subdue the "noble savages."

Like most optimists riveted to clearly defined goals, Columbus didn't like problems. Instead, he pushed on, leaving the disaster of La Navidad behind. After searching the area around La Navidad for the bodies of dead Spaniards to retrieve any gold they might have in their pockets and hastily burying the few corpses they found, the Admiral guided his ships along Hispaniola's northern coast.

In the first of many bad executive decisions, Columbus ordered the fleet to drop anchor on January 2, 1494, off a spot he named Isabel in honor of the Queen. Here, the Admiral said, the twelve hundred men would build a trading colony, and he would serve as the first governor in the New World. The site selection couldn't have been worse. The nearest fresh water was a mile away. The anchorage lay wide open to the winter's harsh winds. Malaria-carrying mosquitos infested the nearby swamps.

Columbus justified his ill-conceived decision with arguments that the Indians had told him the location was close to the alleged gold mines and that the land was fertile. Following the Admiral's orders, the Spaniards began building Isabel, the first real town established by Europeans in the New World. Around a Plaza Mayor, the Spaniards built houses and the New World's first church and laid out streets to recreate a bit of Spain in the tropical jungle. It was a new frontier ripened for Spain's military entrepreneurs, but it was not Spain.

There was an enormous language barrier which limited most communications to pointing and gestures. Even the simplest things needed for daily life didn't exist. The Spaniards had to import barrels, nails, knives, needles, cups and plates. There was no beef, pork, wheat or wine. Only fish, cassava and a few vegetables. Because of the irregular diet, the unfamiliar tropical climate and the stinging mosquitos, hundreds of men went down sick and some died. The new town turned into a hospital, requiring the town's chief doctor to work so hard that he demanded that the Admiral double his salary.

The doctors ran out of drugs. Wine casks burst. Weevils bored into the wheat and biscuits. The Caribbean sun rotted the meat and fish. Laboring in the humid heat at hard construction work weakened the sweat-soaked Spaniards. With so many men ill, the Admiral ordered the proud Spanish noblemen to join the work force to dig ditches, grind flour and perform other manual labor. Under the chivalric precepts of medieval Spain, *caballeros* and *hidalgos* didn't dirty their hands with menial work. They were "sons of somebody," and, to them, taking orders from the son of a Genoese weaver and tavern keeper was the ultimate insult to their manhood and to their place in society.

Columbus saw mutiny in the mens' eyes. He hung some and punished others with floggings, adding to the charges against him that of cruelty. Frustrated by the details of governing, the Admiral made three decisions, all bad. To get rid of some of his critics, Columbus sent twelve of the seventeen ships back to Spain with scraps of gold, a few spices and a cargo of Indian slaves which he wanted sold to pay expenses.[18] When the disgruntled colonists returned home, they immediately went to the Sovereigns to spread the tales of massacre, death and anarchy, and to launch vicious personal attacks on the Admiral.

Making his second mistake, Columbus dispatched detachments of armed men to Hispaniola's interior under the command of two noblemen, Pedro Margarit and Alonso de Ojeda, to build a fort closer to the supposed gold mines. For the first time, the Indians saw men on horseback, who the frightened natives believed to be centaurs. There were no gold mines, and the inland invasion infuriated Caonabo and other *caciques*. The raping, pillaging and severe punishment meted out by Margarit and Ojeda's soldiers created a battle zone in a tropical jungle as dense and forbidding as that in Vietnam.

While his soldiers fought through brambles and vines in the interior, Columbus blundered again. Just as he did when faced with bad news at La Navidad, Columbus left Isabel with three caravels to do what he knew best—explore. Mistrusting everyone but his inner circle of friends and family, Columbus put his younger brother Diego in charge of Isabel. "His brother, Don Diego, a man more suited to the cloister than to a colony, [was] unable to cope with the situation," Morison says.

During the Admiral's absence, the weak-willed Diego received word that the Spaniards at the inland fort were cutting off the natives' ears for minor offenses and enslaving the wives and daughters of *caciques*. Diego ordered Margarit to cease the brutality. But Margarit, an aristocrat, treated the Diego's letter as a personal attack by a low-born foreigner on his honor as a gentleman, an offense to chivalry's code of *pundonor*. In a rage, Margarit marched to Isabel, seized three caravels and, along with the disaffected Fray Buil, returned to Spain to spread the word of the Columbus brothers' incompetent administration.

Like most determined entrepreneurs, Columbus had no patience when it came to dealing with others. Listening to, and resolving, the niggling complaints of lesser men only diverted his attention from his primary goal, finding the riches of the Orient. It was beneath the dignity of the Sovereigns' personal representative to waste his time with malcontents. Furthermore, Columbus was convinced that God personally ordained him to carry out the great enterprise.

It was not in the Almighty's plan that he should bog himself down with the minutia of petty politics or diplomacy. As a visionary, he was locked on to his objective, and he knew where it was—Cuba. Convinced that Cuba was an outer province of China, the Admiral set sail in the three caravels, including his favorite ship, the Nina, on April 24, 1494, to find the Great Khan. For almost five months he cruised Cuba's southern coast, touched at Jamaica and returned to Isabel in September, 1494, with nothing.

During Columbus' sojourn to Cuba, a fleet of three supply ships landed at Isabel with his brother Bartholomew on board. When the Admiral returned to Isabel, aching with the arthritis that would plague him the rest of his life, his inability to delegate authority to anyone outside his family and a few intimate friends led him into another blunder. Columbus appointed Bartholomew governor, serving up to the Spaniards three members of the Columbus clan as targets for their resentment. In late 1494, another small fleet arrived, bearing the first European women to land in the New World since the Norsemen.[19] The fleet's captain, Antonio de Torres, also brought a letter from Isabel and Ferdinand suggesting that their Admiral and Viceroy return to Spain. Columbus had little to show for his efforts. A few gold trinkets, some cotton cloth, exotic parrots, yes. But nothing of real value. He knew that, back in Spain, Margarit, Fray Buil and other disaffected returnees were manufacturing "lies" about his inability to manage the new colony.

In a desperate attempt to produce something of value, Columbus made another bad decision in February, 1495. Mounted on the first horses to trot through the New World's jungle trails, the Admiral and his soldiers rounded up fifteen hundred Indians, selected five hundred of the healthiest and loaded them on slave ships to be sold at auction in Seville. The historian Bernaldez reported from Seville that the Indians were "naked as they were born ....They were not very profitable because almost all died...."

Columbus did not return to Spain with the slave ships. He remained at Isabel to direct a punitive expedition inland to retaliate against Indian violence. "Men from the Iron and Steel Age descended upon men from the Stone Age," Bradford says. With Santiago Matamoros' specter hovering over them, the Admiral led an army of twenty-five horsemen, two hundred footmen, an assortment of Indian allies and a pack of vicious hounds to Hispaniola's interior. With their superior technology, the Spaniards defeated a sizeable native force in the first major battle between Indians and Europeans. They captured the Indians' most forceful *cacique*, Caonabo, and dragged him back to Isabel shackled in irons.

After subduing the Indians and extracting as much gold as possible, Columbus returned to Isabel. During his military campaign in the island's interior, a crown servant, Juan Aguado, had arrived. Influenced by Fray Buil and Margarit's assaults on the Admiral, Ferdinand and Isabel sent Aguado as their special envoy to Isabel "to see and report" on the colony. Columbus was furious. Aguado's mission pricked the Admiral's enormous pride and his overweening sense of dignity. He, and only he, was the Sovereigns' representative. He must, he knew, return to Spain immediately to regain the Sovereigns' trust and to see if the mystical attraction between him and Isabel was still there.

Before Columbus left the colony, he gave instructions to Bartholomew to abandon the squalid, miserable site at Isabel and relocate the colonial capital on Hispaniola's south coast. The new town, Santo Domingo, would serve as the first colonial capital from which Spain's military entrepreneurs would conquer the new frontier and brand it with Spain's version of the frontier mentality. Still at Isabel, the Admiral ordered his carpenters and shipwrights to build a new vessel, christened the India, the first modern ship built in the New World. Along with the India, Columbus left Hispaniola aboard his treasured Nina, with Caonabo and a cargo of thirty Indians sloshing in the swill of the ships' the holds. On June 11, 1496, the two caravels made port at Cadiz.

During the long voyage eastward, Columbus brooded on the reasons for his misfortune. After searching his soul, and praying for Divine wisdom, the deeply religious side of his character convinced him that God was punishing him for his excessive pride. It was God's vengeance that denied him gold and the route to the Orient, that placed him in disfavor with the Sovereigns and that numbed his limbs with arthritis. When he arrived in Spain, the tall, gaunt Admiral donned the coarse brown robes of a Franciscan monk to give an outward sign of his new-found humility.

Dressed in Franciscan garb, a penitent Columbus caught up with the itinerant Spanish court at Burgos. When the Sovereigns granted him an audience, Columbus approached Isabel and Ferdinand with trepidation. Had Fray Buil and Margarit's cutting tongues rendered permanent damage? Had Aguado's poisonous reports of incompetence, cruelty and arrogance created suspicion? Would God deny him the Sovereigns' favor? Was the old magic between him and his patroness still there? It was. When their blue eyes met, Columbus knew that the magnetism that attracted Isabel still worked. She treated him graciously (*con blandura*), expressed pleasure at his return and displayed a keen interest in the gold dust and nuggets, exotic Indians and other strange items he presented. Although Ferdinand was interested in the gold, the King was noticeably cold to this Admiral and Viceroy who seemed unable to manage affairs in the colony.

Columbus immediately proposed a third voyage. But in 1496 a new and costly expedition was low on the Sovereigns' agenda. Fighting the French in Italy and arranging dynastic alliances with England, Portugal and the Hapsburg's Holy Roman Empire were more important. Columbus followed the court from place to place, and attended the wedding of Prince John and Margaret of Hapsburg in 1497.

Despite this honor and the Queen's gracious treatment of him, he could only wheedle occasional audiences to plead his case for men and ships. Here, on land, the beached Admiral was at his worst. Fending off the sneers of his detractors, who called him "The Admiral of the Mosquitos," and begging for attention at court drew out the most unpleasant side of his character, making him irritable and bitter. In heated debates with the nay sayers, Columbus beat back their allegations that his discoveries hadn't yielded near the returns garnered by the Portuguese from West Africa. After months of arguing and petitioning, the Sovereigns finally granted his request.

Columbus left Seville and set off on his third voyage to his Viceregal domains on May 30, 1498. He dallied two days in Gomera with Beatriz de Peraza, and made plans for a more southerly route.[20] Leaving Gomera, Columbus set his course south and west. His three caravels dipped down to within about eight degrees north of the Equator, steered back to the northwest and made landfall at Trinidad on July 31, 1498. The Admiral edged his ships through the Serpent's Mouth, the treacherous strait between Trinidad and Venezuela, and cruised the Gulf of Paria, noting the enormous gush of fresh water which flowed from the Orinoco River up to twenty miles out to sea.

Till then, all the Admiral had found were islands. And, because of his confused medieval notions of geography which he took from Esdras, Marco Polo and Ptolemy, Columbus didn't know that he and his crewmen were the first Europeans to set foot in South America. In his journal of the third voyage, he concluded that the earth was not round "but that it is the shape of a pear which is everywhere very round, except where the stalk is, for there it is very prominent...and on [the top of the world] is placed something like a woman's nipple...."[21] Then, based on his observation of the massive flow of fresh water from the Orinoco, the Admiral arrived at the astonishing conclusion that he was near the Biblical "earthly paradise," the Garden of Eden.

Some scholars claim Columbus' alleged discovery of an "earthly paradise" was, at worst, the raving of a madman or, at best, reflected a mind clouded by medieval theology.[22] More likely, with his expertise in self-delusion and his instinct for grabbing the slightest evidence to prove his point, he convinced himself that God was giving him hints that he was close to the Garden of Eden. More practically, he knew it would please the pious Queen to know that the Garden of Eden might reside in her new realms. After this miraculous "discovery," the Admiral sighted on the North Star and conned his vessels into port at Santo Domingo on August 31, 1498. When he arrived, Columbus was sick, worn out. The jabbing pains of arthritis had kept him awake at nights and his grey-blue eyes remained perpetually red and tired after years of squinting into the sun's glare off the Ocean Sea.

When the Admiral went ashore he found that, under the governorship of his brother Bartholomew, the colony had disintegrated during his two-year absence. The Indians rebelled against the high Spanish taxes, payable in gold or cotton cloth. Failure to pay the exorbitant levies was punished with lashes or a death sentence. While the Indians strained under the Spanish yoke, seventy disaffected Spaniards organized the first American revolution, and set up a separate state some one hundred miles to the west of Santo Domingo.[23] Harking back to the ecstasy of their Moorish heritage, the rebels surrounded themselves with harems of native women and sometimes forced them to lay nude on beds of flowers during ritual love ceremonies.

After Columbus' return to Santo Domingo, the anarchy and bloodshed continued. As Columbus always did when faced with adversity, he became more secretive, keeping his counsel and revealing only what he thought the men needed to know. The Admiral secluded himself to escape the tedium governance and the sneers of his surly subordinates. He withdrew into a closed circle that included only his two brothers and a few trusted friends. Outside this circle, the Spanish "sons of somebody" balked at the orders issued in grating Genoese accents by the trio of low-born foreigners. If the Spaniards refused to comply with the Columbus brothers' orders, the brothers "were always quick to torture, hang and behead.... [T]hey behaved like enemies of the King and Queen."[24]

When news of the chaos in the colony leaked back to Isabel and Ferdinand, they sent Francisco de Bobadilla to Santo Domingo to investigate what they now perceived as a hopeless administration which could not discipline either Indians or Spaniards. Bobadilla, a nobleman who served as a knight of the Calatrava military order, stepped ashore in August, 1500, to be greeted by the bodies of two Spaniards swinging from Santo Domingo's gallows. After the stern Old Christian surveyed the anarchy, he arrested Columbus, clapped the Admiral of the Ocean Sea in chains like a common criminal and shipped him and his brothers back to Spain.

Shortly after Columbus landed at Cadiz in October, 1500, he went to Seville to be with old friends who would lend a sympathetic ear. Humiliated, he wrote a scathing letter to Dona Juana de Torres, a governess of Prince John and a confidante of the Queen. The letter poignantly reveals his bitterness:

> "It is now seventeen years since I came to serve these princes with the Enterprise of the Indies; they made me pass eight of them in discussion, and at the end rejected it as a thing of jest. None the less I persisted....Over there [the New World] I have placed under their sovereignty more land than there is in Africa and Europe....I, by the divine will, made that conquest. At a time when I was entitled to expect rewards and retirement, I was [unjustly] arrested and sent home loaded with chains, to my great dishonor....The accusation was brought out of malice, on the basis of charges made by civilians who had revolted and wished to take possession of the land....By whom and where would this be considered just? I have lost in this enterprise my youth, my proper share in these things, and my honor.... I beg [you Dona Juana]...to read all my papers, and to consider how I, who came from so far to serve these princes,...now at the end of my days have been [cheated] of my honor and my property without cause.... If I had stolen the Indies and given them to the Moors, I could not have met with more enmity in Spain."[25]

Even though Franciso de Bobadilla's chains weighed him down, Columbus remained dramatically defiant. To mark

Bobadilla's degradation of his person, he refused to take off the chains. "I have been placed in chains by order of the Sovereigns," Columbus said, "and I shall wear them until the Sovereigns themselves should order them removed."[26] On December 17, 1500, royal pages ushered the Admiral and Viceroy into the throne room of the Alhambra in Granada. Rather than trying to shame the Sovereigns as he did in his letter to Juana de Torres, Columbus humbled himself; breaking into tears and kissing the royal couples' hands. Was the magic still there?

Supposedly, the Queen cried at the sight of the dejected man kneeling before her, his face framed by a mane of white hair and beard. Isabel was courteous, gracious as usual. She listened sympathetically to his tale, consoled him and restored his property to him. As to whether he should continue to govern the Viceroyalty, the Sovereigns evaded the issue and made no commitment regarding Columbus' power to rule. Because the Sovereigns side stepped the issue, Columbus sensed that the mystical attraction between him and Isabel had weakened.

When Columbus detected Isabel's disapproval of his executive abilities, he knew he was lost "for in truth she, more than the King ever [did], favored and defended him, and so the Admiral trusted especially in her."[27] Columbus was only the first of many Spanish administrators to fail. "The deterioration of the South American Continent over subsequent centuries may be put down to two factors," Bradford says. "[The] inefficient Spanish colonial administration and the ministrations of a Church so rigid that...it never made any attempt to understand the nature of man in a different area of the world. Many Spanish prelates...were as proud and power-conscious as any of the worst Popes of Rome."[28]

After the meeting, the Sovereigns paid little attention to their beached Admiral, occupying themselves with the Italian wars and the marriage of Princess Catherine of Aragon to the English princes. "There is always something going on here [at court] that puts everything else in the back-ground," Columbus wrote to a trusted friend. "The Princess [Catherine] left this morning, so perhaps now something will be done about the Indies."[29] The months dragged by until, in September, 1501, Isabel and Ferdinand issued an order naming Nicolas de Ovando governor of Hispaniola. Now, Columbus knew for certain that the Sovereigns believed that he was incapable of administering his lands and vassals in the New World.

Although the royal order stripped him of the right to govern, Columbus still retained his titles of Admiral and Viceroy and his right to receive his income as stipulated in the Capitulations. He could have retired to a life of relative ease in his dotage, surrounded by his sons and old friends to nurse the arthritis that sapped his strength. Men of little vision would have quit. But, at age fifty, the old lion decided to make one last charge. He would return to the sea, where he excelled, which invigorated his imagination. He would return to the work at which he was a master, discovery.

To restore his dignity, and to give himself one last chance to win back all of his rights and privileges, the Admiral proposed a fourth voyage. After his return from the third voyage, Columbus was sick, depressed and confused. He became even more irascible and his mind wandered off in bitter tirades against Bobadilla, Fray Buil, Margarit and his other enemies. But, with his mind focused on the fourth voyage, the obsessive side of his nature took control.

Columbus pulled out all the stops. The bourgeois businessman side of his character came to the fore, and he launched a promotional barrage to sell his plan to Isabel and Ferdinand. He drafted and redrafted a prospectus he felt would please the Sovereigns. He badgered friends at court to batter down Isabel and Ferdinand's wall of indifference. He wrote to Alexander VI, pleading with the Spanish Pope to intercede with the Sovereigns on his behalf. He wrote a letter to the royal couple on the art of navigation to remind them of his skills. To appeal to the Queen's piety, he compiled what he called *The Book of Prophecies*, listing every passage in the Bible which even remotely related to a Divine prediction supporting his great enterprise.

Columbus was back in his element, wheeling and dealing to promote one last glorious trip across the Ocean Sea. He called it *El Alto Viaje* (The Ultimate Voyage).[30] Unlike the second and third voyages, *El Alto Viaje* would not be geared for colonization, pacification or conversion. It would have a single purpose—discovery. Isabel now clearly understood the strengths and the flaws of her Admiral. In the Queen's judgment, Columbus was inept at handling details and managing men, and she knew that he hated the drudgery of administration. What she had was a man of action; an explorer and a discoverer.

After months of negotiation, Isabel and Ferdinand accepted the plan. The agreement between the crown and Columbus strictly limited *El Alto Viaje* to the discovery of islands and continents. The Sovereigns' instructions only authorized him to take formal possession and report back if he discovered new lands. Isabel and Ferdinand's orders also prohibited the Admiral from stopping at Santo Domingo on the outbound trip, and stipulated that he could not capture Indians for the slave trade.[31]

Columbus signed a new will, and, in command of a fleet of four caravels crewed by one hundred fifty men, left Cadiz on May 11, 1502.[32] For this trip, the Admiral, always suspicious of people he didn't know, packed the caravels with trusted friends and family; his fifteen-year-old illegitimate son Ferdinand, his brother Bartholomew, his loyal servant Diego Tristan, his friend Diego Mendez, several compatriots from Genoa and a number of shipmates from previous voyages. The caravels, swift shallow-draft vessels designed for exploration, arrived at the island of Martinique on June 15, 1502.

Despite the Sovereigns' prohibition on his docking at Santo Domingo, Columbus tried to enter the port to take on fresh provisions and repair his vessels. When Governor Ovando refused his request, Columbus pointed his four caravels west, and landed on the coast of Honduras in early August, 1502. Even though Governor Ovando forced him to stand offshore and his arthritis pains continued to nag him, *El Alto Viaje* began with the Admiral at his optimistic best, stubbornly convinced that he and God would redeem his former glory.

Columbus was still convinced that Cuba was an appendage of Asia, and that, if he sailed due west of Hispaniola, he would find the strait to the Indies. "With a last spurt of imagination Columbus [thought] that, if he could discover this passage, he could sail around the globe and return to Spain from the East."[33] The Admiral was so certain that *El Alto Viaje* would meet with success, he carried with him a letter of introduction he persuaded Isabel and Ferdinand to write to Vasco da Gama, the Portuguese sailor who made the trip around Africa to Calcutta and back to Lisbon in 1498-99, and who had left on a second voyage to India earlier in 1502. But *El Alto Viaje* became a voyage of disaster.

Of the one hundred-fifty men who sailed from Cadiz, about thirty-five never returned, the victims of drowning, disease or skirmishes with the Indians. The four caravels weathered several major hurricanes, but the pounding sea took its toll on ropes, sails and men.[34] During one of the storms, Columbus wrote, "For nine days I was lost, without hope of life....[I was] in a sea turned to blood, boiling as a cauldron on a mighty fire....[The sky] blazed like a furnace, and the lightening darted forth in such flashes that I wondered...whether it had destroyed my masts and sails....[I]t cannot be said that it rained, but rather that there was a second universal deluge. The crews were already so broken in spirit that they longed for death...."[35]

The fleet cruised the Honduran, Nicaraguan, Costa Rican and Panamanian coasts, with the tall Admiral on the sterncastle of his flagship vainly looking for the strait he was sure would lead him to the Indies. All he found were mosquito infested swamps, impenetrable jungles and mostly hostile natives. The ships had been at sea for months without beaching for recaulking to protect them against seaworms. An onslaught of sea worms forced the Admiral to abandon one of the caravels, and the three remaining "ships [were] rotten, worm-eaten, all full of holes."

Columbus was sick with arthritis and malaria, and the illness and hardship of the voyage numbed the fifty-one-year-old Admiral's mind. He began hearing voices. "I was...on [a] dangerous coast, utterly alone, in a high fever and in a state of great exhaustion," Columbus wrote. "Hope of escape was dead.... Exhausted, I fell asleep, groaning. I heard a very compassionate voice saying: 'O fool [who is] slow to believe and to serve thy God, the God of all!'...I heard all this as if I were in a trance...."[36]

Sick and depressed, Columbus, for one of the few times in his life, gave up. The elements and his old man's body had beaten him. *El Alto Viaje* was a failure. On Easter, 1503, the three crippled caravels left the Panamanian coast. The Admiral intended to sail directly to Santo Domingo, but the leaking hulls of his ships forced him to put into port in Cuba, where he abandoned a second caravel. Again he put out to sea, but the wooden planks were "riddled with [more] holes than a honeycomb, and the crews were spiritless and despairing," Columbus said. "With three pumps, pots and kettles, and with all hands working, they could not keep out the water which came into the ships, and there was no...remedy for the havoc which the worm had wrought."[37]

On June 22, 1503, the sinking caravels made port at St. Ann's Bay in Jamaica. The Admiral ordered the useless caravels run aground to serve as housing until, by the Divine will, they were rescued.[38] Marooned, the survivors stayed in Jamaica for just over a year, when two caravels from Santo Domingo liberated them from their island prison on June 28, 1504. After recuperating in Santo Domingo, Columbus returned to Spain, arriving on November 7, 1504. Less than three weeks later, Queen Isabel, Columbus' protector and patroness, died.

Ferdinand, mired in a struggle with the supporters of Philip the Handsome and Joan the Demented to retain his right to rule Spain, ignored the Admiral. From his sickbed in Seville, Columbus bombarded his friends at court with letters asking them to intercede with Ferdinand to restore his full rights and privileges. Amerigo Vespucci, who was in Seville, carried one of those letters to court. "He [Vespucci] is a very honorable man and always desirous of pleasing me," Columbus said of the man who cheated him out of part of his glory.

On May 20, 1506, at age fifty-four, the Admiral of the Ocean Sea died in Valladolid.[39] His legacy: The Stone Age pre-Columbian world of the Americas was forever altered; and the minds and imaginations of post-Columbian Europeans were forever expanded. Christopher Columbus discovered a "New World" by accident, and, by accident, his discovery made Europe a "New World."[40]

BIBLIOGRAPHY

Barber, Richard, *The Knight and Chivalry*, Harper and Row, New York, 1970.

Bendiner, Elmer, *The Rise and Fall of Paradise*, G. P. Putnam's Sons, New York, 1983.

Bennassar, Bartolome, *The Spanish Character*, University of California Press, Berkeley, 1979.

Boorstin, Daniel J., *The Discoverers*, Random House, New York, 1983.

Bradford, Ernle, *Christopher Columbus,* Viking Press, New York, 1973.

Braudel, Fernand, *The Perspective of the World*, Vol. 3, Harper & Row, New York, 1984.

Cardini, Franco, *Europe 1492*, Facts on File, New York, 1989.

Castro, Americo, *The Spaniards*, University of California Press, Berkeley, 1971.

Castro, Americo, *The Structure of Spanish History,* Princeton University Press, New Jersey, 1954.

Cohen, J. M., *The Four Voyages of Christopher Columbus,* The Cresset Library, London, 1988.

Crow, John A., *Spain, The Root and the Flower,* University of California Press, Berkeley, 1985.

de Madariaga, Salvador, *Spain, A Modern History*, Frederick A. Praeger, New York, 1963.

Dickens, A. G. (editor), *The Courts of Europe 1400-1800*, Greenwich House, New York, 1984.

Duby, Georges, *The Chivalrous Society*, University of California Press, Berkeley, 1977.

Durant, Will, *The Story of Civilization,* Part IV, Part V, Part VI, Simon and Schuster, New York, 1950.

Elliott, J. H., *Imperial Spain, 1469-1716*, St. Martin's Press, New York, 1964.

Fernandez-Armesto, Filipe, *Ferdinand and Isabella*, Dorset Press, New York, 1975.

Fraser, Antonia, *The Warrior Queens*, Alfred A. Knopf, New York, 1989.

Fuson, Robert H., *The Log of Christopher Columbus*, International Marine Publishing Co., Camden, Maine, 1987.

Gibbon, Edward, *The Rise and Fall of the Roman Empire,* Dell Publishing Co., New York, 1963.

Granzotto, Gianni, *Christopher Columbus, The Dream and the Obsession,* Collins, London, 1986.

Hare, Christopher, *The Queen of Queens and the Making of Spain,* Charles Scribner's Sons, New York, 1906.

Hillgarth, J. N., *The Spanish Kingdoms 1250-1516,* Clarendon Press, Oxford, 1978.

Hole, Edwyn. *Andalus; Spain under the Muslims,* Robert Hale Ltd., London, 1958.

Hooper, John, *The Spaniards, A Portrait of the New Spain,* Penguin, London, 1987.

Jane, Cecil, *The Four Voyages of Columbus,* Dover Publications, Inc., New York, 1988.

Jane, Cecil, *The Journal of Christopher Columbus,* Bonanza Books, New York, 1960.

Kamen, Henry, *Inquisition and Society in Spain,* Indiana University Press, Bloomington, 1985.

Kamen, Henry, *Spain, 1469-1714, A Society in Conflict,* Longman, London and New York, 1983.

La Souchere, Elena de, *An Explanation of Spain,* Random House, New York, 1964.

Lloyd, Alan, *The Spanish Centuries,* Doubleday, New York, 1968.

Lunenfeld, Marvin, *The Council of the Santa Hermandad*, University of Miami Press, Coral Gables, 1970.

Machiavelli, Niccolo, *The Prince*, P. F. Collier & Son, New York, 1910.

Mariejol, Jean Hippolyte, *The Spain of Ferdinand and Isabella,* Rutgers University Press, New Brunswick, N.J., 1961.

McEvedy, Colin, *Atlas of Medieval History*, Penguin Books, Harmondsworth, Middlesex, 1961.

McKendrick, Melveena, *Concise History of Spain*, American Heritage, New York, 1972.

Michener, James A., *Iberia, Spanish Travels and Reflections,* Random House, New York, 1968.

Morison, Samuel Eliot, *The Admiral of the Ocean Sea,* Little, Brown and Co., Boston, 1942.

Painter, Sidney, *Medieval Society,* Cornell University Press, Ithaca, New York 1951.

Peters, Edward, *Inquisition*, University of California Press, Berkeley, 1989.

Pitt-Rivers, J. A., *The People of the Sierra,* University of Chicago Press, Chicago, 1961.

Plunkett, Ierne L., *Isabel of Castile,* G. P. Putnam's Sons, New York, 1915.

Posse, Abel, *The Dogs of Paradise*, Atheneum, New York, 1989.

Prescott, William H., *Ferdinand and Isabella*, J. B. Lippincott & Co., Philadelphia, 1881.

Rienits, Rex and Thea, *The Voyages of Columbus,* Crescent Books, New York, 1989.

Roth, Cecil, *The Spanish Inquisition*, W. W. Norton & Co, New York, 1964.

Rybczynsski, Witold, *Home,* Viking Penguin Inc., New York, 1986.

Sale, Kirkpatrick, *The Conquest of Paradise*, Alfred A. Knopf, New York, 1990.

Smith, Bradley, *Spain, A History in Art,* Doubleday, (No date).

Smith, Rhea Marsh, *Spain, A Modern History,* University of Michigan Press, Ann Arbor, 1965.

Spitz, Lewis W., *The Renaissance and Reformation Movements,* Rand McNally, Chicago, 1971.

Taviani, Paolo Emilio, *Christopher Columbus, The Grand Design*, Orbis, London, 1985.

Tuchman, Barbara W., *A Distant Mirror,* Ballantine Books, New York, 1978.

Tuchman, Barbara W., *The March of Folly*, Alfred A. Knopf, New York, 1984

Virgil, *The Aeneid,* Vintage Books, New York, 1990.

Webb, Walter Prescott, *The Great Frontier*, Houghton Mifflin Company, Boston, 1951.

Footnotes

Isabel, Ferdinand; The Early Years

[1] Crow, John A., *Spain, The Root and the Flower*, p. 34. The compiler of the Spanish songs was Alfonso de Baena, a converted Jew *(converso)*.

[2] Prescott, William H., *Ferdinand and Isabella*, Vol. II, p. 109.

[3] As was common at the time, mothers and daughters had the same name. In the text, references to Isabella mean Isabel's mother.

[4] Michener, James, *Iberia*, p. 106.

[5] Prescott, William H., *Ferdinand and Isabella*, Vol. I, p. 124.

[6] Plunkett, Ierne L., *Isabel of Castile*, p. 22.

[7] Hare, Christopher, *The Queen of Queens and the Making of Spain*, p. 57.

[8] Ibid., p. 194. Some of the beautifully bound volumes Isabel collected still exist in the library at the Escorial.

[9] Some scholars argue that Isabel did not learn Latin until she was in her twenties, and that she learned to read and write it within a few years thereafter. However, her life was filled with activity and it seems doubtful she could make herself fluent in Latin while running Spain at the same time. At the very least, she must have learned rudimentary Latin as a girl. See Mariejol, Jean, *The Spain of Ferdinand and Isabella*, p. 308.

[10] There are several versions of the Battle of Covadonga. Some historians believe that it was only a minor skirmish between Christians and Moors, not a major battle. But, by Isabel's time, the battle was surrounded by myth and legend.

[11] Lloyd, Alan, *The Spanish Centuries*, p. 50.

[12] Crow, John A., *Spain, The Root and the Flower*, p. 91.

[13] Prescott, William H., *Ferdinand and Isabella*, Vol. I, p. 167. As in most

inflationary times, people borrowed all the money they could, knowing they would have to pay back in depreciated currency.

[14] Plunkett, Ierne L., *Isabel of Castile*, p. 28-29.

[15] Hernando Pulgar lived from 1430 to 1491 and served as secretary and official court historian of Ferdinand and Isabel. Isabel designated Pulgar the court historian in 1482. His *Cronica de los Reyes Catolicos* is a major source for events occurring during the royal couple's reign.

[16] Prescott, William H., *Ferdinand and Isabella*, Vol. I, p. 165.

[17] Plunkett, Ierne L., *Isabel of Castile*, p. 32.

[18] Ibid., p. 57.

[19] Prescott, William H., *Ferdinand and Isabella*, Vol. I, p. 189.

[20] Ibid., Vol. I, p. 195. Isabel's chaplain, Alonso de Coca, visited both the Duke of Guienne and Ferdinand and made the reports .

[21] Prince Charles of Aragon was betrothed to Isabel of Castile as part of John of Aragon's plan to unite the two kingdoms.

[22] Taviani, Paolo, *Christopher Columbus*, p. 489.

Chapter 2: The Road to Succession

[1] Prescott, William H., *Ferdinand and Isabella*, Vol. I, p. 228.

[2] Plunkett, Ierne L., *Isabel of Castile*, p. 89. Segovia's historian, Colmenares, says that Ferdinand was twenty-two, but he was actually twenty-three.

[3] *Ibid.* p. 92.

[4] Prescott, William H., *Ferdinand and Isabella*, Vol. I, p. 251.

[5] Lunenfeld, Marvin, *The Council of the Santa Hermandad*, p. 76.

[6] Prescott, William H., *Ferdinand and Isabella*, Vol. I, p. 265. King Alfonso's letter is quoted.

[7] The portion of the treaty dividing up the Atlantic Ocean would remain a source of dispute between the two countries for years.

Chapter 3: Tightening the Grip

[1] Crow, John A., *Spain, The Root and the Flower*, p. 127. The sections of Crow's book dealing with the cities is the most sprightly written with regard to the "feel" of a medieval Castilian city, and many of the shorter quotes herein are from Crow.

[2] Louis Mumford's article entitled "The Medieval Town," appeared in *Horizon Magazine* , July, 1961, and is quoted by Crow, p. 130.

[3] Crow, John A., *Spain, The Root and the Flower*, p. 70.

[4] Smith, Bradley, *Spain, A History in Art*, devotes a chapter to medieval Castilian music and illustrates the chapter with pictures of the musical instruments.

[5] Cardini, Franco, *Europe 1492*, p. 202, quotes Mandeville, and has illustrations of the imagined monsters.

[6] Like governments of any age, after the kings got their citizens to move into the towns and cities, they raised taxes.

[7] Mariejol, Jean, *The Spain of Ferdinand and Isabella*, p. 288.

[8] Lloyd, Alan, *The Spanish Centuries*, makes constant mention of Isabel's graciousness.

[9] Hare, Christopher, *The Queen of Queens, and the Making of Spain*, p. 2. Peter Martyr, an Italian scholar who tutored the royal children and wrote a substantial history of the Sovereigns' reign, is quoted.

[10] A recent effort to canonize Isabel met with failure when Pope John Paul refused to elevate her to sainthood. Her harsh treatment of Jews and Moors came back to haunt her five hundred years later.

[11] Jane, Cecil, *The Four Voyages of Columbus*, Vol. II, p. lix. Jane's analysis of Isabel's personality is well reasoned.

[12] Taviani, Paulo, *Christopher Columbus*, p. 195.

[13] Kamen, Henry, *Spain, 1469-1714*, p. 60, quotes the Admiral of Castile.

[14] Governmental corruption is still endemic in Latin America.

[15] Mariejol, Jean, *The Spain of Ferdinand and Isabella*, p. 169.

Chapter 4: Columbus, 1451-1476

[1] The portly merchant ships were generically called *naos*.

[2] Taviani, Paolo, *Christopher Columbus*, p. 20, and Morison, S. E, *The Admiral of the Ocean Sea*, p. 7, both agree that Columbus was born between late August and late October of 1451 in Genoa, although Taviani, p. 233, says there may be a case for establishing his birth somewhere between 1450 and 1452. One writer, Fuson, Robert H., *The Log of Christopher Columbus*, p. 13, says some authors have placed the date of birth as early as 1435 and as late as 1460. Some writers and scholars claim that Columbus was born in places as disparate as France, other parts of Italy, Spain, Greece, England, Chios, Armenia, Corsica, Switzerland,Germany, Majorca and Portugal. Taviani, p. 231, provides a bibliography of the "legends and fantasies" about the place of Columbus' birth and notes that the Spanish historian, A. Ballesteros Beretta, after 80 pages of discussion, concludes that "no one can cast the least shadow of doubt" that Columbus was born in Genoa. In his will, Columbus wrote "...from it (Genoa) I came and in it I was born." Some scholars claim that Columbus was Jewish (see Taviani, p. 253 for a discussion). He may have had Jewish ancestors, as many people did, but this seems irrelevant, since Columbus was an extraordinarily pious Christian, and lived his life as such. Since Columbus was a private citizen from a lower middle class family, there is very little in writing about his early years. This is not unusual, since almost everyone was illiterate, and the period (the 1450s onward) was an "oral" one. With the sketchy information available, scholars have had a field day dissecting and analyzing every shred of evidence, sometimes twisting logic to the extreme to make their point and find their place in the annals of academia by proving a new theory. With detective work that would please Scotland Yard, these ambitious scholars, eager to make their mark among their peers, carp over the minutia of Columbus' life with glee. Their writings are filled with "maybe," "probably" and "possibly," but they plow ahead with their theories. In the late 1800s, some revisionist Columbus scholars, led by Henry Vignaud, began writing of Columbus as an obsessive madman. One of the latest books, *The Conquest of Paradise*, by Kirkpatrick Sale, uses Columbus as a metaphor for the transference of all of Europe's evils to the New World. This black portrait of Columbus, as well as those that show Columbus as a demigod, are both incomplete and inaccurate. Sale is perhaps the most guilty, presenting hypotheses and sly innuendos as facts, so that he can sustain his flawed thesis that

Columbus was the man who brought almost nothing but Europe's vileness to the Garden of Eden inhabited by the noble savages of the New World. Admittedly, there are only about twenty documents shedding any direct, hard light on Columbus' early life, and much of the information regarding this period comes from things Columbus said as an older man or as hearsay (somebody saying what Columbus said to them), but, rather than engage in an academic diatribe (except in this footnote), the author has chosen to tell the Columbus story as he believes it to be logical, taking into account Columbus' character and statements and the available pieces of evidence. The author agrees with Cecil Jane's comment in *The Four Voyages of Columbus*, p. xxix, that "All that concerns the origin and early life of Columbus is enveloped in a cloud of obscurity so dense that it appears to be little possible that it will ever be dissipated." However, the author believes that Columbus was born in 1451, was Genoan and was not Jewish. He also believes that Columbus probably did not go to Tunisia in the service of Rene d' Anjou, and that Columbus did go to Chios, England, Iceland, the Canaries, the Azores, West Africa, Madeira and the Cape Verde Islands. The reader should know that many scholars agree.

[3] Rienits, Rex and Thea, *The Voyages of Columbus*, p. 14.

[4] Bradford, Ernle, *Christopher Columbus*, p. 11.

[5] Diego's Italian name was Giacomo, but it was changed to Diego when he joined Christopher in Spain. Bartholomew's Italian name was Bartolomeo. Christopher's Italian name was Cristoforo. Since the Colombos married in 1445 and Christopher was not born until 1451, it is possible that other children were born during that six year span, but, if so, died in childbirth or as infants. There is no evidence that there were other children.

[6] Susanna Colombo is mentioned in only three documents.

[7] Taviani, Paolo, *Christopher Columbus*, p. 25. Taviani has written the most comprehensive and detailed modern account of Columbus' early life.

[8] All exchanges of property were recorded in notarial deeds which served as a form of public registry of property for the conveyance of titles.

[9] Christopher's mother, Susanna, died sometime between 1474 and 1483.

[10] Morison, S. E., *The Admiral of the Ocean Sea*, p. 14. Granzotto, Gianni, *Christopher Columbus*, p. 25, argues that the relationship between father and son was not good because there is no correspondence between them.

[11] Venice had an armed navy to protect its sea-lanes.

[12] Taviani, Paolo, *Christopher Columbus*, p. 315.

[13] Bradford, Ernle, *Christopher Columbus*, p. 12, tells the St. Christopher legend in detail. Colombo was a fairly common name in Italy at the time. In 1492, one Vincenzo Colombo, no relation to Christopher, was executed as a pirate on Genoa's docks. The name means dove. Columbus is the Latinized form of the name and is used in the English speaking world. When Columbus went to Spain he "Spanishized" his name to Colon, in the same way that many immigrants to the U.S. Anglicized their names.

[14] Granzotto, Gianni, *Christopher Columbus*, p. 2. The colony was called Pera.

[15] *Ibid.*, p. 2.

[16] Taviani, Paolo, *Christopher Columbus*, p. 314-315. The Genoese was Guglielmo Embriaco, who was nicknamed "The Hammerhead." The First Crusade took place in 1101.

[17] The Genoese were also under heavy pressure from their chief rivals for the eastern trade, the Venetians.

[18] Taviani, Paolo, *Christopher Columbus,* p. 34. Somewhat more poetically, Morison, S. E., *The Admiral of the Ocean Sea,* p. 16, writes that Genoa "bathes her breasts in the sea, and spreads her arms to embrace it."

[19] The comment was made in a letter, dated about 1501. See Morison, S. E., *The Admiral of the Ocean Sea,* p. 18, for another translation of the letter.

[20] The house claimed to be that of Columbus in Genoa now has five stories, but may have had only two or three during Columbus' time.

[21] There were no explosives and the cost of marble, chipped out of the mountains by hand, was high. Bricks were cheap.

[22] A young boy Columbus may have run across another famous explorer, John Cabot, who was born in Genoa one year before Columbus in 1450.

[23] Morison, S. E., *Christopher Columbus*, p. 15, tells the story of one Genoese who, when giving testimony in a trial in Rome as late as 1910, needed a translator.

[24] Boorstin, Daniel, *The Discoverers,* p. 224.

[25] Taviani, Paolo, *Christopher Columbus,* p. 72, discounts the Prester John part of the story as "pure supposition."

[26] Granzotto, Gianni, *Christopher Columbus,* p. 24. Jane, Cecil, *The Four Voyages of Columbus*, Vol. I, p. lxxxi argues that Columbus was illiterate when he left Genoa.

[27] In a biography of his father, Ferdinand Columbus wrote that his father attended the University of Pavia. Scholars completely discount this claim. Taviani argues that, perhaps, Columbus attended the weaver's guild school in the Vicolo di Pavia in Genoa, and that Ferdinand Columbus made a mistake.

[28] In 1470 the Colombo family moved to Savona a few miles west of Genoa. There Columbus met Michele da Cuneo, who later went on the second voyage to the New World.

[29] Scholars debate exactly when Columbus first went to sea. In a letter to Ferdinand and Isabel, Columbus said he went to sea at age ten. Bradford thinks the trip to Chios could have taken place at any time between 1470 and 1478. There are no documents between 1474 and 1483 regarding the Colombo family, and there is no document saying exactly when Christopher first went to sea. There is even doubt whether Columbus ever went to Chios, but the author, and most other scholars, believe that he did, and that he went in 1474, although a Genoese fleet went to Chios in 1475 and Columbus could have been on that trip. Granzotto, Gianni, *Christopher Columbus*, p. 26, claims that Columbus went to Chios in 1473 on a ship named the Roxana, but cites no evidence to support the claim. In his writings, Columbus refers several times to his visit to Chios, but does not give an exact date.

[30] Columbus' name does not appear in the manifest of the Genoese convoys that went to Chios in 1474-1475, so scholars speculate that he was an ordinary seaman or a merchant, whose name would not have been on the lists. The records of some ships that went to Chios during that period show unnamed weavers were aboard.

[31] Today, Chios is a Greek island.

[32] These monopoly corporations were similar to the English trading companies, such as the East India Company, which were chartered to exploit

the riches of a particular area.

[33] Jane, Cecil, *The Four Voyages of Columbus,* Vol. II, p. lxxiii.

[34] Corsairs were an accepted institution at the time, with almost legal status. Pirates, on the other hand, were not sanctioned by any government, and kept everything they stole for themselves.

[35] Granzotto, Gianni, *Christopher Columbus,* p. 28, argues that it makes no sense that Columbus was a captain of a corsair in the early 1470s and that, when he went to Chios in 1474, he was not even listed on the manifest as an officer or able-bodied seaman. In a 1495 letter, Columbus claims that, in one night's sailing, he would have covered 180 nautical miles, and both Morison and Granzotto say this couldn't have happened in the ships of the day.

Chapter 5: Columbus, 1476-1484

[1] Columbus' name does not appear on the manifest as a seaman. The capacity in which he went on the trip is not known for sure, but it is possible that he was a representative of the Spinola or Di Negro families from Genoa, who were allied with the Fregoso party and with whom Columbus' father may have put him in contract for a job.

[2] On some maps of the day, Cape St. Vincent was marked as "Finisterre," the end of the world.

[3] Taviani, Paolo, *Christopher Columbus*, p. 286, discusses the different arguments regarding the incident. It is not certain whether four or five corsairs sank. Some writers claim that Columbus was not aboard the Genoese ship but, somehow, inexplicably, was part of the crew of one of the corsairs. Some scholars claim the incident never took place and was a fabrication by Columbus or his biographers to make his life more dramatic. It is believed that the biographer, Las Casas, gave a correct description of the battle, but that Columbus' son, Ferdinand, incorrectly described a battle in 1485 which took place off the coast from Lisbon. Most scholars believe that Columbus was aboard the Bechalla, a ship which was flying the Flemish flag. At the time, Genoa was allied with France and the fleet had a letter of safe conduct from King Louis XI, and, theoretically, was immune from attack by the French-Portuguese corsairs. But, with the Bechalla flying the Flemish flag, the corsairs used this as an excuse to attack. The commander of the corsairs was Guillaume de Casenove, sometimes known as Coulon or Coulomb. That the battle took place is not in doubt, as it is mentioned in several documents.

[4] The Portuguese Parliament petitioned the King to throw out the Genoese in 1481 for stealing trade secrets, but business espionage was common practice all during the period Portugal was expanding its trade routes.

[5] Bradford, Ernle, *Christopher Columbus,* p. 33. There are two theories as to the legend of Prester John. One is that, in present-day Ethiopia, a Christian king ruled, and that tales of this king trickled across the Sahara Desert. Another, which Marco Polo endorsed, is that Prester John was an oriental Khan who was converted to Christianity and lived near the Great Wall of China.

[6] Boorstin, Daniel, *The Discoverers,* discusses Prince Henry the Navigator beginning at p. 156.

[7] Taviani, Paolo, p. 300. Prince Henry may not have personally moved permanently to Sagres until 1433, but the exact date is not known. Organiza-

tional efforts at Sagres did begin as early as 1419 or 1420.

[8] Prince Henry's brother Pedro collected many books for him, including *Il Milione* by Marco Polo.

[9] Boorstin, Daniel, *The Discoverers*, p. 162. The Catalan Jew was Jehuda Cresques, the son of another famous cartographer, Abraham Cresques.

[10] The Madeira Islands were shown on a Genoese map published in 1351, and may have been discovered by the Carthagenians. The Canary Islands were known to the Phoenicians, Greeks and Romans. Fourth century coins made in Carthage have been found in the Azores. Other "discoveries" by Prince Henry's crews may not have been new, but, by his time, most of the ancient discoveries were known only as legends.

[11] Bojador, a Portuguese word, means "Bulging ."

[12] Gomes Eanes de Zurara, as quoted in Boorstin, Daniel, *The Discoverers*, pp. 166-167, and Morison, S. E., *The Admiral of the Ocean Sea*, p. 30.

[13] Columbus made the annotation regarding Ireland in his copy of *History of Memorable Things that have happened in my time* by the author-Pope, Pius II. Whether Columbus went to England, Ireland and Iceland is debated by some scholars, but most, citing quotations like the one set forth above, and other evidence, believe that Columbus visited these three places.

[14] Boorstin, Daniel, *The Discoverers*, p. 103. The mapmakers were not sure where St. Brendan's Island was, but they uniformly put it on their charts. The famous map drawn by Martin Benheim in 1492 located the island near the equator, but some maps located it west of Ireland and others located it near what is now the West Indies. The mythical island showed up on a map made as late as 1759.

[15] The quotation of Columbus' comments on Iceland is a compilation of those used by Taviani, Paolo, *Christopher Columbus*, p. 82, and Morison, S. E., *The Admiral of the Ocean Sea*, p. 24. The author believes the compilation is more easily understood than a strict quote from either source. The original of Columbus' memoirs was lost, but the quote survived in his son Ferdinand's biography of his father. Scholars have used this quote to argue that Columbus never went to Iceland or Ireland because there are several mistakes. For example, the tides in Iceland do not rise and fall 26 fathoms, but only about eight fathoms. Also, Iceland is between about 64 and 66 degrees north, not 73 degrees as Columbus incorrectly claimed. Some scholars jump on the fact that Columbus says that the sea was not frozen, which, they say, was probably incorrect, but one scholar, F. Mangnusen, asserts that the winter of 1477 was very mild. Further, Columbus may have been wrong about the month in which he claims he visited Iceland. Most trips from Bristol to Iceland were made in the spring or autumn when the seas were calmer. Some scholars use these mistakes to prove their case that, in general, much of what has come down about Columbus is a fraud to make him look more heroic. See Taviani, p. 81 et seq. and p. 318 et seq., for an exhaustive discussion of the issues, and very logical explanations as to why the mistakes were made. Taviani and a string of other scholars believe that Columbus made the trip to Ireland and Iceland.

[16] Boorstin, Daniel, *The Discoverers*, p. 205 et seq, tells the Viking story in detail.

[17] Prince Henry nominated Perestrello to the governorship, but his post was confirmed by the King. Moniz was Felipa's mother's family name. As

with many women of the day, little is known about Felipa. The author hopes the reader will forgive the footnotes disclaiming precise knowledge of a place, date or event involving Columbus' early life. But the reader may be assured that the lack of data is equally frustrating to a historian. For five hundred years scholars and writers have investigated and debated every corner of Columbus' life, and, as mentioned in a prior footnote, the author has chosen what appears to him to be the most logical version of the various alternatives. One further scholarly debate involves the date of Columbus and Felipa's marriage. The spectrum ranges from 1476 to 1485, but the author believes that the marriage took place in September or October of 1479. Taviani, Paolo, *Christopher Columbus*, who has done the most masterful job of pulling together, sorting out and reaching conclusions regarding Columbus' early life, discusses the marriage possibilities beginning at p. 101.

[18] As an older man, Columbus seems to have convinced himself that there was noble blood in his lineage, and his son Ferdinand perpetuated the idea in his biography of his father.

[19] At that time, scholars and laymen alike had only a fuzzy notion of India, the Indies, the Orient, China and Japan, and often used the terms interchangeably. The 1474 letter was written to a priest, Fernao Martins, who was a confidant of King Alfonso, and who later became a cardinal.

[20] The actual distance from the Canaries to Japan is about 10,600 miles on a straight line. Most writers in Columbus' day referred to Japan as Cipangu, and China as Cathay.

[21] Granzotto, Gianni, *Christopher Columbus*, p. 57.

[22] The Toscanelli quotes from the 1474 letter are from Taviani, Paolo, *Christopher Columbus*, pp. 159-160. The quote from Toscanelli's first letter to Columbus is from Morison, p. 64. The quote from Toscanelli's second letter to Columbus is from Taviani, p. 162-163. The Latin text written by Columbus was discovered in 1860 in Seville. It differed from the text of the Toscanelli letter quoted by Ferdinand Columbus and Las Casas in their biographies of Christopher Columbus. Some scholars used the differences to argue that the Toscanelli correspondence was a fraud or a fake. Most scholars, however, accept the Toscanelli correspondence as real, and ascribe the differences to bad transcriptions or translations. Another issue which is debated by scholars is when Columbus actually saw the first Toscanelli letter and map. The best evidence seems to be that Columbus got it some time in 1480. See Morison, S. E., *The Admiral of the Ocean Sea*, p. 63, Granzotto, Gianni, *Christopher Columbus*, p. 56, and Taviani, Paolo, *Christopher Columbus*, p. 403, for discussions of the Toscanelli correspondence. It is not certain whether Columbus copied in Latin the original of the 1474 letter or the duplicate Toscanelli sent him later.

[23] Exactly when Columbus learned to read and write Latin, Castilian and Portuguese is not known. Castilian was spoken by many Portuguese aristocrats at the time Columbus lived in Lisbon. Even when Columbus wrote in Castilian, he sometimes used Portuguese spellings of words.

[24] The meeting with King John may have taken place in 1485. There is no transcript of the conversation(s) between Columbus and King John, but historian Joao de Barros discusses the conversation(s) in general terms. See Footnote 27 below. However, historians, Columbus' contemporary biogra-

phers and Columbus' later writings and annotations discuss the arguments which Columbus had formulated to prove his case. Rather than leave these arguments out of the text because we do not know precisely what Columbus and King John said, the author believes that it is more important that the reader understand the issues which Columbus confronted and the rebuttals and evidence he used. For example, it is known that cloves were thought to be a cure for the Black Death, and were a meat preservative. Years later, Columbus wrote that he believed that King John knew more about discovery than anyone else. Further, it is difficult to believe that an intense, insistent man like Columbus would not have mentioned to the King the dead bodies which had washed ashore in the Azores and the other stories which Columbus had in his arsenal of "proof." Columbus, a sincere Christian, would surely have pointed out that his trip would spread the Catholic religion. There is substantial scholarly controversy over the exact rewards Columbus demanded of King John. Columbus' biographer, Las Casas, lists the demands made on King John, which are substantial, and which are almost the same demands he later made on Isabel and Ferdinand. Using this, some scholars argue that Las Casas' list was not correct and is, incorrectly, a restatement of Columbus' requests for riches and titles from the Spanish Sovereigns.

[25] Jane, Cecil, *The Four Voyages of Columbus,* p. lii-liii.

[26] The Portuguese captain was Diogo Cao.

[27] The Portuguese historian was Joao de Barros who Taviani and Morison call "the Portuguese Livy." Barros wrote *Decades of Asia* between 1539 and 1552, and discussed the negotiations between King John and Columbus. This quote is a mixture of the translations used by Morison and Taviani.

[28] Granzotto, Gianni, *Christopher Columbus,* p. 58, quoting a letter written by Columbus years later to King Ferdinand. See Taviani, Paolo, *Christopher Columbus,* p. 428, for a slightly different version of the quote.

[29] The three-man committee was made up of the Bishop of Ceuta, and two Jewish scientists, Jose Vizinho and a Master Rodrigo. The Bishop of Cueta was once the confessor of La Beltraneja. Vizinho was a well-known and respected astronomer and cosmographer. Master Rodrigo was the court physician and an expert in astronomy and cosmography.

[30] Rienits, Rex and Thea, *The Voyages of Columbus*, p. 21. Some writers say Felipa died in 1483. An additional reason for Columbus' despondency, some scholars claim, was that King John, using information he got from Columbus, granted a Portuguese group headed by Fernao Dulmo and Joao Estreito the right to sail west. This supposed treachery made Columbus furious, and was an added incentive for him to leave Portugal and go to Spain. But, since Columbus maintained a friendly relationship with King John after he left Portugal, and because many of the details related to the voyage by Dulmo and Estreito are unclear (the trip didn't take place until 1487, two or three years after Columbus left Lisbon), the author discounts this explanation of why Columbus left Portugal.

Chapter 6: Columbus, The Spanish Years

[1] The scholars' estimates of when Columbus went to Spain range from 1484 to 1486. Most scholars believe that Columbus went in 1485, although

there is debate over the time of year he went.

[2] Taviani, Paolo, *Christopher Columbus*, p. 430. Columbus' fear of King John detaining him may have been real. If Columbus stole the 1474 Toscanelli map and letter, and if he had it on his person, there would have been reason for fear. King John may not have wanted Columbus to take his expertise to rivals in other countries. Another theory is that Columbus was afraid King John would arrest him because he learned secret information on his trip to St. George of the Mines. One theory holds that Columbus fled his creditors, and was forced to leave in secret. Yet another theory is that the Moniz family, the maternal line of Columbus' wife Felipa, were allied with the Braganza faction which unsuccessfully tried to unseat King John, and, therefore, Columbus was tainted. On the other hand, in 1488 King John wrote Columbus a friendly letter, and did not arrest him after his return from the first voyage in 1493. It should be noted that Las Casas' biography is highly favorable to Columbus, and, therefore, many scholars question at least portions of its credibility.

[3] There is much scholarly debate as to whether Columbus first went to La Rabida on the day he arrived or whether he went to the town of Huelva where Felipa's relatives lived.

[4] Taviani, Paolo, *Christopher Columbus*, p. 169. Some authors claim that Columbus told Marchena of his theories only in the secrecy of the confessional, but this is doubtful because a discussion of the subject would have required several days of discourse.

[5] Columbus' statement was an exaggeration, which was not unusual for Columbus, because many other Spaniards bought in to Columbus' ideas.

[6] Morison, S.E., *The Admiral of the Ocean Sea,* p. 80. There is a great deal of historical confusion about whether Father Perez was at La Rabida when Columbus first went there or whether Columbus met him later. It is disputed whether Marchena was at La Rabida when Columbus first arrived or whether they met later. Until fairly recently, some scholars thought Father Perez was Father Marchena. Prescott, William H., *Ferdinand and Isabella*, Vol II, p. 119, treats Perez and Marchena as the same person. Father Perez was an advocate for Columbus and helped him substantially through the years.

[7] Some scholars believe that Columbus went to Huelva first, and then to La Rabida.

[8] Muliart's name is sometimes spelled Muliantes, Muliar, Molyart or Molyarte. He is generally believed to have been Flemish, and Granzotto, Gianni, *Christopher Columbus*, p. 63, states that his original Flemish name was Muller. Granzotto says that another of Felipa's relatives, Pedro Correa, lived in Huelva. Correa married Felipa's half-sister, the daughter of an earlier wife of Bartolomeo Perestrello, Felipa's father. Unfortunately, Granzotto does not cite any evidence to support his argument that Correa lived in Huelva. It is not clear whether Columbus left his son Diego in the care of Muliart or the Franciscans at La Rabida or in the care of Muliart who then turned Diego over to the Franciscans for schooling.

[9] The Duke of Medina Sidonia was Don Enrique de Guzman, the scion of the Guzman family. Most scholars, including Morison, S. E., *The Admiral of the Ocean Sea*, p. 82, agree that Columbus approached Medina Sidonia in 1486, but Taviani, Paolo, *Christopher Columbus*, p. 479, seems to imply that Columbus did not approach the Duke until 1488 or 1489.

[10] Don Luis de la Cerda, who was later made a duke in 1491.

[11] Taviani, Paolo, *Christopher Columbus*, p. 171, espouses another theory of how Columbus approached Isabel. Under Spanish law, Taviani says, Columbus had the right to petition directly to the throne, and he did so. Supposedly, Father Marchena was Columbus' advisor with respect to his legal rights. The author has found no other source supporting this argument.

[12] Plunkett, Ierne L., *Isabel of Castile*, p. 295.

[13] There is academic debate over whether Columbus met the Sovereigns on January 20, 1486 or later in the year.

[14] Granzotto, Gianni, *Christopher Columbus*, p. 73, quotes Andres Bernaldez, who wrote *The History of the Catholic Kings*, and who was a historian and a friend of Columbus.

[15] Bradford, Ernle, *Christopher Columbus*, p. 65, quotes Las Casas.

[16] After the War of Granada ended, Talavera was appointed Archbishop of Granada.

[17] The Treaty of Alcacovas served as the peace treaty between Portugal and Spain after Ferdinand and Isabel defeated King Alfonso and La Beltraneja.

[18] The committee met at different times over several years, and it is believed that the cast of characters may have changed from time to time. Rather than take the reader through the speculation and conjecture, about which there are few facts, as to when and where the commission met, the author has chosen to treat it as a single body and, with few exceptions, has not tried to distinguish the dates upon which it met. Jane, Cecil, *The Four Voyages of Columbus*, Vol. II, p. xv, outlines the argument put forward by Las Casas, and followed by many scholars, that the royal committee treated Columbus harshly because they "were unwilling to hear and that they were intellectually incapable of understanding the case...[they were] victims of their own preconceived ideas...[and were] ignorant and obstinate...."Cecil Jane, however, makes the case that both Talavera and Maldonado were learned, tolerant men of great wisdom.

[19] Bradford, Ernle, *Christopher Columbus*, p. 66, believes that Columbus did not produce the Toscanelli map.

[20] *Ibid.* p. 66 and Morison, S. E., *The Admiral of the Ocean Sea*, p. 88, quote testimony testimony given in 1515 by Dr. Rodrigo Maldonado. Maldonado was the Governor of Salamanca and was a member of of the commission. Also, Diego de Deza may have served on the commission.

[21] See Taviani, Paolo, *Christopher Columbus*, p. 193, regarding Columbus' sources of support.

[22] Isabel attended the wedding of one of Cardinal Mendoza's illegitimate children. Jane, Cecil, *The Four Voyages of Columbus*, Vol. II, p. xxvi, describes the moral attitudes at the time.

[23] Beatriz Enriquez de Harana's life, like that of most medieval women, is shadowy. Very little is known about her. Therefore, writers have had an open playing field to speculate on the reasons Columbus did not marry her. Some feel that Columbus never married Beatriz because she was too low born for the man who received the noble title of Admiral of the Ocean Sea. Another theory is that Columbus was carrying on an affair with Beatriz de Bobadilla, Isabel's friend, and Columbus did not want to make Bobadilla mad and lose a good contact. Taviani, Paolo, *Christopher Columbus*, p. 188, argues that Spanish

law prevented Columbus from marrying Beatriz after he became a nobleman with the title of Admiral of the Ocean Sea. Some speculate that Beatriz was a noblewoman, others a chambermaid and others a barmaid in a tavern. Some biographers invented a marriage with Beatriz, but there is no evidence to prove it, and, in fact, there are several legal documents which mention Beatriz, but never as the wife of Columbus.

[24] The instruction to Diego was not in the main body of Columbus' will, but in a codicil, an amendment, to his will. The quote is a compilation of those by Morison, S. E., *The Admiral of the Ocean Sea*, p. 84, and Granzotto, Gianni, *Christopher Columbus*, p. 75. Morison says the codicil to Columbus' will was written in 1506, but Granzotto says it was 1505. See Taviani, Paolo, *Christopher Columbus*, p. 287, for a slightly different version of the quote.

[25] There are rumors, but no proof, that Columbus had an affair with Beatriz de Bobadilla, the Marquisa de Moya. Similar stories, which are false, hold that Columbus may have had an affair with Isabel.

[26] Hare, Christopher, *The Queen of Queens and the Making of Spain*, p. 239. The chamberlain was Juan Cabrero.

[27] Taviani, Paolo, Christopher Columbus, p. 480. The quote is from Gonzalo Fernandez de Oviedo, author of *The General and Natural History of the Indies*. Oviedo, a nobleman who was about fifteen when Columbus made his first voyage, wrote his history in the early 1500s.

[28] Las Casas is quoted by Morison, S. E., *The Admiral of the Ocean Sea*, p. 88.

[29] Hare, Christopher, *The Queen of Queens and the Making of Spain*, p. 239. If, in fact, Columbus went to Spain in 1484, then he would have suffered for eight years until 1492. But the author believes that Columbus did not go to Spain until 1485. Columbus was frequently inaccurate in stating when certain things happened.

[30] Jane, Cecil, *The Four Voyages of Columbus*, in his Introduction to Vol. II, makes a strong argument that the royal committee and the Sovereigns did not give Columbus a definite answer, and may have never told him the results of the committee's deliberations. Jane's analysis is interesting because he takes into account the personality of the Sovereigns and Columbus and the intellectual climate of the time to reach his conclusions.

Chapter 7: The Aristocracy

[1] Prescott, William H., *Ferdinand and Isabella*, Vol I, p. 234.

[2] Mariejol, Jean, *The Spain of Ferdinand and Isabella*, p. 229.

[3] Prescott, William H., *Ferdinand and Isabella*, Vol. I, p. 164.

[4] Lloyd, Alan, *The Spanish Centuries*, p. 58.

[5] Kamen, Henry, *Spain 1469-1714*, p. 22.

[6] Lope de Vega wrote years later, but clearly expressed the thinking during the Sovereigns' time.

[7] Michener, James, *Iberia*, p. 423. The building was a palace when Isabel was born, and was later converted to a convent.

[8] Several of the authors noted in this chapter give varying estimates of the wealth of certain noblemen. Although the estimates vary somewhat, they are all very high.

[9] Mariejol, Jean, *The Spain of Ferdinand and Isabella*, p. 270, lists the

most noble families, the titles they held and the year in which they were awarded. The Duke of Medina Sidonia was the leader of the Guzman family clan. Normally, noble families had one leader who held the highest title, Duke, while other members of a clan held lesser titles, such as Count or Marquis. Families also networked their sons into high posts in the Church, military orders and government, creating a web of ties throughout Spain.

[10] Prescott, William H., *Ferdinand and Isabella*, Vol. I, p. 302.

[11] Pedro de Mendoza held several Church posts, but for clarity's sake he is herein referred to as Cardinal Mendoza or the Primate of Spain.

[12] These loans were called *censos*.

[13] This same scorn for trade and business existed during the reign of the Sovereigns, and before.

[14] Elliott, J.H., *Imperial Spain*, p. 22.

[15] Prescott, William H., *Ferdinand and Isabella*, Vol. I, p. 492 at footnote 32. Gonzalo Fernandez de Oviedo, the royal chronicler of the Indies, wrote this report of the Duke of the Infantado's splendor at the battle of Illora. Oviedo is a major source of information for the Sovereigns' reign.

[16] Isabel later appointed Talavera Archbishop of Granada. The "Talavera commission," which he chaired, investigated Christopher Columbus' evidence supporting his rationale for a voyage across the Atlantic Ocean.

[17] Mariejol, Jean, *The Spain of Ferdinand and Isabella*, p. 245.

[18] Bennassar, Bartolome, *The Spanish Character*, p. 170 et seq, comments in detail on the Spanish love of luxury.

[19] Elliott, J. H., *Imperial Spain*, p. 171.

[20] Bennassar, Bartolome, *The Spanish Character*, p. 103 et seq, and Mariejol, Jean *The Spain of Ferdinand and Isabella*, p. 231. Both discuss the relationships between masters and servants.

[21] Many of these objects are on display in the medieval section of the Metropolitan Museum of Art in New York. The chapel described in the succeeding paragraph has been set up in the Metropolitan.

[22] Smith, Bradley, *Spain, A History in Art*, p. 86 et seq.

[23] Mariejol, Jean, *The Spain of Ferdinand and Isabella*, , p. 308.

[24] Kamen, Henry, *Spain 1469-1714*, p. 58.

Chapter 8: Chivalry

[1] Bennassar, Bartolome, *The Spanish Character*, p. 213. The quote is from the *Siete Partidas*.

[2] Barber, Richard, *The Knight and Chivalry*, p. 339 et seq.

[3] Bennassar, Bartolome, *The Spanish Character*, p. 178 . The trial took place in 1530, but adultery by a woman met with the same harshness in the late 1400s.

[4] Mariejol, Jean, *The Spain of Ferdinand and Isabella*, p. 235.

[5] The concept of "machismo," extreme maleness, still exists in many Spanish and Hispanic men.

[6] Bennassar, Bartolome, *The Spanish Character*, p. 92.

[7] Today in Mexico a vile thing is a *desmadre*, and men still come to blows over crude references to one's mother.

[8] Barber, Richard, *The Knight and Chivalry*, p. 181. The knight's name has come down in English as Philip Boyle in a book written by Viscount Dillon

in 1900. Since the challenge was issued in England in the 1400s, his Spanish name has been lost.

Chapter 9: The Holy Brotherhood

[1] In Spanish the Holy Brotherhood's name is *Santa Hermandad.* Despite the religious connotation of the name, the Holy Brotherhood was a police force.

[2] Lunenfeld, Marvin, *The Council of the Santa Hermandad,* p. 92. Lunenfeld's book is the best source on the Holy Brotherhood.

[3] The Holy Brotherhood's headquarters in Toledo has been preserved much in the same state it existed during the reign of Ferdinand and Isabel.

[4] Mariejol, Jean , *The Spain of Ferdinand and Isabella,* p. 23. The court physician was Francisco Lopez de Villalobos.

[5] *Ibid.*, p. 22.

[6] Prescott, William H., *Ferdinand and Isabella,* Vol. I, p. 277, says the Brotherhood's jurisdiction extended to villages with less than one hundred residents. But, Lunenfeld, Marvin, *The Council of the Santa Hermandad,* p. 31, says that it was less than fifty residents.

[7] Lunenfeld, Marvin, *The Council of the Santa Hermandad,* Chapter 2, discusses the restructuring of the Brotherhood in detail.

[8] Elliott, J.H., *Imperial Spain,* p. 75.

[9] Ordinary citizens, taxpayers, were called *pecheros.*

[10] Other new crimes over which the Brotherhood would have jurisdiction, included usurpation of tax gathering, private imprisonment without the order of a judge for more than twenty-four hours and attacks on Brotherhood officials.

[11] Lunenfeld, Marvin, *The Council of the Santa Hermandad,* p. 38. The quote is from Alonso Palencia's *Cronica Enrique IV* .

[12] Prescott, William H., *Ferdinand and Isabella* , Vol. I, p. 283.

[13] Lunenfeld, Marvin, *The Council of the Santa Hermandad,* p. 73.

Chapter 10: Justice, The Royal Council

[1] Mariejol, Jean, *The Spain of Ferdinand and Isabella,* p. 177-178.

[2] Kamen, Henry, *Spain 1469-1714,* p. 29 et seq.

[3] Medieval Castilians' penchant for litigation still exists in some countries, notably the United States of America.

[4] Prescott, William H., *Ferdinand and Isabella,* Vol I, p. 292.

[5] Mariejol, Prescott, Elliott and Kamen each devote chapters to the workings of the Royal Council.

[6] Elliott, J. H., *Imperial Spain,* p. 80.

[7] Antonio de Nebrija lived from 1446 to 1536 and observed the entire reign of Isabel and Ferdinand. He was a humanist and grammarian, and reformed the teaching of Latin in Spain and authored the first Castilian grammar book.

Chapter 11: The Military Orders

[1] Prescott, William H. , *Ferdinand and Isabella,* Vol. I, p. 307, at footnote 36.

[2] Bennassar, Bartolome, *The Spanish Character,* p. 81.

[3] The legends of Santiago vary from author to author. This version is a compilation of the stories told by Crow, Michener, Lloyd, Smith and Prescott.

[4] Crow, John A., *Spain, The Root and the Flower,* p. 84. It is not certain

that the Battle of Clavijo took place.

[5] *Ibid.*, p. 85-6. There are other stories regarding the origin of the cockleshell as the symbol of Santiago.

[6] Mariejol, Jean, *The Spain of Ferdinand and Isabella*, p. 228.

[7] Michener, James, *Iberia*, p. 721.

[8] Elliott, J. H., *Imperial Spain*, p. 77 regarding income; and Mariejol, Jean, *The Spain of Ferdinand and Isabella*, p. 271 regarding the number of vassals. These estimates appear to have been made about 1523, a few years after Ferdinand and Isabel's reign, but they reflect the magnitude of the wealth of the military orders. Elliott expresses the amounts of income in ducats, but the author has converted these into maravedis at the rate of 375 maravedis to one ducat in order to be consistent with all other references herein to Castilian currency.

[9] Little in-depth research has been done regarding the military orders, and, therefore, accounts of who and how they were controlled are sketchy. Since the military orders were an integral part of Castilian society, an investigation into their affairs would make a fascinating study.

[10] Mariejol, Jean, *The Spain of Ferdinand and Isabella*, p. 155. There is some argument that the Royal Council of the military orders was not established until the later reign of Charles V.

[11] *Ibid.*, p. 269.

Chapter 12: The Beginning

[1] Crow, John A., *Spain, The Root and the Flower*, p. 24. This date is not precise, and other authors assign different time periods to the Stone Age drawings at Altamira.

[2] Lloyd, Alan, *The Spanish Centuries*, p. 35.

[3] Crow, John A., *Spain, The Root and the Flower*, p. 28, quoting the Roman poet Horace.

[4] Virgil, *The Aeneid*, Book VI, p. 190, written during the reign of the Emperor Augustus.

[5] Smith, Bradley, *Spain, a History in Art*, p. 47.

[6] He built Hadrian's wall in England.

[7] Gibbon, Edward, *The Rise and Fall of the Roman Empire*, p. 71.

[8] Hadrian sent forty thousand Jews from the tribe of Judah and ten thousand from the tribe of Benjamin to Spain. See Hole, Edwin, *Andalus; Spain under the Muslims*, p. 21

[9] St. Vincent was actually executed in the Roman city of Saguntum which is near the present day site of Valencia.

[10] The other two Germanic tribes were the Alans and the Suevis.

[11] Hole, Edwyn, *Andalus, Spain Under the Muslims*, p. 19. There is some dispute over the etymology of the name.

[12] McKendrick, Melveena, *Concise History of Spain*, p. 21.

[13] Numerous histories, songs and poems, including a poem by Sir Walter Scott, tell varying stories of the rape and Roderick's defeat.

[14] Crow, John A., *Spain, The Root and the Flower*, p. 43, footnote 17.

[15] The number of Muslim soldiers is disputed, and may have been as high as twelve thousand.

[16] National Geographic, Vol. 174, No. 1, July 1988, p. 92.

[17] Crow, John A., *Spain, The Root and the Flower*., p. 42. So says the Spanish "*General Chronicle*", published in the 1200s, in an attempt to explain

the reasons their Christian ancestors capitulated with almost no resistance.

[18] Prescott, William H., *Ferdinand and Isabella,* Vol. I p. 376, footnote 2.

[19] Bendiner, Elmer, *The Rise and Fall of Paradise,* p. 46.

[20] Crow, John A., *Spain, The Root and the Flower,* p. 48.

[21] Berbers, Syrians and true Arabs fought with one another.

[22] This was to become the symbol of the Ommayad dynasty in Al Andalus.

[23] Emirs were viceroys who owed allegiance to the Caliph of Damascus (or Baghdad when the capital was moved). Caliphs were emperors. Neither Rahman I nor his successors had the temerity to declare themselves Caliphs of Al Andalus until many years later.

[24] Melveena McKendrick,*Concise History of Spain,* p. 31.

[25] The King of Aragon captured Valencia and incorporated it into his kingdom. The other areas mentioned were incorporated into Castile. Castile and Aragon were united during the reign of Ferdinand and Isabel.

[26] James Michener, *Iberia* , p. 172.

[27] One of Spain's most prominent scholars, Americo Castro, in *Spain in Its History: Christians, Moors and Jews,* and other writings, argues the case that the Arabs had a strong influence on Spain. However, Claudio Sanchez Albornoz, in *Spain: An Historical Enigma,* believes that the Islamic heritage was not decisive with respect to Spain's character.

[28] Although much of the Muslims greatness in Spain occurred while Cordoba was the capital, their influence continued while Seville and Granada were the capitals of Arab Spain. Rather than try to distinguish between the times or places in or at which a particular bit of Arab influence was introduced to the Peninsula in the text, the author has chosen to present the following material in such a way that it gives an overall picture of Muslim contributions and accomplishments without regard to the tedium of dates or cities, except where necessary.

[29] The exact figures quoted in this paragraph are debated by scholars, but the author has included the above estimates to give the reader a general idea of the size and magnificence of Cordoba in the 900s.

[30] Some scholars believe there were only thirteen hundred columns.

[31] Crow, John, A., *Spain, The Root and the Flower,* p. 61.

[32] Ibid. p. 33.

[33] A Jewish doctor restored the sight of Ferdinand's father, King John of Aragon.

[34] Born 1126, died 1189.

[35] Born 1135, died 1204.

[36] de Madariaga, Salvador, *Spain, A Modern History,* p. 17.

[37] Almost all Spanish words beginning with "al" or ending with "i" are of Arabic origin.

[38] Hole, Edwyn, *Andalus; Spain under the Muslims,* p. 106-7.

[39] Ibid., p. 105.

[40] Ibid., p. 116.

[41] Bendiner, Elmer, *The Rise and Fall of Paradise*, p. 212 et. seq. One Jew, Hasdai ibn Shaprut, became the "viceroy of the Jews" under Caliphs Rahman III and Hakam II. "His most casual look might make or break a poet or rabbi...and, on occasion, [his influence] could set a militia in motion."

[42] Crow, John A., *Spain, The Root and the Flower,* p. 82.

[43] Ibid., p. 111. Ferdinand, Queen Isabel's husband, had Jewish blood.

[44] Lloyd, Alan, *The Spanish Centuries,* p. 18

[45] McKendrick, Melveena, *Concise History of Spain,* p. 63.

[46] See Webb, Walter Prescott , *The Great Plains* and *The Great Frontier*, for a discussion of the effect of the frontier on the mentality of Americans. Webb was heavily influenced by the American historian, Frederick Jackson Turner, who developed the theory in the early 1900s. The parallels and differences between the Spanish frontier and the American frontier would be the subject of an interesting book.

[47] Some historians, including Americo Castro, argue that the Spanish disinclination toward manual labor came from the early Christians' disdain of Moors and Jews who worked with their hands for a living. Since work was the task of the conquered castes, the Spanish felt that work was not an index of essential worth, as was the making of war.

[48] Spain's two greatest modern historians, Americo Castro and Claudio Sanchez Albornoz, disagree as to the magnitude of the Arab effect on Spanish history, but both agree with regard to the impact of the Reconquest. Castro says the Reconquest "was a loom on which the history of Spain was warped." His antagonist, Sanchez Albornoz, says "I consider the Reconquest the key to the history of Spain...."

[49] The importance of the Castilian Parliament (Cortes) should not be overemphasized. It had the right to approve taxes and budgets, but the king usually had the final word.

Chapter 13: The War of Granada, The Early Years

[1] Lloyd, Alan, *The Spanish Centuries* p. 6-7.

[2] Prescott, William H., *Ferdinand and Isabella,* Vol. I , p. 385-6, footnote 26. Some scholars have other arguments as to the derivation of the name Granada.

[3] Smith, Bradley, *Spain, A History in Art,* p. 98-99. The African tribesmen were called the Benimerines.

[4] Prescott, William H., *Ferdinand and Isabella,* Vol. I, p. 390, footnote 30.

[5] Kamen, Henry, *Spain, 1468-1714,* p. 32, says there were only five hundred thousand residents of the Kingdom of Granada. Other authors claim there were three to four million Granadians.

[6] The exact number of battle towers at the city of Granada and troops in the Kingdom Granada is disputed by scholars, but the estimates set forth in the text give the reader a reasonable idea of the magnitude.

[7] Hillgarth, J.N., *The Spanish Kingdoms,* p. 370.

[8] Known also as Abu-l-Hasan and Mulay Hassan.

[9] In 1476.

[10] Hare, Christopher, *The Queen of Queens and the Making of Spain,* p. 114; and Ierne Plunkett, *Isabel of Castile,* p. 162. Their translations vary slightly.

[11] The name Alhama comes from the Arabic word *hammam,* baths, and the town was a watering hole for aristocratic Arabs.

[12] Moorish writers claim that the Spaniards massacred all of Alhama's townsmen.

[13] See Prescott's descriptions of this, and other, battles. Using contempo-

rary accounts of the various battles, Prescott provides the most stirring versions of the fighting between Spaniards and Muslims. His book was originally written in 1840, but is still an excellent "read" with respect to the drama of battle and some of the men involved in those battles.

[14] Saroya was originally a Christian captive named Isabel de Solis. After her capture by the Moors she took the name Saroya, meaning "morning star" or "light of the morning." Hare, Christopher, *A Queen of Queens*, p. 129. Her name is sometimes spelled Zoraya. There is some confusion among scholars as to whether Saroya was the name of the young slave girl who Abul Hacen fell in love with or of the older mother of Boabdil.

[15] His official name was Muhammed XII, but his nickname was Boabdil, or sometimes "El Chico" to distinguish him from his uncle of the same name, who was nicknamed El Zagal.

[16] Arabic for "the Valiant" or "the Bold."

[17] Abul Hacen and El Zagal had defeated the Spanish at Antequera earlier in 1483 and their popularity was substantially enhanced by the victory.

[18] Some accounts say that it was the Mingozalez River.

[19] Hillgarth, J. N., *The Spanish Kingdoms* , p. 381.

[20] The chaplain, Alonzo de Coca, was sent to Aragon to report on Ferdinand's suitability as a mate for Isabel.

[21] Quintilian was a Spaniard who went to Rome in the first century A.D. and became a leading rhetorician and thinker on education.

[22] Jane, Cecil, *The Four Voyages of Columbus*, Book II, p. xxxiv.

[23] Machiavelli, Niccolo, *The Prince*, p. 75 et. seq.

[24] Hare, Christopher, *The Queen of Queens and the Making of Spain*, p. 152.

[25] Hillgarth, J. N. , *The Spanish Kingdoms*, p. 368.

[26] *Ibid.*, p. 371.

[27] Crow, John A., *Spain, the Root and the Flower*, p. 128.

[28] The Papal Bull was renewed in subsequent years, including a Bull by Pope Innocent VIII in 1485.

[29] Lloyd, Alan, *The Spanish Centuries*, p. 17-8.

[30] Hillgarth, J. N., *The Spanish Kingdoms*, p. 372.

[31] Mariejol, Jean, *The Spain of Ferdinand and Isabella*, p. 270.

[32] Hillgarth, J. N., *The Spanish Kingdoms*, p. 376. Plunkett, Ierne L, *Isabel of Castile*, p. 193 says that lombards could fire 140 shots per day.

[33] Mariejol, Jean, *The Spain of Ferdinand and Isabella*, p. 202.

[34] *Ibid.*, p. 203, quoting Amador de los Rios.

[35] Plunkett, Ierne, *Isabel of Castile*, p. 195.

[36] Kamen, Henry , *Spain 1469-1714*, p. 34 and Prescott, William H., *Ferdinand and Isabella, Vol II*, p. 60-61.

[37] Hillgarth, J. N., *The Spanish Kingdoms*, p. 378. In 1483, the cities furnished 1,700 horse and 12,000 foot soldiers. In 1489, the nobles furnished about 7500 horse and some 5,800 foot soldiers.

[38] Lunenfeld, Marvin , *The Council of the Santa Hermandad*, p. 78. The ten thousand figure is for 1490.

[39] *Ibid.*, p. 44.

[40] Hillgarth,J. N., *The Spanish Kingdoms*, p. 378. This occurred during the latter part of the War of Granada.

[41] Kamen, Henry, *Spain 1469-1714*, p. 34.

[42] The troops from royal lands, the Holy Brotherhood, the military orders

and mercenaries were under the direct command of Ferdinand.

[43] Mariejol, Jean, *The Spain of Ferdinand and Isabella,* p. 197.

[44] Plunkett, Ierne L, *Isabel of Castile,* p. 195.

[45] Hillgarth, J. N., *The Spanish Kingdoms,* p. 380. The estimated cost of the entire war was eight hundred million maravedis. The cost of cereals for the siege of Baza was eighty million maravedis.

Chapter 14: The War of Granada, The Final Push

[1] Smith, Bradley, *Spain, A History in Art,* p. 124. Other scholars have different numbers of horsemen and foot soldiers.

[2] At that time a seaport, but now land locked.

[3] Hare, Christopher, *The Queen of Queens and the Making of Spain,* p. 173.

[4] Also known as Hamet el Zegri.

[5] Lloyd, Alan, *The Spanish Centuries,* p. 14, argues that the naval blockade was Isabel's idea.

[6] Prescott, William H., *Ferdinand and Isabella,* Vol II, at p. 23.

[7] *Ibid.,* Vol. II, p. 28. Some estimates run as high as ninety thousand men. Lloyd, Alan, *The Spanish Centuries,* p. 16, says there were seventy thousand men. See Hillgarth, J. N., *The Spanish Kingdoms,* p. 375-376 for perhaps the most up to date estimates of troop strength during 1482-1492.

[8] Taviani, Paolo, *Christopher Columbus,* p. 483 says that it was not a prisoner, but a Muslim agent sent to assassinate Ferdinand and Isabel. Lloyd, Alan, *The Spanish Centuries,* p. 16, says the Moor was a Moorish fanatic who got into the Spanish camp under the guise of wanting to wish the Sovereigns well. Plunkett, Ierne L., *Isabel of Castile,* p. 211-213, confirms the story that the assassin was a Muslim fanatic named "El Gerbi."

[9] Plunkett, Ierne L., *Isabel of Castile,* p. 214. The commander Ferdinand sent was the Chief Commander of Leon, Don Gutierrez de Cardenas.

[10] Prescott, William H., *Ferdinand and Isabella,* Vol. II, p. 30. Fernando de Pulgar was appointed the official court historian in 1482. He was also a private secretary to the Sovereigns.

[11] *Ibid.,* Vol. II, p. 38, footnote 28.

[12] And, evidently, Isabel's also. Some apologists claim that it was Isabel who resisted the pleas of her clergy to put all the Malagans to the sword.

[13] See Mariejol, Jean, *The Spain of Ferdinand and Isabella,* p. 193, for a description of the soldiers commanded by various Grand Masters of themilitary orders and by noblemen. Some estimates credit the Spanish army with only 53,000 troops.

[14] Gonzalo Fernandez de Cordoba did not receive the title of El Gran Capitan until later, during the Spanish wars of conquest in Italy.

[15] Also known as Cidi Yahye and Yahya an-Naiyar. Cid Hiaya later became a Christian and married one of Isabel's ladies in waiting. He was known in Spain as Don Pedro de Granada.

[16] Taviani, Paolo, *Christopher Columbus,* p. 193.

[17] Prescott, William H., *Ferdinand and Isabella,* Vol. II, p. 74.

[18] *Ibid.,* Vol. II, p. 65.

[19] *Ibid.,* Vol. II, p. 67.

[20] Plunkett, Ierne L., *Isabel of Castile,* p. 220.

[21] Elliott, J.H., *Imperial Spain,,* p. 36-7. Boabdil was also captured by the

Sovereigns in a battle at Loja in 1486, and he made similar promises to be a vassal of Ferdinand and Isabel. The 1483 treaty has been lost. Boabdil entered into a third treaty in 1487 with the Sovereigns. Between the three treaties, Boabdil made himself a tool of the Spanish. The history of El Zagal and Boabdil's mutual treachery and their alliances and disalliances with the royal couple would fill a book in itself.

[22] Hare, Christopher, *The Queen of Queens, and the Making of Spain,* p. 222. The nobleman was Musa ben Abil Gazan.

[23] Some historians claim Ferdinand had only fifty thousand men. Like almost all statistics from that period, the exact number cannot be determined with certainty. Numerical figures are set forth to give the reader an approximation of the size of the armies, and the author believes that the larger number of eighty thousand is more appropriate to defeat Granada's two hundred thousand inhabitants.

[24] Lunenfeld, Marvin, *The Council of the Santa Hermandad,* p. 78. The Sovereigns had direct control over the troops of the Holy Brotherhood, but the men furnished by nobles were not subject to the royal couple's direct commands.

[25] Called an *espingarda,* the crude weapon was little more than a wooden stock with a long barrel. These early guns were heavy and inaccurate.

[26] Kamen, Henry, *Spain 1469-1714,* p. 34.

[27] Smith, Rhea Marsh, *Spain, A Modern History,* p. 107. Fernandez de Cordoba developed many of the tactics he would use in the Italian wars during the War of Granada, learning much from Swiss mercenaries.

[28] The Holy Brotherhood militia was abolished in 1497. However, because Ferdinand had direct control over the Holy Brotherhood's soldiers during the War of Granada, he and Isabel introduced many innovations that were later adopted by Spain's armies during the wars in Italy and North Africa.

[29] Prescott, William H., *Ferdinand and Isabella,* Vol. I, p. 492, footnote 32. Gonzalo Fernandez de Oviedo, is describing the Duke of the Infantado at the battle of Illora in 1486, but the description could have applied equally to the splendor of many counts, marquis, dukes and clergymen at Granada.

[30] Lloyd, Alan, *The Spanish Centuries,* p. 7.

[31] Peter Martyr, sometimes called Pietro Martire, was one of the Prince's teachers. He was from northern Italy and studied in Rome before going to Castile.

[32] Prescott, William H., *Ferdinand and Isabella,* Vol. II, p. 95.

[33] The heir apparent, John, and his four sisters, Isabel, Joan, Maria and Catherine.

[34] Prescott, William H., *Ferdinand and Isabella,* Vol. II, p. 91. Santa Fe means Holy Faith.

[35] Plunkett, Ierne L., *Isabel of Castile,* p. 225-226.

[36] Subject to the supervision of a Spanish governor.

[37] *Ibid.,* p. 228.

[38] Hillgarth, J. N., *The Spanish Kingdoms,* p. 373.

[39] *Ibid.,* p. 388.

[40] This story regarding the place Boabdil stopped and wept may be nothing more than legend, but it is oft repeated by many historians.

[41] Prescott, William H., *Ferdinand and Isabella,* Vol. II, p. 98. Hillgarth, J., N., *The Spanish Kingdoms,* p. 390, citing two other historians, says that Boabdil died forty years later in Fez and makes no reference to Boabdil dying

in the service of another emir.

[42] Kamen, Henry, *Spain, 1469-1714,* p. 36. This immigration figure is for the 1485-1498 period.

[43] Inigo Lopez Mendoza, a member of the powerful Mendoza clan, who later became the Marquis of Mondejar.

[44] See Jane, Cecil, *The Four Voyages of Columbus,* Vol. I, pp. l-lii, for a disposition on Isabel's militant views.

Chapter 15: Columbus, The Soverigns Consent

[1] Rienits, Rex and Thea, *The Voyages of Columbus,* p. 28

[2] In his biography of his father, Ferdinand says Columbus read Ptolemy, Marinus of Type, Strabo, Ctesias, Onesicritus, Nearchus, Pliny, Alfragan, Aristotle, Averroes, Seneca, Solinus, Marco Polo, Sir John Mandeville, Peter Aliacus and Julius Capitolinus. Columbus also read d'Ailly and Piccolomini. Many of Columbus' books are at the Biblioteca Colombina in Seville.

[3] Some experts claim that Columbus did not write all of the 366 notes. Some scholars devote pages to debates over whether Columbus or his brother wrote the notes and some question whether they are fraudulent. These scholars are in the minority. See Taviani, Paolo, *Christopher Columbus,* p. 450, for a listing of the scholars who contest the margin notes, which are sometimes called "postils."

[4] Granzotto, Gianni, *Christopher Columbus,* p. 49. Throughout the sections of this chapter discussing the arguments back and forth between Columbus and his critics, the author has taken some license with respect to exactly what Columbus or his detractors may have said, rather than polluting the text with "maybe," "perhaps" or "might have." Although the exact words of the exchanges are not known, in general the arguments against the voyage and Columbus, are known.

[5] There is scholarly controversy over whether Columbus was searching specifically for the riches of China, Japan and the Spice Islands or was looking for some nebulous "islands and lands" to the west. The author believes that, without question, Columbus was seeking the riches of the lands he had read about and he did not have some vague desire to discover islands and lands which might or might not have any value. Almost all scholars agree with the author on this point.

[6] A great line by Granzotto, Gianni, *Christopher Columbus,* p. 50.

[7] The miles used are nautical miles which equal 6080 feet, whereas English miles equal 5280 feet.

[8] Marinus of Tyre was a Greek geographer who lived in the 100s, and is credited with being the first mathematical geographer. Ptolemy lived after Marinus, and refuted many of Marinus' calculations, but Columbus paid scant attention to this fact.

[9] Columbus' geographic mistakes were among the most fortunate errors in history. Had he known the true distance, in excess of ten thousand miles, he would never have attempted the voyage, and no one would have supported such a voyage. At the time, nobody knew the Americas existed.

[10] The two merchants were Fernao Dulmo and Joao Estreito. Little is known of their attempt. Since it appears that they tried to sail west from the Azores, where the winds blow predominantly from the west to the east, they failed.

[11] King John's letter is quoted in full by Taviana, Paolo, *Christopher*

Columbus, p. 476.

[12] There is no direct evidence that Columbus went to Portugal. However, Morison, S. E., *The Admiral of the Ocean Sea,* p. 75, and Rienits, Rex and Thea, *The Voyages of Columbus,* p. 32, believe that Columbus went to Lisbon in December of 1488. In a margin note to d'Ailly's *Imago Mundi* Columbus, or perhaps Bartholomew, wrote "I was present in all of this [when Bartholomew Diaz returned from his voyage to the Cape of Good Hope]."

[13] It is believed that Bartholomew went to England in February of 1488. Since King John sent his letter to Columbus in March of 1488 expressing an interest in supporting a voyage west, it is not clear why Bartholomew would have gone to England at a time when King John was, apparently, looking favorably on Columbus' proposal.

[14] Ferdinand Columbus claims the English were interested, but Oviedo says they weren't. In any event, there is no evidence that Columbus ever came close to reaching an agreement with the English. King Henry VII was a notorious cheapskate, "parsimonious" most writers say more delicately, and may have turned down the venture on economic grounds. Supposedly, in 1488, while Columbus was with the court at Murcia, he met a Spanish sailor who told him of lands to the west of Ireland that the sailor had seen. There is no proof positive that the episode took place.

[15] Ferdinand and Isabel's letter is quoted in full by Taviani, Paolo, *Christopher Columbus,* p. 192.

[16] Bartholomew Columbus remained in France until 1493 where he received word that his brother successfully made the trip west and returned.

[17] Fuson, Robert H., *The Log of Christopher Columbus,* p. 51. Columbus made this statement in the preamble to his ship's log for the first voyage, written sometime in August of 1492.

[18] It is not known whether the original Talavera commission, perhaps with different members, or a new special commission or the Royal Council finally gave the Queen and King their advice that the voyage was not feasible.

[19] Santangel was of Jewish origin, but was a *converso* who converted to the Catholic faith. He was the son of a wealthy merchant who worked his way up in the court bureaucracy. The exact wording of the exchange between Santangel and the Queen is not known, but the arguments presented in the text were all issues which would, in the author's view, have been made.

[20] Prescott, William H., *Ferdinand and Isabella,* Vol II, p. 126.

[21] The Royal Patent (*Titulo*) is quoted in part by Taviani, Paolo, *Christopher Columbus,* p. 495, and Morison, S. E., *The Admiral of the Ocean Sea,* p. 105. The Royal Patent is dated April 30, 1492. The Sovereigns also issued a Letter of Credence and three Royal Decrees on April 30, 1492, which established Columbus' credentials and authorized the outfitting of ships. The letter addressed in blank to foreign princes is quoted by Morison, p. 107. It is not known exactly when Columbus gave his full list of demands for titles and rewards to the King and Queen. Being a shrewd businessman, he may have asked for his compensation after the Sovereigns definitely approved the concept.

[22] Bradford, Ernle, *Christopher Columbus,* p. 80.

[23] Fuson, Robert, *The Log of Christopher Columbus,* p. 228. Fuson estimates that Spain received a 1,733,000 percent return on its money during the 1500s.

[24] Exactly who put up the money is not known. Nor is it known precisely how much money each investor furnished. Morison, S. E., *The Admiral of*

the Ocean Sea, p. 102, believes that Isabel offered to finance the voyage by pledging her jewels, but that she did not actually do so. The author believes that the argument that most of her jewels were already pawned for the War of Granada is more convincing.

[25] See Morison, S.E., *The Admiral of the Ocean Sea*, p. 110, for a more extensive translation of the letter to the citizens of Palos, dated April 30, 1492.

[26] The first two quotes are from testimony given in a trial in 1515 by Juan Rodriguez and Cristobal de Triana. The third quote is from a 1535 trial in which Hernando Valiente testified as a witness. The quotes are set forth in Taviani, Paolo, *Christopher Columbus*, p. 203. Columbus may have met Martin Alonso Pinzon prior to 1492 during one of his visits to Palos and La Rabida, see Morison, S. E., *The Admiral of the Ocean Sea*, p. 99, and Granzotto, Gianni, *Christopher Columbus*, p. 87.

[27] Hernando Janes de Montiel is quoted by Taviani, Paolo, *Christopher Columbus*, p. 204, and Francisco Medel at p. 205. These quotes are taken from lawsuits filed years later seeking to depreciate the importance of Columbus' role in the great enterprise and enhance the importance of the Pinzons. Therefore, some of the testimony must be taken with a grain of salt. Undoubtedly, if the Pinzons, with their reputations and prestige, had not agreed to participate in the voyage, it would have been very difficult for Columbus to recruit a full complement of men. Columbus recruited some of the crew, including his mistress Beatriz Enriquez' de Harana's cousin, Diego de Harana, who served as marshall of the fleet.

Chapter 16: Columbus, Palos to The Canaries

[1] Morison, S. E., *Admiral of the Ocean Sea*, p. 172.

[2] In old Castilian, "Y" was used instead of an "I."

[3] Most versions of the log are written in the third person, but Fuson, Robert H., *The Log of Christopher Columbus*, uses the first person. The author has chosen to follow Fuson's format. Rather than footnoting each quotation from the log and cluttering the text, the author has elected to leave out as many footnotes as possible. Generally, the reader can find the quotations easily by referring to the applicable dates. The author believes that Fuson's version of the log is the best, but readers may also refer to Jane, Cecil, *The Journal of Christopher Columbus*, and Morison, S.E. , *The Admiral of the Ocean Sea*. On occasion, the author has used portions of a particular quote from more than one source when the author felt it made the meaning more clear.

[4] Although Columbus says he will map the lands he discovered, only one map, a sketch of the northwest coast of Haiti, survives, and the authenticity of that map is questioned by some scholars.

[5] None of the three vessels has survived and, therefore, the exact specifications of the ships are not known. Several scholars have made estimates of the the ships' details, based upon information regarding caravels and merchantmen of the time.

[6] There is general agreement among scholars that the entire crew numbered between eighty-seven and ninety. However, some scholars put the number as high as 120. Fuson, Robert H., *The Log of Christopher Columbus*, p. 223 et seq discusses the crew and includes a roster of the men known or suspected to have been among the crew.

[7] Scholars and writers debate whether Columbus was truly an expert navigator. Morison believes he was among the greatest navigators who ever

lived, but others, noting that there is no proof that Columbus actually was a sea captain or pilot prior to the first voyage, express doubt as to Columbus' navigational skill and/or skills as a seaman. Although there is no direct proof that Columbus had experience in these areas, he did make many long voyages as a younger man. Because the ships of the time were so small, the captains and pilots fraternized with all aboard and, doubtless, discussed the intricacies of sailing. It is known that Columbus was a diligent student, and he may have devoted some of his studies to the art of sailing and navigation. In the log, Columbus' computations of where the fleet was located were often closer to correct that those of the other pilots and captains. Given all this, the author believes that Columbus was a fine seaman and navigator. The mere fact that he was able to go to the New World and return is, the author believes, proof that he had extraordinary skills in these areas. His feat would compare to placing a modern man on the back side of an unmapped planet and asking that man to travel thirty-two hundred miles to and from a particular point with little more than a compass to guide him.

[8] Some scholars believe that Luis de Torres also spoke Aramaic, a semitic language which became the speech of Syria, Palestine and Mesopotamia.

[9] Some Columbus-bashing scholars claim that a large percentage of the crewmen were desperate criminals, reasoning that only a man condemned to death would sign on for such a dangerous voyage. There is no factual support for this view.

[10] A few scholars have confused Gomera's governess, Beatriz Bobadilla de Peraza with Queen Isabel's best friend, Beatriz de Bobadilla, and claimed that they were the same person. However, the author's research shows that they were two different women.

[11] Abel Posse's novel is titled *The Dogs of Paradise*. Posse, a retired Argentine diplomat, won the Romulo Gallegos Prize in 1987 for the best novel written in Spanish.

Chapter 17: Columbus, The Canaries To The New World

[1] Morison, S. E., *The Admiral of the Ocean Sea*, p. 177, mentions the two Spanish gentlemen.

[2] Taviani, Paolo, *Christopher Columbus*, p. 61. Scholars debate whether Columbus made a trip to Tunis, and whether he was able to jigger the compass during that voyage.

[3] Morison, S. E., *The Admiral of the Ocean Sea*, p. 173, translates several chants, prayers and ditties.

[4] Columbus' assumption that the weeds were attached to the seabed was wrong. It is argued that Columbus wishfully thought that the sea was shallow enough for the weeds to cling to the bottom, indicating that he was near land. Scientists have later determined that the weeds in the Sargasso Sea float and have no roots to attach to the bottom of the ocean.

[5] It can be argued that Columbus' discovery of the trade winds was almost as important as his discovery of the New World. The winds and routes he discovered were used by sailing ships for centuries, until the age of steam. If the constant trade winds hadn't existed, the safest route to the Indies would have been to hug the West African coast, round the Cape of Good Hope and sail back north to India and China.

[6] Magellan carried thirty-five extra needles, but there is no record of how many Columbus carried.

[7] Taviani, Paolo, *Christopher Columbus,* p. 214.

[8] Some Columbus-bashers argue that the threats of mutiny and murder he recorded in the log were lies designed to enhance his image of bravery when faced with danger to his person.

[9] Lloyd, Alan, *The Spanish Centuries,* p. 72, quotes an unnamed person he calls a follower of the Pinzons. It appears that the quotation is from one of the later trials which attempted to discredit Columbus and build up the role played by the Pinzons, but Lloyd's text on this point is not clear.

[10] Despite his initial doubt that the light he saw indicated land, Columbus later claimed that his sighting of the "wax candle" was the first sighting of land and claimed the royal couple's ten thousand maravedis prize.

[11] The first quote is from Jane, Cecil, *The Four Voyages of Columbus,* Vol. I, p. xiv. The second quote is from Fuson, Robert H., *The Log of Christopher Columbus,* p. xiii.

Chapter 18: Columbus, The Caribbean

[1] Las Casas says the Indians were "dumbstruck" by the Spaniards beards, clothes and white skin. Granzotto, Gianni, *Christopher Columbus,* p. 143.

[2] As in earlier chapters related to Columbus, the quotes from Columbus' log are from Fuson, Morison, Jane, Granzotto and *The Journal of Christopher Columbus,* by Cecil Jane. The dates upon which Columbus wrote certain entries are those used by Fuson. However, the reader should understand that, in some instances, there is confusion as to exactly which date Columbus actually wrote an item in the log.

[3] The Indians' name for the island was Guanahani, the native word for iguana, Morison, S. E. , *Admiral of the Ocean Sea,* p. 233. There is much scholarly debate over which Bahamian island Columbus first found. Among the candidates (using their modern names) are Watlings Island (named after an English pirate, John Watlings, who used it as his headquarters), Samana Cay, the Turks and Caicos Islands (of which there are several choices), Cat Island, Mayaguana Island, Concepcion Island and Plana Cay. This list is not exhaustive. Many scholars believe that the first island found was either Samana Cay or Watlings Island. See Fuson, Robert H., *The Log of Christopher Columbus,* p. 199-208, for an excellent discussion of the various possibilities, complete with maps. There are 723 islands and cays in the Bahama Islands, and, since Columbus' description of the island he called San Salvador is somewhat general, it has left room for much scholarly investigation.

[4] The Indians belonged to the Taino culture and spoke a dialect of the Arawak language. They probably immigrated from the South American mainland to the Bahama Islands after pushing out a more primitive tribe called the Siboneys.

[5] In addition to numerous comments on the physical features of the Indians, Columbus comments at length on the flora and fauna of the islands. Some authors argue that his remarks about the lands he discovered show a poetic side of Columbus' nature, and others credit him with having an unusual sensitivity to nature, with powers of observation beyond that of most men. The author has chosen to leave out most of the comments on flora an fauna, but the interested reader can obtain a sense of Columbus' powers of observation by reading Fuson's full, and most readable, translation of the log.

[6] Morison, S. E., *Admiral of the Ocean Sea,* p. 231.

[7] Jean Jacques Rousseau wrote a number of books, the most famous of which is *The Social Contract,* published in 1762. Rousseau rhapsodized on a "state of nature," epitomized by the American Indians before the Europeans came. In a "state of nature," Rousseau argued, men have certain inalienable rights. Since these rights cannot be given away, they cannot be abused by government. And, since all rights of governments come from the authority granted to them by the people through what he called a "social contract," the people are the true sovereigns, and governments have no legitimacy unless the governments follow the contracts which the people grant to them. See Gershoy, Leo, *The French Revolution and Napoleon,* p. 71-75. Thomas Jefferson and many other American revolutionary leaders read and followed much of what Rousseau had to say. Modern environmentalists have seized on Columbus as the metaphor for all of Europe's evils being transported to the "noble savages" living in a "state of nature." See Sale, Kirkpatrick, *The Conquest of Paradise.* Recently, the National Council of Churches condemned Columbus' discovery as "an invasion and (an) occupation, genocide, economic exploitation and a deep level of institutional racism and moral decadence." In an essay in *Time Magazine,* May 27, 1991, Charles Krauthammer says the left is making Columbus the villain whose crime was the rape of America. Krauthammer, however, debunks the Columbus bashers, saying : "The real question is, What eventually grew on this bloodied soil? The answer is, The great modern civilizations of the Americas—a new world of individual rights, an ever expanding circle of liberty and, twice in this century, a savior of the world from totalitarian barbarism." Even though Columbus bashing sells more books, the author agrees with Krauthammer.

[8] The Tainos used paint on their bodies as a suntan lotion to protect their skin from the searing sun.

[9] The log entries for October 15-16, 1492, are confused, and it is not totally clear whether Columbus left San Salvador on the 15th or the 16th.

[10] Fuson gives the modern-day names of the islands Columbus discovered. Morison has prepared maps, with dates, showing where he believes Columbus went.

[11] The American Navy used hammocks until just before World War II.

[12] Bradford, Ernle, *Christopher Columbus,* p. 122, compares Columbus' excursion through the Caribbean to a man staggering through a dark room, "a room with which he thinks he is familiar, but which in fact is in a house that he never even knew existed." This comparison is apt. Note that Columbus makes confusing and incorrect statements, sometimes believing that he is in Japan, China or islands close to them.

[13] Scholars debate where Columbus first landed in Cuba, but many believe that it was near the town of Antilia at the Bahia Bariay in Oriente Province.

[14] The interpreter was Luis de Torres. The crewman was Rodrigo de Jerez. The ambassadors found a few huts, cotton and natives who pointed to the south when asked about gold and spices. The embassy returned to the ships on November 5.

[15] Coconuts were not introduced to the Caribbean until years later.

[16] Rienits, Rex and Thea, *The Voyages of Columbus,* p. 46. Some commentators believe that tobacco produced more wealth for Spain than did gold.

[17] Babeque is today's Great Inagua Island and Bohio is Hispaniola. Bohio is sometimes spelled Bofio.

[18] Hispaniola means New Spain. Columbus called the island by its Spanish name, Espanola. Hispaniola is the Latinized version which is used in English.

[19] Fuson, Robert H., *The Log of Christopher Columbus,* p. 131, says Columbus identified the Bay of Mosquitos (*Baie de Moustiques* in French) as *Puerto de la Concepcion* (Port of the Conception). Columbus sailed the Tortuga Channel between Hispaniola and Tortuga Island to the north. Tortuga Island later became a notorious hideout for Caribbean pirates.

[20] *Ibid.,* p. 130. Fuson says that what Columbus called the Port of St. Nicholas is now the Baie du Mole in Haiti.

[21] *Ibid.,* p. 143. Columbus reported on this harbor, which he called Cape Caribata (present-day Pointe Saint Honore), on December 20, 1492.

[22] Granzotto, Gianni, *Christopher Columbus,* p. 162.

[23] Columbus says an additional five hundred Indians swam the three miles out to the ships.

[24] Columbus refers to the Indian leader he was about to meet as king and lord. In the text, for clarity, the author refers to the "king" as the *cacique* or by his name, Guacanagari.

[25] Morison, S. E., *Admiral of the Ocean Sea,* p. 300, agrees. Columbus used the word "banco" (bank or sand bar) to describe the obstacle upon which the Santa Maria grounded. However, due to the damage done to the Santa Maria, it appears that it was actually a coral reef.

[26] Columbus sometimes refers to the Canibs as the Caribes. In the text, the author refers to them only as the Canibs, the root word for cannibals in modern English.

[27] On January 2, 1493.

[28] The Viking colonies were the first known settlements in America, but they lasted only a few years.

[29] Bradford, Ernle, *Christopher Columbus,* p. 142. The events narrated in this section took place over a period of several days. As Bradford notes, the shipwreck forced Columbus to become a colonist.

[30] This quote is from the December 31, 1492, entry in the log, and the succeeding quote is from the January 3, 1493, entry.

[31] The complete list of Columbus' charge to the colonists is set forth in the January 2, 1493, version of Fuson's translation of the log, p. 162.

[32] Columbus made these vitriolic comments, but only in writing, in the log, over a several day period in early January 1493.

[33] On January 14 and 15 Columbus planned to find the Island of the Canibs, but, because the ships were leaking, and the crew started grumbling about not heading directly home, Columbus decided to sail for Europe.

[34] A sailor named Pedro de Villa won the third lottery, and Columbus agreed to pay his expenses to make a pilgrimage to the church of Santa Maria de Loreto in the province of Ancona.

[35] Note that Columbus was wrong in his statement that both his sons would be orphans. Beatriz Enriquez de Horana was still alive, and, therefore, his illegitimate son Ferdinand would not have been an orphan. Also, Ferdinand was born in Spain, and was not a foreigner.

[36] Morison, S. E., *Admiral of the Ocean Sea,* p. 328, tells the true story of "a fly-by-night London publisher [who] had the impudence to claim that he had secured [Columbus' parchment in 1892]....It was written in English, he explained, because the Admiral thought that the manuscript would stand a better chance of being understood if couched in that universal maritime language. A 'facsimile edition,' printed...in imitation script on imitation vellum, entitled *My Secrete Log Boke* and suitably adorned with genuine barnacles and

seaweed, found many credulous purchasers...."

[37] If some scholars are to be believed, Columbus and Diaz may have met in 1488 when Columbus allegedly went to Portugal. The author does not believe that Columbus made the 1488 trip to Lisbon, and that the first meeting of the two men took place in 1493.

[38] When Columbus refused to submit to Diaz request, the Portuguese asked that the Nina's captain, Vicente Pinzon, come aboard Diaz' boat, and Columbus rejected this request also.

[39] King John was referring to the 1479 Treaty of Alcacovas.

[40] The court historian was Ruy de la Pena. His name is sometimes spelled Rui de Pina.

[41] The Spanish port was Bayona, near modern-day Vigo.

[42] Martin Alonso died about four or five days after his return. Even though Martin Alonso Pinzon died, his spirit would haunt Columbus and his relatives for decades. Litigation, debating the issue of which man should receive the glory for the discovery, dragged through Spanish courts for years. Some historians believe that subsequent Spanish monarches, when they figured out how much wealth the Columbus family had, sponsored and promoted the lawsuits to depreciate Columbus' role and bring back more of the wealth and power to the royal family. While Martin Alonso was in Galicia, he wrote to Ferdinand and Isabel asking permission to travel overland to visit them, but the King and Queen rejected Pinzon's request, making it clear that they would stick by Columbus.

[43] Boorstin, Daniel, *The Discoverers,* p. 236. In addition to the letter to the Sovereigns, Columbus sent a copy of it to his financial patron, Luis de Santangel. Columbus' original letter was in Spanish, but was translated into Latin as an eight page pamphlet, titled *De Insulis Inuentis,* and widely distributed. During 1493 and 1494, the letter was published in Rome, Paris, Basel and Antwerp. In this letter, Columbus brought the art of hyperbole to a new level as he described the lands he found: Cuba was "very fertile to a limitless degree." Harbors were "beyond comparison with others which I know in Christendom." Mountains were "very lofty...beyond comparison with the Island of Tenerife." There were "trees of a thousand kinds...and they seem to touch the sky." He sprinkles adjectives with abandon; beautiful, marvellous, a wonder to behold, cannot be believed, great mines of gold. Jane, Cecil, *The Four Voyages of Columbus,* Vol. II, p. 2, sets forth the complete Spanish and English texts of the letter.

[44] Bradford, Ernle, *Christopher Columbus,* p. 167. Las Casas is quoted.

Chapter 19: The Church, The Inquisition

[1] Cardinal Cisneros' full name was Francisco Jimenez de Cisneros. Some authors refer to him as Cardinal Jimenez or Ximenez. He lived from 1436 to 1517.

[2] Mariejol, Jean, *The Spain of Ferdinand and Isabella,* p. 251. Elliott, J. H., *Imperial Spain,* p. 88, estimates the Church's combined income at 2.25 billion maravedis. Elliott's estimates are expressed in ducats which the author has converted into maravedis at the rate of 375 maravedis to one ducat. See Hillgarth, J. N., *The Spanish Kingdoms,* p. 629, for a description of Cas-tile and Aragon's money, in which he sets the conversion rate at 375 to l.

[3] Kamen, Henry, *Inquisition and Society in Spain,* p. 45. Other religious orders included the Carthusian, Jeronimite and Cistercian. Kamen says that estimates by some writers that the Church had up to a half or a third of the

national income are too high. In any event, the Church's revenues made up a large portion.

[4] Ferdinand's bastard son Alfonso was succeeded in the post of Bishop of Zaragoza by his own bastard son.

[5] Prescott, William H., *Ferdinand and Isabella,* Vol. I, p. 314.

[6] Hillgarth, J. N., *The Spanish Kingdoms,* p. 99.

[7] *Ibid.,* p. 100.

[8] Such fraternities, sometimes called confraternities, still exist in Spain. The brothers of the confraternities, hooded and robed in silk or satin, can still be seen marching in religious processions, carrying ornate statutes of the Virgin or the saints.

[9] The flagellants' descendents still exist in some mountainous areas of New Mexico, where they call themselves "penitentes" (ones suffering penitence). The practice also still exists in Spain, Latin America and other places.

[10] Sixtus IV was Pope from 1471 to 1484. Innocent VIII succeeded him from 1484 to 1492, and, in 1492, with a great deal of manipulation by Isabel and Ferdinand, Alexander VI, a Spaniard, succeeded to the Holy Office. In the text, the author deals primarily with Sixtus, but all three Popes gave way to worldly pleasures. Readers may get a good feel for these Popes in Tuchman, Barbara, "*The March of Folly,*" p. 52 et seq.

[11] Hillgarth, J. N., *The Spanish Kingdoms,* p. 93. The satirist, Fray Inigo de Mendoza, was writing about the prior Archbishop of Toledo, Alfonso Carrillo, but the same comment could have applied to Cardinal Mendoza. Cardinal Mendoza fathered his three illegitimate sons by two women. Mariejol, Jean, *The Spain of Ferdinand and Isabella,* p. 255.

[12] *Ibid.,* p. 93. A popular preacher in the early 1400s, Vicent Ferrer, made the comment.

[13] At the time of the Battle of Toro, Mendoza was the Archbishop of Seville, and later became the Archbishop of Toledo, Primate of Spain, in 1482 when his predecessor, Alfonso Carrillo, died.

[14] Hillgarth, J.N., *The Spanish Kingdoms,* p. 105. The Franciscan reformer was Eiximenis who died in 1409.

[15] At the time of the synod, the Primate of Spain, Alfonso Carrillo, was still in revolt against Ferdinand and Isabel.

[16] Prescott, William H., *Ferdinand and Isabella,* Vol. I, p. 316.

[17] For many years before the Sovereigns came to power, the Castilian kings controlled Church patronage in territory conquered from the Moors.

[18] In 1482, the Sovereigns obtained the right to appoint the Bishop of Cuenca, in 1484 the Bishop of Seville, in 1486 the Bishops of Granada and the Canary Islands and, in 1501 and 1508, Papal Bulls gave them patronage (*patronato*) over the New World. The Bulls regarding the New World granted to the crown in perpetuity all tithes levied in the New World, and, in effect, made the Spanish sovereigns the Popes of the New World. No clergyman could go to the New World unless the King of Spain agreed, there was no Papal ambassador in the New World and the crown had the right to veto Papal Bulls which applied to the New World. See Kamen, Henry, *Inquisition and Society in Spain,* p. 45, Elliott, J. H., *Imperial Spain,* p. 87 and Prescott, William H., *Ferdinand and Isabella,* Vol. I, p. 314 regarding the Church generally.

[19] The Spanish religious orders split into two groups; the more liberal, lax Conventuals and the more conservative, strict Observants. In Papal Bulls issued in 1497 and 1517, the Pope ordered that the rules of the Observants should be followed. The Observants movement began in the Order of St.

Francis and spread to other orders of monks. Although the Franciscan Order began as a mendicant order, renouncing the ownership of property and living by begging, by the reign of the Sovereigns the Franciscans had accumulated goods, property and income, and lived in luxurious monasteries. With the support of Isabel and Cardinal Cisneros, who was a Franciscan, the Observants' zeal and conviction carried the day against the more liberal Conventuals. Mariejol, Jean, *The Spain of Ferdinand and Isabella*, p. 259.

[20] Although Cardinal Cisneros was intent on reform, he was guilty of absenteeism. He didn't visit his See until two years after his appointment, and spent most of his time at court or at war. To strengthen Church reforms, Cardinal Cisneros was instrumental in creating the faculty of theology at the University of Alcala.

[21] Elliott, J. H., *Imperial Spain,* p. 94, and most other authors argue that the reforms of the Sovereigns were substantial. However, Kamen does not agree. The reader should note that the Spanish Catholic Church was no different from those in other European nations, and that corruption and abuses were widespread, bringing into play Martin Luther's reforms.

[22] Hillgarth, J. N., *The Spanish Kingdoms,* p. 451. The quote from Bernaldez is set forth. Bernaldez, although anti-semitic himself, is one of the few contemporaries who felt any sympathy toward the expelled Jews. Pope Alexander VI mentioned the expulsion as one of the reasons he bestowed the title of "The Catholic Kings" on Ferdinand and Isabel. Nobody is sure how many Jews lived in Spain in 1492. The estimates run from a few thousand to several hundred thousand. Many Sephardic Jews immigrated to the more tolerant Netherlands, and, later, some of their descendants found their way to the United States, notably Justices Cardozo and Bandeis of the Supreme Court.

[23] England expelled its Jews in 1290 and France in 1306.

[24] Kamen, Henry, *Inquisition and Society in Spain,* p. 9. In the mid-1400s, only about fifteen percent of the tax farmers were Jews, but many others were converted Jews. Kamen argues that the Jews were, as a whole, not as rich as popular sentiment claimed, and that they mostly worked in the "small trades and minor professions."

[25] The exact number of Jews who converted is not known, but a substantial number of Jews did convert.

[26] Hillgarth, J. N., *The Spanish Kingdoms,* p. 95. A former rabbi who converted, Pablo de Santa Maria, became the Bishop of Burgos in the mid-1400s, and another *converso,* Alonso de Oropesa, was in charge of the Jeronimite order. During the Sovereigns' reign, several Jews held important posts; Abraham Senior was the treasurer of the Holy Brotherhood, David Abulafia was in charge of supplies for troops during the War of Granada and Isaac Abrabanel administered the taxes on sheep.

[27] Moors who converted to Christianity were called *moriscos.* After Luther's Reformation, Protestants also suffered under the Inquisition.

[28] Kamen, Henry, *Inquisition and Society in Spain,* p. 103. In Aragon, there was less pressure on the Moors to convert because they were a source of cheap farm labor. *Mientras mas Moros, mas ganancia* (More Moors, more profit), the saying went.

[29] *Ibid.,* p. 12.

[30] Mariejol, Jean, *The Spain of Ferdinand and Isabella,* p. 45. In 1478 Ferdinand and Isabel obtained a Papal Bull from Sixtus IV authorizing them to establish the Inquisition.

[31] Torquemada held the post of Inquisitor General from 1483 to 1498. When he died, Diego de Deza held the post until 1507. Cardinal Cisneros assumed the reins of the Inquisition from 1507 to 1516 in Castile. The Inquisition is often referred to as the "Suprema" or the "Holy Office."

[32] Hillgarth, J. N., *The Spanish Kingdoms,* p. 457 and Kamen, Henry, *Inquisition and Society in Spain,* p. 14. Some scholars argue that Isabel and Ferdinand were not as anti-semitic as their countrymen, while others accuse them of vitriolic racism. The facts are, at best, fuzzy; on the one hand the Sovereigns seemed to want to protect the Jews and took many of them into their confidence, but on the other hand they expelled and persecuted Jews. Being the pragmatists that they were, Isabel and Ferdinand may have been more tolerant toward Jews during the War of Granada, when they needed financial help from the Jews. After the war ended, Isabel and Ferdinand may have reasoned that the Jews' help was no longer needed. Among the reasons the Sovereigns took a hard line against Jews and *conversos* are: the pressure from ordinary citizens; the financial pressures ie. freeing the crown and its allies in the nobility from debts owed to Jews and permitting them to buy up Jewish-owned property cheap or to confiscate their property; the Sovereign's unbending drive to homogenize Spain; and their desire to purify Christianity.

[33] Kamen, Henry, *Inquisition and Society in Spain,* p. 14-15, tells the story and indicates that it may be a legend, and quotes Ferdinand's letter to the Count of Aranda.

[34] *Ibid.,* p. 17. The Sovereigns' order of expulsion prohibited the Jews from exporting gold, silver and precious stones, but many of them smuggled out these valuable items, some by swallowing them. The quote is from a rabbi whose father was an exile.

[35] Although many Jews left Spain, many *conversos* who stayed took the vows of Christianity and continued in their old religion. Three of Isabel's secretaries were *conversos* and *conversos* held the five most important posts in the government at one point.

[36] At the outset, the Sovereigns and the Pope quarrelled over who would control the Inquisition. Also, the Aragonese resisted the Inquisition's establishment. Following their policy of controlling all major institutions in Spain, Isabel and Ferdinand successfully asserted their authority over the Inquisition and imposed it in Aragon. The Inquisition had existed for several centuries before Ferdinand and Isabel, but it was under direct Papal supervision and control.

[37] Early on, the Inquisition issued Edicts of Grace, and later Edicts of Faith, which varied slightly. The procedures and time periods varied from city to city and throughout the years. Although Inquisition tribunals were set up in many places at different times, the principal and most long lasting tribunals were in Barcelona, Cordoba, Cuenca, Granada, Llerena, Logrono, Madrid, Murcia, Santiago, Seville, Toledo, Valencia, Valladolid, Zaragoza and Palma, Majorca. Rather than point out the permutations and when they occurred, the author has chosen to present a composite which gives the reader an understanding of the Inquisition.

[38] Roth, Cecil, *The Spanish Inquisition,* p. 76. The quote is from a 1519 Edict issued in Valencia. The Edict details every imaginable religious transgression and covers 6.5 pages of Roth's text.

[39] Kamen, Henry, *Inquisition and Society in Spain,* p. 164.

[40] Early on there were only two inquisitors, but in the late 1500s there were

three.

[41] The Inquisition also called on local parish priests to act as *comisarios* (commissioners) on its behalf and to supply it with information.

[42] Kamen, Henry, *Inquisition and Society in Spain,* p. 179.

[43] Peters, Edward, *Inquisition,* p. 92 and Kamen, Henry, *Inquisition and Society in Spain,* p. 161. Some writers argue that the Inquisition's jails may have been better than those of the secular courts. Apologists for the Inquisition have made the case that the procedures, jails and tortures of the Inquisition were in many cases better than those in other European countries, and, indeed, this is sometimes true. They also note that many of the attacks on the Inquisition came from Protestant countries, particularly England, after the Inquisition began including Lutherans and other Protestants in its lists of heretics. Therefore, the argument goes, the Spanish got a "bum rap" because so much of the focus centered on Spain. Many other Catholic countries, including Portugal and Italy, sponsored Inquisitions. Although these facts are true, the brutality of the Spanish Inquisition cannot be denied.

[44] Kamen, Henry, *Inquisition and Society in Spain,* p. 172. The quote was written by a Portuguese prisoner held in Lisbon in 1802. Kamen states that this description would be typical of the conditions in a Spanish Inquisitorial prison.

[45] Roth, Cecil, *The Spanish Inquisition,* p. 98. This account of the fire torture was written in the 1700s, but it was used in earlier times.

[46] Note that the secretary's report of Elvira del Campo's torture ends with the word "suspended." Under the Inquisition's rules a person could be tortured only once unless new evidence came to light. The inquisitors got around this rule by "suspending" rather than "ending" the torture.

[47] Hillgarth, J.N., *The Spanish Kingdoms,* p. 431, says that between 1487 and 1499 in Barcelona there were no acquittals and only about two acquittals a year in Toledo between 1484 and 1531.

[48] Other penalties included prohibition from holding public office, engaging in certain professions, wearing elaborate clothing , riding horses, bearing arms and giving testimony as a witness in court. Frequently, these penalties applied to a guilty person's descendants.

[49] *Sanbenito* is a contraction of the Spanish words *saco bendito* (sacred jacket).

[50] The delivery of condemned persons to the civil authorities was called, in the Inquisition's euphemistic parlance, "relaxing."

[51] Kamen, Henry, *Inquisition and Society in Spain,* p. 189, says that only one or two percent of the accused were burned at the stake. There is no accurate count of the number of persons who were burned or convicted of lesser crimes by the Inquisition. The Inquisition lasted for some four hundred years, and many of its records have not survived. Making the task more difficult, *autos de fe* were held in many Spanish cities and towns and in many places in Latin America. Undoubtedly, however, thousands of persons suffered under the Inquisition.

[52] Roth, Cecil, *The Spanish Inquisition,* p. 108. For lesser crimes, private *autos de fe* were held. The types of public ceremonies varied over the years. During the Sovereigns' reign, the ceremonies were not as elaborate or lengthy as they later became.

[53] There were two types of repentance, light *(de levi)* and heavy *(de vehementi).* If a person repented *de vehementi* and relapsed into heresy, he was almost automatically subject to condemnation at the stake.

[54] Roth, Cecil, *The Spanish Inquisition,* p. 119.
[55] Kamen, Henry, *Inquisition and Society in Spain,* p. 195-6.

Epilogue

[1] Prescott, William H., *Ferdinand and Isabella*, Vol. III, p. 174-175.

[2] When Ferdinand died twelve years later, the Sovereigns' bodies were placed in a grand tomb in the Cathedral Church of Granada.

[3] Prescott, William H., *Ferdinand and Isabella*, Vol. III, p. 192.

[4] Rivalry and cultural differences between Castile and Aragon and Catalonia existed for centuries before and after 1492. The differences still exist in modern Spain. Because the conflicts are so deep and so complex, the author has chosen not to deal with the issue of regional rivalries in this book.

[5] Wool was a major business in Spain, centered in Burgos. The Sovereigns' policy was to support the *mesta,* the Spanish organization of sheep herders.

[6] The area comprising much of present-day Holland, Belgium and the French province of Burgundy was part of the Hapsburg empire. Writers refer to it variously as Flanders, Burgundy, the Netherlands and the Low Countries. The author refers to this area herein as the Low Countries. The Hapsburgs also held dominions in Austria and central Europe.

[7] Hillgarth, J.N., *The Spanish Kingdoms*, p. 593.

[8] Only Isabel or her descendants could pass title to the Castilian crown, while Ferdinand, as the King of Aragon, had the right to pass title to that crown. Therefore, Ferdinand could rule only as a regent of Castile on behalf of his daughter Joan.

[9] Ferdinand obtained jurisdiction only over the southern part of Navarre. The northern portion remained independent until Henry of Navarre became King of France in 1589 and ruled as Henry IV.

[10] The major Italian campaigns took place in 1495-1497 and 1501-1504. In 1537, the Spanish King organized the Spanish army into *tercios*, units of three thousand men whose arms, fire power, maneuverability and organization made them the most effective fighting force in Europe.

[11] Ferdinand began the extension of Spain's foreign service before Isabel died. At the time, kings normally sent an embassy to another country only for the period of time needed to negotiate a treaty or settle a dispute.

[12] The Hapsburgs ruled until the 1700s when the Bourbon dynasty took over the throne. After Ferdinand's death, the nobles again split into factions, and Charles was not firmly seated on his throne for several years.

[13] Fonseca was a *letrado*, a university trained man who came up through the clergy. He served as the Archdeacon of Seville and later as the Bishop of Burgos.

[14] The statement was made by Michele da Cuneo, an Italian friend of Columbus who came from the town of Savona where the Admiral lived as a boy. Cuneo and Dr. Diego Chanca both wrote reports of the second voyage.

[15] Morison, S.E., *TheAdmiral of the Ocean Sea*, p. 407. Human flesh was one of the Indians' few sources of protein.

[16] The tribe is variously called the Canibs and the Caribs.

[17] Morison, S.E., *The Admiral of the Ocean Sea*, p. 417, and Bradford, Ernle, *Christopher Columbus*, p. 189. "The rape of the Indies had begun," Bradford says.

[18] This act made Columbus the initiator of the slave trade between Spain

and the Indies. In addition to bringing slaves and gold, the Spaniards and their human cargo brought back a new germ, syphilis. Scholars debate whether the Spaniards transmitted the disease to the Indies or vice versa. However, shortly after the twelve ships returned from Isabel, syphilis became widespread in Europe.

[19] It is not entirely clear whether women came to the New World on the small fleet in 1494, but some scholars believe they have evidence that there were women aboard.

[20] Columbus had six ships for the third voyage. At Gomera he split his fleet in two, sending three ships directly to Santo Domingo while he took a more southerly route. Professor Morison believes that there was no romance between Columbus and Beatriz de Peraza during the layover in Gomera, based solely on the absence of any mention of their love affair by contemporary chroniclers. It is true, however, that Columbus never saw Beatriz de Peraza after the third voyage.

[21] Jane, Cecil, *The Four Voyages of Christopher Columbus*, Vol. II, p. 30.

[22] Boorstin, Daniel J., *The Discoverers*, p. 242, et seq., says that Columbus' observations were "no random fantasy but the only rational explanation to reconcile the existence of some vast source of fresh water with Christian doctrine, with his Ptolemaic geography...and [with] the certainty of a direct sea passage...to the Indian Ocean." Boorstin gives a good, clear description of the geographical context in which the Admiral had to operate.

[23] While Santo Domingo was falling apart, the Sovereigns licensed others to poach on Columbus' private domains in the New World. Amerigo Vespucci made one of those voyages in 1499, wrote a travel diary (which he back-dated to the time Columbus made his third voyage in 1498) that became famous throughout Europe and robbed the Admiral of the distinction of having the New World named after himself. The word "Amerigo" soon became corrupted into America. Vespucci was from an influential Florentine family, and was sent to Spain in 1492 to represent the Medici family business. During this period (the late 1490s and early 1500s), Peralonso Nino, who went on the first voyage, discovered the Amazon, and Rodrigo de Bastidas sailed along the coast of Venezuela. Alonso de Ojeda, using Columbus' maps, with Vespucci on board, found rich pearl beds along the coast of Venezuela. Pedro Cabral, a Portuguese navigator, explored the coasts of southern Brazil, and John Cabot touched North America under the English flag in 1497.

[24] Granzotto, Gianni, *Christopher Columbus*, p. 240.

[25] Morison, S.E., *TheAdmiral of the Ocean Sea*, p. 575-6, and Bradford, Ernle, *Christopher Columbus*, p. 253.

[26] Granzotto, Gianni, *Christopher Columbus*, p. 242. Columbus' bastard son Ferdinand wrote that, to memorialize his humiliation, Columbus said that he wanted the chains buried with him in his coffin. This was not done. It is not known whether Columbus wore the chains when he met with the Sovereigns, but the contemporary historians did not mention the chains when they described the meeting between the Sovereigns and Columbus.

[27] Morison, S,E., *TheAdmiral of the Ocean Sea*, p. 577.

[28] Bradford, Ernle, *Christopher Columbus*, p. 234.

[29] Columbus made the comment in a letter to his old friend, Fray Gaspar Gorricco.

[30] Literally, *El Alto Viaje* can be translated as The High Voyage. But the author believes that Columbus intended the phrase to have the stronger meaning of The Ultimate Voyage.

[31] The Sovereigns' orders permitted Columbus to stop at Santo Domingo on the homeward bound part of his voyage to reprovision and repair his fleet.

[32] The fleet left Seville on April 2, 1502, went to Cadiz and attempted to enter the open sea on May 9, but unfavorable winds forced them to remain in port until May 11. The estimates of the number of men on the forth voyage range from one hundred thirty-five to one hundred fifty.

[33] Granzotto, Gianni, *Christopher Columbus*, p. 249.

[34] The modern word hurricane derives from the Indian word *hurucan*.

[35] Jane, Cecil, *The Four Voyages of Christopher Columbus*, Vol. II, p. 86. The quotation is from a letter written by Columbus on July 7, 1503, to Isabel and Ferdinand. The storm referred to took place off the coast of Central America.

[36] Ibid, p. 90-92.

[37] Ibid, p. 94-96.

[38] During the stay in Jamaica, the natives began grumbling over the intruders' demands for food and threatened to attack. Columbus consulted one of his books and discovered that there would be an eclipse of the moon on February 29, 1504. He told the natives that God was not happy with them, and that the Almighty was going to blot out the moon. When the eclipse occurred, the terrified Indians ceased their grumbling and agreed to continue supplying food to the Spaniards. Mark Twain used this gambit in his novel *A Connecticut Yankee in King Arthur's Court,* but Twain had his character use a solar eclipse.

[39] Fuson, Robert H., *The Log of Christopher Columbus,* p. 237, et seq., tells the story of Columbus' death in detail. Fuson also traces the progress of the Admiral's remains from their first burial in Valladolid (1506) to Santo Domingo (sometime between 1541 and 1547) to Cuba (1795) to Seville (1899).

[40] Peter Martyr first used the expression "New World" in a November, 1494, letter. A few years later, Martyr published a book in Venice called *De Orbe Novo (The New World)*.